CONTENTS

AUSTRIA

Austria inherited an empire which included, under the authority of a single sovereign in Vienna, countries as different as southern Italy and Galicia, Hungary and the Netherlands, but was reduced to a modest size in 1919. Nevertheless, she reflects the character of her former empire and the place she occupies in the Europe of today is due as much to her historic past as to her geographical position.

Enchanting Landscapes. – From the Vorarlberg, which is resembling eastern Switzerland, to the Burgenland whose features are already those of the European Balkans, and from the Drava Valley to the foothills of the Bohemian massif and the Carpathians, the landscape varies continuously.

Here are the Tyrolean Alps, their snowy summits, given over to skiers and lovers of mountaineering; the Salzkammergut, dotted with lakes and pastoral villages; the Danube Valley, marked in the Wachau by ruined castles and by vineyards; the Vienna Woods, of which you can hardly think of without humming a waltz; the moving beauty of Salzburg, the town of Mozart and the prince-archbishops; the charm of Graz, the capital of verdant Styria; the prestige of Vienna, impregnated with world history and rich in priceless art treasures, and the wistful horizons of the Burgenland, stretching before the Iron Curtain.

Art Treasures. – Cities like Innsbruck, Graz, Salzburg and, above all, Vienna are of interest to tourists: they have fine buildings and incredibly rich museums. Smaller towns like Feldkirch, Hall in Tirol, Rattenberg, Steyr, Freistadt, St. Wolfgang and Bruck and der Mur proudly display their links with the past.

Innumerable castles, surviving from the Middle Ages, dot the landscape and are powerfully placed on spurs guarding important routes.

Many of them have been turned into hotels or restaurants which can be enjoyed by tourists when making a halt.

The parish churches and above all the abbeys, for the most part Baroquised, contain decoration and furnishings – picture galleries, statues and altarpieces – evidence of one of the most brilliant periods of religious art.

The sumptuous Baroque decoration becomes ethereal during a mass with the choir singing and organ playing...

A Smiling Welcome. – To the charm and interest of scenes and buildings is added the attraction of a kind and smiling welcome, showing the pleasant habit of the Austrians, which they call *Gemütlichkeit,* of taking things as they come.

The tourist is rarely treated as a foreigner in Austria. Mixing freely with the natives, he takes part in a lively folklore, especially in the Tyrol. In a wine growing village of the Viennese suburbs he may spend an evening in a wineshop *(Heuriger),* sipping this year's wine to the sound of violins and accordions.

Good humour is the rule with this artistic people.

Its variety makes Austria an attractive country for holidays. The sophisticated go to the art and museum towns and the fashionable resorts on the Carinthian lakes. Those who are looking for the beauties of nature have a wide choice of small, hospitable mountain villages which offer, in summer, opportunities for numerous excursions, and in winter excellent ski-runs.

The New Face of Austria. – Austria is not only a country of artists or lovers of opera. After seventeen years of war and occupation, the country is now tending to base its economic and technical development along the lines of larger and richer lands.

Tourists visiting Austria can witness these changes by driving along the great mountain roads such as those of the Silvretta, the Grossglockner, or the Felber Tauern, the Brenner motorway, or the new highway which follows the Danube through the Wachau. As they cross the great Europa Bridge which spans the Sill Valley, they will see such bold undertakings as the Kaprun Dam, high in the mountains, or that of Altenwörth on the Danube, and go through industrial towns in full development such as Linz and Graz, whose suburbs of modern buildings are constantly growing.

A buffer state between the east and the west, Austria, since 1945, has played an important role as an international meeting point *(see tourist calendar of events p 31).*

WHEN TO VISIT

Due to its climate and picturesque and very varied scenery, Austria is popular at all seasons of the year.

Austria, two thirds covered by mountains, is justly favoured for its ski slopes in **winter.** The sweep of resorts, enjoyed equally by those just learning to ski as by the highly skilled, begins on the frontier around the Arlberg Pass, itself famous in sporting history *(p 19).* The resources of the Tyrol, the most popular area, benefited considerably from the last Olympic Games held at Innsbruck.

The Salzburg region has also developed as a winter resort area.

In the **spring** the longer days make it possible to ski at a high altitude. The season is also enlivened by carnival processions.

Summer is the ideal time of year for mountain pleasures. Smiling Carinthia, with its warm water lakes, attracts swimmers, water-skiing enthusiasts and anglers. Colder, but more romantic, are the lakes of the Salzkammergut, which are, above all, picturesque. Mountaineers will choose, according to their taste, the glaciers of the Ötztal or the High Tauern or the slopes of the Karwendel, the Kaisergebirge, the Dachstein or the Gesäuse.

Autumn, with the sun shining and a nip in the air, lights with a particular beauty the old stone buildings in the art and museum towns. Night falls swiftly, however.

A journey through the vineyards of the Burgenland or Lower Austria with the descent of the Danube beneath the Wachau heights is unforgettable at this time of year which is marked in Vienna by the reopening of the theatrical and musical seasons (1 September and October respectively).

PRACTICAL INFORMATION

BEFORE STARTING

You may consult the A.N.T.O. (Austrian National Tourist Office) in London: 30 Saint George Street, W1R 9FA, ☎ 629 0461; in Paris: 47 av. de l'Opéra (2e), ☎ 742-78-57; in New York: 545 Fifth Avenue, N.Y., 10017 ☎ 697–0651.

Information bureaux *(Verkehrsverein)* to which one may write, are to be found in all Austrian tourist resorts. They possess information about their own resorts. The sign 🛈 indicates local offices on maps in this guide; telephone numbers and addresses are given in section headings.

PASSPORTS AND CUSTOMS

As administrative and customs formalities are subject to variation, readers are advised to apply to the Automobile Association, Royal Automobile Club, or other motoring association for the latest information.

The Österreichischer Automobil-Motorrad-und-Touring Club **(ÖAMTC)** is the largest motoring organization in Austria, with headquarters in Vienna (Wien 1, Schubertring 3, ☎ 7299). Most of the Provinces have their own automobile associations, affiliated to the ÖAMTC, and all are prepared to give assistance to touring motorists in trouble.

Each member of a touring party must have a Passport or British Visitor's passport to enter Austria.

Official documents are no longer required for cars but vehicles and their contents may be examined by Customs Officials.

British tourists need only carry a valid driving licence and the log-book of the car to enter Austria; although not required it is advisable to take the Green International Insurance card. U.S. tourists need an International Driving Licence or a valid driving licence (should be accompanied by a translation).

Present regulations for tourists have been much simplified, so that the above documents now suffice for France and most of the countries of Western Europe, though travellers are of course subject to the usual Customs formalities on crossing frontiers.

If you take a caravan to Austria, the log-book and Green Card are sufficient. A camping or caravan card or international camping carnet is generally required, and a modest daily charge made, if you use one of the selected camping sites recommended by the camping associations *(see following page)*.

Currency. – Hotels, restaurants and shops do not always accept foreign currency and it is wise, therefore, to change your money and cheques at the banks and exchange offices to be found in the larger stations and at the frontier.

The exchange rate in April 1982 was: 29.70 Austrian Schillings to the £1 and 16.70 to the U.S. 1 $.

A FEW PRICES

One night's stay for a tourist (dinner, room, breakfast) in a hotel like the 🏠 and 🏠 hotels in the Michelin Guide *France*	300–400S
Simple meal (soup, main dish of the day, bread and beer)	80–100S
Complete meal including a local speciality (trout, fried chicken, house *Platte*, etc.)	100–150S
One 1/4-litre–just under 1/2-pint – *(Viertel)* of good vintage white wine	20–25S
Coffee (according to the method of making)	15–30S
Beer (1/2-litre – just under 1 pint)	12–25S
Petrol, gasoline (per litre – 1 3/4 pints)	10,70–11,10S
Oil (per litre can)	40–50S
Greasing and oiling	80–200S
Postcard (foreign postage)	4S
Letter (foreign postage)	6S
Telephone call abroad (3 minutes) (Vienna-London)	42S

LOCAL CRAFTS

An official craftsmen's centre shop, a **Heimatwerk,** will be found in each provincial capital (ask the local tourist office for the exact address). The list below gives a general idea of local crafts.

Burgenland. – China (Stoob), osiery (Piringsdorf), jade jewellery and serpentine marble (Bernstein).

Carinthia. – Costumes, ceramics, carved coffrets; wrought-iron (Friesach).

Lower Austria. – Petit point, Augarten porcelain, embroidered blouses.

Salzburg. – Pewter, china, regional costumes.

Styria. – Printed linens, jewellery (Bad Aussee), carved wooden masks (Mitterndorf), painted pottery (Gams), loden (Ramsau and Mandling), hand woven linen (Radkersburg).

Tyrol. – Mangers in wood, tablecloths and embroidered fabrics, wrought-iron; majolica (Schwaz), cut and engraved glassware (Kufstein and Kramsach).

Upper Austria. – Painted glassware and painted wooden coffrets: handwoven linen (Haslach); leather-work, candles (Braunau); wood carvings (Zell am Moos); wrought-iron, steel-engravings (Steyr); china (Gmunden); head dresses and silver jewellery (Bad Ischl).

Vorarlberg. – Wooden articles, painted glassware, hand weaving; dolls (Bregenz); embroidery (Schwarzenberg and Lustenau).

WHEN YOU STOP

Choice of an Hotel. – *(See vocabulary on p 12)*. The traditional hotel in Austria offers the traveller the accommodation he is entitled to expect, with the advantage, in first class hotels, of little strangeness as regards cuisine, service and language (especially in the Tyrol and the Vorarlberg where English is spoken or at least widely understood).

Life in local inns should be tried for its particular charm. It is a way of life which has vanished elsewhere, but remains unspoilt here. *Gasthof* does not mean low class hotel, for though no luxury *Gasthof* exist there is a great deal of variety in their accommodation, comfort and cuisine. The foreigner should play the game according to the rules and not expect special attention.

At a halt or during a country holiday you may accept the hospitality offered by the local people in the *Fremdenzimmer* or *Zimmer frei*. This method of lodging, which often has the charm of the unexpected, is preferred by some.

Brochures. – Our readers should consult the hotel lists distributed by the Austrian National Tourist Office.

To get a general idea of the accommodation resources of a resort, including the rooms available in private houses, apply to the local tourist bureaux *(p 5)* for their brochures which may also be available at the overseas agencies of the national tourist office.

Tips. – Service (10–15%) is generally included in hotel and restaurant bills. But in Austria, it is usual to give more than the expected tip in hotels, restaurants and cafés. Taxi-drivers, porters, barbers and theatre attendants also expect tips.

Camping. – The Austrian National Tourist Office distributes folders listing organized camping grounds with details, in each case, of the site and the standard of the facilities provided.

International Camping Guides are also published by some of the large motoring organizations, as for example **ADAC** (published by the German Automobile Club). This guide, sold in Austria through **ÖAMTC** lists some 445 camping sites for Austria alone.

Caravanning. – *See p 11.*

Pleasure Craft. – Motor boats are under strict rules, if not forbidden, on Austrian lakes.

Postal System. – All Post Office equipment (vans, letter-boxes, telephone kiosks, stamp machines) may be recognized in Austria by their yellow colour.

All letters, parcels and cards sent to Austria must be addressed with the following postal code: A – the internationally recognized abbreviation for Austria – the town or area's given postal number and then its name.

Poste Restante. – The plans in this guide show, for each town, where you can collect letters adressed *poste restante (Postlagernd)*. Code numbers for the towns are given in the index to this guide, pp 175–177.

For the larger towns write out the full address. It reads as follows – Mr. X, Postlagernd and then you add: A – 1010 Wien, Fleischmarkt 9; A – 9020 Klagenfurt, Dr. Hermanngasse; A – 6010 Innsbruck, Maximilianstrasse 2; A – 5010 Salzburg, Residenzplatz 9; A – 8010 Graz, Neutorgasse 46.

Telephone. – All telephone communications are automatic. Each area has its own code, which consists of 4 or 5 numbers beginning with a zero (printed on letter heads in parenthesis or followed by an oblique).

Except for local calls, the code must always be composed before the number of the correspondent.

Working hours and Public Holidays. – Throughout Austria shops close on Saturday afternoons. Banks are usually open from 8am to 12.30pm and 1.30 to 3pm (5.20pm Thursdays).

Legal public holidays are: 1 January, 6 January, Easter Monday, 1 May, Ascension, Whit Monday, Corpus Christi, 15 August, 26 October, 1 November, 8 December and Christmas and Boxing Days.

Before going to Vienna take note of the days and times that its museums and galleries close especially during Easter and Whitsun *(see notice p 150)*.

SHOOTING AND FISHING

Shooting. – Any foreigner who has time for it can go in search of excitement in the Tyrol, shooting chamois (August-December), grouse *(Auerhahn)* or gamecock *(Birkhahn)* at the spring thaw, or deer-stalking in the wooded solitude of the Pre-Alps. Official regulations are strict and complicated, and it is essential to make one's preparations well beforehand with the help of the Landesfremdenverkehrsamt (Regional Tourist Bureau) of the federal province in question. The owner of a shoot often assumes responsibility for issuing the various permits required *(total cost: 450 to 1 500S)*, as well as requiring a fee for the shooting and game bagged *(total cost: 1 000 to 100 000S for large game)*.

Fishing. – Anglers on holiday cannot fail to be envious when they discover the running water and lakes of the Austrian mountains. Trout, and even the common grayling, are plentiful in many torrents, while the lakes teem with salmonidae of other kinds (lake trout, large grayling) and a local kind of pike, all of which appear frequently on hotel menus.

Angling in Austria is subject to two permits: one, official, valid for a whole federal province, the other local and obtainable from the owner of the fishing rights. *For further details, consult the brochure "Fishing in Austria" of the Austrian National Tourist Office.*

6

RULES OF THE ROAD

– Do not forget to equip your car with a nationality plate.

– A valid driving licence is required.

– A Green Card (an internationally recognized certificate of insurance) is highly recommended.

Road Traffic. – Priority must be given to traffic coming from the right, unless otherwise indicated. On mountain roads vehicles travelling uphill have priority. The **speed limit** in built up areas (indicated by place name signs at the beginning and end of such areas) is 50 kph - 30 mph; on motorways 130 kph - 80 mph; and on all other roads 100 kph - 60 mph.

A driver convicted of driving while under the influence of alcohol is severely punished.

The use of **dipped head lights** is compulsory in conditions producing poor visibility – fog, rain, snowfall. Fog-lamps may be used in conjunction with sidelights (but not headlights). **Converter lenses** are required under continental regulations.

In Town. – Supervised **parking zones** exist in all larger towns – a parking disc *(Parkscheibe)* can be obtained at the local tourist office, police station or tobacco shop *(Trafik)*. Parking is prohibited anywhere where there is a sign: *Beschränkung für Halten oder Parken* (restriction for stopping or parking). Trams are still numerous, have priority and must be passed on the right only between their stopping points. In Vienna parking is prohibited in any street with tramways.

The use of the horn is prohibited in towns and tacitly proscribed on main roads except in moments of danger. Unguarded level crossings sometimes have flashing lights. Red lights mean STOP, white or yellow that the light signals are working and that the road is clear for the car to cross the line.

Safety measures. – Motorists must be in possession of an officially approved breakdown triangle and a first aid kit.

Automobile Clubs. – The ÖAMTC central bureau is in Vienna – Schubertring 3 ☎ 7299 or for road information only ☎ 72997.

CARAVANNING

Austrian alpine roads have gradients of more than 1 in 5 (see Michelin map **426**). It is possible that there are steep or narrow sections which are not necessarily indicated on the map or road sign. In addition many passes are not recommended for, or are closed to, caravans.

Even the better alpine roads (the access ramps to the Tauern Railway Tunnel) are subject to pile ups and delays making it difficult to circulate with a caravan.

The table below indicates – in direction west–east – the main difficulties of these **Alpine** routes.

Name of pass	Altitude of pass in meters	Alpine Routes	Page (1)	o Closed o Not re-commended
Hochtannbergpass	1679	Dornbirn – Reutte	55	o
Bielerhöhe	2036	Silvretta Road	**48**	o
Seefelder Sattel *(2)*	1180	Innsbruck – Mittenwald	**142**	o
Timmelsjoch *(3)*	2474	Ötztal Valley – Italy	116	o
Gerlospass *(4)*	1628	Zell am Ziller – Zell am See	71	o
Hochtor	tunnel 2505	Grossglockner Road	**77**	o
Radstädter Tauern *(5)*	1739	Radstadt – St Michael im Lungau	**118**	o
Katschberg *(5)*	1641	St Michael im Lungau – Spittal an der Drau	**118**	o
Turracher Höhe	1763	Mur Valley – Carinthian Lakes		o
Kartitsch-Sattel	1526	Kötschach – Sillian	71	o
Loibl	tunnel 1067	Klagenfurt – Yugoslavia		o
Gaberl-Sattel	1547	Direct Route- Upper Mur Valley – Graz	116	o
Präbichl	1232	Enns Valley – Leoben	65	o
Rottenmanner Tauern	1265	Upper Mur Valley – Enns Valley	**82**	o
Aflenzer Seeberg	1253	Mariazell – Aflenz	45	o

(1) When the road described entails an altitude-gradient profile the page numbers are given in heavy type.

(2) Access to Seefeld is done via Mittenwald–Innsbruck.

(3) Caravans not exceeding 3.40 m - 11.40 ft in height can circulate in the Ötztal as far as Untergurgl.

(4) Access to the Gerlos shelf and to Gerlos itself is done in the direction east–west.

(5) A-10 motorway is recommended.

Michelin road map 426 Austria

at a scale of 1/400 000 (1 in: 6.30 miles)

– *Road network with their characteristics: snowbound, gradients, hilly roads...*

– *A wide variety of tourist information: scenic routes, ski-lifts, viewpoints, refuge huts...*

– *A detailed inset of Vienna and suburbs*

– *An index with map co-ordinates.*

The perfect companion to this guide.

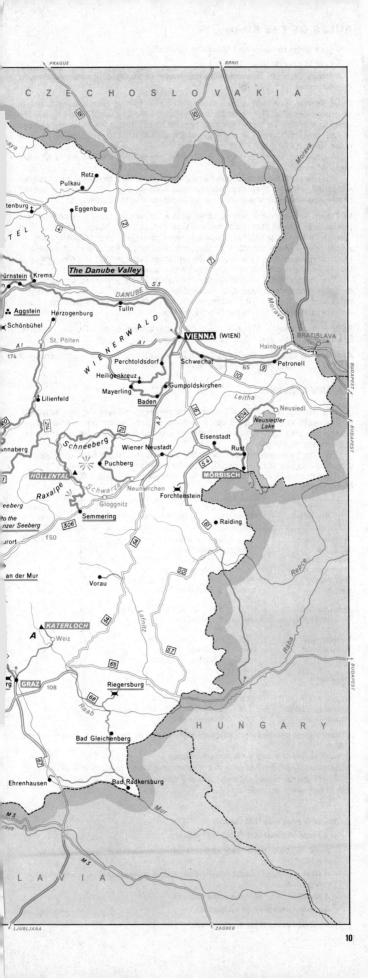

VOCABULARY *Useful hotel terms are underlined*

Ansichtskarte	picture postcard	Kreuzgang	cloister
Ausfahrt,		Kur	cure and place to stay
Ausgang	exit	Landhaus	seat of provincial govern-
Ausflug	excursion		ment
Auskunft	information	Links	to, on the left
Bahnhof	railway station	Markt	market square, market town
Brücke	bridge	Maut	toll (road, bridge)
Brunnen	fountain, well	Mesner	sacristan
Burg	fortified castle	Münster	cathedral
Café	tea and coffee shop	Offen	open
Denkmal	monument, memorial	Pass	pass or small ravine
Dom	cathedral, largest local	Pension	*pension,* family hotel,
	church		usually with full board
Einfahrt, Eingang	entrance	Postlagernd	*poste restante,* to be called
Essen	to eat (Mittagessen: lunch		for
	Abendessen: dinner)	Quelle	spring, fountain
		Rathaus	town hall
Fähre	ferry	Rechts	to, on the right
(Wasser) Fall	(water) fall, cascade	Schloss	château, castle
Festung	fortress, fortified town	Schlucht	gorge, defile
Firn	snowfield	Schlüssel	key
Fremdenheim	*pension* – where only	Schwimmbad	swimming pool
	breakfast is served	See	lake
Frühstück	breakfast	Sommerfrische	summer holiday (in the
Frühstück,			country)
Pension	see *Fremdenheim*	Speisesaal	restaurant or dining room in
Garten	garden		a hotel
Gasse	street, alley	Spielbank	casino
Gasthaus	café, inn	Stausee	artificial lake formed by a
Gasthof	inn		dam
Gaststätte	restaurant; buffet	Stift	abbey, monastery
Gebühr	tax, tip, toll	Strandbad	bathing beach
Geradeaus	straight ahead	Strasse	road, street
Geschlossen	closed	Stube, Stüberl	small dining room in a
Gesperrt	barred, closed		restaurant decorated in
Gletscher	glacier		the local style
Gobelins	tapestry (in general)	Tal	valley
Grüss Gott	"God bless": traditional	Talsperre	dam
	greeting	Tor	gate, town gateway
Guten Tag	Good morning	Treppe	steps, stairs
Haus	house	Verboten	forbidden
Hof	courtyard, hôtel, farm	Wald	forest
Höhe	height, altitude	Wechsel	exchange (money)
Höhenweg	road running along the	Wildfütterung	winter forage point for
	crests, across the side of		larger game (enabling
			one to see, at pre-
Höhle	cave		determined points, the
Hütte	mountain refuge, factory		animals which live in the
Jause	tea, light meal		forest)
Kanzel	pulpit, belvedere	Wintersportplatz	winter sports resort
(Musik) Kapelle	orchestra, fanfare	Wirtschaft	modest inn
Kar	small mountain	Zimmer frei	rooms to let (room free)
	amphitheatre (in		(sign outside private
	limestone area)		houses)
Kirche	church	Zimmernachweis	reservation of rooms (made
Klamm	gorge, ravine		by Tourist Offices and the
Kloster	abbey, monastery		special bureaux of the
Kofel, Kogel	dome-shaped mountain		main railway stations)
Krankenhaus	hospital		

SPECIAL WARNING SIGNS

Anfang	Start	LKW	Heavy lorries
Ausgenommen	Residents only	PKW	Tourist cars
Anrainer		Rechts, links	
Aussicht	Viewpoint	einbiegen	Turn right or left
Bauarbeiten	Road works	Rollsplitt	Loose gravel
Einbahnstrasse	One-way street	Sackgasse	Dead end
Ende	End of restriction	Schlechte	
Freie Fahrt	No restrictions	Wegstrecke	Road in bad condition
Frostschäden }	Icy roads	Schlechte	
Frostaufbrüche }		Fahrbahn	
Fussgänger-Zone	Pedestrians only	Steinschlag	Falling stones
Gefährlich	Danger	Umleitung	Detour
Geradeaus	Straight on	Verengte	
Glatteis	Black ice	Fahrbahn	Road narrows
Kurzparkzone	Restricted parking, disc	Vorrang	Priority
	obligatory	Vorsicht	Caution

CULINARY TERMS *p 32.*

BOOKS TO READ

In English

THE HABSBURG TWILIGHT – TALES FROM VIENNA **Sarah Gainham** *Weidenfeld & Nicolson 1979*
VIENNA – THE IMAGE OF A CULTURE IN DECLINE **E. Crankshaw** *Macmillan 1976*
THE FALL OF THE HOUSE OF HABSBURG **E. Crankshaw** *Macmillan 1981*
UNKNOWN AUSTRIA **Barbara Whelpton** (3 vols.) *Johnson Publications 1969*
THE HABSBURG MONARCHY 1809-1918 **A.J.P. Taylor** *Pelican 1976*
MUSIC AND MUSICIANS IN VIENNA **Richard Rickett** *Georg Prachner 1981*
A BRIEF SURVEY OF AUSTRIAN HISTORY **Richard Rickett** *Georg Prachner 1978*
CHRONICLE AND WORKS (vol. 2) HAYDN AT ESTERHAZY 1776-1790 **H.O. Robbins Landon** *Thames & Hudson 1978*

In German

DIE GROSSEN DER WIENER MUSIK **Richard Rickett** *Georg Prachner 1977*
DEHIO Guides (DEHIO HANDBUCH): Niederösterreich, Oberösterreich, Tyrol, Salzburg, Steiermark, Wien, Kärnten, Burgenland, Graz – detailed inventory, but hard reading.
 Many good monographs have been published and are to be found on sale at the entrance to the relevant monuments.

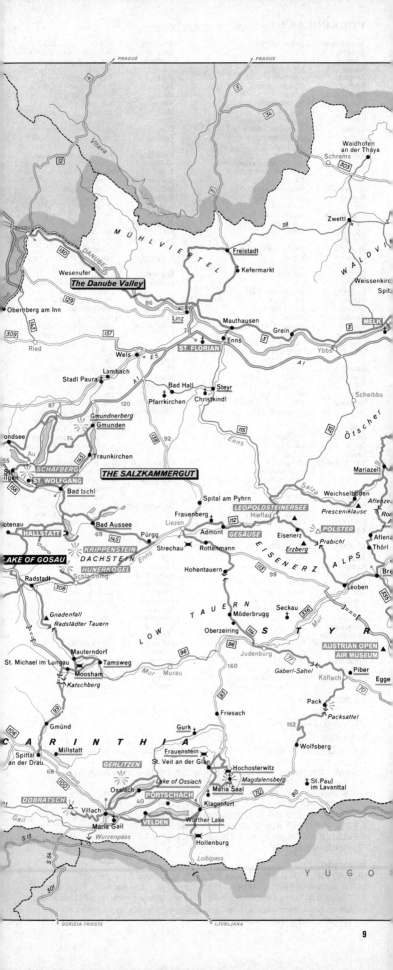

THE AUSTRIAN REPUBLIC

See the map on p 3, which shows the boundaries and the capital of each Federal Province.

Since it adopted, in 1920, a federal constitution similar to that of Switzerland, the Austrian Republic has been a Federal State consisting of nine autonomous provinces. The arms of each of these *Länder* is illustrated below, together with the official letter used as a sign on cars.

BURGENLAND (B)

SALZBURG (S)

BURGENLAND – 3 965 km^2 - 1 531 sq miles – pop 272 274.
Until 1918 this region was part of the kingdom of Hungary. It owes its name to three castles *(Burgen)* built some way from the frontiers of the province.

CARINTHIA (Kärnten) – 9 533 km^2 - 3 681 sq miles – pop 536 727.
The province has the only considerable national minority in Austria (4% of the inhabitants speak Slovene). Nonetheless a plebiscite held in 1920, of the southern areas claimed by Yugoslavia showed equally strong unity with Austria.

LOWER AUSTRIA (Niederösterreich) – 19 170 km^2 - 7 402 sq miles – pop 1 439 137.
This is the cradle of the nation *(p 22)*. It is also the most prosperous agriculturally.

UPPER AUSTRIA (Oberösterreich) – 11 978 km^2 - 4 624 sq miles – pop 1 270 426.
This region between the Salzkammergut and Bohemia is highly developed agriculturally and industrially.

SALZBURG – 7 154 km^2 - 2 763 sq miles – pop 441 842.
The former domains of the prince-archbishops of Salzburg were united with Austria only in 1805. Their economy was based on salt.

STYRIA (Steiermark) – 16 386 km^2 - 6 326 sq miles – pop 1 187 512.
The "green province" of Austria, where the timber industry, cattle-raising and now particularly metallurgy, play a leading part, is one of the oldest industrial countries in Europe.

TYROL (Tirol) – 12 648 km^2 - 4 883 sq miles – pop 586 139.
This ancient mountaineers' country is a stronghold of the Roman Catholic and patriotic traditions in Austria.

VIENNA (Wien) – 414 km^2 - 165 sq miles – pop 1 515 666.
The services and ministries of the Federal Government, of the *Land* (District) of Vienna and of the *Land* of Lower Austria have their headquarters in the capital.

VORARLBERG – 2 601 km^2 - 1 004 sq miles – pop 305 615.
Smallest of the federal provinces, the *Ländle* (the little country) is by no means the least lively.

KÄRNTEN (K)

STEIERMARK (St)

NIEDERÖSTERREICH (N)

TIROL (T)

OBERÖSTERREICH (O)

WIEN (W)

VORARLBERG (V)

THE AUSTRIAN DEMOCRACY

Austria is a Federal State formed by nine provinces or *Länder (see above)*. Each province seeks to maintain its independent character but strictly within the framework of the Austrian state as a whole.

"The Land". – The population of the province or the *Land* elects the members of the **Provincial Diet** every 4 or 6 years. The number varies between 36 and 56 in proportion to the size of the population of the province. Only the Diet of Vienna has 100 members.

The diet elects the members of the **Provincial Government** on the basis of proportional representation. This government is the administrative organ of the *Land;* it has to have the confidence of the diet, and takes its decisions on the majority vote.

Federal organization. – The **Federal Assembly** is constitued by the members of the National Council and of the Federal Council, who share the legislative power.

The National Council has 183 members elected for 4 years by universal suffrage by men and women over twenty years of age. It is convoked or dissolved by the Federal President.

The Federal Council is formed by 54 representatives elected by the provincial diets. Its role is to safeguard the rights of the provinces in the administrative and legislative fields *vis-à-vis* the Federation. On the federal level, it has the right to propose laws and its approval is necessary for international agreements and treaties.

The Federal President or President of the Republic, elected by the people for 6 years, holds the executive power with the Federal Government. He represents the Republic abroad and commands the armed forces; he appoints the important civil servants and the Chancellor and promulgates the laws.

The Federal Government is made up of a Chancellor, a Vice-Chancellor, Ministers and Secretaries of State, appointed by the Federal President on the advice of the Chancellor.

The respective competence of the *Land* and the Federation are clearly set out. The Federation is only concerned in general fields: foreign affairs, based on a policy statement of strict neutrality proclaimed in 1955, and public security... In certain fields, the Federation makes the laws and the provinces carry them out (road traffic).

In order that the functions of the provincial and federal organizations do not overlap, the Constitution allows the Federal Council the right of opposition to the National Council and the right of opposition by the Federal Government to laws passed by the provincial diets.

PLAN OF LOCAL MAPS

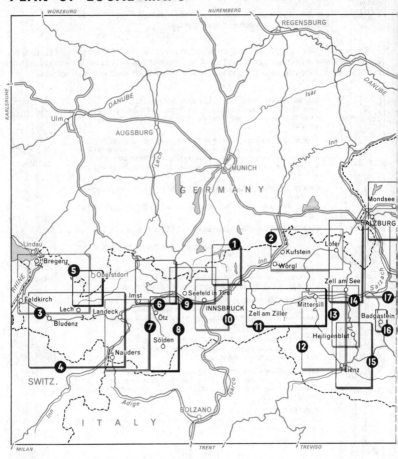

The companion guides in English in this series are
Austria, Germany, Italy, Portugal, Spain, Switzerland

Other Michelin Green Guides available in English
Brittany, Canada, Châteaux of the Loire, Dordogne, French Riviera, Normandy, Provence, London, New England, New York City, Paris.

TO BE FOUND IN THIS GUIDE

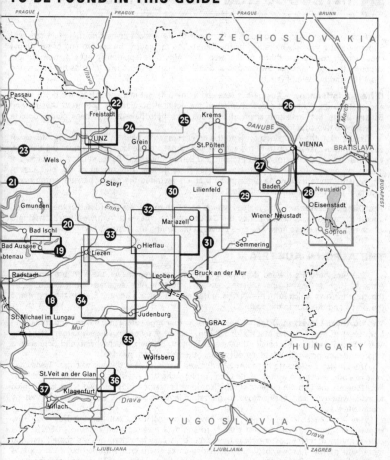

No. of map above	TITLE OF MAP	Page reference
20	The SALZKAMMERGUT to the South (Dachstein Massif)	138–139
21	The SALZKAMMERGUT to the North	136–137
22	The MÜHLVIERTEL	105
23	The Valley of the DANUBE Passau – Linz	60
24	Linz – Grein	60
25	Grein – Krems	61
26	Krems – Vienna – Hainburg	62
27	The WIENERWALD	169
28	NEUSIEDLER Lake	112
29	The SCHNEEBERG Neunkirchen – Semmering	140
30	The ÖTSCHER Massif St. Pölten – Mariazell	114
31	The AFLENZER SEEBERG Road Bruck an der Mur – Mariazell	45
32	The SALZA VALLEY Hieflau – Mariazell	126
33	EISENERZ ALPS Liezen – Leoben	64
34	The HOHENTAUERN PASS Road Judenburg – Liezen	83
35	The PACKSATTEL and STUBALPE Roads Judenburg – Wolfsberg	116
36	ST. VEIT AN DER GLAN (Excursions)	125
37	WÖRTHER SEE and OSSIACHER SEE	172

Join us in our never ending task of keeping up to date.
Send us your comments and suggestions please.

Michelin Tyre P.L.C.
Tourism Department
81 Fulham Road, LONDON SW3 6RD

Aut. An. 2

INTRODUCTION TO THE TOUR

Austria comprises: to the north, a fragment of the ancient crystalline mountain range of Bohemia and a vast plain drained by the Danube; to the south, the eastern end of the Alpine chain which covers two-thirds of the area. The Alps here apparently have a more simple structure than in France or Switzerland and their outlines slope down towards the east to the great Hungarian plain of Puszta.

Different influences. – Austria has received many different influences from the north, south and east, as great natural areas overflowed the political frontiers. To the north, Austria and Bavaria share the limestone chain of the Alps and there have always been close contacts between the two countries.

To the east, the Alps slope away to the great Hungarian plain of Puszta, giving Austria an eastern window largely open to the cultural and climatic influences coming from the Balkans. Vienna arose at the crossroads of Germanic and Balkan influences. To the south, Austria has lost means of access to the Adriatic since 1919. Nevertheless, the spread of the old Austro-Hungarian Empire far beyond present-day frontiers favoured the earlier penetration on many counts of the Mediterranean civilization.

The Danube Plateau. – This plateau, which backs on to the last buttresses of the Bohemian massif to the north, is deeply cut by the Danube, which crosses it from west to east and into which most of its rivers flow. The area provided the setting for Austria's early history.

THE ALPS IN AUSTRIA

The Alps here are divided from north to south into three chains: the Northern Limestone Alps, the High or Central Alps, and the Southern Limestone Alps, separated from each other by the great furrows which form the Valleys of the Inn, the Salzach and the Enns in the north; and the Drava and the Mur in the south.

The Northern Limestone Alps. – These overflow to a large extent into Bavaria and spread out from west to east into the massifs of Rätikon, Lechtal, Karwendel, Kaisergebirge, Steinernes Meer, Tennengebirge, Dachstein, the Alps of Ennstal, Eisenerz, Hochschwab and Schneeberg where the dark green forests stand out against the grey limestone cliffs.

The Limestone Alps do not form an unbroken barrier that is difficult to cross. Transverse valleys along which the waters of the Lech, Tiroler Ache (the Alz in Bavaria), Saalach and Enns flow towards the Danube plateau, cut the Northern Limestone Alps into distinct massifs which tourists with cars can easily cross to go round and whose cliffs have been explored by mountaineers.

The Alps east of the Tiroler Ache have a characteristic outline: the Dachstein, the Hochschwab and the Raxalpe rise sharply to summits of more than 2 000 m - 6 562 ft. The porous nature of their limestone rocks makes these plateaux into stony deserts, scored here and there with narrow furrows, between which rise small sharp crests formed by water courses through the limestone. Here, the flow of the water is almost entirely subterranean and results in the formation of numerous caves, the most well-known being the Dachstein.

The climb by cable-car to the Krippenstein or the Raxalpe will reveal all the originality of this formation.

The Northern Limestone Alps are bounded to the south by the deep furrow through which flow the Inn between Landeck and Wörgl (130 km - 81 miles), the Salzach between Krimml and St. Johann im Pongau (80 km - 50 miles) and the Enns between Rachstadt and Hieflau (110 km - 68 miles). This gash which separates the Limestone Alps from the High Alps benefits road traffic and allows tourists to drive along the chain for its entire length.

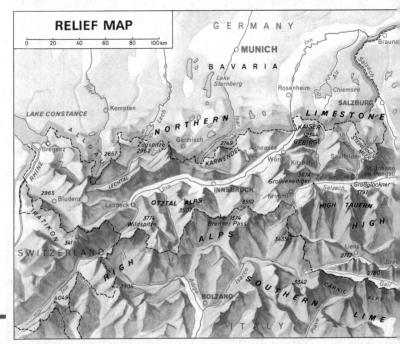

16

The High or Central Alps. – The High Alps, mostly of crystalline rocks, appear as a succession of ridges topped by glaciers. Difficult of access, and forming the highest summits in Austria, they comprise from west to east: the Ötztal Alps (Wildspitze, 3 774 m - 12 382 ft), the High Tauern (Grossvenediger, 3 674 m - 12 054 ft – and Grossglockner, 3 797 m - 12 458 ft) with its dazzling glaciers and the Lower Tauern. The line of the crests hardly drops below 3 000 m - 10 000 ft – for a distance of more than 250 km - 150 miles; passes are rare making the barrier no easy matter to cross. The Brenner Pass (1 374 m - 4 508 ft), mediaeval route towards Venice, links the Valley of the Inn and the Adige. The Grossglockner road and the Felber Tauern tunnel enable tourists to cross the imposing massif of the High Tauern.

To the south of the High Alps, the furrows of the Drava, Mur and Mürz Rivers play a role that is comparable to the great valleys of the north and form the natural link between Vienna and Venice or Milan.

The Southern Limestone Alps. – The Carnic Alps and the Karawanken are only Austrian on their northern slopes, Austria having had in 1919 to cede the southern part of the Tyrol to Italy and the Julian Alps to Yugoslavia.

SOME PECULIARITIES OF THE MOUNTAIN CLIMATE

Compared with the weather in the nearby plains, the mountain climate varies considerably with difference in altitude, physical relief or exposure to sunshine. Such phenomena as the breezes and the *Föhn* can have an effect on tourists.

Mountain Breezes. – At the end of the morning, the warm expanded air of the valleys creeps up the natural corridors to the heights, causing the formation of clouds round the summits. This increase in cloud in the afternoon is a sign of settled fine weather (it should incite walkers to go up to the belvederes very early in the morning). About 5pm this valley breeze ceases to blow, and coolness suddenly sets in: it is now the turn of the mountain breeze, cold and generally stronger, to sweep the valley in the opposite direction.

The Föhn. – This wind is most strongly felt north of the Alps, in the Alpine Valleys of the Rhine, the Inn (especially in the Ötztal) and the Salzach.

The phenomenon is caused by the passage of a deep barometric depression along the north slope of the Alps. Rid of its moisture on the Italian slope of the range, where there are now constant storms and rain, the air drawn in by this depression spills over the crest-line and, rising in temperature owing to compression as it loses altitude (1 °C per 100 m or 5 °F per 100 ft), is transformed into a dry and burning wind, while the atmosphere becomes wonderfully clear.

In the mountains everyone is on the alert. Torrents are in spate, avalanches rumble and the risk of fire is great. Citizens live in such a state of nervous exhaustion that examinations are suspended in the schools at Innsbruck. The *Föhn* can be adduced as a defence in criminal trials.

But the *Föhn* also has some good effect: it melts the snow and enables flocks to be sent up to the Alpine pastures early. Thanks to it, some valleys, suitably situated, can grow maize and fruit trees far beyond the normal boundaries.

THE GLACIERS

About 10 000 years ago the Alpine glaciers overflowed, reaching colossal proportions – the glacier that filled what is now the Inn Valley was 1 700 m - 5 578 ft thick.

A glaciated valley has a unique geometric form that sets it apart from a valley that was cut solely by running water. Its gross shape as well as specific features on its walls and floor reflects the sculpturing effect of a valley glacier. By endless friction these enormous masses have cut great amphitheatres *(Kar) (illustration 1)* with its flattened trough (A) and steep sides (B) such as that which closes the Brandnertal *(p 52)*; they moulded great valleys called "feeding trough" valleys *(illustration 2)* with its U-shaped "scoop" with wide base (C) and steep sides (D) (Saalach Valley *p 121)*; or little hanging valleys cut so steeply that they overhang the principal valley, producing occasionally magnificent cascades (Achensee *p 94)*. The glaciers did not use the already existing relief pattern, instead they made their own course grinding the rocks into steps, thus providing ready made facilities for hydro-electric installations.

The glaciers carry along a rocky debris, which, when deposited, forms moraines *(illustration 3)*. A valley glacier builds at its snout an end moraine, marking the limit to which the glaciers advanced, and forming natural dams against which have accumulated the vast expanses of water of the Salzkammergut (in Austria) to the north (Attersee *p 138)* or the Bavarian plateau – and a lateral moraine (E) along the glacier sides in contact with the valley walls.

Two lateral moraines joining at the confluence of two valley glaciers combine to form a medial moraine (F).

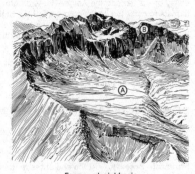

Former glacial basin.

A. Flattened trough.
B. Steep sides.

Former glacial valley.

C. U-shaped "scoop" with wide base, often embanked.
D. Shoulder.

Moraines.

E. Lateral moraine.
F. Medial moraine.

AUSTRIAN CONIFERS

Fichte
(Spruce)

Typical species on slopes facing north; resonant wood is used for sounding boards in pianos and the bodies of violins; in construction and for boats and barrels and as pulpwood.

Lärche
(Larch)

The only European conifer that sheds its leaves in winter – the wood coarse grained, strong, hard and heavy is used in ship construction, telephone poles, mines, timber and railway ties.

Schwarzkiefer
Schwarzföhre
(Austrian Black Pine)

It is the tree of the last limestone ranges bordering the Viennese basin; well liked for reafforestation under difficult conditions (chalky topsoil).

Zirbe
(Stone Pine)

This pine often grows alone at the upper limit of forest vegetation where it is battered by the wind; its smooth wood is much liked for carving and rustic furniture.

MOUNTAINEERING

In spite of political frontiers the Bavarian and Austrian Alps and the Dolomites form a single playground in Central Europe, with about 1 100 refuges. In Austria, 850 mountain-guides and ski-guides are at the disposal of tourists.

The Heroic Period. – The conquest of the Grossglockner (3 797 m - 12 458 ft) in 1800 was a victory not only over the difficulties presented by the mountain itself but also over the superstitions that surrounded it. However, it was only in the second half of the 19C that climbing became widely popular among the students of the Universities of Munich, Vienna, Innsbruck and Graz. The students were daring and also lacked money and as a consequence, to the horror of experienced French and Swiss mountaineers, frequently climbed in the eastern Alps without guides.

Today all the rock-walls of the Austrian Alps are listed in specialized guides – it is enough to remember that the Viennese have the Raxalpe climbing course and the Gesäuse school, 90 and 200 km - 56 and 124 miles respectively from home.

Contempt for Danger. – After the First World War, turning their backs on the atmosphere of disorder in the towns, young German and Austrian climbers undertook desperate enterprises, sometimes alone, with a contempt for danger bordering on frenzy. This daring brought about much of the tragic atmosphere associated with the rock-walls of the Dolomites and even more with the north wall of the Matterhorn, the Great Jurasses and the Eiger, regarded as the last great problems of the Alps and only conquered in 1931, 1935 and 1938 respectively. But technique was being perfected and mountaineering became a sport. In 1925, Wilo Welzenbach of Munich drew up a scale in six degrees of which the sixth corresponded with the limit of human endurance. This coldly objective classification shocked some of the idealists but has gradually come to be accepted.

Several German and Austrian expeditions have taken part in the conquest of the peaks in the Himalayas and the Karakoram. They attacked Nanga Parbat (8 125 m - 26 657 ft), the highest peak in Kashmir, which, with walls 5 000 m - 16 400 ft high, affords the greatest relative difference of level in the world. In 1895 the British Alpine climber Albert F. Mummery attempted to climb the mountain, he died trying. Many other climbers tried but none succeeded (due to terrible weather conditions or avalanches); it was a Tyrolese, Hermann Buhl, who completed the climb alone in 1953. This great mountain climber disappeared in 1957 after conquering the Broad Peak (8 047 m - 26 401 ft). In 1975 the Gasherbrum (Hidden Peak alt 8 068 m - 24 470 ft) was climbed by Reinhold Messner and Peter Habeler.

SKIING

Skiers from other countries, often drawn to Austria in the first place by the country's reputation for economic holidays, soon find themselves in sympathy with their hosts. The beginners appreciate, with pleasure, the fantasy tempering the hardness of learning to ski, for a sense of humour and peasant's friendliness are still to be found among instructors.

The Arlberg Period (1920-1930). – Although not the pioneer of Austrian skiing, **Hannes Schneider** (1890-1955), a man of the Arlberg, was the first to devise a coherent doctrine of Alpine skiing. He banned the Scandinavian Telemark swing (a turn made by lifting the weight from the outside and leaning over the inside ski) and drew on the technique of the snow plough for the *Stemmbogen* and the *Stemmschwung*. These, by enabling the pupil always to control his speed, gave him the necessary confidence for progress.

Schneider was alive to modern methods of communication. In 1926 he made a film, *The Wonders of Skiing,* which had a huge success. In 1927 Schneider met Arnold Lunn *(p 47),* founder of the Kandahar Ski Club who had revolutionized competitive skiing by codifying the downhill race and the slalom. The two men agreed to introduce at St. Anton a combination of the downhill run and the slalom, in 1928, the Arlberg-Kandahar, which has since become, thanks to its sporting nature, an unofficial world championship race of the Alpine countries.

About 1930 many contacts were made between the Tyrolese masters and instructors and the champions of other Alpine countries. Toni Seelos, an expert at the slalom whose elegant style was to influence the until then somewhat rough Arlberg technique, was in charge at Seefeld which became an advanced training centre and attracted men who were highly skilled including the young Frenchman Émile Allais. Allais, by critical observation and experiment, helped to create a new style: skidding, *Stemmschwung* with parallel skis – known as pure drops – diving with the body forward, etc.

Since 1956 Austrian skiing has maintained its excellent reputation. The *Wedeln (scull),* whose theory was devised by the instructor, Kruckenhauser, and the "Jet Welden" are systems used by skiers throughout the world *(1).*

The Austrian Snows. – In addition to Innsbruck which was re-equipped for the 1964 and 1976 Winter Olympic Games, Austria also offers a selection of smaller winter sports resorts which are all well equipped. Such are St. Anton, Seefeld and Kitzbühel, to which must be added spa resorts, notably Badgastein with its numerous ski-lifts and mountain villages such as Saalbach. These villages are scattered in such a way and the mountains are so inhabited that there has been no necessity, apart from the isolated cases of Zürs and Radstädter Tauernpass (the resort of the Obertauern), to build special ski resorts which might spoil the local atmosphere for the many foreigners who come to Austria not only for the excitement of skiing but also for the traditional friendliness of the mountaineers.

Following the general fashion, the cable-cars rise to heights of 3 000 m - 10 000 ft – and more. Such are the cable-cars from Kaprun up the Kitzsteinhorn which enable the tourist to ski far up the mountain, even in summer. They function also in the Upper Stubai Valley (Hochstubai installation), in the Upper Tux Valley and above Mayrhofen (Gefrorne Wand glacier), to mention but a few.

Cross-country Skiing. – The relatively gentle slopes of the Eastern Alps provide excellent terrain for cross-country skiing. Small hospitable villages as well as larger resorts (Seefeld, Kitzbühel) are well equipped with trails.

---

(1) For more details on the modern Austrian Technique read The New National Austrian Ski System *edited by the Austrian Association of Professional Ski Teachers (Kaye & Ward).*

HISTORICAL FACTS

The Habsburgs

1273-1291	**Rudolf I,** the founder of the Habsburg dynasty, divides Austria and Styria between his sons.
1335	Carinthia and Carniola annexed to the Habsburg domains.
1358-1365	Reign of Rudolf IV. The Tyrol annexed to Austria in 1363.
1440-1493	Friedrich III, Duke of Styria, inaugurates a policy of political succession and intermarriages which will raise the Habsburgs to the highest ranks in the west. His son Maximilian was the first to profit.

Expansion of Influence

1493-1519	By his marriage, **Maximilian I,** Emperor of the Holy Roman Empire, gains possession of most of the Burgundian States (Low Countries, Franche-Comté). He marries his eldest son, Philip the Fair, to the Infanta of Spain. Their son, Charles V, obtains the whole of their possessions.
1519-1556	Reign of **Charles V.** The Turks besiege Vienna in 1529.
1556	Abdication of Charles V and partition of the Empire. Ferdinand I, Charles's brother, is crowned Emperor and becomes head of the Austrian branch of the House of Habsburg. The founder of the Austrian monarchy, he also reigns over Bohemia and Hungary. Philip II, Charles's son, is given Spain and Portugal, northern Italy, Naples and Sicily, the Low Countries and Burgundy.
1618-1648	The Thirty Years War caused by the mutual antagonism of the Protestants and the Catholics and European fears of the political ambitions of Austria.

Consolidation of the Empire

1657-1705	Reign of Leopold I. Vienna again besieged by the Turks in 1683. The Hungarian monarchy falls to the Habsburgs in 1687.
18C	Throughout this century, Austrian policy is overshadowed by three great problems: the Succession to the Empire, the territorial threat from the Turks, the Piedmontese and the French, and the unified administration of different countries.
1713	To make sure that his daughter, in the absence of male heirs, shall receive the Imperial Crown, Karl VI sacrifices territorial rights to the great European countries and promulgates the Pragmatic Sanction. When the King dies, Maria Theresa has to defy its signatories in order to keep her empire. War of the Austrian Succession (1740-1748) and Seven Years War (1756-1763).
1740-1780	**Maria Theresa** ably supported in governing her States (Parliament), becomes popular owing to useful financial administrative reforms. In the authoritarian manner of enlightened despotism, her son, Josef II, continues this reorganization.
1781	Abolition of serfdom.
1786	Suppression of 738 convents and monasteries of contemplative orders, for the benefit of parochial organization.
1792-1835	Reign of Franz II. In 1805, as compensation for the losses of territory suffered by her under the Treaty of Pressburg, Austria is given the domains of the Archbishopric of Salzburg. In 1806, Franz II renounces the title of Head of the Holy Roman Empire and adopts that of Emperor of Austria under the name of **Franz I.**
1809	**Metternich,** the Chancellor, practically directs Austrian policy and works for revenge against France. Rebellion of the Tyrolese, led by Andreas Hofer, against the Franco-Bavarian alliance (Year Nine).

Troubles and Downfall of the Monarchy

1814-1815	**Congress of Vienna.** Austria recovers the territories lost in her wars with France and takes a leading position in the Germanic Confederation of which Metternich was the mastermind.
1848-1849	Revolution in Vienna. Fall of Metternich, Hungarian rebellion suppressed with the help of Russia.
1848-1916	Reign of **Franz-Josef.**
1866	War between Austria and Prussia. Austria is defeated at Sadowa, gives up her intervention in German politics and casts her eyes upon the Balkans.
1867	Creation of the dual Austro-Hungarian monarchy, with common defence, foreign and economic policies.
1878	Occupation of Bosnia and Herzegovina by Austria.
1914	The assassination at Sarajevo (Bosnia) of the Crown Prince, Franz Ferdinand, unleashes the First World War.
1916-1918	Reign of Karl I and collapse of the Dual Monarchy.

The Republic

1919	Treaty of St-Germain-en-Laye. Cession of South Tyrol to Italy. After a plebiscite, southern Carinthia, which was to be ceded to Yugoslavia, remains Austrian. Karl Renner becomes the first State Chancellor.
1933	Chancellor Dollfuss inaugurates an authoritarian régime, hostile both to the Social-Democrats and to the Nazis.
1934	Social Democratic Party banned. Nazi *Putsch.* Assassination of Chancellor Dollfuss. His successor, Schuschnigg, tries to avoid war with Germany.
1936	Germany recognizes the territorial sovereignty of Austria.
1938	Hitler in fact invades Austria, the campaign is known as Ostmark; Austria becomes a province of the Greater German Reich. A referendum approves the Anschluss (annexation).
1943	At the Moscow Conference, the Allies undertake to restore to Austria, after the war, its independence and its frontiers of 1 January 1938.
1945	The Russians occupy Vienna on 11 April. On 27 April a Government is formed under the premiership of Karl Renner. The democratic constitution of 1920 is put into practise. Austria and Vienna are divided into four occupation zones.
15 May 1955	**Belvedere Treaty.** Evacuation of occupying troops. Proclamation of Austrian neutrality.

HISTORICAL FACTS

Historical Events in Britain and in America

Richard, Earl of Cornwall and brother of Henry II of England, as King of the Germans invested Ottaker (King of Bohemia, 1253) with the Duchies of Austria and Styria.	**1260**
Columbus sighted the New World.	**1492**
First colonists settle in North America.	**1583**
War of Spanish Succession. Duke of Marlborough in command of the English and Dutch armies saved Vienna from the French at the victory of Blenheim (1704).	**1701–1714**
War of Austrian Succession. The Austrian cause was supported by England and Holland against Prussia, France and Spain. At Dettingen (1743) an army of British, Austrians and Hanoverians commanded by George II was victorious over the French. This was the last time an English king fought in person on the battlefield. At Fontenoy (1745) an English-Austrian army suffered defeat. British naval superiority and gains in North American and India laid foundations of British Empire.	**1740–1748**
Seven Years War. Britain and Prussia ranged against France, Austria and Russia. British sea power (Quiberon Bay, 1759) and conquests of Wolfe and Clive gave to Britain her Canadian and Indian possessions.	**1756–1763**
American Declaration of Independence.	**1776**
Napoleonic Wars. Four times defeated under Franz I (the Emperor Franz II), Austria was supported by England to re-enter the fight against Napoleon and shared in his overthrow (1813-1814). The Duke of Wellington took part in the Congress of Vienna to resettle European territories, under which Austria received Lombardy and Venetia.	**1792–1815**
Crimean War. Austrian intervention forced Russian withdrawal from Balkan invasion, together with the sinking of the Turkish fleet at Sinope. Britain and France declared war on Russia in 1854.	**1853–1856**
Civil War.	**1861–1865**
The First World War began with Austria's attack on Serbia after the assassination at Sarajevo of Franz Ferdinand, heir to the Austrian throne.	**1914–1918**
Stock market crash.	**1929**
World War II. Austria liberated by Allied armies in April 1945. Austria and Vienna divided into four zones: British, French, American and Russian.	**1939–1945**

GREAT DAYS AND ADVERSITIES

The Eastern March. – The Danube Valley was opened to Roman expansion. The mixing of peoples which Europe saw after the Celtic occupation had most effect in Austria.

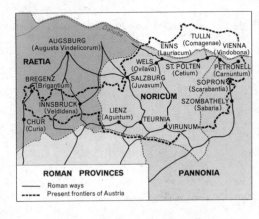

After defeating the Avar tribes, who lived in the area that is now Hungary, Charlemagne reinforced the defensive system of his empire by forming, on the banks of the Danube, the Eastern March – Ostmark or Ostarichi – whose name became Österreich in German and finally Austria in English.

The House of Babenberg (976–1246). – This family brought unity to a country wrestling with opposing influences and cleverly preserved it through the quarrels of the Papacy and the Empire which set popes against emperors. They chose, as residences, Pöchlarn, Melk, Tulln, the Leopoldsberg and finally Vienna. They were devout and favoured the foundation of abbeys such as Kremsmünster, St. Florian, Melk, Göttweig, Klosterneuburg, Heiligenkreuz, Zwettl and Lilienfeld.

Under Heinrich II Jasomirgott, Austria was elevated to the rank of a hereditary Duchy.

The last of the Babenbergs, Frederick the Warrior, was killed while fighting the Magyars. The vacancy he left aroused the envy of the kings of Bohemia and Hungary.

Ottokar of Bohemia got the better of his rival and imposed his rule on the former possessions of the Babenbergs, but ended by finding an opponent in Rudolf of Habsburg, who had been chosen by the Prince-Electors to succeed the Babenbergs.

Rudolf the Founder. – Rudolf, who was crowned in 1273, immediately attacked Ottokar, occupied Vienna and won the victory of Marchfeld in 1278. The opening phase had begun of what was to be the remarkable destiny of the House of Habsburg.

A.E.I.O.U. – *Austria Est Imperare Orbi Universo* – Austria shall rule the world. The career of the Habsburg dynasty *(see genealogical tree opposite)* in less than three centuries was such that it could adopt this proud device; to the political wisdom of its representatives wearing the imperial crown, it added great diplomatic skill. A clever marriage policy brought Austria, in the 16C, more territory than the most fortunate of wars: Maximilian I, a prince who was a friend of the arts *(p 36)*, acquired the Franche-Comté and the Low Countries by his marriage with Mary of Burgundy, daughter of Charles the Bold; his son, Philip the Fair, married Joan the Mad, Queen of Castile, the child of this union being Charles V. As Holy Roman Emperor, King of Spain, possessor of Naples, Sicily and Sardinia and immense territories in the two Americas, Charles V, the successor of the Habsburgs through his father, was the most powerful sovereign in Europe. This vast

Empire remained united but a short time beneath a single crown. On the abdication of Charles V, the territories were divided between Charles's son, Philip II, and his brother, Ferdinand I, who reigned over the Habsburg's German possessions and Bohemia and Hungary.

"Long Live Our Maria Theresa!". – This was the cry of the Hungarian noblemen, preparing in 1740 to defend the rights of their young sovereign, aged 23. Maria Theresa, the daughter of Karl VI, found a difficult situation when she came to the throne.

The Elector of Bavaria, who had himself chosen as Emperor under the name of Karl VII, showed himself, at first, to be a dangerous rival.

War broke out between Austria on the one hand, Bavaria, Prussia and France on the other. Maria Theresa faced it with tireless energy, and her forty-years' reign brought positive gains. She allied her husband, Duke François of Lorraine, with her Empire, and after his death, her son, Josef II. Remarkably supported by first class ministers and generals, she carried out useful financial and administrative reforms.

The Struggle with France (1792–1815). – For the twenty-three years during which Revolutionary, then Imperial, France was at war with the rest of Europe, Austria was, together with England, her most determined opponent.

It was France which on 20 April 1792 declared war on Franz II, Emperor of Austria and Germany. The war went badly for the Austrians: beaten at Jemappes in 1792, at Marengo and Hohenlinden in 1800 and threatened, after Napoleon's daring campaign, in Italy in 1797.

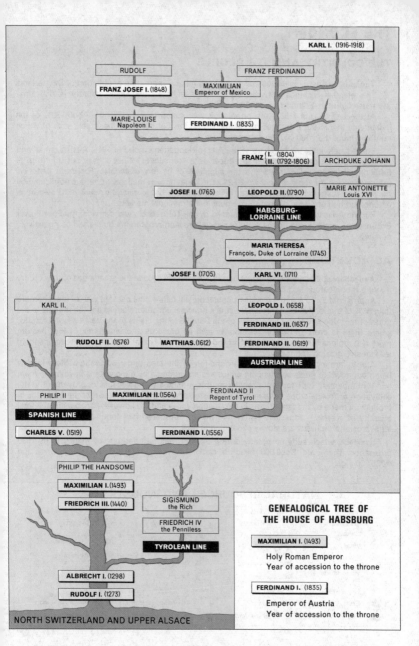

The accession of Napoleon to the imperial throne in 1804 was a heavy blow to the Habsburg monarchy. Napoleon I opened his reign with the victories of Ulm and Austerlitz (1805) and forced Franz II to sue for peace and renounce the crown of the Holy Roman Empire. In 1809 the defeat of the French on the battlefields of Essling and Aspern and the successes of the Tyrolese partisans under the leadership of Andreas Hofer brought new hope to the Austrians. But the victory of Napoleon at Wagram was followed by the Treaty of Vienna. In 1810 the victor married the daughter of the vanquished. But Metternich refused to accept humiliation and after the Russian campaign of 1812 threw all the forces of Austria against Napoleon. In 1814 the Austrian troops under Schwarzenberg entered Paris.

The Congress of Vienna *(p 149)* consolidated not only the triumph of Metternich, who was virtually directing the politics of all Europe, but renewed the power of the Habsburgs.

The Century of Franz-Josef. – Franz-Josef's reign of sixty-eight years (1848–1916), one of the longest in history, ended in failure, since the Habsburg monarchy collapsed two years after his death. Nevertheless, history remembers this sovereign, loved and respected by his people, and the profound social, economic and political changes made in his reign.

Few monarchs have had to face so many political difficulties: the revolution of 1848, on his accession to the throne, marked by a terrible revolt of the Hungarians, which was checked by aggressive Russian intervention; the *Ausgleich* (compromise) of 1867 which created a dual Austro-Hungarian government; disastrous wars in Italy against Napoleon III in 1859 and against Prussia in 1866; family misfortunes: death of the Emperor's brother, the Emperor Maximilian of Mexico, shot in 1867; death of his only son, the Crown Prince Rudolf, at Mayerling in 1889; assassination of his wife, the Empress Elizabeth (the beautiful Sissi) at Geneva in 1898; assassination of his nephew, the Archduke Franz Ferdinand at Sarajevo in 1914. Yet his reign resulted, at home, in economic prosperity and a gentle way of life, reflected in the middle class of the period, and by an artistic revival and development of town-planning of which, in Vienna, the layout of the Ring was typical *(p 152)*.

THE ECONOMY

THE COUNTRY AND ITS PEOPLE

The area of Austria is 84 000 km^e - 32 432 sq miles – more than double that of Switzerland.
The greatest distance between the frontiers of this club-shaped country is 580 km - 316 miles (London–Edinburgh = 600 km - 373 miles).

At the last census (1981) the population was stated to be 7 555 000. About 30% of the inhabitants live in the five cities of Vienna, Graz, Linz, Salzburg and Innsbruck, each of which numbers more than 100 000 inhabitants.

Immediately after the break-up of the Austro-Hungarian Empire in 1919, Austria, small and mountainous, appeared on the map almost as a "remainder" since it was cut off from its traditional commercial markets and the suppliers of its raw materials. *(For more historical information see the table of facts pp 20-21.)* The situation was made even more complicated by the fact that Austrian industry had been developed in the 19C to meet the needs of its own huge empire and had not been geared to compete in international markets.

Recent vicissitudes – conditions imposed by the Third Reich, war damage, the Four Power Occupation – have forced on the country a reconstruction programme that is still being actively pursued.

AGRICULTURE

Agriculture still plays an important part in Austrian life despite the great areas of the country that are mountainous and unsuitable.

Approximately 10% of the working population still follows the peasant way of life and more than 90% of the food is homegrown. Austria's principal agricultural areas are the regions to the north of the Alps and along both sides of the Danube to the plains of the eastern border areas, where there is crop and cattle farming as well as orchards and vineyards. In the medium mountain regions there is cattle breeding and forestry, while in the high mountain regions there is extensive grazing and forestry.

Arable farming represents less than one-fith of the area under cultivation. More land is being put down to grass because the difficulties encountered by the peasants have made them go, in numbers, to look for more regular returns in industry and because improvement in the cultivation of forage crops have improved livestock. Nevertheless, because of the increases in production made by the large farms in the Danube Valley and the Lower Austrian plain, the total quantity of cereals – especially barley and maize – produced has continued to rise slightly. Vineyards and orchards are slowly expanding in area.

Livestock, which suffered greatly during the war, has returned approximately to its 1939 prosperity. There are 2 560 000 head of cattle, of which 1 000 000 are dairy cows, and 4 025 000 pigs.

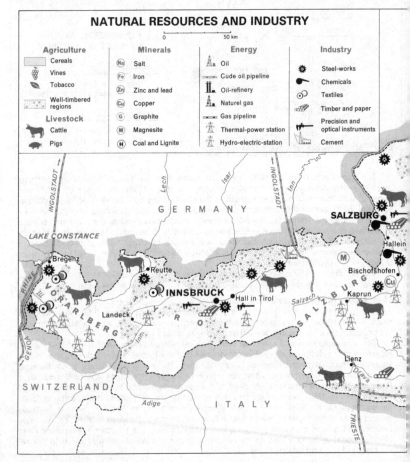

NATURAL RESOURCES AND INDUSTRY

FORESTRY

One-quarter of the people of Austria gain their livelihood from the forests which, consisting largely of conifers, cover nearly 45% of the country and represent one of the greatest national resources. The place of timber in the Austrian economy is only surpassed in Europe by its importance in Finland and Sweden.

Timber, particularly rough-sawn timber, is one of Austria's main exports and represents 5.2% of the total. The industry rivals, in importance in the Austrian economy, the iron industry if the subsidiary papermaking and packaging industries are included. There is still scope for great advance in the exploitation of forestry products locally before export.

POWER RESOURCES

From the time **water power** first began to be developed for hydro-electric energy, progress has been most encouraging. There are at present more than 1 000 power stations in operation.

If dams were constructed on all the sites theoretically suitable, production could rise to 50 000 million kWh (output in the United Kingdom in 1980 = 441 875 million kWh), which would make Austria, for its size, one of the larger producers of electrical energy in Europe. Actually only about 60% of the national resources have been developed, but already there are spectacular achievements to be seen such as that at Kaprun *(p 173)*, that in the Upper Valley of the Ill *(p 47)* at Malta, at Zemm and, in the central areas, running with the flow of the Danube, the dams and power stations at Ybbs Persenbeug and Aschach *(pp 61 and 60 respectively)* Wallsee-Mitterkirchen, Ottensheim-Wilhering, etc.

Nearly half of the railways are electrified and approximately 90% of the traffic is carried in modern equipment. Electrical consumption per person per year is on average slightly below that of Western Germany and well below that of the United Kingdom.

Oil, another of the natural resources which has been developed since 1938 – to the exclusive advantage of the Germans and Russians for many years – remains a trump card in the Austrian economy though production is declining.

In 1979 the wells, mostly concentrated in the Matzen area, Aderklaa and Zistersdorf in Lower Austria, produced approximately 1 720 000 tons of crude oil. The greater part of this was refined at Schwechat, the large suburd of Vienna. The construction in 1970 of a pipeline leading off to Vienna from the great trans-alpine Trieste-Ingolstadt oil pipeline (TAL) has allowed the refinery at Schwechat, whose capacity is nearly 14 million tons, to work to full production and also supply one quarter of the total Austrian car, industrial and domestic oil requirements.

The production of **natural gas** now stands at 2.4 milliard m³ - 85 milliard cu ft. Natural gas drilled in Austria is either piped to local factories and power stations or to industrial centres in other parts of the country. However, a part of the country's demand is met by supplies from abroad – importation has become essential. Part of the country's gas requirement is supplied by the USSR to Italy (Trans-Austria Gas Pipeline – TAG) pipeline and by the USSR to West Germany (West Austria Gas Pipeline – WAG) pipeline.

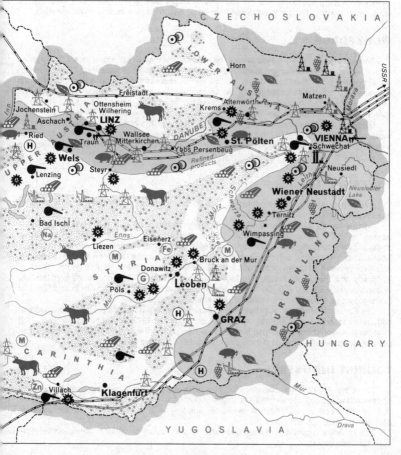

MINING AND HEAVY INDUSTRY

Austria is a country with a long tradition in mining and heavy industry; in the Tyrol especially deposits of gold, silver and copper were mined intensively up to the 17C. Salt mining (p 27) and the mining of non-ferrous minerals are still carried on there, in particular in the production of **magnesite**. Austria, with 1 105 000 tons in 1979, was among the greatest producers in the world. This mineral is used in the fire-proof linings for blast-furnaces and smelting ovens. It is also used in construction work. So far as building resources are concerned, Austria is self-sufficient in cement.

Current development of **heavy industry** in Austria is governed, above all, by production in the metallurgical basin in Styria where the well known Iron Mountain, the Erzberg is situated. The biggest opencast mine in Europe, it supplies the blast furnaces of Donawitz which produce steel sections and those of Linz producing sheet metal.

In 1979 Austrian steel production reached a total of about 5 million metric tons (U.K.: 11 million metric tons). The insufficient production of iron ore and, above all, the lack of scrap-iron for the smelting ovens, have stimulated research especially at the School of Mining Engineering at Leoben. Austrian engineers have perfected the "Linz-Donawitz" technique (L-D-Verfahren), now used under licence by more than 200 steel firms abroad, and that of metallurgical powders (Plansee works near Reutte).

TEXTILE AND CHEMICAL INDUSTRIES

Austria has succeeded, since the industrial revolution, in modernizing the manufacturing industries, even those as traditional as textile. In the great chemical industry entirely new equipment has recently been installed.

Textile Industries. – These go back to a famous craft tradition, for the materials woven in Vorarlberg were much sought after in the fairs of central Europe in the time of the Thirty Years War. Even today Viennese embroidery and lace from Vorarlberg are amongst the most important, in monetary value, of Austria's textile exports.

At the time of the industrial revolution in the 19C, production of yarn and cloth was concentrated in the Vorarlberg (the cotton-belt) which, in this, followed a parallel course to the neighbouring Swiss cantons of Appenzell and St. Gallen, and in the region of Vienna, where the proximity of a large town directed production particularly towards the manufacture of fabrics for clothes and furnishings.

The textile industry today in all employs about 45 000 workers and, with an export trade (including clothing) which amounts to more than 19 milliard Austrian Schillings is one of Austria's primary exports.

The Chemical Industry. – While the soda and chlorate industries and their derivatives have benefited from their proximity to the old salt mines of the Salzkammergut (Hallein), the chemical industry is modern. The nitrogen works at Linz produces 1.5 million tons and more than covers the domestic requirements for chemical fertilizers, exporting the surplus as does the Lenzing factory producing approximately 105 000 tons of staple fibre a year, making it amongst the largest in the world. Rubber is produced in greatest quantity at the factory at Wimpassing.

WORKFORCE

The Austrian economy's expansion in recent years has led to full employment, this applies also to industry: steel construction and machinery – 12.5%; electrical industry – 11.2%; iron and metal goods –10%; chemical industry – 9.7%. The increase in production is due mostly to the increase in productivity, especially in the metallurgical, chemical and paper industries. The provinces where the greatest industrial progress has been made since 1936 are the "Land" of Salzburg, where manpower has more than trebled, Upper Austria and the Tyrol.

Outside agriculture and industry is the third section of the community, which includes all those not actually engaged in production – people in the professions, in commerce, banking and insurance and transport – who contribute to raising the standard of living and soon equaling that of Switzerland.

EXTERNAL TRADE

Austrian external trade amounted in 1979 to approximately £206 milliard for imports as against £206 milliard for exports.

Austria has to import foodstuffs – particularly cereals, fruit and early vegetables (these amount to 5.8% of her total imports), coal, machinery and cars. She exports machinery, metallurgical products, textiles, wood and paper bricks and magnesite panels, and optical instruments. Her trading partners, in order of importance, are: the Common Market countries – with first Western Germany, then Italy, France, Switzerland and the United Kingdom.

Trade with the United Kingdom in 1980 amounted to £279 681 000 for imports from the U.K. to Austria and £307 267 700 for exports from Austria to the U.K. Trade with both EFTA and Eastern Europe is becoming steadier but still amounts to very little.

The Common Market's important role in Austria's foreign trade has prompted the national authorities to seek a special trade agreement, concluded in 1972, with that organization – full membership would not be compatible with Austria's policy of neutrality. Certain products can pass freely between Austria and the Common Market Countries without taxation.

TOURIST INDUSTRY

There are 21 911 hotels, country inns and *pensions,* besides countless rooms in people's houses (about 45 000), to support the tourist industry. In 1980 visitors from abroad occupied 76% of the hotel accommodation available, bringing with them revenue to the value of 83.3 milliard Austrian Schillings.

The currency brought in by tourism enables the country to absorb almost entirely the external trade deficit.

SALT AND SPAS

Among the mineral resources drawn upon in Austria, salt-mining is now only of minor importance. Nonetheless, since prehistoric times the precious mineral has played such a part in the civilization of the eastern Alps and in trading that tourists can hardly overlook the various enterprises still being worked in the Salzburg area. Moreover, in the medical sphere, the salt waters of Bad Aussee, Bad Ischl and Hall in Tirol in the Tyrol form the basis of useful cures.

Place-names often include the syllable *Salz* or *Hall* – synonymous terms, meaning salt, salt-works. Tours through the mine galleries varied by slides on toboggans down slippery slopes and the crossing of illuminated underground lakes always attract tourists. The miners sticks faithfully to their traditional vocabulary – the greeting *"Glück auf"* (have the good luck to come up again) can still be heard – and dress uniform and they still believe the innumerable legends about the world below ground with its gnomes and goblins.

Melting Mountains. – Except in the natural springs *(Solequellen)* of Bad Reichenhall, the mineral deposits in the Austrian Alps consist of a mixture, called *Haselgebirge,* of salt, clay and gypsum. The miners begin by making a pit in the bed, which they flood and keep supplied regularly with fresh water. This water dissolves the rock on the spot and, being now saturated with salt (27%), sinks to the bottom of the basin, from which it can be pumped, while impurities are left behind. The brine *(Sole)* is brought to the surface and pumped into the vats of the salt factories *(Sud-hütten),* for the production of domestic or industrial salt.

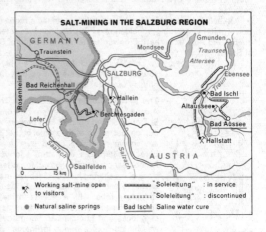

SALT-MINING IN THE SALZBURG REGION

The First Pipelines. – The difficulty of supplying fuel, arising from the huge consumption of the wood burning furnaces, and the desire to bring the centres of production within reach of those where salt was consumed in the lowlands, led the authorities from the 17C onwards to process the brine far from the mines, which were often isolated in the mountains. For this they built conduits of wood, lead or cast iron known as *Soleleitung,* the longest of which ran for 79 km - 49 miles from Bad Reichenhall to Rosenheim, in Bavaria and worked from 1810 to 1958 *(see Michelin Green Guide to Germany).* Pumping stations *(Brunnhaus),* kept up a constant flow of brine, over hill and dale. To prevent too sudden a drop the aqueducts included long mountainside sections as in the *bisses* (water-conduits) of the Swiss Valais. The footpaths or *Soleleitungsweg* which followed them made splendid *corniche* routes; such are the mine-road from Hallstatt to Bad Ischl, clinging to the mountainside above the Lake of Hallstatt.

When the salt had been refined it was sent on by water – as on the Inn below Hall in Tirol *(p 80)* and the Lower Traun *(p 137)* – or in carts. Many salt-roads *(Salzstrassen)* in Austria, one of the best known being the Ellbögen road *(p 91),* recall memories of this traffic, so fruitful for the country's economy and the public treasury.

Spas. – Tourists concerned about their health will find in Austria a wide selection of resorts equipped for the most varied treatment. In the skiing season many of these country resorts (Badgastein) keep their warm water swimming pools open.

Sulphur-springs. – These are used mainly to remedy ailments of the joints, muscles and nervous system and skin troubles at resorts such as Baden whose thermal beach draws many Viennese and, in the Salzkammergut, at Bad Ischl, Bad Goisern, etc.

Salt-springs. – Waters impregnated with sodium chloride (salt) from natural springs or "mother-waters", the residues of the refining of industrial salt, are exploited together with the salt-mines. They are used in douches and baths and are good for gynaecological and infantile diseases and for inhaling, when they clear the bronchial tubes. To this group may be added the bicarbonate bearing waters, like those of Bad Gleichenberg in Styria, which are also recommended for drinking to treat the stomach, intestines and kidneys.

Iodized-springs. – These are invaluable for curing metabolic and circulation disorders, and for vision and glandular troubles. They are particularly well represented by Bad Hall in Upper Austria.

In addition to the true mineral springs, some hot springs such as those at Badgastein also have radioactive properties.

Special Treatment. – The baths and applications of mud are current practise in many resorts. Patients suffering from inflammation of the joints or the after-effects of wounds have good hopes of a final cure.

The naturist and dietetic **Kneipp Cure** was perfected by Sebastian Kneipp, the parish priest of the Bavarian village of Wörishofen from 1855 to 1897. The system uses every kind of hydrotherapy in specialized establishments.

Places to stay

A wide variety of places to stay
– resorts, spas and ski areas –
have been selected to make your holiday more pleasant.

A map on pp 40–41 shows the location of the places listed on pp 39 to 43.

PICTURESQUE AUSTRIA

THE DECOR

Austria still lives in a setting, piously preserved and renewed, of a God-fearing nation.

The Signs of Faith. – The roofed crosses set up at the roadside or in open fields *(Wiesenkreuz)* bear a figure of Christ which can often be renewed, thanks to the work of local woodcarvers. They are numerous in the Tyrol.

In Carinthia popular piety more often brought about the erection of a *Bildstock*. This is a tall post whose top, protected from the weather by a small wooden roof, has several facets decorated with religious paintings by local artists.

Christ is also prominent inside Tyrolean houses, including the public rooms of inns. Here the crucifix is placed in a corner and leans into the room in a protective attitude. This is called the *Herrgottswinkel* (God's corner).

On belfries often shine the initials JHS (or a triangle representing the Holy Trinity) in a setting of golden rays. This tradition was established in the Eastern Alps from the 15C onwards after the preaching of St Bernard of Siena.

Roofed cross.

Following a mediaeval custom, many churches have a funeral chapel, sometimes still in use as an ossuary or charnel-house *(Karner)* as at Hallstatt.

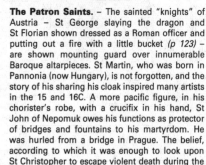

The Holy Family.

The Patron Saints. – The sainted "knights" of Austria – St George slaying the dragon and St Florian shown dressed as a Roman officer and putting out a fire with a little bucket *(p 123)* – are shown mounting guard over innumerable Baroque altarpieces. St Martin, who was born in Pannonia (now Hungary), is not forgotten, and the story of his sharing his cloak inspired many artists in the 15 and 16C. A more pacific figure, in his chorister's robe, with a crucifix in his hand, St John of Nepomuk owes his functions as protector of bridges and fountains to his martyrdom. He was hurled from a bridge in Prague. The belief, according to which it was enough to look upon St Christopher to escape violent death during the day, is vouched for by traces of several gigantic paintings on church walls (Imst).

Bildstock.

Considerable devotion to the Madonna is everywhere evident; one also sees signs of a special devotion to St Anne, the Virgin's mother. She often appears in the representation of a trinity of the Holy Family (Anna Selbdritt): the Saint carries the Virgin on one arm, the Infant Jesus on the other.

Austria also has its **civic heroes,** in particular Andreas Hofer who organized the Tyrolean resistance against Napoleon and Archduke Johann, a friend of the people and of progress.

Towns and Cities. – In Styria, Carinthia and the Danubian countryside the most interesting town planning is most often that based on a main road.

When the place was first developed the old road was widened to form a sort of esplanade, known as the *Anger* (lawn). When all the land on each side of the *Anger* was built over, the form known as the *Strassenplatz* (street-square) was reached. These street-squares, shaped like spindles or regular oblong rectangles, form the heart of the town between the gateways, once fortified, leading to them. The monuments representing municipal dignity are generally to be found there: the *Pestsäule* (Plague Column) set up like that in Vienna *(p 147)* at the end of the 17C; also fountains, etc.

Town Planning in the Lower Inn and Salzach Valleys.
(Rattenberg – view from the castle)

Tyrolean Urbanism.
(Kitzbühel – the Stadtplatz)

Façades are surmounted by a horizontal ledge which masks a sloping roof *(Grabendach - p 120)*.
The whole scene with its Italian echoes, forms a strong contrast with the picturesque style of Kitzbühel (adjacent). Rattenberg is the Austrian town where this method of roofing is best preserved.

The main streets of the old cities of the Tyrol (Kitzbühel) are lined with substantial houses, often covered with outside paintings.
The gabled roofs, placed side by side, form a picturesque broken skyline.

From Ludwig Reiter, Dr Moser, Georg Angerer, Franz Nussbaumer and Cosy-Kunstverlag (Salzburg) photos.

Rural Scenes. – Field fences often hem in the by-roads of Austria, which have no verges. In the country round Salzburg, especially the Tennengau and the Pinzgau, these fences are made of laths interwoven in a distinctive way.

When haymaking, the mountain farmers, anxious to get good forage, remove the hay from contact with the damp soil by piling it on stakes furnished with wooden pegs. Another method is to hang the hay on wires, like linen hung out to dry.

In the Carinthian Alps cereals are grown on the sunny slopes up to a height of 1 500 m - 4 500 ft – but the harvest often has to be gathered early on account of frost. The sheaves are spread out on wooden driers with horizontal struts, sometimes covered and the grain is able to ripen.

Fencing at Abtenau.

Drying-rack for cereals.

Hay in Carinthia.

Farms and Chalets. – From the Tyrol, dotted with mountain chalets, to Lower Austria and the Burgenland, which have been cultivated by huge farming interests, Austria displays a great variety of country dwellings *(see Austrian Open Air Museum p 76)*.

House in the Bregenzerwald at Bezau.

Tyrolean chalet.

In this part of the Vorarlberg, with its Germanic civilization, the peasant's house hardly differs from the Appenzell type found on the Swiss bank of the Rhine. The façades covered with shingles, where each row of windows peeps from under a protective ledge, are typical.

The Lower Inn Valley was colonized by the Bavarians, and the farmhouses are like those in the Chiemgau Alps (e.g. in the Reit im Winkl area, *local map p 92*).
A fine type of house, with a low-pitched roof decorated with a little belfry and often weighted with blocks of stone. Long balconies run the length of the upper storey.

Farm on the Danube Plain.
(Countryside south of the Danube)

Heuriger in Lower Austria.
(Beethoven's house at Heiligenstadt.)

These big quadrangular farm buildings *(Vierkant)* round a central courtyard stand alone in the middle of each estate in the hilly country between Linz and St. Pölten.

This style survives up to the suburbs of Vienna. The small, low buildings are symmetrically placed on either side of a yard open at the street end by a coach-house door.

From "Monopol", Landesfremdenverkehrsamt Klagenfurt, Tiroler Verkehrswerbung Innsbruck, Hiller, Austrian National Tourist Office and the Geographical Institute of the University of Vienna photos.

PEASANT TRADITIONS

Traditions of more or less peasant origin and religious fêtes are still faithfully observed in Austria, especially in the mountain areas.

End of Winter. – In February, to drive out the bad genies of winter and prepare for the return of spring, carnival processions *(Faschingsumzüge)* make the valleys ring with their joyful din. The traditional figures, ringing cow-bells and hand-bells, wearing carved wooden masks and with huge crowns of flowers and foliage on their heads, perform, in accordance with unchanging custom, dances symbolizing the struggle against the evil spirits of winter. The masked processions of Nassereith and Telfs attract large crowds *(see tourist calendar of events opposite)*.

(After Sickert photo)

Carnival masks from Nassereith.

Spring Festivals. – When winter has been unceremoniously dismissed, the first tufts of grass make their appearance and Easter is celebrated – the festival of the Resurrection and also that of nature renewed. A huge bough, decorated with box leaves, ivy and *pretzels* and solemnly carried by village children, often takes the place, in the country, of the simple branches blessed in church on Palm Sunday. The palm branches are afterwards planted in the fields, where they will protect the seeds from the frost.

In spring, blossoming nature calls out Sunday walkers, and long lines of the faithful in their best clothes trail along the roads. The Corpus Christi processions are particularly picturesque at Traunkirchen and at Hallstatt, where they are held in boats. At Brixen im Thale, near Kitzbühel, there is a mounted procession by the local peasantry.

Summer and Autumn. – As summer approaches, celebrations and festivals multiply in the towns, but become rarer in the country. However, the bonfires celebrating the return of that season twinkle gaily on midsummer's, St John's, night. Round Innsbruck the floodlit mountain crests make sparkling garlands in the sky, while fireworks light up the valleys during the Sacred Heart.

Joyous, noisy festivals mark the end of work in the fields (Salzburg countryside) or of the wine harvest (Burgenland, Lower Austria). In September and October they crown the hard work of the summer. In the mountains cowbells are heard as the herds come down from the Alpine pastures.

Before the loneliness of winter this is the time for the great fairs (Ägydimarkt at Graz, Jahrmarkt at Aussee, Weisenmarkt at St. Veit).

In early autumn a smell of apples may greet visitors at the entrance to a church. The peasants bring their products to the harvest festival: apples, nuts, grapes and wheat are piled up on special tables.

The same spirit of thanksgiving is shown at the festival of St Leonard, when peasants and their wives and farm workers, dressed in their best, go joyfully to church in flower decked carts to celebrate mass in honour of St Leonard, the patron saint of livestock.

Festivities at Christmas and New Year. – On the evening of 5 December, the passing of St Niklaus (St Nicholas) marks the beginning of the Christmas celebrations. He goes from door to door, giving apples, nuts and cakes to good children. There is then a wonderful display of carved wood cribs in houses and churches, and wakes and vigils follow one another until Christmas.

Another children's tradition, the *Sternsingen* (carols), closes this period of the festival. On the eve of Epiphany, children go from farm to farm, thus commemorating the starlit march of the three Kings of the East. In every house they sing the traditional carol "May Gaspar, Melchior and Balthazar guard you and bless you", and when they have gone, the master of the house chalks the initials of the three Kings and the date on the door. A new year can then begin under divine protection.

COSTUMES

Regional costumes are still objects of admiration and respect in Austria. On fête days the velvet corsages of the women of Ischl, the embroidered silk blouses of the Wachau, the beribboned corselets of the Montafon and the lace aprons of the Burgenland bear witness to the richness of local folklore. Men wear leather or *Loden* wool breeches, tight at the knee, and often supplanted nowadays by shorts which are more convenient for the brisk movements of Tyrolean dancing. They have broad braces and leather belts decorated with applied designs (ivory chamois, Edelweiss in felt) and short jackets, without collars or lapels, of many coloured *Loden* wool.

The province, and even the valley from which the men come, may be recognized by their hats, adorned with various trophies (badger-brush in Bavaria, grouse feathers in the Wipptal), black or green, conical or flat.

Though not connected with any special folklore tradition, the **Dirndl** is always popular with foreign visitors. The rather old-fashioned charm and gay and contrasting colours of this dress, which, while defying fashion, has remained original while adapting itself to modern conditions, attract and hold attention. A pleated skirt, an apron printed in light colours (blue and white, pink and white), knotted at the waist, a slightly open-necked and pleated white corsage with full sleeves and a buttoned or laced corselet form the basis of the *Dirndl*, which is subject to a thousand local or personal variations.

As original as the *Dirndl* for women, but much more dressy, since it is not out of place at an evening reception and has been called the Alpine dinner-jacket, is the **Steirer Anzug**, which is the city suit of Austrian men. Great and small proudly wear the grey *Loden* trousers or breeches (dark brown in Carinthia) embroidered in green, white socks and long, rather flaring coat with green embroidery and gilt buttons. The equivalent feminine costume differs from that for men by hardly more than the skirt **(Steirer Kostüm)**.

The *Loden*, wool sweater and peasant blouse with its unique embroidery, buttons and belts make up the Austrian look honoured in the Viennese and Salzburg shops.

TOURIST CALENDAR OF EVENTS

DATE	PLACE	NATURE OF EVENT

Folklore

DATE	PLACE	NATURE OF EVENT
January 6 (every 4 years – next in 1986)	**Badgastein** (p 51)	*Perchtenlaufen:* carnival procession.
February (in turn) 1983 / 1984 / 1985	**Nassereith** Map 426 / **Imst** / **Telfs** 16, 30, 31	*Schemenlaufen* / *Schleicherlaufen* / *Schellerlaufen* — carnival procession symbolizing the combat between the evil spirits and the spirits of fertility.
1st Sunday in May	**Zell am Ziller** (p 71)	*Gauderfest.*
Whit Monday	**Freistritz an der Gail** (West of Villach – map 426 34, 35)	*Kufenstechen:* jousting in which galloping horsemen pierce a barrel with a lance.
End of May through September (next in 1985)	**Erl** (North of Kufstein – map 426 18) (local map p 92)	Mysteries of the Passion.
Thursday in Corpus Christi week	Regions with strong Roman Catholic traditions, especially: **Brixen im Thale** (map 426 18)	*Antlassritt:* mounted procession.
	Hallstatt (p 81)	
	Traunkirchen (p 146)	Processions in boats.
Saturday and Sunday after Corpus Christi, Saturday and Sunday end of July	**Tamsweg** (145)	*Samsonumzug:* processions.
Eve of the summer solstice: June 20	**Tyrol**	Feast of St John: floodlighting of the mountains.
June 24	**Zederhaus** map 426 northwest of 34	*Prangstangentragen:* staves which may be 8 m - 25 ft tall, entirely covered with flower petals are borne in procession to the churches, where they are afterwards left on view until 15 August.
End of June	**Tyrol**	*Herz-Jesu Feuer:* floodlighting of the mountains.
August 15	**In the whole country**	Processions (regional costumes).
End of September – beginning of October	**Burgenland and Lower Austria**	Grape gathering festival: processions, wine fountains, fireworks.
December 5	**Mitterndorf** (East of Bad Aussee – map 426 21)	*Nikolospiel:* the passing of St Nicholas in the streets *(5.30 to 8.30pm)* provokes a series of noisy and colourful demonstrations.
December 27–January 14	**Thaur** (East of Innsbruck – map 426 31)	Mangers on display: local families welcome visitors on this occasion.

Music – Opera – Theatre

DATE	PLACE	NATURE OF EVENT
Week before Easter	**Salzburg** (p 129)	Easter Festival.
Mid-May to mid-June	**Vienna** (p 147)	Vienna Festival.
Mid-July to mid-August	**Bregenz** (p 53)	Festival (on the shores of Lake Constance).
End of July to end of August	**Salzburg** (p 129)	Salzburg Festival: mainly works of Mozart and Richard Strauss.
Saturdays and Sundays (8.30 pm) end of July through August	**Mörbisch** (Burgenland) (p 111)	Operettas on Neusiedle Lake.
July through August	**Ossiach** (Carinthia) (p 113)	Concerts in the church (festival "Carinthian Summer").
October to mid-November	**Graz and environs** (p 73)	Festival "Styrian Autumn".

Fairs

DATE	PLACE	NATURE OF EVENT
2nd week in March	**Vienna** (p 147)	International Spring Fair.
End of April-beginning of May	**Graz** (p 73)	Spring Fair.
End of August–beginning of September (every two years)	**Wels** (p 170)	International Agricultural Fair.
Mid-September	**Vienna** (p 147)	International Autumn Fair.
End of September beginning of October	**Innsbruck** (p 85)	Innsbruck Fair.
	Graz (p 73)	Autumn Fair.

Sports events

During the winter season, Austria is the site of many different kinds of winter sports events: alpine skiing, cross-country skiing, sledding, bobsledding, speed skating, and ice hockey.

DATE	PLACE	NATURE OF EVENT
January (alternating with other Alpine resorts)	**St Anton am Arlberg** (p 122)	Arlberg–Kandahar Race (an international competition decided on the results of a downhill and slalom).
January	**Kitzbühel** (p 95)	Hahnenkamm Race (World Cup Series: men's).
Mid-August	**Zeltweg-Knittelfeld** (Northeast of Judenburg – map 426 36)	Austrian Grand Prix Automobile Race (race counting for the world championship of Formula 1 on the Österreich-Ring).

FOOD AND DRINK

Foreign tourists on their first visit to Austria are often puzzled by the dishes they are offered. At breakfast amidst the rolls may be caraway-sprinkled brioche, an egg and the highly recommended *Schwarzbrot* (black rye bread). At 11 is the traditional *Gabelfrühstück* (breakfast with a fork) – hot spicy goulashes and hot sausages – especially welcomed after a hike. At lunch there is soup (*Fritattensuppe, Nudelsuppe,* etc....) and a copious main dish, whether it be half a chicken, a veal or pork scallop fried in breadcrumbs *(see below)*. If you are still hungry at 4 *(Jause)* stop in a tea room *(Konditoreien)* or coffee house and savour the exquisite *Sachertorte,* linger over the *Linzertorte* or taste the light and flaky *Strudel.* Dinner is lighter in fare, it is often cold with a variety of salads, cold meats and sausages *(Burenwurst, Krakauer, Dürre, Polnische, Salami ...)* and terminates tastefully with cheese *(Topfen).*

Austrian Cuisine. – Profiting by the contributions of the many peoples who lived in the Empire, Austrian cuisine has inherited the German, Magyar, Italian, Czech and Serb traditions. Oriental flavourings bring the dishes a savour which pleases the inborn Viennese instinct for good living. Sweets, desserts and pastry are in great favour.

Meat. – The *Wienerschnitzel* (Viennese fillet of veal) is on every menu. Fried in egg and breadcrumbs, it is usually served with potato salad.

The traditional *Gulasch,* of Magyar origin, is a stew highly flavoured with a Hungarian red pepper or paprika sauce and garnished with tomatoes, onions and potatoes. It is also served, very hot, as a consommé.

Graz and Styria offer delicious chickens or ducks fried in breadcrumbs. In the shooting season venison is plentiful in all parts of the country.

Sweets and Dessert. – The *Sachertorte* (Sacher cake) was invented by Prince Metternich's chef. It is a huge biscuit, stuffed and iced with chocolate, of a discreet, sweet and delicate flavour. The recipe remains a secret.

The *Linzertorte,* a tasty apricot jam and almond tart, apple *Strudels* or pies made with cherries or sweet white cheese, stuffed with Corinthian raisins, Alsatian plums and apricot fritters, the *soufflée* omelette known as a *Salzburger Nockerl* and the *Kaiserschmarrn,* another sweet omelette containing raisins and served cut into dice, give an idea of the variety of Austrian desserts.

Austrian Beverages. – The national drink in Austria varies whether it be white wine, beer, apple juice or coffee.

Wine. – Wine growing today covers about 37 000 ha - 90 000 acres in Lower Austria, in the Weinviertel, on the slopes near Vienna, and in the Burgenland and Styria. White wine (85%) is met with much more frequency than red. Annual production is of the order of 1 million hectolitres - 22 million gallons. There are many white vintages classed in importance: Grüner Veltliner (Valteliné), Müller-Thurgau, Welschriesling, etc.

Most vintages yield pleasant table wines which are often light and sparkling. "Wine of the year" (new wine) is drunk in the typical wineshops called *Heurigen,* very popular among Viennese *(p 152)* and tourists alike. These wineshops can be recognized by a tuft of greenery hanging over the door. Wine tasting becomes a meal by the addition of various cold meats, often sold at the door, in an atmosphere where the choruses of popular songs are taken up to the music of what is known locally as *Schrammelmusik,* played by a group consisting of at least an accordion and a violin.

The district of Wachau, in the Danube Valley produces wines with a delicate bouquet (Spitz, Dürnstein, Weissenkirchen, Krems, Langenlois).

Grinzing makes a pleasant sparkling wine, and Gumpoldskirchen, south of Vienna, a stronger wine.

Red vintages – especially the Blauer Portugieser and the Blaufränkisch – are of high quality and the wines they produce are increasingly in vogue. In Lower Austria the best known are those of Bad Vöslau, south of Vienna, Retz (the Retz wine is known as *Spezi,* i.e. a special), of Haugsdorf and of Matzen, in the Weinviertel. In the Burgenland the wines of Pöttelsdorf, Oggau and particularly Rust, and in Styria those of Leibnitz, have a great reputation.

Beer. – Coming from Styria, is the Gösser beer made in Leoben while the Reininghaus and Puntigam are both made in Graz.

Apfelsaft. – This is apple juice, pure and simple, it is quite popular among the Austrians. They often drink it "gespritzt" which is half water and half seltzer.

A Few Culinary Terms

Apfelsaft: apple-juice
Backhendl: fried chicken in breadcrumbs (Styria)
Faschiertes: mince, meat-balls
Frittate: pancakes cut into strips and put into soup
Gebäck: rolls, biscuits (must pay for bread eaten)
Gulasch: stew with highly seasoned sauce
Hirschbraten:
  Rehbraten: roast venison
Kaffee: in Vienna coffee is described as:
  Mokka: black (percolated) coffee
  Kapuziner: coffee with whipped cream
  Brauner: coffee with a little milk
  Mélange: half coffee, half milk
  Obers gespritzt: coffee with a lot of cream
  Mokka gespritzt: coffee with rum
  Einspänner: coffee with whipped cream served in a glass
  Türkischer: Turkish coffee
Kaiserschmarrn: sweet omelette containing Corinthian raisins
Knödel Nockerl: dumplings
Leberkäse: ("liver cheese"). Slice of meat or liver paste, served hot

Mehlspeise: collective name for sweet dishes served as a hot dessert
Mus: marmalade
Palatschinken: thin pancake filled with apricot jam
Pfannkuchen: pancakes
Platte: grilled meats, richly garnished
Salzburger Nockerl: soufflée omelette
Schlag (obers): whipped cream
Semmel: bread roll
Strudel: thin pastry rolled and stuffed
Tafelspitz: boiled beef with a small slice of liver, sauté potatoes, vegetables and tartare sauce
Torte: cake
Wienerschnitzel: Viennese fillet of veal fried in breadcrumbs

MEAT CAN BE

gebacken: fried in breadcrumbs
gebraten: roast or braised
geröstet: sauté
gekocht: boiled
geselcht, geräuchert: salted and smoked
am Grill, gegrillt: grilled

ART

ARCHITECTURE

Austria, cradle of widely differing civilizations, has shown, in the course of centuries, a taste in architecture which often reflected external influences, and which has drawn the best from them. In certain periods, however, a style on a par with national aspirations has been developed. This was particularly true of the 18C, when, under the enlightened guidance of the Habsburgs, Austrian Baroque appeared with such vigour as to relegate earlier achievements to a lower plane.

The Roman occupation left traces at Carnuntum (Petronell), in the Danube Valley below Vienna – then called Vindobona – especially in Carinthia, at Teurnia (near Spittal), Aguntum (near Lienz) and Magdalensberg, which overlooks St. Veit an der Glan.

The Romanesque style. – From the 12C onwards religious architecture enjoyed great expansion in Austria as in all Christian Europe. The main centres of the Romanesque style were the episcopal seats of Salzburg, Passau and Brixen. The style also developed thanks to the foundation of many Benedictine, Cistercian and Augustinian convents and monasteries or the transformation of those already in existence: such as those at Melk, Gurk, Klosterneuburg, Zwettl, Seckau and Heiligenkreuz.

Mural paintings developed most extensively in the Archbishopric of Salzburg (Gurk). Salzburg was already an art centre, while Vienna as yet had no bishop.

The Gothic Style. – In the 14 and 15C the Gothic style invaded Austria. The Cistercians drew inspiration from the French pointed arch and the Franciscans kept on with their traditional Italian architecture; but most Gothic churches are of the hall-church *(Hallenkirche)* type with nave and aisles of equal height, as in Vienna in St Stephen's Cathedral (note the chancel), in the Augustinian Church, the Church of the Minorites, and the Church of Our Lady of the River Bank.

Until the 16C there was a preference for the sectional vaulting where decorative ribs form a pattern of groined or star vaulting whose richness of design contrasts boldly with the bare walls. This **Late Gothic** *(Spätgotik)* developed into a style of long straight lines – the exact opposite of the ornamental opulence of the Flamboyant Gothic to be seen in France at this period.

Paired naves were the fashion in the Alps: two naves at Feldkirch, four at Schwaz.

The great Gothic altarpieces, which were a synthesis of all the plastic arts – architecture, sculpture, painting – have, for the most part, suffered mutilation. Two are pleasant works: that at Kefermarkt and especially that at St. Wolfgang, painted and carved in 1481 by a Tyrolese, Michael Pacher, the greatest late Gothic artist.

A few 15C secular buildings have fortunately been preserved, such as the Bummerlhaus at Steyr and the Kornmesserhaus at Bruck and der Mur. Oriel windows *(Erker)* were added at this period to the façades of mansions and other buildings, such as the delightful Little Golden Roof at Innsbruck.

The Renaissance. – The architectural heritage of a Renaissance inspired by Italian models was not to be preponderant in Austria, except at Salzburg, which the prince-archbishops dreamed of making a new Rome. In spite of a great outpouring of ideas, reflected in the character of the Emperor Maximilian I (1493–1519), the Gothic tradition dominated in the 16C. Even Maximilian's tomb at Innsbruck, which is regarded as a typical product of the German Renaissance, remained subject, with its display of ancestors, to the arrangement of the famous tombs of the Dukes of Burgundy (to be seen in Dijon), surrounded by "weepers".

The Baroque Miracle. – The Baroque style, dominated by irregular contours and variegated forms, seeks to express movement above all. It is picturesque and theatrical, appeals more to the senses than to the spirit, and in its extreme manifestations may end in vulgarity or excessive delicacy (Rococo). In most cases, however, it is attractive and amusing.

Baroque originated in Italy from the "manner" of Michelangelo and his disciple Giulio Romano, and was introduced into the Habsburg Empire (Central Europe, Flanders, Spain) by Charles V and his descendants. Baroque art, which was essentially religious at that time, served the protagonists of the Counter-Reformation, against Protestanism. To the bareness of Lutheran buildings was opposed the exuberance of Roman Catholic churches, whose pomp struck the popular imagination.

It was after the rout of the Turks under the walls of Vienna in 1683 that the Baroque style began to spread. Alongside innumerable churches, local master masons and Italian architects like Carlone raised palaces and mansions characterstic of the taste of rich Austrians for emphatic solutions.

(After D. Sochor, Arch. S.I. Innsbruck)

Innsbruck. - The Little Golden Roof.

If French influence prevailed over Italian taste in the domain of civil architecture (Nymphenburg and Schönbrunn are inspired by Versailles), the Italians took the lead in the building of churches, often owing much to Borromini, Guarini or Juvara.

The churches, whose exteriors are striking in their great simplicity of fine, are frequently crowned with bulbous belfries. Their interiors are confusing in their extreme lavishness of decoration. Vast pictures on vaulting and domes, sculpture, stucco and marble make up for the absence of stained glass windows. The warm tones of the painted compositions are enhanced by the gilding of the statues and contrast with the rough-cast walls.

Austrian Baroque. – This style is characterized by relative sobriety and a breadth of conception. It is distinguished by great names, in architecture as well as in sculpture and painting.

Johann Bernhard **Fischer von Erlach** (1656–1723), after a stay in Italy and a study of French achievements, created a national style of which the Holy Trinity at Salzburg *(see illustration)* is one of the prototypes (built between 1694 and 1702). Although his plans for the Palace of Schönbrunn were not realized, many buildings in Vienna bear the mark of his genius: the Church of St Charles, the National Library (then the Imperial Library), the Schwarzenberg Palace, etc... Most of these buildings were completed after his death by his son, Joseph Emmanuel (1693–1742), who also realized most of the Hofburg (Imperial Chancellery and the Indoor Riding School).

Johann Lukas von **Hildebrandt** (1668–1745) settled in Vienna in 1696 and worked with Fischer von Erlach. In Vienna he designed the two palaces at the Belvedere, and at Salzburg the Mirabell Château; his work was considerable and had an influence on the artists of his generation.

(After D.A.P.R.A. photo)

Salzburg. - The Church of the Trinity.

Jakob **Prandtauer** (1660–1726) worked at the Abbey of St Florian before achieving his masterpiece, the Abbey at Melk, which was completed by his son-in-law, Munggenast. The latter afterwards used his talents at Dürnstein and Altenburg.

Painters and sculptors took part in the sumptuous interior decoration of palaces and churches. Rottmayr was the favourite collaborator of Fischer von Erlach and the precursor of a specifically Austrian Baroque style. Other artists creating during this time were Balthasar Permoser, who carved the *Apotheosis of Prince Eugene* (1721), which decorates the Museum of Baroque Art in Vienna *(p 162);* Daniel Gran, who

FINE BAROQUE CHURCHES

Linz, MELK, St.Florian, Pfarrkirchen, Vienna, Salzburg, Mariazell, Spital am Pyhrn, Bregenz, Volders, Stams, Zell am Ziller, Graz, Innsbruck, Klagenfurt

painted the frescoes in the dome of Vienna's National Library *(p 155),* Paul Troger and Johann Schmidt (alias Kremser Schmidt) whose altarpieces enhance many of the churches found in Lower Austria. It is with Anton **Maulpertsch** that Austrian painting of this period attains its peak. Georg Raphaël Donner is best known for the fine fountain in the Neue Markt in Vienna.

The Rococo Style. – Inspired by the French *Rocaille,* this style shows decorative refinements carried to the limit in these last examples of Bavarian Rococo: painting in *trompe-l'œil* (false relief), marble, stucco, bronze and wood are used in profusion by artists who were frequently masters of several arts.

The stuccoists brought together garlands, medallions, vegetation and shell-work, Baldachins, sham draperies, superimposed galleries, niches overladen with gilding and painted in pastel shades add to the prevailing impression of being in a theatre rather than a church. The chancel is striking with its richly decorated high-alter.

A typical example of the Rococo style which was created during the reign of Maria Theresa (1740–1780), is Schönbrunn *(p 162).*

Neo-Classicism and Romanticism. – After the excesses of Rococo came the triumph of a Classicism, inspired by Greece and Rome, a frigid style characterized by the columns and pediments of antiquity. This tendency, which had little in common with the Austrian and even less with the Viennese character, was patronized by certain Germain rulers, including Ludwig I of Bavaria who transformed Munich.

The first half of the 19C, and more exactly the period between the Congress of Vienna (1814–1815) and the revolution of March 1848, corresponds with the era of the *Vormärz* (the time before March), the Biedermeier flourished. The **Biedermeier style** is a bourgeois style. It enthrones family life and the comfort of the home, at least as they were then understood: furniture, often made of light wood, has flowing lines, bric-à-brac and miniatures line the shelves of glass-fronted cupboards.

The most well-known painters of this period were Ferdinand Georg Waldmüller and Rudolf von Alt.

Contemporary Architecture. – At the beginning of the 20C there was a reaction against the tendency to pastiche or imitation, which had spread under the reign of Franz-Josef, especially in Vienna when the great buildings were constructed round the outside of the Ring (Votive Church, new Town Hall, Opera).

With the Vienna Secession movement – one of the founders being Gustav Klimt (1862–1918) – a new style was born known as Art Nouveau or Jugendstil.

The new principles called for restraint and internal architecture in harmony with the function of the building. The most eminent representatives of this school in Austria are Otto Wagner and Clements Holzmeister (born 1886) the architect of the new Festival Hall at Salzburg and numerous modern churches in Austria.

MUSIC

MIDDLE AGES

12 and 13C The *Minnesänger* (minstrels) draw their poetic inspiration from the *Lied,* the true expression of popular feeling.

14 and 15C The *Meistersinger* (master singers) introduce polyphony to the Empire.

17C

The birth of a new music. The Italian musical technique – Neapolitan opera, the *bel canto,* the sonata, concerto – is triumphant. Meanwhile the Austrians are past masters in the art of organ building – the most famous instrument is the one at St. Florian *(p 123).*

GLUCK AND THE REFORMING OF THE OPERA

Vienna is the locale for the reform of opera, thanks to the German, Christoph Willibald Gluck.

1714–1787 **Gluck** considers opera as an indivisible work of art, both musical and dramatic; he seeks, above all, the natural effects, truth, simplicity and a faithful expression of feeling.

1754 Gluck is named *Kapellmeister* of the Opera at the Imperial Court.

1774 Two of his operas are performed in Paris: *Iphigenia in Aulis* and *Orpheus.* The enthusiasm of the Gluckists clashes with the Puccinists (traditionalists)

HAYDN AND MOZART

They create during the apogee of Classical Art.

1732–1809 Conductor and composer attached to the service of Prince Esterhazy at Eisenstadt for thirty years, **Haydn** is the creator of the string quartet and lays down the laws of the classical symphony, showing a remarkable care for balance and grace.

1756–1791 **Mozart** brings every form of musical expression to perfection – its pleasant and sparkling motifs ripple beneath a rhythmic counterpoint of charming liveliness. *(Details of his life p 130).*

THE ROMANTIC MOVEMENT

At this time, Vienna is the musical capital of Europe.
Numerous are the foreign musicians who adopt Vienna as their home.

BEETHOVEN (1770–1827)

1808 *Fifth and Sixth Symphonies.*

1824 The *Ninth Symphony* – with chorus, stamped both with a power of expression and a depth of feeling seldom equalled, is the zenith of his work.

SCHUBERT (1797–1828)

Blessed with a great sensibility and an outstanding improviser, Schubert rediscovers in the *Lieder* the old popular themes of the Middle Ages. His *Lieder,* even more than his symphonies, masses, impromptus and compositions of chamber music make him secure as the leading lyrical composer of the 19C.

1832 Found his *Unfinished Symphony* at the home of a friend.

THE KINGDOM OF THE WALTZ AND OPERETTA

1820 In Vienna, a musical genre, the **waltz,** which had its origins in popular triple-time dance, is triumphant.
Adopted first in the inns and then in the theatres on the outskirts of the city, the waltz scores such success that it appears at the Imperial Court.
Two men, **Joseph Lanner** (1801–1843) and **Johann Strauss** (1804–1849), help to give this music form such an enviable place that the waltz known everywhere as the "Viennese Waltz" enjoys world wide popularity.
The Strauss sons, Joseph and Johann, carry the waltz to a high degree of technical perfection, taking it further and further from its origins to make of it a symphonic form. The **operettas** by **Johann Strauss, the son** *(Die Fledermaus – the Bat; the Gypsy Baron),* by Suppé, by Benatzky *(The White Horse Inn)* and by Franz Lehar brilliantly reflect the Viennese heart, light and sentimental and in perfect accord with the smiling Austrian countryside.

SYMPHONIC RENEWAL

1824–1896 **Anton Bruckner,** is one of the most fertile composers of church music – nine long symphonies, masses, a *Te Deum.* He spent many years as organist of St. Florian and at Linz Cathedral before his appointment as professor at the Vienna Conservatory.

1833–1897 Settled in Vienna, **Johannes Brahms** composes a large body of works of a lyrical nature inestimable in its impact (1868, *Ein deutsches Requiem – A German Requiem).*

1842 Founding of the Vienna Philharmonic Orchestra playing under the guidance of illustrious conductors (Richard Strauss, Furtwängler) chosen by the players themselves.

1860–1903 **Hugo Wolf** a tormented spirit who became insane, composes fine *Lieder* in his lucid periods, based for the most part on the works of Goethe.

1860–1911 **Gustav Mahler,** who composed *Lieder* and nine symphonies, is the last representative of the symphony.

THE CONTEMPORARY ERA

1919 Founding of the Vienna Symphony Orchestra.
Herbert von Karajan has ensured its success abroad, in concerts in which modern music is often honoured.
Contemporary musical research is issued for the most part from the twelve tone Austrian school represented by **Arnold Schönberg** (1874–1951), **Alban Berg** (1885–1935) and **Anton von Webern** (1883–1945) who aim to revolutionize musical language (atonal and polytonal music).

TOURING PROGRAMMES

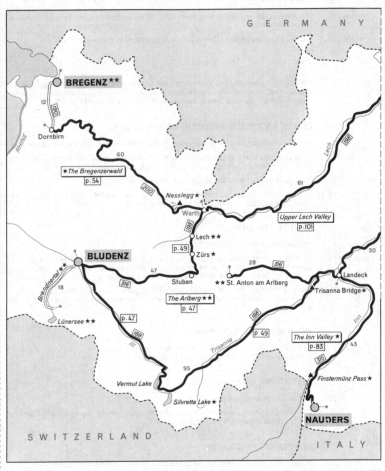

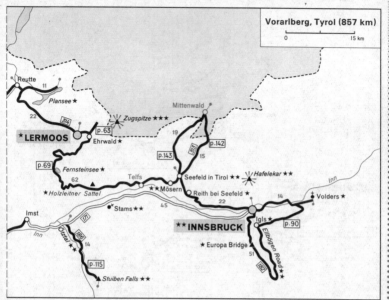

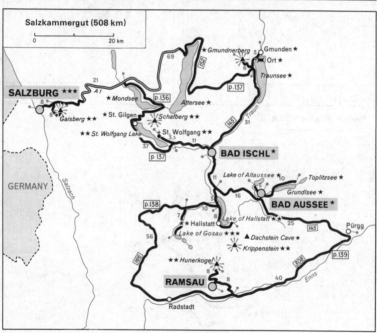

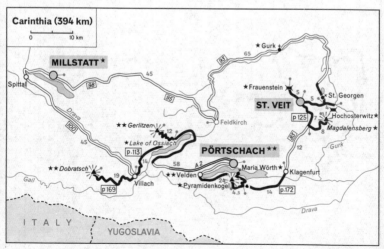

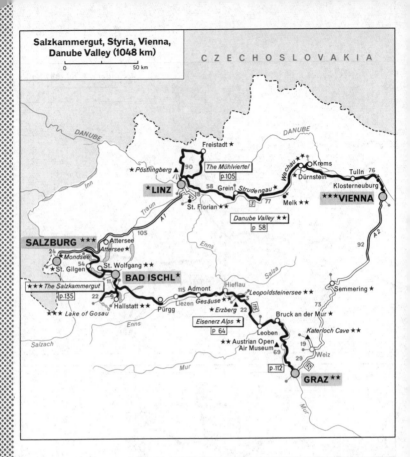

Salzkammergut, Styria, Vienna, Danube Valley (1048 km)

0 — 50 km

CZECHOSLOVAKIA

DANUBE

★ Pöstlingberg ▲

Freistadt ★

The Mühlviertel
p.105

90

★ LINZ

58 Grein *Strudengau* ★

St. Florian ★★

Krems ★★
Dürnstein
Wachau

Tulln 76
Klosterneuburg

***VIENNA

77
Melk ★★
s

Danube Valley ★★
p 58

A1

Traun

Inn

DANUBE

Attersee
Attersee ★

105

Enns

Salza

92

A2

SALZBURG ★★★

24
Mondsee
★ St. Gilgen 54

St. Wolfgang ★★

BAD ISCHL ★

11.

The Salzkammergut ★★★
p.135

22 9

Hallstatt ★★

115 Admont
Liezen *Gesäuse* ★★
Pürgg 3

Hieflau
Leopoldsteinersee ★★

★ Semmering ★

73

Salzach

★★★ *Lake of Gosau*

Enns

Erzberg ★
22

Eisenerz Alps ★
p 64

Leoben

Bruck an der Mur ★

Katerloch Cave ★★

Mur

★★ *Austrian Open
Air Museum*

69

19
29 Weiz

p.112

GRAZ ★★

Mur

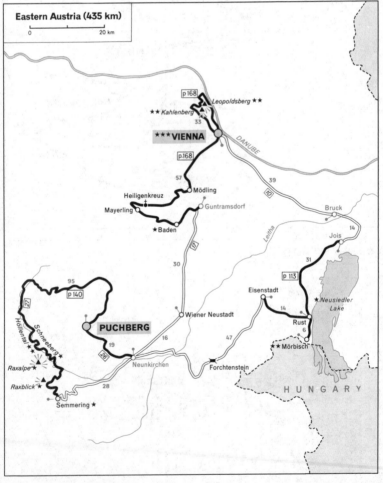

Eastern Austria (435 km)

0 — 20 km

p 168
Leopoldsberg ★★

★★ *Kahlenberg*

33

***VIENNA

DANUBE

p.168

57

Mödling

39

Heiligenkreuz

Mayerling

Guntramsdorf

Bruck

14

Jois

★ Baden

30

31

p 113

Eisenstadt

★ *Neusiedler
Lake*

95

p 140

Schneeberg

PUCHBERG

Wiener Neustadt

16

47

14

Rust

Höllental ★★★

Raxalpe ★

Raxblick ★

19

26

Neunkirchen

28

Forchtenstein

6
★★ *Mörbisch*

HUNGARY

Semmering ★

38

PLACES TO STAY

It can be assumed that most of the resorts listed below have a swimming pool (or a beathing beach beside a lake) as well as a tennis court.

See notes p 40

Column key:
- **56** = See description p
- **㉟** = No. of fold in Michelin map
- ⚕ = Doctor
- ℞ = Chemist (1)
- ◇ = Picturesque town
- ≼ = Extensive views
- 🌲 = Woodland nearby
- ● = Lakeside setting
- ⛵ = Sailing school (2)
- ⛰ = Mountaineering (3)
- ⛷ = Summer skiing (4)
- 🎣 = Fishing
- 🐴 = Horse riding
- ⛳ = Golf course and No. of holes
- ♠ = Casino

SUMMER

Resort	Ref.	Altitude	Doctor	Chemist (1)	Picturesque town	Extensive views	Woodland nearby	Lakeside setting	Sailing school (2)	Mountaineering (3)	Summer skiing (4)	Fishing	Horse riding	Golf	Casino
Abtenau	138	715	⚕	℞	◇	≼	🌲	–	–	–	–	🎣	🐴	–	–
Admont	45	641	⚕	℞	–	–	🌲	–	–	⛰	–	🎣	🐴	–	–
Aflenz	46	765	⚕	℞	–	–	🌲	–	–	–	–	🎣	🐴	–	–
Aigen im Mühlkreis	60	596	⚕	℞	–	–	🌲	–	–	–	–	🎣	🐴	–	–
Alpbach	46	973	⚕	℞	◇	–	🌲	–	–	–	–	–	🐴	–	–
Altaussee	50	723	⚕	℞	–	≼	🌲	●	–	⛰	–	🎣	🐴	–	–
Altmünster	137	443	⚕	℞	–	≼	–	●	⛵	–	–	🎣	🐴	–	–
Attersee	138	404	⚕	–	◇	≼	–	●	⛵	–	–	🎣	🐴	–	–
Aussee (Bad)	50	659	⚕	℞	–	–	🌲	–	–	⛰	–	🎣	🐴	–	–
Grundlsee	50	740	–	–	–	≼	🌲	●	⛵	⛰	–	🎣	–	–	–
Baden	51	233	⚕	℞	–	–	🌲	–	–	–	–	–	🐴	–	♠
Badgastein	51	1013	⚕	℞	–	≼	–	–	–	⛰	–	–	🐴	9	♠
Bezau	55	651	⚕	℞	–	–	🌲	–	–	–	–	🎣	🐴	–	–
Bregenz	53	398	⚕	℞	–	≼	–	●	⛵	–	–	🎣	🐴	–	♠
Döllach im Mölltal	110	1013	–	–	–	–	🌲	–	–	⛰	–	🎣	🐴	–	–
Ehrwald	63	996	⚕	℞	–	≼	🌲	–	–	⛰	–	🎣	🐴	–	–
Ellmau	93	812	⚕	℞	–	–	🌲	–	–	⛰	–	🎣	🐴	–	–
Faaker See	171	554	⚕	℞	–	–	🌲	●	⛵	–	–	🎣	🐴	–	–
Filzmoos	138	1055	–	–	◇	≼	🌲	–	–	⛰	–	🎣	🐴	–	–
Freistadt	70	560	⚕	℞	◇	–	🌲	–	–	–	–	🎣	🐴	–	–
Fulpmes	91	937	⚕	℞	–	–	🌲	–	–	⛰	–	🎣	🐴	–	–
Fuschl am See	136	670	–	–	–	–	🌲	●	–	–	–	🎣	🐴	9	–
Gargellen	48	1480	–	–	–	–	🌲	–	–	⛰	–	🎣	🐴	–	–
Gaschurn	48	986	⚕	℞	–	–	🌲	–	–	⛰	–	🎣	🐴	–	–
St. Gallenkirch	48	884	⚕	–	–	–	🌲	–	–	⛰	–	🎣	🐴	–	–
Gerlos	71	1245	–	–	–	–	🌲	●	⛵	⛰	–	🎣	🐴	–	–
Gleichenberg (Bad)	72	317	⚕	℞	–	–	🌲	–	–	–	–	–	🐴	–	–
Gmunden	72	440	⚕	℞	◇	≼	–	●	⛵	–	–	🎣	🐴	–	–
Goisern (Bad)	139	500	⚕	℞	–	–	🌲	–	–	⛰	–	🎣	🐴	–	–
Golling	128	481	⚕	℞	◇	–	🌲	–	–	⛰	–	🎣	🐴	–	–
Gosau	138	767	⚕	–	–	≼	🌲	–	–	⛰	–	🎣	🐴	–	–
Graz	73	364	⚕	℞	◇	≼	–	–	–	–	–	–	🐴	–	–
Hall (Bad)	79	388	⚕	℞	–	–	🌲	–	–	–	–	–	🐴	–	–
Hall in Tirol	80	581	⚕	℞	◇	–	–	–	–	⛰	–	–	🐴	–	–
Hallstatt	81	511	⚕	℞	◇	≼	🌲	●	–	⛰	–	🎣	🐴	–	–
Heiligenblut	81	1288	⚕	℞	–	≼	–	–	–	⛰	–	🎣	🐴	–	–
Hinterstoder	139	585	⚕	℞	–	–	🌲	–	–	⛰	–	🎣	🐴	–	–
Hintertux	㉛	1494	–	–	◇	–	–	–	–	⛰	⛷	🎣	–	–	–
Hofgastein (Bad)	82	860	–	℞	–	–	–	–	–	⛰	–	🎣	🐴	–	–
Innsbruck	85	574	⚕	℞	–	≼	–	–	–	⛰	–	–	🐴	18	–
Igls	90	899	⚕	℞	–	≼	🌲	–	–	⛰	–	🎣	–	9	–
Ischl (Bad)	91	469	⚕	℞	–	–	🌲	–	–	⛰	–	🎣	🐴	9	–
Ischgl	49	1377	⚕	℞	–	–	🌲	–	–	⛰	–	🎣	🐴	–	–
Kaprun	173	786	⚕	℞	–	–	🌲	–	–	⛰	⛷	🎣	–	–	–
Kirchberg in Tirol	㉒	837	⚕	℞	◇	–	🌲	–	–	⛰	–	🎣	🐴	–	–
Kitzbühel	95	762	⚕	℞	◇	–	🌲	–	–	⛰	–	🎣	🐴	9	♠
Kleinkirchheim (Bad)	㉟	1073	⚕	–	–	–	🌲	–	–	–	–	🎣	🐴	–	–
Kleinwalsertal (Hirschegg, Riezlern, Mittelberg)	97	1084 à 1218	⚕	℞	◇	≼	🌲	–	–	⛰	–	🎣	🐴	–	♠
Kössen	91	589	⚕	℞	–	–	🌲	–	–	⛰	–	🎣	🐴	–	–
Krems	98	221	⚕	℞	◇	–	–	–	–	–	–	🎣	🐴	–	–
Krumpendorf	172	440	⚕	℞	–	≼	–	●	–	–	–	🎣	🐴	–	–
Lech	101	1447	⚕	℞	–	–	🌲	–	–	⛰	–	🎣	🐴	–	–
Lermoos	102	995	⚕	℞	◇	≼	🌲	–	–	⛰	–	🎣	🐴	–	–
Leutasch	143	1126	⚕	℞	◇	≼	🌲	–	–	⛰	–	🎣	🐴	–	–
Lienz	102	678	⚕	℞	–	–	🌲	–	–	⛰	–	🎣	🐴	–	–
Iselsberg	110	1118	–	–	–	≼	🌲	–	–	–	–	🎣	🐴	–	–
Lochau	54	418	⚕	℞	–	≼	–	●	⛵	–	–	🎣	🐴	–	–
Lofer	106	625	⚕	–	◇	≼	🌲	–	–	⛰	–	🎣	🐴	–	–

PLACES TO STAY

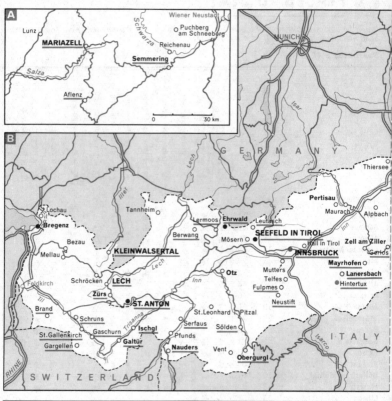

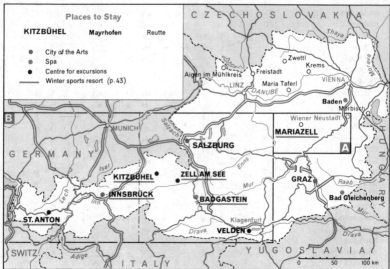

NOTES

SUMMER

1. *The resident doctor usually sells prescribed medication when there is no chemist.*
2. *Only sailing schools belonging to the Association of Austrian Sailing Schools are mentioned.*
3. *Only those centres offering climbing or glacier excursions and with mountain guides are mentioned.*
4. *Skiable area accessible only by roads, cable-cars or chair lifts.*

WINTER

1. *See above.*
5. *The brown symbol indicates the feeding of game (Wildfütterung - p 12) in the immediate vicinity.*
6. *The first figure indicates the number of cable-cars or other lifts available to skiers and non-skiers; the second figure indicates the number of lifts for which one must be mounted on skis (ski-lifts, etc.).*
   Resort equipment is constantly changing, the figures, therefore, only give an indication of what is available.
7. *It can be assumed that the resorts listed offer outdoor skating facilities.*

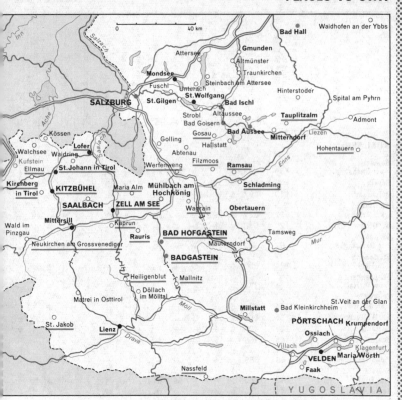

	56 = See description p	⑮ = No. of fold in Michelin map ④②⑥	Altitude	= Doctor	= Chemist (1)	= Picturesque town	= Extensive views	= Woodland nearby	= Lakeside setting	= Sailing school (2)	= Mountaineering (3)	= Summer skiing (4)	= Fishing	= Horse riding	= Golf course and No. of holes	= Casino
SUMMER																
Lunz	㉓		598	⚕	℞	–	–	🌲	●	–	–	–	–	–		
Mallnitz	146		1190	⚕	–	–	–	🌲	–	–	🏔	–	–	–		
Maria Alm	122		802	⚕	–	◇	«	–	–	–	–	–	–	🐎		
Maria Taferl	61		443	–	–	–	«	🌲	–	–	–	–	–	–		
Maria Wörth/Reifnitz	172		458	⚕	–	◇	–	–	●	⛵	–	–	🐟	–	18	
Mariazell	107		868	⚕	℞	–	«	🌲	–	–	–	–	–	🐎		
Matrei in Osttirol . .	67		977	⚕	℞	–	«	–	–	–	🏔	–	–	🐎		
Maurach	94		958	⚕	℞	–	«	🌲	●	–	🏔	–	–	🐎		
Mauterndorf	119		1122	⚕	℞	◇	–	🌲	–	–	–	–	–	🐎		
Mayrhofen	108		630	⚕	℞	–	«	–	–	–	🏔	–	–	🐎		
Mellau	55		690	⚕	℞	–	«	🌲	–	–	–	–	–	🐎		
Millstatt	110		604	⚕	℞	–	«	🌲	●	⛵	–	–	–	🐎		
Mitterndorf	139		797	⚕	℞	–	–	🌲	–	–	–	–	–	–		
Mittersill	72		790	⚕	℞	–	«	–	–	–	🏔	–	–	🐎		
Mondsee	111		493	⚕	℞	◇	«	–	●	⛵	–	–	–	🐎		
Mörbisch	111		118	⚕	–	◇	–	–	●	⛵	–	–	–	–		
Mösern	143		1204	–	–	–	«	🌲	–	–	–	–	–	–		
Mühlbach am Hochkönig	128		859	⚕	℞	–	«	–	–	–	🏔	–	–	–		
Mutters	90		830	⚕	–	–	«	🌲	–	–	–	–	–	–		
Neukirchen am Grossvenediger . . .	72		856	⚕	℞	–	–	–	–	–	–	–	–	🐎		
Neustift	90		993	⚕	℞	–	–	–	–	–	🏔	🎿	🐟	🐎		
Obergurgl	116		1927	⚕	℞	–	–	–	–	–	🏔	–	–	🐎		
Ossiach	113		508	–	–	–	–	🌲	●	⛵	–	–	–	🐎		
Ötz	115		820	⚕	℞	◇	–	–	–	–	🏔	–	🐟	🐎		
Pertisau	94		929	–	–	–	«	–	●	–	🏔	–	🐟	🐎	9	
Pfunds	84		971	⚕	℞	◇	–	🌲	–	–	–	–	🐟	🐎		
Pörtschach	117		458	⚕	℞	–	«	–	●	⛵	–	–	🐟	🐎		
Puchberg am Schneeberg . . .	140		585	⚕	℞	–	–	–	–	–	–	–	–	🐎		

Column key:
- 56 = See description p
- (circled) = No. of fold in Michelin map
- = Altitude
- = Doctor
- = Chemist (1)
- = Picturesque town
- = Extensive views
- = Woodland nearby
- = Lakeside setting
- = Sailing school (2)
- = Mountaineering (3)
- = Summer skiing (4)
- = Fishing
- = Horse riding
- = Golf course and No. of holes
- = Casino

SUMMER

Place	Page / Fold	Altitude	Doctor	Chemist (1)	Picturesque town	Extensive views	Woodland nearby	Lakeside setting	Sailing school (2)	Mountaineering (3)	Summer skiing (4)	Fishing	Horse riding	Golf course / No. holes	Casino
Ramsau am Dachstein	139	1083	●	–	●	●	●	–	–	●	●	–	●	–	–
Rauris	(53)	948	●	●	–	–	●	–	–	●	–	●	–	–	–
Reichenau	140	487	●	●	–	–	●	–	–	●	–	–	●	–	–
St. Anton am Arlberg	122	1287	●	●	–	–	●	–	–	●	–	●	–	–	–
St. Gilgen	124	548	●	●	●	●	●	●	●	–	–	●	●	–	–
St. Jakob in Defereggen	67	1389	●	●	–	–	●	–	–	●	–	●	–	–	–
St. Johann in Tirol	124	660	●	●	●	–	●	–	–	–	–	●	–	–	–
St. Leonhard im Pitztal	(30)	1371	●	–	–	–	–	–	–	●	–	–	–	–	–
St. Veit an der Glan	124	476	●	●	●	–	–	–	–	–	–	–	●	–	–
St. Wolfgang	125	549	●	●	●	●	–	●	–	–	–	●	●	–	–
Salzburg	129	424	●	●	–	●	–	–	–	–	–	●	●	9	●
Schröcken	55	1269	–	–	–	–	–	–	–	●	–	–	–	–	–
Schruns and Tschagguns	48	689	●	●	–	–	●	–	–	●	–	●	–	–	–
Seefeld in Tirol	142	1180	●	●	–	●	●	–	–	–	–	–	●	18	●
Semmering	141	985	●	●	–	●	●	–	–	–	–	–	–	9	–
Serfaus	84	1427	–	●	●	●	–	–	–	●	–	●	–	–	–
Sölden	116	1377	●	●	–	–	–	–	–	●	●	●	–	–	–
Spital am Pyhrn	143	647	●	●	–	–	●	–	–	●	–	●	–	–	–
Steinbach am Attersee	137	510	●	–	–	●	●	●	–	–	–	●	–	–	–
Strobl	137	544	●	●	●	●	●	●	●	–	–	●	●	–	–
Tamsweg	145	1021	●	●	●	–	●	–	–	–	–	●	–	–	–
Tannheim	(15)	1097	●	●	–	–	●	–	–	●	–	●	–	–	–
Telfes	90	994	●	●	–	●	●	–	–	●	–	●	–	–	–
Thiersee	100	677	●	–	–	●	●	●	–	–	–	●	–	–	–
Traunkirchen	146	430	●	–	–	●	●	●	●	–	–	●	–	–	–
Unterach am Attersee	136	479	●	●	–	●	–	●	–	–	–	●	–	–	–
Velden	171	450	●	●	–	●	–	–	●	–	–	●	●	–	●
Vent	115	1893	–	–	–	●	–	–	–	●	–	●	–	–	–
Wagrain	127	838	●	–	●	–	●	–	–	–	–	●	●	–	–
Waidhofen an der Ybbs	(22)	358	●	●	–	–	●	–	–	–	–	●	–	–	–
Waidring	92	778	●	–	●	–	●	–	–	–	–	●	–	–	–
Walchsee	93	660	●	●	–	–	–	●	–	–	–	●	–	–	–
Wald im Pinzgau	72	885	●	●	–	–	●	–	–	●	–	●	–	–	–
Werfenweng	128	901	–	–	–	●	●	–	–	●	–	●	–	–	–
Zell am See	173	757	●	●	–	●	–	●	●	–	–	●	–	–	–
Zell am Ziller	71	575	●	●	–	–	●	–	–	–	–	●	–	–	–
Zwettl	174	520	●	●	–	–	●	–	–	–	–	●	–	–	–

When visiting Europe

Michelin Red Guides

Benelux, Deutschland, España/Portugal, France, Great Britain and Ireland, Italia
(hotels, restaurants, lists of sights).

Michelin Green Guides

Austria, Germany, Italy, Portugal, Spain, Switzerland
(sights and touring programmes described)

Michelin Main Road Maps

Greece 980, Great Britain/Ireland 986, Germany 987, Italy 988, France 989, Spain/Portugal 990, Yugoslavia 996.

	See description p	No of fold in Michelin map	Altitude	Doctor	Chemist (1)	Picturesque town	Extensive views	Woodland nearby (5)	Indoor swimming pool	Cross-country skiing	Chair lifts (6)		Artificial skating rink	Casino
Aflenz	46		765	●	●	—	—	●	—	—	0	9	—	—
Badgastein	51		1013	●	●	—	≼	●	●	S	2	18	—	♣
Berwang		(16)	1336	—	—	—	—	●	—	—	0	10	—	—
Brand	52		1037	—	—	—	≼	●	●	—	0	8	—	—
Ehrwald	63		996	●	●	—	≼	●	●	S	3	7	⛸	—
Ellmau	93		812	●	●	◇	—	—	—	—	1	9	—	—
Filzmoos		(20)	1055	—	—	◇	—	●	●	S	0	16	—	—
Fulpmes	91		937	●	●	—	—	●	●	S	0	7	—	—
Galtür		(29)	1583	●	—	—	—	—	●	S	0	5	—	—
Gargellen		(28)	1480	—	—	—	—	●	—	—	0	7	—	—
Gaschurn	48		986	●	●	—	—	●	●	S	0	8	—	—
St. Gallenkirch	48		884	●	●	◇	—	●	—	—	0	16	—	—
Gerlos	71		1245	—	—	—	—	●	●	—	0	15	—	—
Gosau		(20)	767	—	—	—	≼	●	●	S	1	23	—	—
Heiligenblut	81		1288	●	●	◇	≼	—	●	—	0	10	—	—
Hintertux	108		1494	—	—	◇	—	—	●	S	2	4	—	—
Hofgastein (Bad)	82		860	●	●	—	—	—	●	S	2	15	⛸	—
Innsbruck	85		574	●	●	—	≼	—	●	S	2	2	⛸	—
Igls	90		899	●	●	—	≼	●	●	—	1	5	—	—
Ischgl	49		1377	●	●	◇	—	●	—	S	6	22	—	—
Kaprun	173		786	●	●	—	—	—	●	S	3	11	—	—
Kirchberg in Tirol		(18)	837	●	●	◇	—	●	—	S	0	14	—	—
Kitzbühel	95		762	●	●	◇	—	●	●	S	4	25	⛸	♣
Kleinwalsertal (Hirschegg, Mittelberg, Riezlern)	97		1084 à 1218	●	●	◇	≼	●	●	S	2	32	—	♣
Kössen	91		589	●	●	—	—	●	—	S	0	9	—	—
Lanersbach		(31)	1281	●	—	◇	—	—	●	S	0	11	—	—
Lech	101		1447	●	●	—	—	—	—	S	3	18	—	—
Lermoos	102		995	●	●	◇	≼	●	●	S	0	6	—	—
Leutasch	143		1126	●	●	◇	≼	●	—	S	0	9	—	—
Lienz	102		678	●	●	—	—	—	●	S	1	9	—	—
Lofer	106		625	●	●	◇	≼	●	●	S	0	13	—	—
Mallnitz	146		1190	●	●	—	—	●	●	S	1	9	—	—
Maria Alm	122		802	●	●	◇	≼	—	—	S	0	24	—	—
Mariazell	107		868	●	●	—	≼	●	●	S	1	10	—	—
Mayrhofen	108		630	●	●	—	—	—	●	S	2	16	—	—
Nassfeld		(34)	1500	●	—	—	—	●	—	S	0	10	—	—
Nauders	84		1508	●	●	—	—	●	—	S	1	8	—	—
Neukirchen am Grossvenediger	72		856	●	●	—	—	●	●	S	0	14	—	—
Neustift	90		993	●	●	—	—	●	●	S	0	9	—	—
Obergurgl	116		1927	●	●	—	≼	—	●	S	0	11	—	—
Hochgurgl	116		2150	—	—	—	≼	—	●	—	0	5	—	—
Obertauern	119		1738	●	—	—	—	—	●	S	1	21	—	—
Ramsau am Dachstein		(21)	1088	●	—	◇	≼	●	●	S	1	25	—	—
Rauris		(33)	948	●	●	—	—	●	●	S	0	8	—	—
Saalbach-Hinterglemm		(19)	1003	●	●	—	—	●	—	S	1	38	—	—
St. Anton am Arlberg	122		1287	●	●	—	—	●	—	S	6	23	—	—
St. Jakob in Defereggen		(32)	1389	●	●	◇	—	●	—	S	0	14	—	—
St. Johann in Tirol	124		660	●	●	◇	—	—	●	S	3	7	—	—
Schladming	139		749	●	●	—	—	●	●	S	1	15	—	—
Schruns and Tschagguns	48		689	●	●	—	—	—	—	S	4	17	⛸	—
Seefeld in Tirol	142		1180	●	●	—	≼	●	●	S	3	11	⛸	♣
Semmering	141		985	●	●	—	≼	●	●	S	0	7	—	—
Serfaus		(29)	1427	—	●	◇	≼	—	—	S	2	14	—	—
Sölden	116		1377	●	●	—	—	—	●	S	3	18	—	—
Tauplitzalm	139		1647	—	—	—	≼	—	—	S	0	16	—	—
Wagrain		(20)	838	●	—	◇	—	●	—	S	0	22	—	—
Werfenweng		(20)	901	●	—	—	≼	●	—	S	0	13	—	—
Zell am See	173		757	●	●	—	≼	—	●	S	3	25	⛸	—
Zürs	49		1717	●	●	—	—	—	—	—	1	11	—	—

EUROPE on a single sheet
Michelin map No 920 (scale 1/3 000 000)

CONVENTIONAL SIGNS

Sights

*** **Worth a journey**
** **Worth a detour**
* **Interesting**

Italic type indicates natural sights

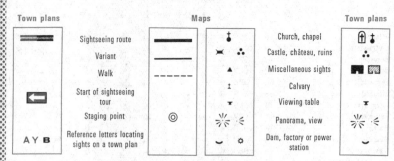

Town plans		Maps		Town plans
	Sightseeing route		Church, chapel	
	Variant		Castle, château, ruins	
	Walk		Miscellaneous sights	
	Start of sightseeing tour		Calvary	
	Staging point		Viewing table	
	Reference letters locating sights on a town plan		Panorama, view	
A Y B			Dam, factory or power station	

Roads

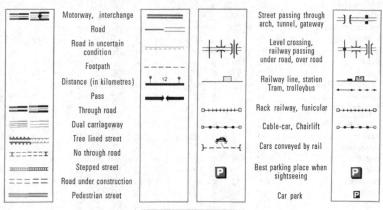

	Motorway, interchange		Street passing through arch, tunnel, gateway
	Road		Level crossing, railway passing under road, over road
	Road in uncertain condition		
	Footpath		Railway line, station Tram, trolleybus
	Distance (in kilometres)		
	Pass		Rack railway, funicular
	Through road		Cable-car, Chairlift
	Dual carriageway		Cars conveyed by rail
	Tree lined street		
	No through road		Best parking place when sightseeing
	Stepped street		
	Road under construction		Car park
	Pedestrian street		

Miscellaneous

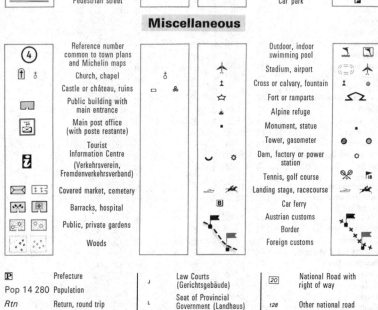

	Reference number common to town plans and Michelin maps		Outdoor, indoor swimming pool
	Church, chapel		Stadium, airport
	Castle or château, ruins		Cross or calvary, fountain
	Public building with main entrance		Fort or ramparts
	Main post office (with poste restante)		Alpine refuge
			Monument, statue
	Tourist Information Centre (Verkehrsverein, Fremdenverkehrsverband)		Tower, gasometer
			Dam, factory or power station
	Covered market, cemetery		Tennis, golf course
	Barracks, hospital		Landing stage, racecourse
	Public, private gardens		Car ferry
	Woods		Austrian customs
			Border
			Foreign customs

P	Prefecture	J	Law Courts (Gerichtsgebäude)	20	National Road with right of way
Pop 14 280	Population	L	Seat of Provincial Government (Landhaus)	128	Other national road
Rtn	Return, round trip	M	Museum	Liezen	Reference point
G	Police station	T	Theatre	△ 1988	Altitude in metres
POL	Police	U	University		
R	Town Hall (Rathaus)				

ß : the letter **ß** (eszett) which is to be found only in the German alphabet, appears in the text transcribed as "**ss**".

TOWNS, SIGHTS

AND TOURIST REGIONS

ADMONT (Styria)

Michelin map **426** fold 22 – *Local map p 64* – Pop 3 105 – Alt 641 m - 2 103 ft – 🔲 ☎ 2164 – *Facilities p 39*

The Benedictine Abbey of Admont was founded in the 11C by St Emma of Gurk *(p 79)* and Gebhard, Archbishop of Salzburg. It became a centre of culture whose fame soon spread beyond the limits of the Enns Valley. The spires of its church are framed by the summits of the Hailer Mauern and the Grosser Buchstein, the northern pillar of the Gesäuse. Matching them in the west, are the towers of Frauenberg *(p 64)* on their hill. There is a particularly good view looking towards Admont from the Hieflau road as it runs along the Gesäuse.

The abbey buildings were completely reconstructed after a fire in 1865. Fortunately the library was spared by the flames and still has its valuable archives.

Abbey Library★★ **(Stiftsbibliothek).** – *Open 1 May to 31 October 10am to 4pm ; 10.30am to noon the rest of the year ; closed Mondays ; 15S.*

The library state room extends 72 m - 75 yds on either side of a central rotunda under a dome. The ceiling paintings by Bartholomeo Altomonte, the body of the library using the deep bays of the windows and the upper gallery with its wrought iron balustrade, contribute to the prestige of this Rococo ensemble (1774), which is worthy of the treasures it contains. Note the celebrated statues of finality – Death, Judgment, Heaven and Hell. These are the work of Joseph Stammel (1695-1765), who revived, in the shadow of the monastery, the art of wood-carving neglected in Austria since the last Gothic blossoming. Worth attention also for freshness of inspiration and clever composition are the manuscripts and printed texts shown under glass. The latter have been selected from the 1 600 MSS and 150 000 volumes which the Benedictines found means to preserve.

The AFLENZER SEEBERG Road ★ (Styria)

Michelin map **426** fold 23

This is the last really moun-tainous road pass in the Aus-trian Alps on the approaches to Vienna. The Aflenzer See-berg (alt 1 253 m - 4 111 ft) or Seeberg Pass makes communi-cation easy between the Maria-zell basin and industrial furrow of the Mur and the Mürz. The views of the Hochschwab crests and the crossing of the Aflenz basin mark pleasant sec-tions on this run.

From Bruck an der Mur to Mariazell

61 km - 38 miles – about 2 1/2 hours – Local map opposite

Start out from Bruck an der Mur (p 56) to the north, on the road to Vienna. Leaving the industrial country (steelworks) of the Lower Mürz at Kapfen-berg, the road finds its way through the narrow Thörlbach Valley, where there are still a few wiremills and nail facto-ries. The picturesque setting of the Thörl gateway marks the exit from this first defile.

Thörl. – Pop 2 407. The lit-tle settlement, now indus-trial, lies in a rocky cleft. It began as a fortified work barring the entrance to the Aflenz basin. Exactly in line with the valley, stand the ruins of the stronghold of Schachenstein on their steep sided spur. The cas-tle was built in 1471. Be-side the road, to the south, an oratory shelters a large Calvary dating from 1530.

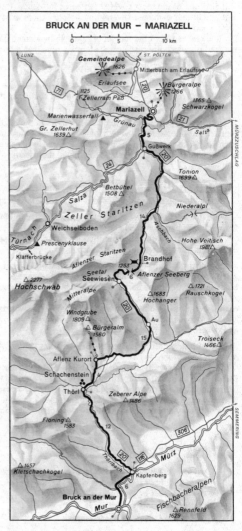

BRUCK AN DER MUR – MARIAZELL

The AFLENZER SEEBERG Road★

Of the gateway (Törlein) from which the village gets its name there remain, on the mountain side, an 18C building through which the roadway passed under an arch, still in existence, and a tower converted into a chapel dedicated to St Barbara.

Aflenz. – Pop 1 064. *Facilities p 39.* Aflenz is a medium altitude resort, very popular in Styria. It enjoys a calm location.

In winter the chairlift to the Bürgeralm serves the sunny Schönleiten plateau, which has a ski tow and in the climbing season saves time for expeditions in the Hochschwab massif.

The church, which is squat and rustic, is one of the latest specimens of Gothic architecture in Austria. The tower is, since the end of the 15C, a defence work. Inside, the decorative artistry of the vault groins merges quite freely into the side walls and the Gothic statues of the twelve Apostles. The south door, with its design of little columns and string-courses superimposed on multilobed archwork, is no less curious. The relief representing the architect, at the keystone, is modern.

From Aflenz to Au the **road**★ runs along the upper banks of a green slope at the base of the last foothills of the Hochschwab. Long, low houses with wide outside galleries are a local characteristic.

At **Seewiesen**, whose Gothic church is reminiscent, both in its shape and in its setting, of the Church of Heiligenblut, the final climb begins. The Seetal, with its evenly inclined slopes, closes in, in the background, between the ramparts of the Aflenzer Staritzen and those of the Mitteralpe (Hochschwab massif).

Brandhof. – This hunting lodge was arranged by Archduke Johann. In it he was secretly married to Anna Plochl in 1827 (p 50).

On the north slope of the pass the route lies first along the sides, then on the floors of little valleys of Alpine pastureland. The climb to Mariazell (p 107) in wide bends emphasizes the very open setting of this famous centre of pilgrimage.

AGGSTEIN Ruins ★ (Lower Austria)

Michelin map **426** fold 10 – 13 km - 8 miles northeast of Melk – *Local map p 61*

The ruins of the stronghold of Aggstein stand in the heart of the Wachau, on a choice **site**★ at 520 m - 1 706 ft altitude on a rock overlooking the Danube from about 300 m - 1 000 ft.

This castle was built in the 12C. Its size and situation made it one of the most formidable and also one of the most coveted fortresses in Austria. It was destroyed by the Turks in 1529 and rebuilt and damaged several times. Today there exist only the lofty shapes of its ruined towers and walls.

It is reached from the hamlet of Aggstein by a steep path (2 hours on foot Rtn). The tip of the spur on which the castle stands forms a remarkable observatory.

ALPBACH (Tyrol)

Michelin map **426** fold 18 – 12 km - 7 miles southeast of Rattenberg – Pop 1 999 – Alt 973 m - 3 192 ft – ⓘ ☎ 5211 – *Facilities p 39*

In the setting of one of the quietest valleys in the Kitzbühel Alps, the mountain village of Alpbach has specialized in entertaining members of universities meeting in a European Forum each year. The setting of the village and the true Tyrolean style of its chalets (illustration p 29) create an atmosphere favourable to unruffled discussion.

ALTENBURG Abbey (Lower Austria)

Michelin map **426** fold 11 – 6 km - 4 miles southwest of Horn – ⓘ ☎ 2765

The Benedictine Abbey of Altenburg was founded in 1144 and was completely rebuilt in the Baroque style between 1650 and 1742.

An alley lined with statues of mythological divinities leads to the entrance hall, the ceiling of which is adorned with delicate stucco.

Abbey church (Stiftskirche). – This is interesting for its architecture and its decoration. The west face, decorated with statues (St Michael, St Benedict, angels) is surmounted by a graceful bulbous belfry. It forms part of a group of buildings framing the prelate's court.

The interior, adorned with marble, stucco and frescos, is of noble proportions. The nave is roofed by an oval dome decorated by Paul Troger with frescos whose central theme is the struggle between St Michael and the dragon. The organ (1773) is remarkable for the elegance and delicacy of the gilded woodwork.

Abbey buildings (Stiftsgebäude). – *Guided tours (1 hour) April through October 9am to noon and 1 to 5pm. Apply to visit in winter. 25S.*

The library with its staircase – decorated with frescos by Paul Troger and Johann-Jakob Zeiller – the crypt and the apartments, served by a grand staircase, combined, will make this an interesting tour to lovers of Baroque art. The **abbey treasures** (additional entrance fee: 15S) (furnishings, statues, documents, liturgical objects in gold and silver plate) representing 850 years of history are exhibited in the prelates apartments (Schatzkammer in der Prälatur).

Michelin road map 426 Austria
at a scale of 1/400 000 (1 in: 6.30 miles)

- *Road network with their characteristics: snowbound, gradients, hilly road...*
- *A wide variety of tourist information: scenic routes, ski-lifts, viewpoints, refuge huts...*
- *A detailed inset of Vienna and surburbs*
- *An index with map co-ordinates.*

The perfect companion to this guide.

Between the Upper Rhine and the Inn corridor the mountainous region of the Arlberg, with which may be grouped the Lechtal Alps and the massifs of the Verwall, the Rätikon and the Silvretta, was for a long time a formidable obstacle to communications.

The road to the Arlberg Pass, which was made fit for wheeled traffic in 1825, and especially the railway tunnel, 10 km - 6 miles long, completed in 1884, provided a permanent link between the Vorarlberg and the Tyrol. The new road tunnel 14 km - 8 1/2 miles long was opened at the end of 1978 ; it also assures communications between these two regions in both summer and winter. *Toll : 140S.*

The danger of snow is less acute than it was for winter traffic. Today few of the people of the Vorarlberg consider, with the touch of humour which greeted the opening of the tunnel, that "Man should not join what God has made separate".

The Cradle of Alpine Skiing. – The teaching of Alpine skiing began at the foot of the Arlberg. In 1901 the Arlberg Ski Club was founded, and a native of Stuben, **Hannes Schneider** (1890-1955), under the direction of Victor Sohm, began to create a technique of movement on the fast slopes of the region, where styles imported from Scandinavia were often inadequate.

Schneider, with the great British sportsman **Arnold Lunn** – who in 1922 introduced slalom gates thereby creating the Alpine slalom race and who also induced in 1930 the Fédération Internationale de Ski to recognize competition in downhill as well as slalom skiing – founded the **Arlberg-Kandahar Cup** which was competed for the first time at St. Anton in 1928 and at regular intervals since at St. Anton, Mürren, Chamonix, Sestriere or Garmisch-Partenkirchen. *(For further details read "Skiing" p 19.)*

Until the Second World War the tourist development of the Arlberg bore the mark of these origins and the summer season, comparatively, languished. The opening of the Silvretta road, by speeding up development in the Montafon (Upper Valley of the Ill), has extended the tourist season to all times of the year.

THE ARLBERG PASS★
From Bludenz to Landeck – *68 km - 42 miles – about 2 1/2 hours – Local map p 48*

To drive through the Klostertal (west slope) at a leisurely pace use the old road which crosses the Innerbraz, Dalaas, Wald and Klösterle and not the Arlberg tunnel road.

Between Bludenz *(p 52)* and Langen you climb in a series of steps through the **Klostertal**, a valley which takes its name from the house built in the Middle Ages by the Hospitallers of St John of Jerusalem to provide help for travellers at a place now called the Klösterle (little monastery). It is interesting to compare the lay out and rate of climb of the old road and that of the tunnel and railway, the latter being obliged to use a flanking route from Bludenz onwards. The whole valley seems to depend on its role as a route of passage, as is shown by the electrical power-stations of Wald and Braz, which supply the power needed by the railway.

From Langen, where the monumental entrance to the Arlberg tunnels opens, to St. Christoph, the landscape is severe in character. Many ravines cut the thinly turfed slopes. The electricity pylons stand on concrete bases with spurs to break avalanches.

Stuben. – Pop 92. The little settlement, nestling behind an anti-avalanche wall on one of the most threatened sections of the road, gets its name from a *Stube* (room) where travellers could warm themselves and get some rest before a final climb.

Very high up, ahead, appear the galleries of the road to the Flexenpass *(p 49)*, which branches off to the left towards Rauz.

After a last climb (with a gradient of 1 in 10), you reach the desolate combe of the Arlberg – Arle means mountain pine in the local dialect – and the pass, at 1 793 m - 5 882 ft altitude.

St. Christoph am Arlberg. – The hospice founded in 1386 below the pass on the Tyrolean slope of the Arlberg, was burnt down in 1957 but has been rebuilt as an hotel with a chapel. The former statue of St Christopher, which was venerated by travellers, had to be replaced by a modern sculpture. This hospice was the nucleus of the present tiny settlement, which, since the early days of skiing, has acted as a mountain annexe of St. Anton. Two ski lifts run from it, and one cable-car leading to the Galzig.

The descent from St. Christoph to St. Anton is majestic. The chief attraction is the appearance of the Patteriol (alt 3 056 m - 10 026 ft), the boldest summit of the Verwall massif.

St. Anton am Arlberg★★. – *Description p 122.*

The **Stanzertal** (Valley of the Rosanna), through which you will run downstream from St. Anton, is one of the most attractive in the Austrian Alps. Thanks to the chalky escarpments of the Lechtal Alps to the north, and to the snowfields of the Hoher Riffler to the south, the landscape is still impressive. But the meadows dotted with little barns and the villages, remarkable for the variety of their settings – for instance, Flirsch is scattered over pastureland, while Strengen lies in a ravine – also render charming glimpses. When the road emerges above the Paznauntal the time has come to enjoy the picture, often illustrated, of the Trisanna Bridge.

Trisanna Bridge★ (Trisannabrücke). – To cross the torrent, the railway has been led at a height of 86 m - 282 ft – through a metal bridge which ends at the feudal Castle of Wiesberg. The bridge, which is light and slender, in no way spoils the romantic setting.

The Sanna Valley, formed by the junction of the Trisanna and the Rosanna, already foreshadows the Inn Valley, which will be reached at Landeck *(p 101)*. The slopes open out and perched villages begin to find room on levels left free by the forest. Note in passing the picturesque site of **Pians**, at the mouth of a tributary gorge.

THE MONTAFON AND THE SILVRETTA ROAD★★
From Bludenz to Landeck – *95 km - 59 miles – 4 hours – Local map p 48*

The Silvretta Road proper (Partenen-Galtür) is closed to caravans ; it takes a toll of 25S per person. Climbing westwards, the roadway with its 30 hairpin curves, may surprise drivers who are not familiar with the Alpine roads. It is generally blocked by snow from November to the end of May.

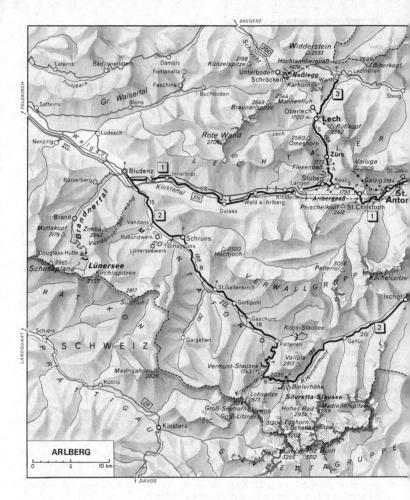

The Silvretta High Alpine Road (Silvretta-Hochalpenstrasse) has joined the Ill Valley (Montafon) and the Trisanna Valley (Paznauntal), using the threshold of the Bielerhöhe (alt 2 036 m - 6 680 ft), where the ruggedness of the high mountain is tempered by the serenity of a dam reservoir.

The run from Bludenz (p 52) to Schruns reveals a Montafon transformed by modern life, especially in the neighbourhood of Vandans. You will see, at this point, the compensating reservoir of the power-station of Rodund (p 49) and a great many high-tension lines.

The Montafon, deeply sunken, is a smiling valley densely populated. The screen formed by the mountains and the mild influence of the Föhn (p 17) encourage fruit growing in basins of medium altitude, while the local breed of cattle, which can be recognized by their toast-coloured hides, do well on the higher pastures. Though the people speak German, the placenames and the

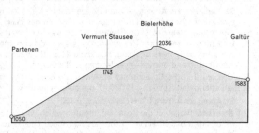

peculiarities of building (a core of masonry pierced with arched doorways is often seen inside a building of dark wood) bear witness to the former Rhaeto-Romansh civilization, which remains alive in the Engadine on the southern slopes of the Silvretta mountain range.

Schruns. – Pop 3 729. *Facilities p 42.* The capital town of the Montafon spreads its houses over a spacious basin, within view of the crests of the Vandanser Steinwand, from which the Zimba peak stands out. The town is pleasing by its liveliness.

The ancient nucleus of the village, with its Dorfstrasse *(closed to motor traffic)* running downhill between the church and the Litz torrent, invites a few minutes' stroll.

From Schruns to Partenen the valley, being narrow and steep-sided, has a more Alpine look. The bulbous belfries and flower decked houses of dark wood dotted on the slopes lend a special charm to the villages of St. Gallenkirch and Gortipohl.

St. Gallenkirch. – Pop 1 992. *Facilities p 42.*

Ahead is the pyramid of the Vallüla, whose foothills seem to wall up the valley.

Gaschurn. – Pop 1 693. *Facilities pp 39 and 43.*

At **Partenen,** where two power stations nestle at the foot of pressure-conduits leading down from Lake Vermunt and Kops Lake, begins a climb of 1 000 m - 3 280 ft. The slope you ascend is covered with scree and has a desolate look which the road has not softened. But the siting, with its many superimposed hairpin bends is impressive.

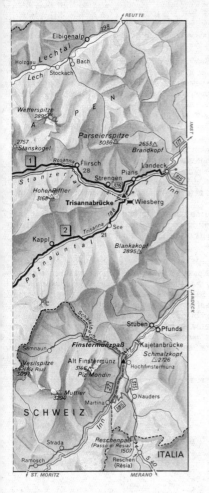

Vermunt Lake (Vermunt-Stausee). – This lake, at an altitude of 1 743 m - 5 718 ft – occupies a middle position between Partenen and the Silvretta Dam and allows a welcome pause in the steep climb. It is from this artificial lake that the waters are led by pressure-conduits to the power station at Partenen. From points near the dam the **view**★ along the wild Kromertal carries as far as the crests of the Grosser Litzner and the Grosses Seehorn.

While the road winds over a ledge worn smooth by former glaciers, look out for the wall of the Silvretta Dam and the crown of summits overlooking the upper lake.

Bielerhöhe. – The artificial stretch of water, **Silvretta Lake**★ (Silvretta-Stausee), formed at the opening of the Bielerhöhe pass has created, at an altitude of 2 036 m - 6 680 ft – a magnificient **scene**★★ in the high mountains.

It is a natural halting place with a large hotel much appreciated as a base for Alpine expeditions and spring skiing in the Silvretta massif.

A walk along the crest of the dam, 432 m - 1 417 ft long and 80 m - 260 ft high – reveals, from left to right and framing the lake : the dark, very sharp pyramid of the Hohes Rad, the Piz Buin, the Eckhorn and the Lobspitze.

The **dam** forms the keystone of the hydro-electrical equipment of the Ill. Step by step, the tapped waters flow until finally freed at the exit from the Rodund power station, between Bludenz and Schruns *(p 48)*.

On the Tyrolean slope of the Bielerhöhe the grassy dell of Kleinvermunt affords, upstream, a few views of the Lobspitze, the Eckhorn and the Madlenerspitze.

Galtür. – Pop 679. *Facilities p 43.*

Between Galtür and Ischgl the symmetrical cradle of the High Paznauntal gradually takes on a covering of woods, in which the clumps of larch make pale patches.

Ischgl. – Pop. 1 136. *Facilites pp 39 and 43.*
As you come down from the Silvretta the appearance of the village, built in terraces on a slight spur, at the foot of its church, is one of the most attractive in the Paznauntal.
Downstream from Ischgl the Trisanna Valley becomes definitely sunken and is more picturesque than hospitable: houses are perched on terraces or sunny protuberances (the village of Kappl) ; the road, running alongside the course of the foaming torrent, now slips under denser woods. After a long section the appearance of the Castle of Wiesberg announces the well known picture of the Trisanna Bridge. In the background are the crests of the Parseierspitze, the highest point (3 036 m - 9 960 ft) of the Northern Limestone Alps in Austria.

Trisanna Bridge★ (Trisannabrücke). – *Description of the bridge and of the end of the tour p 47.*

③ THE FLEXENPASS★

From Rauz to Warth – *17 km - 11 miles – about 3/4 hour – Local map opposite*

Between Lech and Warth the road is liable occasionally to be closed for days or even weeks at a time between November and April on account of the danger from avalanches.
The Flexenpass road, which goes to the resorts of Zürs and Lech, is open all winter due to the protective works against avalanches. It continues beyond Lech into the upper part of the valley. At Warth one can choose between returning back by way of the Bregenzerwald *(p 54)* to Constance Lake or by cutting across the chalky Tyrolean High Alps through the Upper Lech Valley *(p 101)* towards Reutte.
Branching off the Arlberg Road, on the Flexen Road, one arrives at a tight bend before leaving the combe.
From this panoramic bend you can see, in line, beyond Stuben, the Klostertal and the crests of the Rätikon, characterized by the Zimba and the glacial shoulder of the Schesaplana.
Higher up, the **ascent**★ to the pass required the construction of 600 m – 656 yds – of tunnels and protective galleries with windowed openings.
After having reached Flexenpass at 1 773 m - 5 816 ft – one arrives at Zürs.

Zürs★. – *Facilities p 43.* This group of hotels forms a winter resort of first rank in international standing. The sunny, treeless slopes and well developed mechanical equipment (the first modern ski tow installed in Austria was here) explain why this forbidding combe became an established resort.

Lech★★. – *Description p 101.*

The run along the flank of the turfed and steep slopes of the Upper Lech Valley continue north as far as Warth within view of the Biberkopf.

Michelin map 426 fold 21 – *Local maps below and p 139* – Pop 5 047 – Alt 659 m - 2 162 ft
– 🆔 ☎ 2323 – *Facilities p 39*

Bad Aussee is the capital of the Styrian Salzkammergut, a region which is still marked by tradition. It is built at the confluence of two upper branches of the Traun and enjoys a peaked mountain setting. Cutting into the Bad Aussee basin, the Dachstein and the Totes Gebirge throw out a series of well defined bastions, framing picturesque lakes: the Altausseer See and the Grundlsee.

Bad Aussee, which makes equal use industrially and medically of the salt marshes and sodium-sulphate waters brought from the mines of Altaussee, affords an exceptional choice of walks and excursions.

The Faithful Prince. – If Bad Ischl owed its fortune to Franz-Josef, the great man of Bad Aussee was the Archduke Johann *(p 73)*. The long contested romance of the prince with Anna Plochl, the daughter of the local postmaster, and his almost clandestine marriage at Brandhof *(p 46)* in 1827, filled the romantic chronicles of the period. The popularity of the "Prince of Styria" was strengthened by it, and the Republican Austria of today still places the archduke's portrait in the place of honour in its marriage halls.

At Bad Aussee itself it will therefore be no surprise to find the prince's statue in the municipal gardens (Kurpark), the medallion of the couple on the bridge over the Grundlseer Traun (Erzherzog-Johann Brücke) and souvenirs of the Plochl family piously preserved in the former post office, No. 37 Meranplatz.

The Upper Town. – The centre of the town is the Chlümeckyplatz, formely called the Obermarkt, a pleasant place for a stroll. Note a plague column *(p 147)*, which was reconstructed in 1876, and especially the **Kammerhof,** formely the palace of the controller of mines, which in the 17C was given its fine window-frames in red Salzburg marble with cable mouldings. Over the main door are the arms of the Habsburgs and of Styria. The Kammerhof today houses the **local museum** (Heimatmuseum). Behind the Kammerhof, go by way of the Chlümeckyplatz, is the new thermal establishment. The Hofer House, nearby, in the 16C the home of the director of the mines, has preserved mural paintings of the period. Seen on the outside are St Sebastian, St Anne's Family Group, St Florian; inside are Samson and Delilah and a hunting scene *(ask inside to visit).*

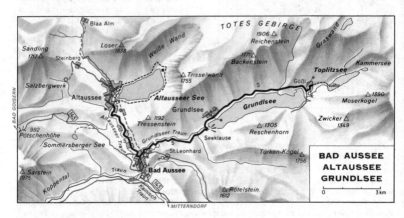

EXCURSIONS

Grundlsee★. – *5 km - 3 miles for the Grundlsee resort; 10 km - 6 miles for the Gössl fork. Local map above.*
Leave Bad Aussee by the Grundlseer Strasse. When you arrive at Seeklause (a landing-stage at the head of the lake) you get an end-on **view**★★ of the whole Grundlsee basin, overlooked from the left by the Backenstein promontory, whose foot the road skirts after passing through the resort of Grundlsee.

Grundlsee. – Pop 1 282. *Facilities see at Bad Aussee p 39.*

In the distance are the long vistas of the pale summits of the Totes Gebirge. Turn back at the end of the lake, at the Gössl fork.

The **trip**★★ will be still more interesting if you take the time *(about 3 hours Rtn after leaving Bad Aussee)* to go to the hamlet of Gössl and from there either in a coach, or a 20 minutes walk, to the wild **Toplitzsee**★. The views from the lake can only be seen by taking the motorboat excursion *(24S)*. Beyond the last isthmus lies the little **Kammersee** hemmed in between the walls of the Totes Gebirge.

Lake of Altaussee★ (Altausseer See). – *5 km - 3 miles to the north – Local map above.*
The road ends at the much scattered resort of **Altaussee** (pop 1 906 – *facilities p 39*) from which you can make a tour of the lake *(about 3 hours on foot – an inn provides a halfway halt)*, or undertake the popular tour *(guided tours (1 hour) 10 May to 18 September 9am to 4pm; 60S brochure available in English)* of the nearby salt-mines *(Salzbergwerk)* which were used by the Germans, as a place of safety for art collections during the Second World War; among them was a splendid polyptych, *Adoration of the Lamb,* from the cathedral at Ghent, recovered in 1945 by the Americans.

BAD – see under proper name.

The towns and sights described in this guide are shown in **black** *on the maps.*

BADEN ★ (Lower Austria) ─────────────────────

Michelin map **426** fold 25 – *Local map p 169* – Pop 23 235 – Alt 233 m - 764 ft – ▣ ☎ 41127 – *Facilities p 39*

Baden is a hydromineral resort in the middle of a pleasant region of hills surrounded by forests and vineyards. Modern spa equipment, games and sports grounds, a fine park and interesting walks fanning out in all directions, keep up its reputation with the Viennese.

The Resort. – Already known and used in the Roman era, the hot springs, the waters of which carry sulphur, chlorine and sulphates, gush forth at a temperature of more than 36°C–96.8°F. The 15 springs in use yield nearly 6 500 000 litres - 1 430 000 gallons daily.

The waters of Baden are used in the form of warm baths or in applications of sulphurous mud. They are prescribed for the treatment of rheumatism and its consequences, the degeneration of joints and the results of injuries.

Baden has had famous guests: Mozart and Beethoven *(a small memorial museum has been installed at No. 10 Rathausgasse. Open 9 to 11am and 3 to 5pm; closed Thursdays in summer and Mondays, Wednesdays, Fridays and Sundays in winter; 8S).* From 1813 to 1834 Baden was chosen by the Imperial Court as its summer residence. *For a tour in the Vienna Woods see p 168.*

BADGASTEIN ★★ (Salzburg) ─────────────────────

Michelin map **426** fold 34 –Pop 5 600 – Alt 1 013 m - 3 323 ft – ▣ ☎ 67520 – *Facilities pp 39 and 43*

Badgastein is one of the towns with the most reminders of taking the waters, as practised by those taking cures in the 19C. It stands on a **site★** on the north slope of the Tauern. Great hotels and shops are arranged in a curve on the flanks of a wooded amphitheatre. The Gasteiner Ache, dropping from the top of the steep slope, falls in a cascade in the very centre of the town.

Sports. – Badgastein has a rather unique indoor swimming pool: carved into the rock and filled from the hot springs (radium emanation, i.e. radon).

In 1958 winter sports equipment was marked by the championships of the F.S.I. (International Skiing Federation). The east slopes of the valley are served by the chair lifts of the Höllbrunn and the Grau-kogel. Opposite these the Stub-nerkogel cablecars take skiers and lovers of panoramas to an altitude of 2 246 m - 7 369 ft.

Since 1971 the search for ski resorts has been solved with the development of **Sport-gastein** (alt 1 588 m - 5 210 ft) in the Nassfeldtal *(toll road from Böckstein: 30S).* The resort is well equipped with a chairlift (alt 2 150 m - 7 052 ft) and a ski tow which goes up to the Kreuzkogel mountainside (alt 2 686 m - 8 812 ft).

The Cure. – This is practised mostly in the hotels and *pensions* directly connected with the hot springs. The waters, which have been visited since the 13C, owe their efficacy not so much to their mineral content, which is low, as to the therapeutic effects of the radon. According to the type of treatment, the radon is absorbed by the skin or through the digestive or the respiratory system. It stimulates the internal secretion glands and relieves rheumatic pain. Since it cannot be retained by the tissues of the body it is soon eliminated (usually in 2 to 4 hours).

Another cure at Badgastein is practised in the Heilstollen. These are abandoned mine galleries, opening above the Böckstein.

Those taking the cure are carried by a little train to various natural chambers (37.5 to 41.5° C or 100 to 107° F) where the atmosphere has a high radon content.

The healthy mountain climate in the ravine at Badgastein, which is well sheltered from the wind, also helps the treatment.

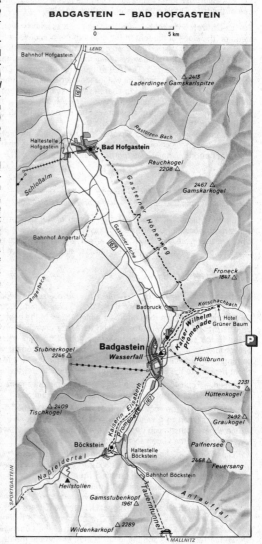

BADGASTEIN – BAD HOFGASTEIN

BADGASTEIN★★

■ **SIGHTS** *time: 1 hour*

Leave the car at the paying car park called "Parkhochhaus" facing the Spa Centre and the Congress (Kur-, Kongress-, und Veranstaltungszentrum).

Lower Waterfall (Unterer Wasserfall) of the Gasteiner Ache★. – After flowing down a slope, the water spreads in a fan shape before falling into the amphitheatre.

Follow the downhill road and, passing to the right of the Neo-Gothic Catholic church, turn to the right into the Kaiser Wilhelm Promenade.

Kaiser Wilhelm Promenade★. – The Kaiser Wilhelm Promenade is level, affording **views**★ of the lower nucleus of the valley, the site of the town of Bad Hofgastein. The slender steeple of St Nicholas, roofed with shingles, makes a delightful foreground scene. A pleasant 45 minute stroll brings you to the Hotel Grüner Baum (swimming pool, miniature golf).

If you have only an hour to spend, leave the promenade, going down to the left after passing the Hotel Germania. At the end of a slight slope turn to the left.

Church of St Nicholas (St. Nikolaus). – This humble 15C church, now disused, is charming. The vaulted nave, star-shaped according to a method of building peculiar to the end of the Gothic period *(p 33)*, is built round a central pillar. Among many traces of mural paintings of the 15 and 16C, the composition depicting the Last Judgment is the easiest to recognize.

Go back to the Kaiser Wilhelm Promenade by the ramp which begins on the left of the "Laurahaus", and return to the car.

Other well laid out routes enable you to reach the Gastein Valley while keeping clear of road traffic. Note particularly that of the Empress Elizabeth (Kaiserin-Elisabeth-Promenade), which joins Badgastein to Böckstein (description p 146) and the Gasteiner Höhenweg which runs down the flank of the mountain from Badgastein to Bad Hofgastein (description p 82). These walks are shown by dotted lines on the local map p 51.

BISCHOFSHOFEN (Salzburg)

Michelin map **426** fold 20 – *Local map p 128* – Pop 9 520 – Alt 544 m - 1 785 ft – ▣ ☏ 2471

It is a surprise to travellers to find, in the highly industrialized small town of Bischofshofen, one of the best Gothic churches in the Austrian Alps.

Parish Church (Pfarrkirche). – This church, with its squat tower, is the lowest of the three which stand on the slope at the foot of the crests of the Mandlwand (Hochkönig Massif).

The transept crossing, under an octagonal dome, is the oldest part of the building (a vestige of an 11C structure). The choir was built in the 14C – its columns are still ringed – and the nave in the hall style of the 15C. The skill of the groined vaulting gives a certain unity to this varied architectural group. On the north wall of the nave a series of murals of the 16 and 17C depict the scenes of the Passion. The side altars in the nave are adorned with excellent Gothic statuary (1480). In the north arm of the transept is the tomb, dating from the middle of the 15C, of Silvester Pflieger, Bishop of Chiemsee. The Baroque altar of St Anne opposite, bears a Holy Family group *(p 28)*, dating from 1500.

In summer *(15 June to 1 October)* the nave holds the *Prangstangen*, processional staves with wool of various colours or garlands of flowers twisted round them, whose use continues in the neighbouring Lungau *(see tourist calendar of events p 31)*.

BLUDENZ (Vorarlberg)

Michelin map **426** fold 28 – *Local map p 48* – Pop 12 893 – Alt 585 m - 1 119 ft – ▣ ☏ 2170

Bludenz placed at a road junction is one of the busiest towns in the Vorarlberg (textile industries, chocolate); it forms an interesting halting place or excursion centre for the motorist, who, starting from there, can make a tour linking the roads of the Arlberg and those of the Silvretta, or penetrate through the Brandnertal, to the heart of the Rätikon Massif.

EXCURSION

Brandnertal★★. – *18 km - 11 miles by narrow roads (blocked by snow) which rise in a gradient of 1 in 8 continuously beyond Brand, plus about 2 hours walk Rtn – local map p 48.*
On leaving Bludenz the road affords a general view of the town, and climbs through a wood cut by clearings. Beyond Bürserberg, with its pretty church, the view opens out in line with the valley to the summit of the Schesaplana, left of the dark mass of the Mottakopf and, in the background, to a great saddle edged with snow. Further on the valley narrows. Through a ravine coming in on the left there is a **view**★ of the Zimba, the little Matterhorn of the Vorarlberg. The slight descent to the Brand basin emphasizes the **site**★ of the village.

Brand. – Pop 646. *Facilities p 39.* This was originally a mere colony of Valaisian exiles *(pp 54 and 97)* and has now become a pleasant mountain resort.

The climb brings the road to the foot of the **amphitheatre**★★ whose sides bar access to the Schesaplana, then to a wild combe with slopes covered with scree. After the Schattenlagant refuge, where tourists can turn back, this combe closes in a "world's end". Leave the car at the lower station of the Lünersee cablecar.

Lünersee★★. – *2 hours Rtn, including 10 minutes by cablecar. The cablecar works from early June to mid-October. The first departure from the lower station is at 8am; the last departure from the upper station at 5pm; 50S Rtn).*
The cablecar leaves the excursionist beside a lake, at the refuge Douglass-Hütte. The Lünersee, in its barren setting of frayed crests of the Schesaplana (alt 2 965 m - 9 728 ft) was, in its natural state, the biggest lake in the Eastern Alps. Since 1958 a dam has raised its water level 27 m - 90 ft, creating a reservoir of 78 million m^3 - 17 160 million gallons – feeding, with a drop of 1 000 m - 3 280 ft – the Lünersee power station (Lünerseewerk) above Tschagguns and the lower station at Rodund (Rodundwerk).

BRAUNAU (Upper Austria)

Michelin map **426** fold 7 – Pop 16 192 – Alt 352 m - 1 155 ft

This is a frontier town, linked by a bridge over the Inn with the Bavarian settlement of Simbach. It has a rather picturesque old quarter and was the birthplace of Adolf Hitler.

Leave the car in the Stadtplatz, which stretches from the bridge (customs post) to the Salzburg Gate.

St Stephen's Church (St. Stephan). – A massive square tower, the third highest in Austria 96 m - 315 ft – and with a Gothic square base, abuts on the chancel which was built at the end of the 15C in the Gothic style. Tombstones are built into the outside walls. The chapel nearest to the chancel in the south aisle contains the tomb of a Bishop of Passau who died in 1485.

BREGENZ ★★ Ⓟ (Vorarlberg)

Michelin maps **426** fold 14, **21** fold 11 and **206** folds 9 and 10 – *Local map p 55* – Pop 24 683 – Alt 398 m - 1 306 ft – ⓘ ☎ 23391 – *Facilities p 39*

Bregenz is the administrative capital of the Vorarlberg. It draws a considerable tourist trade from its position on the shore of Lake Constance or the Bodensee, at the point where the Swabian Sea washes the feet of the mountains.

BREGENZ

Kornmarktstraße	6
Leutbühel	7
Maurachgasse	8
Rathausstraße	9
St. Anna-Straße	12
Seestraße	13
Thalbachgasse	14
Weiherstraße	15

Anton-Schneider-Straße 2
Kaiserstraße 4
Kirchstraße 5

■ THE LOWER TOWN (Innenstadt) *time: 1 1/2 hours*

The Lake Shore. – The lower town, which is the shopping quarter (pedestrian streets), clusters at the foot of the former fortified city (Oberstadt or Altstadt) of the Counts of Bregenz and Montfort.

In the Middle Ages the waters of the "Bodan", as the Romansh (French-speaking) Swiss call it, still lapped against the base of the little Lake Chapel (Seekapelle). The lake shore spreads its shady quays and flowerbeds from the Seeanlagen to the passenger port. A walk on the main mole is particularly pleasant. The view★ from the end extends to the last hills of Upper Swabia and the island of Lindau, in the foreground, with its twin belfries. West of these developments the Strandweg serves the beach and the festival area *(Festspiel- und Kongresshaus)* where every summer open air plays, concerts, operas and operettas are performed.

Vorarlberg Museum★ (Vorarlberger Landesmuseum). – *Open 9am to noon and 2 to 5pm; closed Mondays; 6S.* The collections are particularly well displayed in the prehistory and Roman departments on the 1st floor.

On the 3rd floor may be seen a few lapidary specimens (9C ornamental plaque with interlaced motifs, from Lauterach) and Romanesque and Gothic works of religious art taken from the richest churches in the province. Among these exhibits is a Crucifix from the former abbey church at Mehrerau, dating from the beginning of the 16C.

On the same floor may be seen works of mythological or religious inspiration and portraits (the *Duke of Wellington*) by **Angelica Kauffmann** (1741-1807), considered a native of the Vorarlberg because of her connection with the Bregenzerwald *(p 54)*. She lived in Rome, and Venice, as well as spending 15 years in England. She was a founding member of the RA in 1768 and was follower of Reynolds.

BREGENZ★★

■ UPPER TOWN (Oberstadt) AND CHURCH QUARTER

With its silent squares and deserted streets, this little enclosed town is restful when the season is in full swing on the lake shore.

It can be reached by car via the Kirchstrasse, the Thalbachgasse and the Amtstorstrasse, on the left. Strollers will prefer to walk up the direct way from the central crossroads of the Leutbühel by the paved ramp of the Maurachgasse as far as the Martinstor, a former fortified gateway.

St Martin's Tower (Martinsturm). – *Tours of the tower 1 May to 1 October 9am to 6pm: 7S.*

This 13C structure took on its present appearance, crowned by a heavy bulbous dome, between 1599 and 1602. The chapel arranged in the base of the tower contains a massive Flamboyant ciborium or canopy and an important series of 14C mural paintings, fairly well preserved.

The skylights in the attic afford pretty **glimpses**★ of the remains of the wall and the roofs of the old town, the lake and belfries of Lindau and, in the distance, the Appenzell Alps.

Parish Church of St Gall (Pfarrkirche). – The church faces the fortified town across the Thalbach ravine.

The building is fronted by a porch-belfry. Built of sandstone in the 15C, the church is surmounted by a scalloped Baroque gable. It has a single sunken 18C nave, decorated with the relative restraint which appears in the Vorarlberg churches when compared with Tyrolean and Bavarian churches of the same period. The walnut stalls, which are in valuable marquetry, were done in about 1740 for the nearby Abbey of Mehrerau and have rounded backs decorated with effigies of monks.

EXCURSION

Pfänder★★. – *11 km - 7 miles by a narrow mountain road, plus 1 hour on foot Rtn. Local map opposite. The lake and its environs risk being fogged in during the summer. It is advised to do this excursion either in the early morning or in the evening.*

Leave Bregenz by ① and the road to Lindau, which forms a quay along the edge of the lake. Bear right towards **Lochau** (pop 5 259 - *facilities p 41*) a village on whose territory stands the 16C Castle of Hofen *(not open to the public)* formerly owned by the von Raitenau family, known for the illustrious Archbishop of Salzburg, Wolf Dietrich *(p 129)*. Directly after the church at Lochau turn right into the by-road to Pfänder, which when it passes over open ground affords many views of the lake and of Lindau.

At the top of the climb turn to the right and leave the car 400 m - 450 yds farther on, at the terminus of the authorized road.

Then take the broad uphill path which, by way of the shaded Schwedenschanze terrace, leads to a television tower and the summit (alt 1 063 m - 3 491 ft).

The **panorama**★★ owes a great deal of its attraction to the lake's great sheet of water and to the bird's-eye view of Bregenz. To get a better view towards the south, walk down through the woods to the "Berghaus Pfänder" beside which stands a viewing table; also nearby is an animal park (big game).

From left to right may be seen the curving lines of the Allgäu Alps which seem to sweep right up against the chalk cliffs (Kanisfluh) of the Bregenzerwald, the snow covered Schesaplana, the great furrow of the Rhine and, lastly, the Altmann and the Säntis, which are both situated in Switzerland. When visibility is good, you can even see the Tödi snows (alt 3 620 m - 11 877 ft) in the Glarus Alps.

A cable-car also joins Bregenz to the Pfänder (frequent services from 8.30am to 8pm, prolonged until 10pm in high summer – 64S Rtn). Total time for the excursion: about 1 1/2 hours Rtn, including 1/4 hour by cable and 1/2 hour on foot Rtn.

Car park near the lower station.

The BREGENZERWALD ★ (Vorarlberg)

Michelin maps 426 folds 14, 15, 28 and 29 and 206 fold 10

The Bregenzerwald of Bregenz hinterland is not a forest as its name might suggest, but a natural region like the Black Forest.

The torrent of the Bregenzer Ache, in its broad windings, sometimes skirts the bases of well-defined rocky "bolts", sometimes – and more often – runs along the floors of wide open depressions, finally joining the Rhine Valley through a long, tortuous defile avoided by the roads.

The gentle aspect of its landscapes and the fidelity of its people to the traditional way of life make the Bregenzerwald a pleasant place to stay.

Described p 55 is the Bregenzerwald route east-west; this itinerary can end a tour in Vorarlberg by taking first the Arlberg Road to Rauz then the Flexenpass Road to Warth *(the routes are described, respectively pp 47 and 49)*.

Life in the Bregenzerwald. – The countryside of the Bregenzerwald is very much like the pictures of eastern Switzerland, with its pasture and dairy land.

Houses in the **Mittelwald** (Bezau district) remind one of the farmhouses of the country round Appenzell *(illustration p 29)*.

In the **Hochtannberg**, a high Alpine valley of the Bregenzer Ache, in which the Valaisians settled in the 13 and 14C, as they did in the Brandnertal *(p 52)*, the Kleinwalsertal *(p 97)* and the Grosswalsertal, east of Feldkirch, the wooden chalets with exposed beams and window frames painted in light colours brightening their walls, seem to have been imported straight from the Upper Valley of the Rhône.

The fine traditional costumes of the Bregenzerwald are hardly worn today in everyday life, although there are still a few chances of seeing them on Sundays at church. Remarkable feminine headdresses – wide black straw hats, small crowns, fur hats. and cone-shaped hats – indicate either the social rank of the wearer or the season.

54

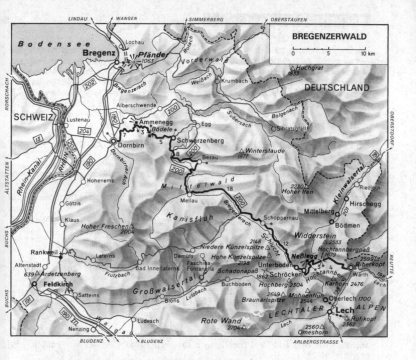

THE ROAD TO THE HOCHTANNBERG★

From Warth to Dornbirn – *60 km - 37 miles – about 2 1/2 hours – Local map above*

The road to Hochtannberg has been greatly improved with the construction of anti-avalanche walls and protective galleries; however it may occasionally be blocked by snow from November to March but it can be cleared quite quickly.

This run, which uses the Hochtannbergpass threshold and the upper gorge of the Bregenzer Ache, follows the windings of the torrent. The crossing of the Bödele Pass lends a mountainous character to this last section of the trip and affords extensive views of the Rhine Valley. Between Warth and Nesslegg the road runs through the Hochtannberg pastureland.

Hochtannbergpass. – Here the road to the Hochtannberg reaches its highest point at an altitude of 1 679 m - 5 508 ft. This section is overlooked by the Widderstein, an outstanding peak of the Vorarlberg. According to local tradition, its rocks scraped the sides of Noah's ark.

Nesslegg★. – This belvedere, marked by the Gasthof Widderstein (Widderstein Inn) at the spot where the road leaves the heart of the Hochtannberg to plunge into the wooded Schröcken tunnel, affords a general **view★** of the upper amphitheatre of the Bregenzer Ache. From left to right you can see the Mohnenfluh, the Braunarlspitze and its snowfields, the Hochberg, the Schadonapass gap and the Hohe Künzelspitze.

From Nesslegg to Schröcken a steep and winding descent through woods affords a few glimpses of the village of **Schröcken** (pop 214 - *facilities p 42*), clustering round its church tower. Downstream from the Hochtannbergbrücke, appears the hamlet of Unterboden, a typical specimen of Valaisian settlement. The sunken sections which follow run through the upper gorges of the Bregenzer Ache, within view of the Künzelspitzen escarpments.

From Schoppernau to Mellau the diverse formation of the Kanisfluh becomes obvious; its northern face forms impressive cliffs. Meanwhile the valley has become populous and covered bridges and houses scattered about make the countryside attractive.

Mellau. – Pop 1 093. *Facilities p 41.*

Farther on, **Bezau** (pop 1 561 - *facilities p 39*) and Schwarzenberg are grouped in more open basins where there are many fruit trees.

Schwarzenberg. – Pop 1 477. The **central square★** displays flower decked houses (Gasthof Hirschen), whose dark walls contrast with the bright roughcast of the church. The latter, which was rebuilt in 1757, has a roomy and well lit nave, characteristic of the local Bregenzerwald school. **Angelica Kauffmann** (1741-1807), the famous artist and herself the daughter of a painter, executed, at 16, the medallions representing the apostles and in 1801, the picture on the high altar. You can see the bust of this local celebrity (born at Chur, but whose father was a native of Schwarzenberg) against the north wall of the nave. *See also the Vorarlberg Museum at Bregenz (p 53).*

The crossing of the Bödele threshold affords, eastwards, clear **views★** of the open basin of the Bregenzerwald and the humps of the Allgäu Alps, where the German frontier runs. In the foreground lies the long ridge of the Winterstaude. On the Rhine slope, after a long run through the forest, the **panorama★** opens out near Ammenegg (Gasthaus Sonnblick). From north to southwest can be seen, in clear weather, Lake Constance, the Appenzell Alps (Säntis and Altmann) and the minor range of the Alvier.

Dornbirn. – Pop 38 663. This is the economic capital and the most populous city of the Vorarlberg. The town is proud of having been able to keep its neat appearance in spite of its industry. Its annual textile fair, in the end of July, is one of the most important in Central Europe.

Beside the parish church, with its Neo-Classical peristyle, is the Rotes Haus (Red House), a small wooden building dating from the 17C and well restored. With its two set back gables, it is a pleasing specimen of the traditional building style of the Alpine Rhine Valley.

The Brenner Pass, at 1 374 m - 4 508 ft, is the lowest route across the Alps and the only one crossed by a main railway line in the open air. It is used at all seasons not only by touring cars but also by heavy traffic. Opened in 1969 is the motorway (Brennerautobahn) from Innsbruck to the pass *(toll: 120S; Rtn 200S)*. The tourist must either drive at a leisurely pace on the old road (No. 182) passing through the routes indicated below, or, to appreciate the Alpine charms of the Sill Valley, take between Innsbruck and Matrei the **Ellbögen road★★** *(p 91)* through Vill, Igls, Patsch and Pfons *(rough and narrow road, driver must be cautious)* and finally, excursions into the tributary valleys of the Sill – the Gschnitztal and the Stubaital *(p 91)*.

BETWEEN INNSBRUCK AND THE BRENNER PASS
by road No. 182 – *37 km - 23 miles – Local map p 90*

4 km 2 1/2 miles	Sonnenburgerhof: from this bend *(south of plan p 86)* there is a remarkable **general view★★** of Innsbruck.
10.5 km 6 1/2 miles	**Europa Bridge★** (Europabrücke), 820 m - 900 yds long, enables the motorway to pass above the Sill Valley at a height of 190 m - 620 ft.
23.5 km 14 1/2 miles	Upstream from Matrei is a view of the mouth of the tributary Valley of the Navis (Navistal), marked by the Churches of St Kathrein and Tiezens.
29 km 18 miles	Stafflach: a view southeastwards, onto the snowcapped Zillertal Alps.
32 km 20 miles	As you leave Gries a noticeboard recalls that this was where Charles V met his brother, the future Emperor Ferdinand I.
34 km 21 miles	Sticking out oddly, at the foot of the ramp, at Luegbrücke (giving on to the motorway), is the little rustic Church of St Sigismund with a Romanesque tower.

BRUCK AN DER MUR ★ (Styria)

Michelin map **426** fold 23 – *Local map p 45* – Pop 15 086 – Alt 487 m - 1 588 ft – ▣
☎ 51811, 51521

Bruck lies at the confluence of the Mur and the Mürz, in the pleasant setting of the Styrian Alps. It is overlooked by the ruins of the old fortress of Landskron.

Bruck is favoured by its situation at the junction of great communication routes and by its proximity to the great steelworks at Leoben. It is a busy industrial town, whose factories, processing iron ore, carry memories of the rich ironmasters and traders in metal. On the main square (Koloman Wallisch Platz) and its nearby streets are the main sights of the town.

(After Dr. A. Defner photo)

Bruck an der Mur. - The Well.

■ **SIGHTS** *time: 1 hour*

Wrought Iron Well★★ (Eiserner Brunnen). – The wellhead was made in 1626 by a local artisan, Hans Prasser, and is considered the masterpiece of all Styria in ironwork.

The forged portion stands on a stone base and is remarkably elegant in execution, particularly the canopy, which has Renaissance motifs.

Kornmesserhaus★ (A). – In spite of remodelling and restorations, this fine building, erected by a rich townsman, Pankraz Kornmess, in the last years of the 15C still has a fine air. The main façade on to the main square has a series of arcades whose decorative arches are adorned with the early rosettes characteristic of Flamboyant Gothic. The loggia which forms part of the 1st floor already shows the influence of the Italian Renaissance.

Old Houses. – There are still a good many old houses, dating from the 15 and 16C.
The **Rathaus** (R-town hall) has a court with three storeys of arcades.

The **Flössmeisterhaus** (B-No. 5), a house adorned with a paired window of the Renaissance period, at the entrance to the Herzog-Ernst-Gasse, also has an interesting interior court.

Parish Church (Pfarrkirche). – *Apply to the sacristan for the key at Kirchplatz No. 1 at the end of the courtyard.*

In the chancel, to the left, is a finely forged wrought iron **sacristy door★**, like its magnificent knocker. It is believed to date from the beginning of the 16C and to come from the Kornmesserhaus.

In the north side chapel is a fine late 18C **altar of the Holy Cross** showing Christ on the Cross, between the Virgin and St John.

BRUCK
AN DER MUR

WIEN 151 km
BAHNHOF
LANDSKRON
Herzog-Ernst-Gasse
PFARRKIRCHE
EISERNER BRUNNEN
Koloman Wallisch Platz
MUR
GRAZ 54 km
Leobner Str.
KLAGENFURT 161 km

CHRISTKINDL (Upper Austria)

Michelin map **426** fold 22 – 3 km - 2 miles west of Steyr

The village of Christkindl – whose name means Infant Christ – has an elegant pilgrims chapel to which a charming tradition is attached.

The Infant Christ's Mail. – The Austrian Postal Service sets up a special office each year at Christkindl, from which one may send Christmas goodwill messages to all parts of the globe. In 1980, 1 721 367 letters were posted from Christkindl – 684 865 being despatched abroad.

The office also undertakes to answer all letters asking for a present (if they enclose a stamp), sent by Austrian children to the Lord Jesus.

Chapel. – The present chapel is dedicated to the Infant Christ. It was built at the beginning of the 18C, in the Baroque style, by Carlone. Four semicircular chapels, roofed with half-domes, stand round a great cupola with a fresco depicting the Assumption of the Virgin. The gilded altar is remarkably carved.

The DACHSTEIN ★★ (Salzburg, Styria and Upper Austria)

Michelin map **426** folds 20 and 21 – *Local map p 139*

The Dachstein Massif, whose highest point reaches 2 995 m - 9 826 ft – is the most revealing example of the limestone plateau in the eastern Alps (*general information p 16*). Its outer ramparts guard not a world of peaks, but great bare, petrified surfaces. The number of cavities found (370 in 1981) shows that a comparison with the Tarn gorges in France is well founded.

THE NORTH WALL★

To the north the Dachstein foothills, more rounded in shape, surround the Lakes of Hallstatt and Gosau. It is on this slope that recent works have opened the road to popular tourism.

A cable-car, serving, as it passes, the Ice Cave of the Dachstein, ends at the belvedere summit of the Krippenstein. It is often used by skiers in winter, who find – beside the wide skiing and excursion grounds of the plateau, served by the terminal of Gjaidalm – a few first class runs in an unusually wild countryside (descents from Krippenstein to the Schönbergalpe and if the snow permits, from Krippenstein to the end of the Traun Valley).

Ascent of the Krippenstein★★. – *From Hallstatt 4 km - 2 1/2 miles in the direction of Obertraun then bear right 2 km - 1 mile, after the end of the lake, then 2 1/2 hours Rtn on foot. Allow 2 hours more if you wish to visit the Dachstein Ice Cave as you go up to the Schönbergalpe.*

The cablecars and mountain hotels are open from 20 December to 15 October. There are departures at least every hour between 8am and 5pm (crowded in high summer – serial numbers are called for passengers). 145S Rtn.

The intermediate station of the **Schönbergalpe**, alt 1 345 m - 4 413 ft is the starting point for the visit to the Dachstein Ice Cave.

Ice Cave at Dachstein★ (Dachsteineishöhle). – *Guided tours in English (1 hour) 1 May to 15 October 8.30am to 4.30pm; 39S; brochure available in English.*

The Ice Cave, which is well equipped with lamps placed behind ice-draperies and hanging icides, is toured along a circular route.

King Arthur's Cathedral and the Great Ice Chapel are among the features of this underground expedition.

The Mammoth's Cave (*joint ticket with the Ice Cave: 52S*) consists of but a small part of a large network of caves: total length 37 km - 23 miles with a drop of 1 180 m - 3 871 ft. The tunnels and bare chambers are impressive in size.

Krippenstein★★. – *From the cablecar station (hotel), 1/2 hour on foot Rtn.*

A chapel stands at the top (alt 2 109 m - 6 919 ft), of this rounded height from where you can enjoy a **general view★★** of the high Dachstein plateau. There emerge the mossy heads of the final peak and also three patches of snow of which the largest is a small glacier, the Hallstätter Gletscher.

To get better **bird's-eye views★★** of the lake at Hallstatt to the north, walk a little farther to the Pioneers' Cross (Pionierkreuz). The path is marked by signs (*allow an extra 1/2 hour*) at the beginning of the Krippenstein road.

Koppenbrüller Cave (Koppenbrüllerhöhle). – *From Gasthaus Koppenrast – 3 km - 2 miles upstream from Obertraun. 1 hour on foot Rtn. Guided tours (1 hour) 1 May to 30 September 9am to 5pm; 39S; brochure available in English.*

The cave, opening in picturesque surroundings in a wooded defile of the Traun, is the only cavern in the Dachstein to be active or still in process of natural enlargement. Crossing the cave is a torrent, which in times of flood rises into the air in the form of a waterspout with a roar which echoes the length of the valley.

Manmade galleries lead from the cave mouth to a great cleft, the Hannakluft, running in a dead straight line, where the underground waters may be seen swirling by.

THE SOUTH WALL★★

The redoubtable south wall of the Dachstein drops vertically (1 000 m - 3 280 ft) to the Alpine pastures of the Ramsau (*facilities: see Ramsau and Filzmoos pp 39, 42 and 43*).

Rising above these escarpments, well known by climbers, the cable-car "the Glaciers" (Gletscherbahn) goes up to Hunerkogel, the peak of the summit ridge, where at the north wall is the small glacier Schladminger Gletscher, which is equipped for skiing in summer.

Ascent of the Hunerkogel★★. – *From Schladming – 16 km - 10 miles by Ramsau and a toll road (22S per person) and 1 hour Rtn, including 10 min by cable-car (8am to 5pm). Rtn 150S.*

From the higher station (alt 2 694 m - 8 840 ft), the **panorama★★** spreads out to the south along the Tauern mountain range (Grossglockner, Grossvenediger) and to the north onto the Salzkammergut Alps (Schafberg, Höllengebirge, Totes Gebirge).

The Danube is the longest river in Central Europe, with a course of 2 826 km - 1 754 miles and the second longest in Europe, after the Volga, which is 3 895 km - 2 292 miles long. It forms a natural link between Germany and southeastern Europe. It crosses or skirts eight states, and three capitals, built on its banks, bearing witness to its international importance. But if it is a link between peoples, it has also often been an obstacle to their coming together.

GEOGRAPHICAL NOTES

An Alpine River. – Rising at an altitude of 1 078 m - 3 537 ft – on the eastern slope of the Black Forest, about 100 m - 100 yds from the actual watershed of the Rhine basin, the Danube is really formed at Donaueschingen by the junction of the Breg and the Brigach. The river, on reaching the Swabian Jura, almost comes to a halt amid the cleft limestone before flowing between the escarpments of a picturesque ravine from Tuttlingen to Sigmaringen. Between Ulm and Vienna, the Danube takes on an Alpine character: it flows fully in early summer and meagrely in the autumn. The variations in flow are caused by the tributaries along its right bank – the Iller, the Lech, the Isar and the Inn, which bring down thaw-waters from the Bavarian and Tyrolean Alps. Their large volume make it, by the time it enters Austria, a powerful river, able to carry a good deal of shipping. At times of spate, alluvial soil gives the river a milky white colour.

From Vienna to the Black Sea. – From the Leopoldsberg bluff, the last foothill of the Alps overlooking Vienna, you can see the first of the alluvial plains which follow after one another between the Alps and the Carpathians. In Hungary is the *puszta*, a grassy steppe where the Danube and its tributaries wind their ways among reeds and marshes. The altitude here is about 100 m - 300 ft above sea-level, and the fall almost nil. From this point on, the continental climate has its effect on the river. The waters are high in May, owing to the thawing of the Carpathian snows and the spring rains. Considerable evaporation in summer nullities the effect of the Alpine spates and causes a lowering of the waters in September.

At the Iron Gates the bed of the Danube narrows until it is only about 100 m - 300 ft across. This forcing of narrow ravines gives back a little vigour to the river, which still has some 1 000 km - 600 miles to go across drier and drier steppes. It runs into the Black Sea through a powerful delta of which the largest three arms – those of Kilia, Sulina and St George – split into innumerable branches which make the whole area look like a lake dotted with islands. Like the Dnieper and the Volga, the Danube each year is frozen for a period which holds up navigation for more than a month. Thus ends this river which has an average daily flow of 6 000 m³ - 2 320 million gallons (the Thames at Teddington: 1 357 million gallons) and a catchment area approximately three and a half times the size of Britain.

HISTORICAL NOTES

An Important Strategic Route. – As early as the Roman era the Danube was playing a first class part in strategy. It formed a protection against the Roman advance, and a barrier against the Barbarians. Under Augustus the Romans were unable to get a footing on the left bank of the river; Trajan succeeded, subdued the Dacians, and in order to watch them more closely, built a huge stone bridge of which the ruins can be seen near the Iron Gates; Aurelius had to retire to the right bank. At the time of Attila the Danubian lands were the crossroads where the peoples, who produced such mixed races as those of the Balkans, were in contact.

Since the Middle Ages all conquerors have regarded possession of the Danube as essential to the success of their undertakings. It was the invasion route chosen by the Turks in 1529 and 1683 *(p 147)*, and then by Napoleon's troops in their march on Vienna. At the time of the Treaty of Paris which ended the Crimean War in 1856, Turks and Russians attached extreme importance to the control of the islands and banks of its delta, although these could be flooded.

The Song of the Nibelungen. – The name Nibelungen applies to a tribe of dwarfs, whose treasure is stolen by Siegfried; later on the name was, thus, applied to the Burgundian warriors, the heroes of the best known of all German epic tales. The song was composed probably towards the end of the 12C and enjoys a fame beyond the Rhineland comparable with that of Roland in France and King Arthur in England. It was inspired by Scandinavian and German legends based on the annihilation of the Burgundian Kingdom by the Huns in the 5C. It tells of the splendour of the Burgundian Court at Worms and of the passions in the hearts of the heroes.

Gunther, King of the Burgundians, will allow Siegfried to marry his sister Kriemhild, on condition that Siegfried will help him woo Brunhild, a queen of outstanding strength and beauty – the conditions are met (Gunther goes through the motions of deeds performed by Siegfried, in an invisible cloak) and the promise is granted. The two queens quarrel: Brunhild reproaches Kriemhild for marrying a vassal and thus Kriemhild reveals the deception of Brunhild by

Siegfried and Gunther. Hagen, Gunther's henchman, discovers Siegfried's one vulnerable spot – kills him and takes the Nibelungen treasure, Kriemhild's wedding present, and hides it beneath the Rhine. For thirteen years Kriemhild worked out her revenge before finally marrying Etzel (Attila), King of the Huns. Kriemhild then invited the Nibelungen to Etzelburg in Hungary, and they journeyed down the long Danube Valley to the castle. Scarcely had the visitors arrived before Kriemhild felt that the moment had come to avenge Siegfried's death. A bitter fight ensued which ended in the annihilation of the Nibelungen, Hagen died and with him the secret of the treasure's burial place.

The Danubian School (early 16C). – The scenes along the Danube from Regensburg to Vienna have inspired a number of painters, mainly Swabians, who had in common a keen sense of nature, conceived not simply as a setting but tingling with hidden life and matching the pictured scene. The artist then made a point of depicting the secret countrysides in which legendary spirits, inseparable from German sensibility, might roam.

Albrecht Altdorfer (1480-1538), a citizen of Regensburg, is the master in whom this poetry is most clearly visible. In the panels of the Passion painted for the monks of St Florian *(p 123)*, the *Battle of Arbela,* the *St George,* and the *Danube Valley* shown at Munich, Altdorfer handles contrasting light in a way so striking as to make him one of the founders of landscape painting, as well as a forerunner of Romanticism. Hans Burgkmair (1473-1531) and Jörg Breu (1475-1537) have a similar aesthetic sense. The latter worked a long time for the Abbeys of Herzogenburg, Zwettl and Melk. A Franconian, **Lucas Cranach the Elder** (1472-1553), is among the Danubian masters. The mysterious depths of water, rocks and woods which form the backgrounds of his works show his affinity with the forest painters.

Navigation on the Danube. – After passing Ulm, due to the addition of the Iller waters, the Danube is navigable. Clumsy craft called Ulm boxes, as well as rafts of logs, used to float as far as Vienna. They had a draught of only about 60 cm - 2 ft and, being unable to go upstream, they were broken up at the end of the journey and sold as firewood.

In 1829 steamships appeared and the passenger and freight traffic grew. The Danube made trading possible between the industrial districts of the upper valley and the agricultural lands downstream. Nonetheless, international use of a river is no simple matter and free navigation remained dependent upon the vagaries of Balkan politics. The 1919 treaties, completing the projects formulated in the Treaty of Paris of 1856, laid down the rules of navigation and foreshadowed the Danube's becoming an international waterway. This statute has never been repealed, although its clauses have been superseded by the creation in 1948 of a new Commission for the Danube controlled solely by the riparian powers. Austria joined this new organization in 1960; West Germany, which has not joined, nevertheless has secured the right of navigation on the river all the way to its mouth. France is represented on the Danube by a few ships which fly the French flag but are, in fact, leased to Rumanian business organizations.

In fact, the present position is that only the Danubian powers enjoy freedom of navigation and commerce on the river. Other reasons make the Danube a much less frequented river than the Rhine: there are large variations of flow and moving sandbanks which are dangerous to navigation and have often to be marked afresh; winter freezing; the river flows into an inland sea; the whole area is sparsely populated and little developed industrially.

Small sea-going ships can, at present, go up as far as Budapest and 1 350 ton barges can reach Regensburg. Ultimately the Rhine-Main-Danube connection, open around 1988, will enable 2 000 ton Rhine barges to go from Rotterdam to the Black Sea.

Boat Trips. – Excluding the trips from Passau to Vienna *(see below)* the tourist can go down the Danube from Passau to the Black Sea by Austrian or Russian boats, with a possible stop-over in Yalta *(duration of cruise: 6 days Vienna to Yalta; up the Danube: 7 days Yalta to Vienna).*

There is also rapid transportation by hydrofoil between Vienna and Bratislava and Vienna and Budapest. *Information at DDSG (see below) and corresponding travel agencies abroad.*

Engineering Works. – For two centuries engineering has been going on to improve the navigability and usefulness of the river. The deepening of the riverbed near Vienna has allowed several of the arms of the river to be drained and thus removed the danger of floodwaters. Since 1945 the major parts of the improvement programme have been undertaken on the one hand by Austria and on the other jointly by Yugoslavia and Rumania, who, between 1964 and 1971, have built the immense dam of Djerdap in the Iron Gates defile.

Austria now has working the Jochenstein Dam on the German frontier, the Aschach Dam, the Altenworth Dam, the largest Austrian civil engineering undertaking on the Danube with an annual output on average of 2 milliard kWh, the Ottensheim-Wilhering Dam, the Abwinden-Asten Dam, the Ybbs-Persenbeug Dam and the Wallsee-Mitterkirchen Dam. Among the projects envisaged for the river's improvement are the Melk and Greifenstein projects. The total output once the projects are all completed, will surpass 15 milliard kWh.

THE DANUBE IN AUSTRIA

The Danube is Austrian for only 360 km - 224 miles from Achleiten, below Passau, to Hainburg, at the gates of Bratislava, that is, for one-eighth of its course. It is a vital artery for the economy of the country. The section of the river, wholly navigable, is used by shipping which serves Vienna, the capital, Linz, a great industrial town, and indirectly the industrial centres of Steyr and St. Pölten. Though the waters of the river do not always display, especially in times of flood, the colour of which *The Blue Danube* sings, its banks, especially between Grein and Krems, often border scenery dear to the Romantics. On the banks have been erected old fortified castles where the shade of a Burgrave still watches, gracious Renaissance dwellings with charming arcaded courts, and fortified churches and abbeys of noble architecture.

Boat Services in Austria. – *From May through September there are regular passenger services run by the DDSG between Passau and Vienna. There is rapid transportation by launch everyday between Passau and Vienna; everyday but Tuesday between Melk and Krems and everyday but Wednesday between Passau and Linz. Cars are not loaded on board, drivers may therefore be asked at Passau to drive the car to Vienna or Linz. For information apply to the DDSG-Reisedienst, A 1021 Wien, Handelskai 265, ☏ (0222) 26 65 36; A 4010 Linz, Nibelungenbrücke, ☏ (0722) 70 011, 21 511; D 839 Passau (Germany), Im Ort 14a, ☏ (0851) 33 035.*

DANUBE Valley★★

☐1 **From Passau (Germany) to Linz** – *86 km - 55 miles – about 3 hours – Local map below*

From Passau to Aschach, the route we propose follows the right bank of the river, which, running in the north against the granite heights of the Mühlviertel, the last foothills of the Bohemian massif, turns in the direction northwest to southeast. In this section of its course the Danube crosses an area formerly filled by glaciers. When the glaciers had melted away, gravel plains formed along the valleys. Meadows, marshes and forests of conifers covered the hills.

Leave Passau *(see Michelin Green Guide to Germany)* by the south, crossing the Inn. Turn immediately to the left towards the Achleiten customs post *(German and Austrian customs controls).*
The river soon appears, wide and majestic, bordered with wooded, rocky slopes, and the road, running along the valley floor, follows all its curves. At Obernzell, which can be seen on the German shore, the river opens out into a

magnificent lake. This is the reservoir of the Jochenstein Dam on the Danube.

   Jochenstein Dam. – This dam, at the foot of which has been installed a power station whose annual production is now 1.6 milliard kWh, was built in common by Austria and Bavaria.
From Engelhartszell to Wesenufer the valley narrows. The *corniche* road, running above the first stretches of water created by the Aschach Dam, affords fine views ; from time to time you may see the outline of a castle. A little after Wesenufer, a pretty village with flowered balconies, the road leaves the shore of the Danube, which makes wide, sunken loops farther north. The road climbs in a wooded gorge and reaches the picturesque Valley of the Aschach, which you leave on reaching the alluvial plain, to cross the Danube below the **Aschach Dam**, one of the largest European low-fall stations. After Ottensheim and its dam, the road leads to Linz *(p 103).*

☐2 **From Linz to Grein** – *67 km - 42 miles – about 2 1/2 hours – Local map below*

Below Linz the valley opens out into a wide basin filled by the alluvial soil of the river and its tributaries, the Traun and the Enns. On this fertile soil cereals, sugarbeet and fruit trees flourish. To the north lie the slopes and wooded ridges of the Mühlviertel and of the Waldviertel.
Leave Linz *(p 103)*, by ②. The road goes through the industrial zone of Linz and crosses the Danube at the Steyregg Bridge. A little after Steyregg, looking back, the road affords a last view of Linz before cutting across a plateau to return to the Danube plain at St. Georgen.

   Mauthausen. – *Description p 108.*
From Mauthausen to Dornach the road crosses a vast cultivated plain (sugarbeet, maize and wheat). Downstream from Dornach the road closely follows the left bank of the Danube, which is hemmed in between rocky, wooded slopes. The approach to Grein is beautiful.

   Grein. – Pop 2833. Grein lies at the foot of a bluff on which the castle is built. This commands the entrance to a ravine which opens into the Wachau. The main square (Stadtplatz) has turreted houses. The church possesses an 18C altarpiece by Bartolomeo Altomonte on the high altar.
The castle *(1/2 hour on foot Rtn)* has four main buildings, flanked by corner turrets, which contrast with the elegance of the Renaissance inner **court★**, with three tiers of arcades. A fountain, an old well and a virginia creeper, hanging over the arches of the ground floor arcade, lend a romantic note to the scene.

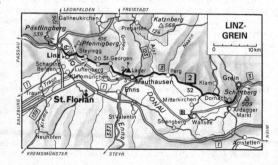

③ From Grein to Krems – *85 km – 53 miles – 1 day – Local map below*

Between Grein and Krems stretches the most picturesque section of the Danube Valley in Austria. It is hollowed out of the granite of the Waldviertel, which forms the last foothills of the Bohemian massif. The Wachau can also be admired from the river itself; with the Danube boat service functioning May through September between Melk and Krems. Information at the DDSG landing stage.

From Grein *(p 60)* to Ybbs, the **Strudengau***, sunken between the high wooded cliffs which overlook it from a height of over 400 m - 1 300 ft often silent and shrouded in mist, provides a heroic and romantic course. The ruins of the Castle of Struden, clinging to their rock, and then those of the Castle of Sarming-stein, catch the eye. The river embraces willow covered islands, then expands into a splendid lake, formed by the Ybbs-Persenbeug Dam, whose power station has an annual output of 1 250 milliard kWh. Particularly outstanding are the locks built to allow the passage of barges.

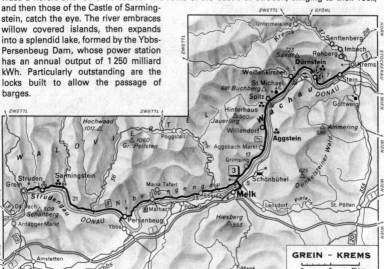

GREIN - KREMS

Persenbeug. – Pop 1 943. This castle overlooking the Danube was built in the 10C and rebuilt in the 17C. The last Austrian Emperor, Karl I, was born here in 1887.

From Persenbeug, lying at the head of a well tilled meandering plain, to Melk, the valley was the scene of certain episodes in the Nibelungen epic *(p 58)*. It was there, in the **Nibelungengau**, that the rides of Gunther and Hagen took place; it is there they collected their knights to go to Attila's court. Atop the hill in Maria Taferl (pop 805 - *facilities p 41*) stands the pilgrims' church.
At Pöchlarn, on the right bank of the river, there settled, in the 10C, the Babenbergs, who began the extraordinary expansion of the Austrian monarchy. It was they who, quite near, founded the Abbey of Melk, whose fine Baroque façade comes into view at Ebersdorf. Its steep promontory base, however, remains long hidden by trees on an island. Take the bridge over the Danube.

Melk**. – *Description p 108.*

Schönbühel. – *5 km - 3 miles from Melk.* From the main road to the Wachau this château built at the beginning of the 19C, appears standing on a projecting rock, above the opposite shore of the Danube. Its pepper-pot towers and bulbous-domed belfry, with rows of fruit trees in the background, make a charming picture.
Below the château a little way from the village, tourists following the right bank of the river can visit a former Servites' convent (now a presbytery), founded in 1666 and also built on a cliff overlooking the Danube. The **church** *(closed in winter; apply at the convent)*, whose ceiling is adorned with frescos, has a moving group behind the altar representing a *pietà*. From a terrace there is a pleasant view of the Wachau.

Take the road on the left bank towards Krems. From Grimsing onwards the famous vineyards begin. Farther on, at the highest point on the opposite shore, is the Fortress of Aggstein. At Willendorf a "Venus", a very primitive earthenware statue dating from about 25 000 years ago, was found in 1906. It is now kept in Vienna at the Natural History Museum *(p 167)*.
The favourable exposure of its slopes and a bed of alluvial soil at their foot have produced in the **Wachau****, terraced vineyards, fields of tobacco and maize and orchards.
Charming villages stand along the riverbanks. Ruins of fortified castles crown the crests, and rounded belfries add their note of fantasy to the countryside.

Spitz. – Pop 2 037. Tourists riding through the Wachau would hardly suspect the presence of the little town of Spitz, hidden behind a curtain of fruit trees. It lies at the foot of terraced vineyards, only the squat shape of the parish church rising above the house roofs. Above, the ruins of the Castle of Hinterhaus stand out against the wooded mountain slope.
Spitz has old houses, with arcades and balconies. The Schlossgasse is one of its most picturesque streets, with the arcades and flying buttresses of a former mansion.
The parish church **(Pfarrkirche)**, a Gothic building of the 15C, has a chancel out of line with the nave; the chancel is elegant and has network vaulting. The organ-loft is adorned with statues of Christ and the Apostles (around 1420). The altarpiece (1799) by Kremser Schmidt *(p 98)* over the Baroque altar shows the martyrdom of St Maurice.

St. Michael. – This fortified church, built about 1500 in the Gothic style, is flanked, near the chevet, by a big round tower.

Weissenkirchen. – *Description p 170.*

Ahead, just after Weissenkirchen, is a beautiful view of Dürnstein.

Dürnstein*. – *Description p 62.*

The slopes are lower near the twin towns of Stein and Krems *(p 98)*.

④ **From Krems to Vienna (Wien)** – *83 km - 52 miles – about 3 hours – Local map below*

Cross the Danube on the great steel bridge at Stein, west of Krems *(p 98)*. A little after Mautern you will see on the right, crowning a wooded hill, the impressive Abbey of Göttweig. Near the river are alluvial terraces on which grow vines and fruit trees, and then meadows and fields of cereals. The road goes near the river, which divides into a network of courses.

Tulln. – *Description p 146.*

When you get near the Vienna Woods, at Greifenstein, the valley narrows and the road is hemmed between the river and high wooded hills, forming the harder terrain of the Wienerwald.

Klosterneuburg. – *Description p 168.*

The road then enters the suburbs of Vienna *(p 147)*.

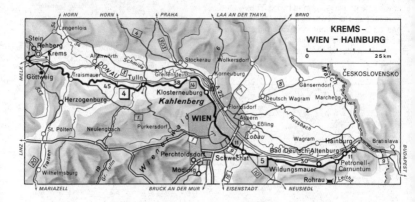

⑤ **From Vienna to Hainburg** – *52 km - 32 miles – about 2 hours – Local map p 62*

Our chosen route follows the right bank of the river all the way. Sometimes the river splits into several arms, embracing many islands, while the valley grows much wider.

Leave Vienna *(p 147)* by ③, road No. 9, to go through Schwechat, which is famous for its breweries. Before skirting the buildings of the international airport of Vienna at Schwechat, one sees indistinctly on the left the outlines of the Island of Lobau where Napoleon's forces, in 1809, recovered their strenght after the unexpected victories of the Austrians at Essling and Aspern.

Wildungsmauer. – In spite of restoration and additions, the Chapel of St Nicholas has preserved the essentials of its Romanesque appearance. The porch and the transept tower date from the 19C.

Petronell. – Pop 1 249. Here and near the neighbouring town of Bad Deutsch-Altenburg, have been unearthed the remains (amphitheatres) from **Carnuntum**, the Roman capital of Pannonia *(map p 22)*.

Rohrau. – *6 km - 4 miles – from Petronell*. Rohrau (pop 1 262) houses in its 16C château, the Harrach Gallery, an important private collection *(open April to 1 November 10am to 5pm; closed Mondays; 25S)* containing: Spanish Baroque, 17 and 18C Roman and Neapolitan and Dutch paintings as well.

There is also the native home of **Joseph Haydn** (exposition of original scores). *Open 10am to 5pm; closed Mondays; 10S.*

Between Bad Deutsch-Altenburg and Hainburg appear, overlooking the Czech shore of the Morava and its confluence with the Danube, the Little Carpathians or first heights of the great Central European range which forms the northern boundary of the Hungarian plain.

Hainburg. – Pop 5 749. This town held a great strategic role in the Middle Ages. It still has its belt of walls and fortified gateways at the foot of its ruined castle.

DÜRNSTEIN ★ (Lower Austria)

Michelin map 426 told 11 – *Local map p 61* – Pop 1 032 – Alt 207 m - 679 ft – 🏛 ☎ 219

The little fortfied town of Dürnstein stands at the foot of a ridge on which are terraced vineyards producing a well known wine *(details of Austrian wines on p 32)*. Crowned by the ruins of a fortress and still girdled by its walls, it lies on a rocky ridge overlooking the Danube, forming one of the most famous scenes in the Wachau *(p 61)*. The modern road to the Wachau avoids the old town by passing under it in a tunnel.

Richard Lionheart a prisoner. – It is said that during the 3rd Crusade, Richard Lionheart, King of England, had a furious altercation with the Duke of Austria, Leopold V. At the attack against Acre in Palestine, Richard is supposed to have removed the Duke's banner from a tower, thus insulting the Duke's honour. By chance, having been shipwrecked on his way back to his kingdom, Richard had to cross the land of his rival. Though disguised as a peasant, he was recognized at an inn near Vienna, arrested and handed over to Leopold, who shut him up in the fortress at Dürnstein. In the spring of 1193 the faithful **Blondel,** playing and singing Richard's favourite songs as he walked at the foot of the castle looking for his sovereign, attracted Richard's attention and was, therefore, able to discover where he was kept prisoner. Unfortunately, the king was transferred and his imprisonment lasted for nearly a year longer in the Imperial Castle of Trifels in the Rhineland Palatinate, before his liberty was granted at the price of an enormous ransom.

■ **SIGHTS** *time: 2 hours*

Hauptstrasse. – This, the main street, runs through the town from end to end and is bounded in the east by an old fortified gateway. It is most pleasing with its old houses, some of them 16C, with their bracketed turrets, oriels and balconies with flowers.

The wrought iron signs of several inns – where it is a pleasure to taste the famous *Heuriger* (current year's wine) of the Wachau – will remind you of the story of Richard Lionheart's imprisonment and the touching story of the faithful Blondel.

Parish Church (Pfarrkirche). – *Guided tours (25 min) 1 April to 31 October 9am to noon and 1 to 6pm; closed Saturday mornings and Maundy Thursday to Holy Saturday; 10S.* The Baroque tower that crowns its façade can be seen from far off. Of the former Augustine Canons' monastery, founded in the 15C, and rebuilt between 1720 and 1725 in the Baroque style, you can admire the porch, adorned with carved columns and statues in the courtyard surrounded by former abbey buildings.

The church is adorned with light stucco; pierced balconies run round the nave above the side altars. The woodwork of the chancel, the pulpit and the high altar makes a contrast in its richness, with the simplicity of the nave. The sacristy, also adorned with delicate stucco, shows valuable marquetry. The cloister has been altered by restorations.

From the balustraded terrace at the foot of the tower of the façade, remarkable for its height and its decoration, there is a pleasant view of the Danube Valley.

Castle Ruins. – *3/4 hour on foot Rtn.* The ruins are reached by a path which begins on the level of the ramparts east of the town and climbs among rocks. From the ruins there is a remarkable **view★★** of Dürnstein and the valley.

EGGENBURG (Lower Austria)

Michelin map **426** fold 11 – Pop 3 729 – Alt 325 m – 1 070 ft – 🅘 ☎ 3501

Eggenburg used to be a fortified town. It still has most of its 15C walls, marked by towers (that of the Chancellor, the Deviner, the Convent), and on a little hill in a loop of the Schmieda, remain the ruins of its castle as well as a smaller more recent château. On the main square (Hauptplatz) are a 16C pillory, a Trinity column and an old house (1547) known as the "Gemalte Haus".

To the east, two Romanesque towers, rise above the parish Church of St Stephen. It is a hall-church with characteristics of the late Gothic style, seen especially in its decoration and furnishings (pulpit 1515). *See Gothic architecture p 33.*

EHRENHAUSEN (Styria)

Michelin map **426** fold 38 – 10 km - 6 miles southeast of Leibnitz – Pop 1 172 – Alt 261 m – 856 ft

Near the Yugoslav frontier a wooded bluff, overlooking the right bank of the Mur and the village of Ehrenhausen, was chosen by the Eggenberg family as the site of a castle and a mausoleum.

Mausoleum. – *Ask at the priest's house (Pfarrhof) for the key.*

This curious funerary monument shelters the tomb of Ruprecht of Eggenberg, who distinguished himself as a general in the struggle with the Turks at the end of the 16C.

The west front, adorned with carved figures, pilasters, leaf and geometrical designs, is framed between two huge statues of ancient warriors, standing on plinths ornamented with battle scenes.

The interior is striking for the number of stuccos on the central dome.

Castle. – The castle, standing near the square keep has preserved an elegant courtyard with Renaissance arcades in three tiers and an old well.

EHRWALD ★ (Tyrol)

Michelin map **426** fold 16 – *Local map p 69* – Pop 2 226 – Alt 996 m - 2 368 ft – 🅘 ☎ 2395 – *Facilities p 39*

Ehrwald, at the west foot of the Zugspitze cliffs, is the best equipped country resort of the Zugspitze Tyrolean district (Tiroler Zugspitzgebiet), of which the basin formed by the Upper Loisach Valley, south of the Bavarian frontier, marks the centre. Among the many local walks, runs and tours, the classic excursion has become the ascent of the Zugspitze by way of the Zugspitzkamm cable-car.

During the skiing season the Zugspitzkamm cable-car offers, to trained athletes, first class ski-runs, whether they are looking for the 3.5 km - 2 1/4 mile descent starting at the intermediate stop, Gamskar (alt 2 016 m - 7 210 ft), or the great Alpine run of nearly 23 km - 14 miles (Gatterlabfahrt) which takes them from the top of the Zugspitze back to Ehrwald *(a guide is advised).*

Ascent to the Zugspitze★★★. – *4.5 km - 3 miles plus 1 1/2 hours Rtn including 1/2 hour by cable-car – Local map p 69*

From Ehrwald the road, pleasantly laid first among larches, then among beeches, leads to the mountain pastures of Obermoos, where the lower Tyrolean cable-car station of the Zugspitze is located. The run is pretty, even if you do not go any farther.

In summer cable-cars leave at least hourly between 8.15 and 11.55am and 1.15 to 5.30pm. Possibly crowded in the season (serial numbers called). 210S Rtn.

Zugspitzkamm★★. – Alt 2 805 m - 9 203 ft. The station, at the terminus of the main cable-car, clings to the wall of an impressive ravine. From the terrace there is a **bird's-eye view★★** of the Loisach Valley. Far away, in line, are the crests of the Ammergebirge and the Lechtal Alps.

Summit of the Zugspitze★★★ (Zugspitzgipfel). – The upper station of the cable-car, coming from Zugspitzkamm, is located in Austria, on the western peak of the Zugspitze (alt 2 962 m - 9 716 ft).

EHRWALD★

The **panorama**★★★ to the south reveals the glacier summits of the High Tauern (Grossglockner and Grossvenediger), the Tyrolean High Alps (Alps of the Zillertal, Stubai and Ötztal), the Ortler and the Bernina, towering over the forward bastions of the Kaisergebirge, the Dachstein and the Karwendel. Nearer, to the east, the mountains of the Arlberg (Silvretta and Rätikon) make way for a view of the Säntis in the Appenzell Alps. In the foreground, the Bavarian Alps, namely the Allgäu and Ammergau mountains can be seen. To the north are the hazy Bavarian lowlands with the shimmering waters of the Ammersee and the Starnberger See.

The arrangements of the summit as well as the ski-fields of Schneeferner, where good snow conditions continue until summer (equipped with numerous ski lifts) is in Bavaria *(customs control). For more details see Michelin Green Guide to Germany.*

EISENERZ Alps ★ (Styria)

Michelin map **426** folds 22 and 23

The Eisenerz Alps, which include the astonishing Iron Mountain, the Erzberg, on which the industrial power of the former Austrian Empire was based, come into contact to the northwest, with the chalky Ennstal Alps, whose impressive walls come one after the other along the Gesäuse defile.

The Präbichl, a pass which leads from the Enns to the Mur, offers a curious route, characterized by long sunken sections between Hieflau and Leoben.

The Iron Mountain. – It is only about a century since the Erzberg took on its present individual appearance.

It was opened up in the Middle Ages by means of little diggings and quarries. These were followed, at the beginning of the 19C by a more carefully designed system of mines and tunnels. About 1870 the engineers, now sure that the whole deposit was uniform, changed to a controlled system of surface mining on the sides of the mountain. Thirty terraces, each about 24 m - 80 ft high now form a great staircase against the Eisenerz sky. The summit of the Erzberg, submitted to this beheading, is gradually sinking from 1 532 m - 5 026 ft before mining began to the present 1 465 m - 4 806 ft.

This surface mining, continuing all year round, accounts for 3.2 million tons of the total output of the ore extracted. It produces 1/3 of Austria's total production (sent to blast furnaces).

Once the iron ore (iron content 32%) is extracted and upgraded by roasting furnaces located at the foot of the mountain it is then sent to the blast furnaces of Linz *(p 103)* and Donawitz *(p 65).*

The Erzberg is the only place in Austria where iron ore is exploited; its reserve will enable it to be a source of profit for about 60 more years.

THE GESÄUSE★
From Liezen to Hieflau – *44 km - 27 miles – about 2 hours – Local map below*

Between Liezen and Admont the road winds along the Enns corridor, with its muddy floor. The two bulbous domes of the church at Frauenberg soon form, on their height, a foreground for the Grosser Buchstein and the Hochtor, which are summits enclosing, farther east, the Gesäuse ravine, of which you can easily see the rocky mouth when you arrive at Admont.

Frauenberg. – *From the touring route, 1.5 km - 1 mile by a narrow and signposted road beginning east of the hill (on arriving at a small pass, turn a sharp left).*
The pilgrims' church was rebuilt by the Abbots of Admont in the 17C, in an Italianate Baroque style. The Calvary terrace at the end of a chestnut avenue forms a belvedere overlooking the Admont basin where you see the steeples of the abbey church and the crown of summits (Haller Mauern, Reichenstein and Hochtor).

Admont. – *Description p 45.*

The best **glimpse of the Gesäuse**★★ is that which, a little before you enter the ravine, reveals the splendid sides of the Hochtor (highest point: 2 369 m - 7 770 ft).
Once on the floor of the gorge the tourist will only enjoy views to the north, towards the Grosser Buchstein.

Haindlkarbrücke. – This bridge over a rushing tributary of the Enns affords a close **view**★ of the formidable walls of the Hochtor, whose smallest projections are used by enthusiastic climbers.

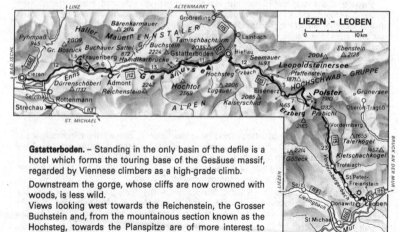

Gstatterboden. – Standing in the only basin of the defile is a hotel which forms the touring base of the Gesäuse massif, regarded by Viennese climbers as a high-grade climb.

Downstream the gorge, whose cliffs are now crowned with woods, is less wild.
Views looking west towards the Reichenstein, the Grosser Buchstein and, from the mountainous section known as the Hochsteg, towards the Planspitze are of more interest to tourists going along the Hieflau towards Admont.

THE IRON ROAD★ (Eisenstrasse)

From Hieflau to Leoben – *50 km - 31 miles – about 2 hours (visit of the mines not included) – Local map p 64*

From Hieflau to Eisenerz the Erzbach Valley has beautiful, winding gorges and offers fine panoramas of the Tamischbachturm. When you reach the basin of Eisenerz, opposite the reddish-brown **Erzberg★**, make a small detour to see the Leopoldsteinersee.

Leopoldsteinersee★★. – This small lake with its deep green waters lies in one of the finest settings in Styria, at the foot of the rock cliffs of the Seemauer in the Hochschwab range.

Eisenerz. – Pop 10 074. The old mining town is grouped closely round the foot of the large Gothic Church of St Oswald, which is unusual for its defences dating from the time of the Turkish threat in 1532. Note, on the southern slope of the valley, the Schichtturm, a bell tower, standing apart on the hillside, whose bell formerly rang to tell the miners to change shifts. On a clear day the pretty Baroque Chapel of St Peter is also visible. *Tours of the mines (1 1/2 hours), 1 May to 31 October, at 10am and at 2.30pm. Apply to the lower station on the former lower slope of Trofeng, near the road from Präbichl. 35S; brochure available in English.*

The steep climb from Eisenerz to the Präbichl Pass (alt 1 232 m - 4 041 ft) is overlooked by the Erzberg, whose manmade steps on this side consist of ridges of sterile rubble, and also by the lovely rock summit of the Pfaffenstein, overlooking to the northwest. To enjoy a general view of the Erzberg you are advised to go by chairlift up the Polster.

Polster★★. – *About 1 1/2 hours Rtn from the Präbichl, including 30 minutes by chairlift and 1/2 hour on foot (the chairlift works regularly in the tourist season: 40S Rtn).*

From the summit (alt 1 910 m - 6 266 ft) crowned with a Calvary, there is a **view★★** of the Erzberg, standing out, in all its red-brown mass, against the greens of the Alpine pastures and woods and the blues of the surrounding lakes.

To the north can be seen the separate sharp rock crests (Griesmauer) of the Hochschwab.

The descent from the Präbichl to Leoben, which, as far as Vordernberg, is adorned by a pleasant Alpine landscape, ends in the impressive industrial setting of the Donawitz-Leoben steelworks.

EISENSTADT Ⓟ (Burgenland)

Michelin map **426** fold 25 – *Local map p 112* – Pop 10 150 – Alt 181 m - 594 ft – 🏢 ☎ 33 84

Eisenstadt has developed on the south slope of the Leithagebirge, whose forests make you think of a huge park. It is at this point that the great Central European Plain begins. The mild climate makes it possible to grow vines, peaches, apricots and almonds.

The proximity of Vienna has checked the economic expansion of the town, which, however, is still the most important market in the region for wine *(détails p 113)*. Since 1925 the political and administrative role of Eisenstadt when it became the capital of Burgenland *(p 13)*, has somewhat revived the city. Neusiedler Lake, nearby, also attracts tourists to the area.

Haydn's Town. – Everything here reminds one of the brilliant composer. Joseph Haydn (1732-1809) lived for thirty years, sometimes at Eisenstadt, sometimes at the Esterhaza Château in Hungary, in the service of Prince Esterhazy. He had been appointed assistant conductor in 1761. His job included conducting the orchestra and directing the chorus; composing music and tending to administrative work (music librarian, supervisor of instruments and chief of musical personnel). In 1766 he was promoted to musical director. Having an orchestra and a theatre at his disposal, Haydn worked without respite and achieved growing fame. His considerable work places him among the greatest names in music. Eisenstadt cherishes memories of the man who was to Mozart a guide, a model and a friend.

■ SIGHTS time: 1 1/2 hours

Château of the Esterhazy Princes (Schloss Esterhazy). – Eisenstadt was one of the favourite residences of this great Hungarian family, who claimed to be descended from Attila and largely contributed to the establishment of the Habsburgs' rule in Hungary. One of its members, Nic Esterhazy, even refused the Hungarian crown from Napoleon I, who offered it to him in 1809.

Wishing to have a residence fit for his rank, Prince Paul Esterhazy commissioned the Italian architect Carlone. On the site of a mediaeval fortress Carlone built, between 1663 and 1672, a great quadrilateral round the court of honour. Each of the four corner towers, at that time, was crowned by a bulbous dome. Between 1797 and 1805 the French architect Moreau modified the building in the taste of that day. The façade to the park was given a portico in the Neo-Classical style with Corinthian columns, and the entrance gateway in the main façade was surmounted by a terrace, supported by Tuscan columns.

Terra-cotta busts, representing the ancestors of the Esterhazy family and several Kings of Hungary, adorn this façade, which is crowned with a small belfry with a rounded dome.

On the far side of the park are the former royal stables, built in 1743.

The château is partly occupied by administration, but the Haydn room is open to visitors.

Haydn Room (Haydn-Saal). – *Guided tours (1/2 hour) in English 1 June to 30 September 9am to 5pm; 10am to 4pm the rest of the year; closed 24, 25, 31 December and 1 January; 10S.* The room is on the 1st floor, facing the entrance. Go in the court up the stairway on the right.

The Haydn Room was the great hall of state in the time of the Esterhazy princes. In the noble setting of this huge hall, decorated in the 18C with stucco, monochrome and frescos, Joseph Haydn, nearly every evening, conducted the orchestra of the princely court, often performing his own works.

EISENSTADT
0   500 m

Esterhazystraße _____ 2
Haydngasse _____ 3
Oedenburgerstraße _____ 4
St. Antonistraße _____ 5

Haydn's House (Haydn-Haus) (A). – In the Haydngasse, a quiet little street, at No. 21 is the modest house in which the composer lived from 1766 to 1778. Go through a covered passage to a charming little court, full of flowers. A small **museum** *(same opening times as the Haydn Room)* contains interesting mementoes of the life and work of the great musician.

Level with the Franciscan church (Franziskanerkirche), turn to the right into the Hauptstrasse. Go up as far as the château where, by way of the Esterhazystrasse, you will come to the Church of the Calvary (Bergkirche). It contains the tomb of Haydn.

EXCURSION

Raiding. – Pop 2 100. *46 km - 29 miles – 2 hours.* Leave Eisenstadt, south, on the Bundesstrasse 59 A, then onto the 331. After Weppersdorf bear left towards Lackenbach to Raiding.

Franz-Liszt museum (Liszt-Geburtshaus). – *Open Easter to 31 October 9am to noon and 1 to 5pm; closed 1 May; 10S.* This small house where Liszt was born in 1811 (died in 1886) was the home offered to his father, who was employed as bailiff to the estate of the princes of Esterhazy. Photos and documents are on display. The old church organ on which Liszt used to play is also here.

EISRIESENWELT Caves ★★ (Salzburg)

Michelin map **426** fold 20 – 6 km - 4 miles northeast of Werfen – *Local map p 128*

Opening at a height of 1 641 m - 5 459 ft on the western cliffs of the Hochkogel (Tennengebirge), above the Salzach Valley, the caves of the World of the Ice Giants, with their 42 km - 25 miles of galleries, are among the world's largest subterranean features. They are especially famous for the fairy-like ice décor which goes back for about 1 km - 1/2 mile and adorns the caves at the entrance, which are the only ones open to tourists.

The ice formations, which in some cases are as much as 20 m - 65 ft thick, have developed as a result of natural ventilation. In summer the air in the deepest cave is swept forward to the mouth and the outside world; in winter the process is reversed and cold air sweeps in so that when, in spring, water from the melting snows enters it freezes immediately. The **journey**★★ up the approach roads, with the views alone, would make the trip worthwhile.

Access. – *The caves are open and the cablecar working from 1 May to early October. It is a 5 hour excursion. Apply for detailed information at the Eisriesenwelt office in the centre of the town (☎ 291). Take warm clothing, sturdy shoes and gloves.*

Guided tours (about 2 hours) 9.30am to 4.30pm in high season; tours less frequent before and after "the season"; 55S.

The ascent is made in 4 stages:

1. 6 km - 4 miles of unsurfaced mountain road rising at a gradient of 1 in 5 1/2 which one can travel either in one's own car or on the "taxibus" which starts from the Hauptplatz in Werfen *(55S Rtn)*.

2. 1/4 hour on foot from the bus terminus to the lower station of the cablecar. The path overlooks the Hohenwerfen Valley and Castle.

3. 4 minutes in the cablecar *(65S Rtn)* to the refuge, where you get your tickets for the caves.

4. 20 minutes walk along a path cut out of the mountainside and affording spectacular views of the valley, the Hagengebirge, the Hochkönig and the Gasteiner Tauern, before you reach the vast and wonderfully sited entrance to the caves.

By the light of acetylene and magnesium lamps you walk straight into the ice area of the caves, climbing up many steps to the Posselt-Halle gallery. The Hymir Halle and the Friga Veil are both examples of fantastic ice architecture enhanced by clever lighting. The highest point 1 775 m - 5 823 ft reached in the tour is at the Ice Gate (Eistor). From then on, the path follows an amazing stratified wall of ice whose every layer is a different tone of blue or white. The Cathedral of Alexander von Mörk is named after the man who explored the caves assiduously and whose ashes were brought back to it. The Ice Palace marks the end of this underworld tour.

ENNS (Upper Austria)

Michelin map **426** fold 9 – 20 km - 12 miles east of Linz – *Local map p 60* – Pop 9 731 – Alt 281 m - 922 ft – 🔟 ☎ 2181 15

Enns, built on the left bank of the River Enns, near its confluence with the Danube, is believed to be the oldest town in Upper Austria. The Romans, in fact, chose this site for a camp; the city, Lauriacum, that developed later was big enough to become the capital of the Roman province of Noricum *(map p 22)*. There it was that St Florian, the patron saint of Upper Austria *(détails p 123)* suffered martyrdom under Diocletian at the beginning of the 4C.

Stadtturm. – Erected at the command of Emperor Maximilian II and built between 1564 and 1568, the city tower stands in the main square, surrounded by fine, Baroque houses.

It is built on a square plan and has four storeys, adorned with arches. A helmet shaped roof surmounts the closed gallery which is placed in the upper part of the fourth storey.

Parish Church (Pfarrkirche). – The church is Gothic, and is remarkable for its unusual plan; it has a double nave, flanked by a single aisle, divided first into two parts, then into three, by slender pillars.

Bahnhofweg _____ 2
Dragoner Straße ___ 3
Forstbergstraße ___ 4
Linzerstraße _____ 5
Steyrerstraße _____ 6
Wienerstraße _____ 7

The road of the Felber Tauern has altered considerably the lives of all living in the eastern Alps: a high level tunnel 5.2 km - 3 miles long goes through the topmost crest of the High Tauern between the Grossglockner and Grossvenediger mountain ranges. The road, open all the year round, has ended the separation of the eastern Tyrol (Lienz) from the northern Tyrol (Innsbruck). The beautiful, wide open Valleys of the Isel and its tributaries, the Defereggental, the Virgental and the Kalsertal once isolated, can now be visited by tourists.

Travellers to Austria may link, on one circular tour, the well known Grossglockner road (*passable in summer only*) and the Felber Tauern road which will enable them also to see the Grossvenediger snows.

From Lienz to Mittersill – *69 km - 43 miles – about 2 1/2 hours – Local map opposite.*

A toll is payable to go through the Felber Tauern Tunnel: 180S for the car and up to 9 passengers. Return tickets are available (600S – valid for 1 year); the return half may be used for the Arlberg tunnel road (p 46) and the Tauern, Brenner and Pyhrn motorway (pp 146, 56, 143).

Starting at Lienz, the road follows for some time the course of the wooded Isel Valley where many houses have been built halfway up the mountainsides.

Matrei in Osttirol. – Pop 4 298 *Facilities p 41*. The most developed tourist centre in the mountain valleys of the western Alps.

On leaving Matrei one sees immediately the Castle of Weissenstein, the former outpost of the bishops of Salzburg on the southern slopes of the Tauern. The road goes up the **Tauerntal★★**. A little further on the Unterer Steinerwasserfall cascade marks the mouth of the Prosseg-Klamm, a gorge which you go through to emerge in an open basin dominated by the hanging glacier from the Kristallkopf. From this point onwards the valley is scattered with ever more primitive alpine chalets.

Excursion★★ towards the Grossvenediger. – *2 km - 1 mile plus 2 hours on foot Rtn.* Leave the rise to the tunnel on your right and continue along the valley floor to the mountain hotel, Matreier Tauernhaus (alt 1 512 m - 4 941 ft). Continue on foot and in 3/4

LIENZ – MITTERSILL
0   12 km

hour you will come to Aussergschlöss (alt 1 695 m - 5 561 ft) where the houses stand in a romantic setting amidst fallen boulders and larch trees and where suddenly you see the Grossvenediger (alt 3 674 m - 12 054 ft – final peak on the far right of the range) draped in all the glory of its glaciers. Farther on, the path, with its occasional terraces, leads to the unusual Aussergschlöss village chapel inlaid beneath an enormous rock, and finally to the tumbledown cottages of Innergschlöss (inn) beyond which is mountaineers' territory.

Stop in the car park at the southern entrance to the Felber Tauern Tunnel: through an opening in the Higher Tauerntal you can see the snow-capped crest of the Grossvenediger.

The tunnel emerges on the northern slopes of the Tauern into the upper clearing of the Amertal amphitheatre. This high mountain valley, more or less deserted, and the Felbertal, less austere, brings you to Mittersill. The town is an important road junction in the Upper Salzach Valley (Oberpinzgau), being the starting point for the road to the Pass Thurn and the Gerlospass.

FELDKIRCH ★ (Vorarlberg)

Michelin maps 426 fold 28 and 21 fold 22 – *Local map p 55* – Pop 23 876 – Alt 459 m - 1 506 ft – ▣ ☎ 23467 – *Facilities p 39*

Feldkirch is the gateway to Austria for travellers coming from the west. Situated on the route through the Arlberg, about halfway between Paris and Vienna, the little fortified town nestles at the foot of Schattenburg Castle, at the mouth of the last ravine of the Ill, but is cut off from the plain of the Rhine by the Ardetzenberg ridge. It has preserved the symmetry of its mediaeval plan and the old-world charm of arcaded squares.

A Clerks' Town. – Since the Middle Ages, Feldkirch has had a "Latin school"; continuing the tradition are the present classical school, through which pass the men of Vorarlberg who aim at higher education, and a school for teachers. Moreover, as the constitution of the Vorarlberg did not systematically centralize all provincial administration at Bregenz, Feldkirch was able officially to remain a capital of lawyers' clerks and finance.

■ THE OLD TOWN *time: 1/2 hour*

The triangular plan of the town dates from the 13C. It is connected both to a hollowed-out site and to the network of roads which meet at Feldkirch. Between the New Town (Neustadt), to the northeast, which has become, with its hotels, the centre of tourist life, and the suburb (Vorstadt) round the Chur Gate in the northwest, the Marktplatz quarter remains the nucleus of the town.

The Hirschgraben (Stags' Ditch) affords the most recognizable traces of the walls. The late 15C **Cats' Tower** (Katzenturm) (A) owes its name to its defence cannon decorated with lions' heads which became known as "the cats". It is also called the Big Tower (Dicker Turm). Beside it is a small square, abutting on picturesque houses with steep pitched roofs.

The **Chur Gate** (Churertor) (B) is distinguished by its stepped gable.

(After Risch-Lau photo)

Feldkirch. - The Marktplatz.

Marktplatz. – This long, rectangular space, bordered with arcades on its long sides, has kept a pleasant serenity. Here and there an inn with a painted façade, a corner tower with a bulbous dome, or a Gothic oriel window catches the eye. To the south the view is bounded by the plain belfry and façade of St John's Church. This is the former church of the monastery of the Hospitallers of St John of Jerusalem, to whom was entrusted the guarding of the way through the Arlberg.

■ ADDITIONAL SIGHTS

Church (Domkirche). – The "cathedral-church" has the double nave, dear to Austrian architects of the 15C, and the fan vaulting characteristic of late Gothic *(details on religious architecture p 33).*

Over the right side altar is a *Descent from the Cross* painted in 1521 by Wolf Huber, an artist of the Danube school who was born at Feldkirch and is regarded as one of the great precursors of German landscape painting.

The pulpit is surmounted by a high canopy in wrought iron.

Castle (Schattenburg). – You approach by car up the Burggasse, a steep slope, or on foot by the Schlosssteig steps.

In spite of its internal refitting as a museum and a restaurant, this castle has kept, on the whole, its former arrangement and the defensive nature of its keep, planted on the top of a rock. The original dwelling or "Palas" is also a tower – recognizable by its tall, conical roof – with walls more than 4 m - 12 ft thick. The advanced defences, guarding the present approach bridge, and the ruined round tower nearby, were built about 1500, when gunpowder was already in use.

Before crossing the bridge there is a **view** of the Rhine Valley

Bahnhofstraße	2
Burggasse	3
Montfortgasse	4
Neustadt	5
Schloßsteig	6
Schmiedgasse	7

in the distance, overlooked by the Hoher Kasten (Alpstein massif, in the Appenzell district). The inner courtyard of the castle (café) is picturesque, with tiers of wooden galleries and vast roofs.

Local Museum (Heimatmuseum). – *Open 9am to noon and 1 to 5pm; closed Wednesdays; 10S; brochure available in English.*

It houses well displayed collections of religious art (especially in the former chapel), of noble and bourgeois furnishings of the Gothic period, of traditional peasant furniture, of arms and armour, and coins and of records of Old Feldkirch. It is pleasant, during the tour, to look at various views of Feldkirch through the windows.

EXCURSION

Rankweil. – *19 km - 12 miles – about 3/4 hour – Local map p 55.*

Leave Feldkirch by the Bregenz road. In the suburb of Feldkirch-Altenstadt take the right fork towards Rankweil. Go up to the church *(access and description p 119).*

On the way back come out of Rankweil by the Satteins road which climbs a low mountain range. After a winding and hilly run through small wooded valleys, the **view** opens out over the Bludenz basin and the Rätikon mountain range.

Bear right at the entrance to the village of Satteins in order to join road No. 1 which returns to Feldkirch.

The road to the Fernpass is varied and picturesque; it is the most hilly section of the former route across the Alps from Augsburg to Venice, which was known in the 15C for its strategic and commercial importance but is today, above all, a tourist link between the great resorts of the Bavarian Alps and Innsbruck.

This road is of vital importance to the Tyrol, since it opens the way to the Upper Valleys of the Lech and the Loisach, which the barrier formed by the Lechtal Alps and the Mieminger Kette cuts off from the Inn Valley. To reach these outer areas, grouped under the name: **Ausserfern** (the district "beyond the Fern"), you follow in turn, after Telfs, the plateau of Mieming, the south slope of the Fernpass proper, and the magnificent way down from the pass to Lermoos, within view of Wetterstein, and finally the Zwischentoren corridor.

From Telfs to Füssen (Germany) – *79 km - 49 miles – about 3 hours – Local map below.*

From Telfs to the threshold of Holzleiten the road runs on gentle, largely inhabited slopes of the Mieming plateau, on which stand the well defined crests of the Mieminger Kette (Hochplattig: 2 758 m - 9 048 ft – Griesspitzen, 2 759 m - 9 052 ft). Near Wildermieming views open out of the Inn Valley, and in the distance, upstream, the snowy heights of the Samnaungruppe. Between Barwies and Obsteig drive slowly so as not to miss the vista of the Inn Valley along a wooded ravine overlooked by the old tower of the fortified Castle of Klamm and the slender chapel for pilgrims at Locherboden.

TELFS - FÜSSEN

Holzleitner Sattel★. – A **landscape★** of larch woods and meadows dotted with hay barns, with glimpses of the Mieminger Kette to the east and Heiterwand to the west, lends idyllic charm to the neighbourhood (alt 1 126 m - 3 694 ft).

Fernstein. – On this easily defensible site is a fortified bridgehead. Below the hamlet is the **Fernsteinsee★;** whose green waters surround a wooded island.

Between Fernstein and Biberwier the Fernpass is marked, on the south slope, by curves and the barrenness which characterizes the little valleys and desolate amphitheatres of the Loreakopf mountain range. On the north slope the bold crests of the Mieminger Kette (Sonnenspitze) and the more massive bastion of the Wetterstein (Zugspitze) rise beyond a dense cloak of forest.

Fernpass. – Alt 1 209 m - 3 967 ft. The most open **view★** of the Sonnenspitze and the Wetterstein can be enjoyed about 1 km - 1/2 mile from the pass, on the north slope.

From above, the road skirts the dark waters of the Blindsee. (The best views of the lake are in the Biberwier–Fernpass direction.) The Weissensee, which is easily reached, is less romantic.

Ehrwald★. – *From Biberwier 3 km - 2 miles; from Lermoos 3.5 km - 2 1/2 miles. Description p 63.*

The road from Biberwier to Lermoos, running a little above the floor of the Lermoos-Ehrwald basin, affords wide-open **views★★** of the Wetterstein and the Mieminger Kette *(details under Lermoos).*

Lermoos★. – *Description p 102.*

To pass from the Loisach basin to that of the Lech, follow the valley named Zwischentoren ("between gates") in memory of the fortifications which once barred the road to the Fernstein and the Ehrenberg cleft. The crossing of the watershed near Lähn is unnoticeable. However, you still have to pass through the bottleneck of the fortified Ehrenberg cleft (Ehrenberger Klause) before you emerge into the Reutte basin.

Ehrenberg Cleft. – The former road on the floor of the ravine can still be seen, barred by dismantled fortifications. These are the only visible traces of the stronghold (visible to the left on the wooded slope) against Bavarian, Swedish and French invasions – once one of the keys to the Tyrol – from the 16C to the end of the 18C. The name of Ehrenberg, as the former seat of the judicial and fiscal authorities in the country, was used until 1850 not only for the town but also for the present Ausserfern district.

Plansee★. – *9 km - 6 miles – bear right on leaving the Ehrenberg cleft.* First the road clings above the wooded ravine, where, at the bottom, a small stream, issuing from the lake, flows. (Pleasant views of Tannheimer Gruppe.) It then forms a lakeside quay (6 km - 3 1/2 miles) as it runs along the uniformly wooded shore where a few hotels and camping grounds attract those to whom a wild setting appeals.

Looking southwest through the small strait which separates the Plansee from the Heiterwangersee one can see as far as the Thaneller mountain.

The road then continues towards Ammersattel (customs – open 1 April to 31 October 6am to 11pm (10pm the rest of the year), Linderhof, and Oberammergau (see Michelin Green Guide to Germany).

Reutte. – Pop 5 145. Reutte is the administrative and tourist capital of the Ausserfern. Its painted houses brighten the run along the Untermarkt and the Obermarkt, where you will also see a few carefully regilded inn signs and window grilles.

The road to Füssen follows the Lech Valley between the Tannheimer Gruppe summits and the steep slopes of the Säuling *(see Michelin Green Guide to Germany).*

FORCHTENSTEIN Castle (Burgenland)

Michelin map **426** fold 25 – 23 km - 14 miles southeast of Wiener Neustadt

The fortress of Forchtenstein rears its walls and towers in wild, romantic scenery, on a bluff in the Rosaliengebirge from which can be seen the wide horizons of the Hungarian Plain.

It was built in the 14C by the Counts of Mattersdorf and enlarged by the Esterhazy family about 1635. It took part in the defence of Austria at the time of the Turkish invasions of 1529 and 1683; and the large collection of arms and armour which comprised the garrison's armoury, together with Turkish pieces, is still housed there.

FREISTADT ★ (Upper Austria)

Michelin map **426** fold 9 – *Local map p 105* – Pop 6 289 – Alt 560 m - 1 837 ft – 🎆 ☎ 2974 – *Facilities p 39*

Freistadt, a former stronghold on the ancient salt route which led from the Alpine countries towards Bohemia, stands in the wild countryside of the Mühlviertel, a granite plateau covered with pasture and forest spreading wide horizons towards the Danube and the Czech frontier.

It still has traces of the ramparts, gateways and towers marking the line of its ditches.

■ **SIGHTS** *time: 1/2 hour*

Hauptplatz★. – This main square, is rectangular and well proportioned. To the southwest stands the tower of the parish church, surmounted by a bulbous dome and a small lantern, while opposite rises the castle tower. The houses lining the Hauptplatz are often fronted by porches or arcades, while their façades, adorned with delicate stucco and painted in pastel shades, add a gay note to the scene. To the west, almost facing the carved fountain dedicated to the Virgin, stands the **Rathaus (R)** and an old house fronted by a porch and flanked by a tower surmounted by a curious bulbous dome.

Cross the Hauptplatz and make for the new Castle (Neue Burg). The **courtyard,** restored, has, on three of its sides, an amusing balcony with a lean-to roof.

Altenhofgasse _____ 2
Böhmergasse _____ 3
Heiligengeistgasse _ 4
Huterergasse _____ 5
Prager-Bundes-Str. _ 6
Samtgasse _____ 7

By the **Schlossgasse,** a quaint and picturesque alley with flower decked balconies and passages, you reach the Böhmergasse and then the Böhmertor, a former fortified gateway. You enter the old town once more, where, in the Waaggasse and the Salzgasse, you will still find houses with oriel windows *(Erker).*

After glancing at the **Dechanthof** (Deanery) **(A),** built in the early 18C, make for the parish church, which you pass on your right before coming back to the Hauptplatz.

Parish Church (Stadtpfarrkirche). – The interior is in the Gothic style, with network vaulting over the chancel. The tower, which stands on the north side of the chancel, dates only from the Baroque period when it was completely transformed.

EXCURSION

Kefermarkt. – *11 km - 7 miles – plus 1/2 hour sightseeing – Local map p 105.*

Leave Freistadt southwards. Soon after leaving the town take the road to Kefermarkt which follows the left bank of the Feldaist. The road runs through woods before reaching Kefermarkt *(description p 95).*

FRIESACH (Carinthia)

Michelin map **426** fold 36 – Pop 7 074 – Alt 637 m - 2 090 ft – 🎆 ☎ 2316, 2213 – *Facilities p 39*

Three castles in ruins, six old churches and the remains of fortifications in which certain moats are still full of water give Friesach an appeal all its own. This concentration of military works, churches and monasteries is explained by the strategic importance of this former outpost of the bishops of Salzburg. Friesach guarded the gap which, between the Mur Valley and Klagenfurt, formed a key section of the road from Vienna to Venice.

The Dominican monastery *(open air plays* – Friesacher Sommerspiele – *in summer)* of Friesach was, in 1216, the first establishment of the Order in a German-speaking country. (In the monastery church are interesting works of art, especially a Crucifix.) The Knights of the Teutonic Order (Deutscher Orden) who, since the First World War under the name of Brothers of the German Order of St Mary of Jerusalem, have adopted a rule conforming to their original traditions of contemplation and good works, have been installed at the south exit from the town since 1255 and have their own church.

The GAILBERGSATTEL Road (Carinthia)

Michelin map **426** folds 33 and 34 – between Oberdrauburg and Kötschach

The road links the Upper Valleys of the Drava (Drau) and the Gail, crossing the pass at 982 m - 3 222 ft.

From Oberdrauburg to Kötschach –*14 km - 9 miles – about 1/2 hour*

The north slope, laid in zigzags under the larches, is for a long time within sight of Oberdrauburg and its ruined castle and is the most attractive part of the road.

Laas. – The church has the same characteristics as the one at Kötschach.

Kötschach. – Kötschach and **Mauthen** form, at the foot of the Carnic Alps, a medium altitude resort (pop 3 633) animated by its role as a road junction at the crossing of the Gail Valley and the way from the Gailberssattel to the Plöckenpass. This may lead motorists coming down from the Grossglockner towards the little known Italian-Yugoslav Friuli frontier region.
The 16C church represents the development of Gothic architecture at its last stage of decorative exuberance. The complicated groining, characteristic of late Gothic, becomes a network which covers the vaulting right down to the pillars. The local red sandstone has been used, notably, for the doorways and buttresses.

Lesachtal. – *53 km - 33 miles to Kartitsch-Sattel.* The by-road that runs up the Lesachtal, the Upper Gail Valley, enters the Drava Valley over the Kartitsch-Sattel (alt 1 526 m - 5 006 ft). *It is only recommended, beyond Kötschach, for drivers who do not mind going through 72 ravines, with gradients of up to 1 in 5 1/2.*

The GERLITZEN ★★ (Carinthia)

Michelin map **426** fold 35 – north of Villach – *Local map p 172*

The Gerlitzen (alt 1 909 m - 6 562 ft) is a summit whose foothills dip into the waters of the lake of Ossiach (Ossiacher See). It stands, in Lower Carinthia, as one of the outposts of the central rock massifs of the Alps. In winter this belvedere is the goal of many local skiers, who, using the cablecars to Kanzel and the many ski lifts, can go up to the sunny slopes.

Ascent of the Gerlitzen. – *12 km - 7 miles – plus 1 hour on foot Rtn. The road that climbs to the Gerlitzen is surfaced; a toll is payable: 40S per car.*
From Bodensdorf, on the north shore of the Ossiacher See, make for Tschöran, where the little mountain road to Gerlitzen starts. This, after winding through woods and pastures, ends at Bergerhütte, at an altitude of 1 764 m - 5 787 ft *(toll road from Tschöran to Bergerhütte: 35S each additional passenger: 15S).* Finish the climb, if necessary, by chairlift *(Rtn fare: 30S).*

The panorama★★. – The circular view embraces, southwards, the three lakes at Ossiach, Worth and Faak and, beyond the Drava Valley, the long barrier of the Karawanken of which the Mittagskogel (2 143 m - 7 031 ft) is the most distinct peak. After the Karawanken, to the west, are the Julian Alps (Triglav – alt 2 863 m - 9 393 ft) and the Carnic Alps. Then to the north comes a confused mass, the district known as the Nockgebiet. The only visible specimens of eternal snows, the little glaciers of Hochalm and the Ankogel (in the High Tauern range), glitter in the northwest.

The GERLOSPASS Road ★ (Tyrol and Salzburg)

Michelin map **426** folds 32 and 33

The Gerlospass links the Zillertal, a prosperous valley, with the Oberpinzgau (Upper Pinzgau), a long cradle in which the Upper Salzach takes in many torrents which have come down from the occasionally visible glaciary summits of the High Tauern (Grossvenediger massif). A visit to the well known Krimml Falls is worth the trip.

From Zell am Ziller to Mittersill –*67 km - 42 miles – about 4 hours – Local map p 72*

The road on the west side of the pass (Zillertal slope), downstream from Gerlos, has narrow sections and a mediocre surface.
Upstream from Gerlos, and on the road descending to Krimml, a toll is payable at the pass: 70S.

Zell am Ziller. – Pop 1 866. *Facilities p 42.* The town, the chief market in the Zillertal, nestles round a **church★** which was boldly built on an octagonal plan in 1782. The huge dome covering the central building was painted by Franz-Anton Zeiller (1716-1793) of Reutte *(p 70),* a cousin of Johann Jakob Zeiller. The figures from the Old and New Testaments are depicted standing round the Holy Trinity.

On the first Sunday in May all the inhabitants of the valley assemble at Zell for the *Gauderfest,* a traditional fête marked by a great folk procession, country wrestling and much drinking of *Gauderbier,* a strong beer (alcoholic content 20°) brewed for this occasion.
On leaving Zell am Ziller the road climbs quickly in hairpin bends up the Hainzenberg slope. It soon leaves behind the pretty pilgrims' Chapel of Maria Rast (the Virgin's Halt – 1739) which guards the Zillertal. It then approaches the hanging Gerlos Valley.

Gerlos. – Pop 749. *Facilities p 43.* This village in a secluded combe receives each winter many sportsmen who find excellent practice grounds and ski runs nearby, especially on the long slopes converging on Gerlos. In the summer sailing takes place on the Durlassboden.

The climb from Gerlos to the Gerlospass begins with a wide curve at the foot of the Durlassboden earth dam. A second bend takes the road up the mountainside above the artificial lake which drowned the Wildgerlostal. The snow covered cliffs of the Reichenspitze, which bar this high valley, and the Wildkarspitze, in the foreground on the left, may be seen at times. The road leaves to one side the Königsleiten and its chairlift, continuing up to the actual Gerlospass (alt 1 507 m - 4 944 ft) farther upward to the top of the Filzsteinalpe its highest point (alt 1 628 m - 5 341 ft – *car park*).

71

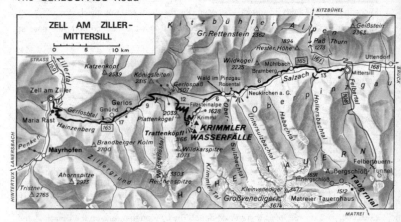

The **descent*** is rapid down the Krimml slope. It brings you in sight first, along all its length, of the Upper Pinzgau cleft and, more especially, of the two main falls of the Krimml. The road, cut into the steep rock mountainsides or avoiding these by way of bridges, finds a better terrain in the Blaubach Ravine (a series of hairpin bends). As you leave the valley, the most remarkable sight to be seen along this road lies before you: the landlocked lake of the Burgwandkehre encircling a rounded hillock, the Trattenköpfl.

Trattenköpfl*. – Alt 1 166 m - 3 824 ft. A close **view*** of the lower Krimml Falls may be had from the car parks at the entrance to the tunnel.

Krimml Waterfalls (Krimmler Wasserfälle)***. – *Description p 99.*

Wald im Pinzgau. – Pop 979. *Facilities p 42.*

From Wald to Mittersill, the Oberpinzgau affords good examples of balconied houses and fences constructed of interwoven laths *(illustration p 29).* As you approach Rasthaus Venedigerblick on the road between Rosental and Neukirchen, take a quick glance at the dazzling summits of the Kleinvenediger and the Grossvenediger.

Neukirchen am Grossvenediger. – Pop 2 230 – *Facilities pp 41 and 43.*

The road arrives at Mittersill, a large crossroad *(pp 67 and 96).*

GLEICHENBERG, Bad ★ (Styria)

Michelin map 426 fold 38 – Pop 1 920 – Alt 317 m - 1 040 ft - 🛈 ☎ 2203 – *Facilities p 39*

The spa of Bad Gleichenberg, not far from the Hungarian and Yugoslav frontiers, is restful and favoured by a mild climate.

It spreads hotels, villas, springs and thermal baths in the shade of its parks, among lawns and flower gardens.

The waters, containing chlorobicarbonate of soda, are used in the treatment of diseases of the respiratory tract, the heart, and, in the form of a drink, as a remedy for affections of the digestive tract.

GMUNDEN ★ (Upper Austria)

Michelin map 426 fold 21 – *Local map p 137* – Pop 12 720 – Alt 440 m - 1 444 ft - 🛈 ☎ 4305 – *Facilities p 39*

In Gmunden, a country resort in the Salzkammergut much sought after by romantic or *Biedermeier (p 34)* artists and poets, the delighted visitor will find a colourful little town with one of the best equipped lake beaches on the north slope of the Alps and wonderful views of the Traunsee. Gmunden, since the 15C, is reputed for its manufacture of artistic pottery.

Esplanade*. – This walk along the lake shore extends for 2 km - 1 mile – first among flowerbeds, then beneath chestnut trees. It leads from the Rathausplatz (main square), which is marked by the town hall, a Renaissance building, with a porcelain tiled clocktower, to the yacht harbour and the beach (Strandbad). In the opposite direction the walk can be pleasantly continued by crossing the river and following it as far as the war memorial (Kriegerdenkmal) or downstream along the Traun River (2 km - 1 mile).

Southwards, the **view*** takes in the crests of the Erlakogel, which resemble the form of a recumbent woman and are known as the Sleeping Greek (schlafende Griechin).

Ort Château*. – Built on a little island linked to the mainland by a breakwater, this *Seeschloss* (Lake Château) forms the typical souvenir picture of Gmunden. Through a doorway in the bulbous tower you can reach the charming inner court, lined on two sides by arcaded galleries superimposed in the style of the 16C.

Archduke Salvator, the nephew of the Emperor Franz-Josef, acquired the estate in 1878. Tired of court life, he lived under the assumed name of **Johann Ort** until he disappeared, in conditions which have never been explained, on a cruise off the coast of South America.

EXCURSION

Gmundnerberg*. – *9 km - 5 miles southwest* – Alt 833 m - 2 733 ft.

Leave Gmunden by the Esplanade and the Bad Ischl road. At **Altmünster** (pop 8 583 – *facilities p 39*) bear right. The road ends in a run along the crest *(turn back, before a sanatorium on the right)* which affords **views*** to the south over the whole of the Traunsee basin. The west bank of the lake is flat and peopled, the east steeply sloped. The Sleeping Greek *(see above)* can be recognized.

GRAZ ★★ P (Styria)

Michelin map 426 fold 38 – Pop 243 405 – Alt 364 m - 1 194 ft – ▣ ☎ 76 591 – *Facilities p 39*

The capital of Styria is in the Mur Valley, close to the last foothills of the Alps in the hilly southeast of Austria.

Its setting, gardens, climate and old quarter make it an attractive town, even though the development of its suburbs have transformed it into an industrial centre with the building of: machines (in Andritz), rolling stock, and motorcycles and cars.

The Romans settled in Styria as early as 16 BC, but avoided the site of Graz and preferred to live farther south, at Flavia Solva (Leibnitz). In the Middle Ages a fishermen's village developed on the left bank, in the narrow strip between the river and the bluff.

In the 12C the bluff was crowned with a fortress, which gave the city its name (*gradetz* or *gradec* meaning a castle in the Slav languages).

A Bastion of Christianity. – In 1480 about 20 000 Turks overran Styria and devastated it; 50 years later Suleiman the Magnificent sacked the whole of the Mur Valley and eastern Styria and until 1683 the Turkish threat continued to hang over the entire province. As early as the 16C a large reserve of arms and munitions had therefore been built up at Graz, which had become the provincial capital of Central Austria. Raw material brought from the Styrian Iron Mountain (*p 64*) was made into the swordblades and halberds, breast-plates and fire-arms by a legion of armourers, blacksmiths and polishers.

Whenever invasion seemed imminent the arms were distributed to volunteers chosen among the people, who reinforced the professional army.

The building in 1642 of an arsenal next to the Landhaus made it possible to bring together arms and munitions which until then had been piled in sheds near the city gates or in the attics of the Landhaus.

A Prince beloved by his people, Archduke Johann. – The thirteenth child of Emperor Leopold II, Archduke Johann (1782-1859), was entrusted with important military commands and took part in the campaigns against Napoleon I. He settled in Graz, where he took advantage of every opportunity to study; he also travelled about Styria and Carinthia with naturalists, archaeologists and designers. His romantic marriage (*p 50*) and his enterprise in creating model farms and building a railway from Graz to Köflach, which gave an essential industrial stimulus to the Eisenerz district, reinforced his popularity.

At Graz itself the foundation of a technical high school and of the large provincial museum, known as the Joanneum Landesmuseum (1811) – made up of 14 departments dispersed in 8 museums – show what an interest he took in the welfare of his fellow citizens, who set up a statue to him in the Hauptplatz.

■ MAIN SIGHTS *time: 2 hours*

Begin the tour at the Hauptplatz.

Hauptplatz★. – This nobly proportioned square, the heart of the city, is surrounded with fine houses roofed with brown tiles. The **Luegg house★,** at the corner of the Sporgasse, has a row of arcades and a façade which was decorated with stucco in the 17C.

If you stand on the pavement on the south side of the square in front of the town hall, which was rebuilt at the end of the 19C, you will see, overlooking the town and seeming to watch over it, the wooded spur of the Schlossberg, at the near end of which stands the tall and well known form of the clocktower (Uhrturm), the emblem of Graz.

Make for the Landhaus, following the **Herrengasse,** a wide, busy street lined with elegant shops and offices.

Landhaus★★. – The Landhaus, the former seat of the Diet of Styria, is a remarkable Renaissance building, built between 1557 and 1565 by the Italian architect Domenico dell'Allio. It is still today the seat of the *Landtag* (Provincial Diet: *p 13*).

The severe and simple main façade, on the Herrengasse, contrasts with the courtyard's southern elegance with its three tiers of arcades, flower decked balconies, staircases and loggias.

In a corner of the courtyard is an old well made by Styrian artisans. It is covered by a remarkable canopy in finely cast bronze, adorned with cherubs and figures of women.

(After Dr. A. Defner photo)

The Landhaus courtyard.

Arsenal★★ (Zeughaus). – *Open April through October Monday through Friday 9am to 4pm (noon Saturdays, Sundays and holidays); 10S; brochure available in English.*

The arsenal was built in 1642. At that time it was one of the largest in the world and it is today the only one still in existence to contain its original installations.

At the beginning of the 18C, when the Turkish danger had finally been removed and when in 1749, the Court at Vienna, having a regular army at its disposal, could guard the frontiers of the Empire without using volunteers, there was some question of dispersing the equipment. But Styria obtained from Maria Theresa permission to keep its arsenal in recognition of the services of the militia.

After the hustle and bustle of the Herrengasse the visitor finds himself taken back four centuries into the secrets of an armoury in perfect order, where the knights and soldiers, gathered in the Landhaus courtyard, could still draw their equipment before going forth to fight the infidels.

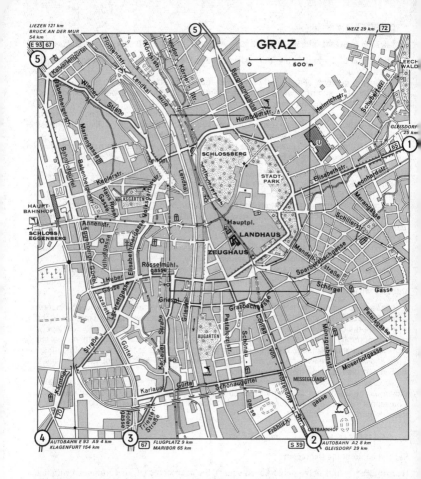

The four storeys of the arsenal contain more than 29 000 weapons of all imaginable kinds: cold steel, arms on poles and fire-arms – arquebuses, pistols and muskets with their powder horn – heavy armour for knights and soldiers, breastplates, and harnesses for use in war or jousting.

Several sets are admirable. There is armour for a horse, hammered out at Innsbruck in 1515 by the imperial armourer, Conrad Seusenhofer. There are also a complete suit of armour, dating from 1560, and a complete suit of parade armour made by the master armourer Michael Witz the younger, of Innsbruck. Finally, there are richly engraved and embossed jousting suits from the workshops at Nuremberg and pistols and chased sporting guns of the 16 and 17C.

From the top storey of the arsenal there is a bird's-eye view of the Landhaus courtyard, while over the roofs you can see the Schlossberg bluff and the clocktower.

From the Schmiedgasse go back to the Hauptplatz into which, on the left, open the Neue-Welt-Gasse (New World Street) and the Franziskanergasse (Franciscans' Street). These picturesque **alleys**★ are cluttered with the stalls of fruiterers and greengrocers. Nearby stands the tower of the Franciscans' church, crowned with a green dome.

Return to the Hauptplatz and follow the Sackstrasse, which leads to the Kaiser-Franz-Josef-Kai, and there take the funicular Schlossbergbahn – up only. *Service continues in summer until midnight; 8S.*

Schlossberg★. – Overlooking the town from about 120 m - 400 ft – this hill, until the Napoleonic wars, bristled with redoubts and fortifications.

During the campaign of 1809, which was marked by the battles of Eckmühl (in Bavaria) Essling and Wagram (near Vienna), Graz was occupied by French troops under Macdonald and the Schlossberg was dismantled except, at the request of the townsfolk, for the clocktower and the appealing octagonal **bell tower,** surmounted by a bulb, and known as the Glockenturm or more familiarly *Lisl.*

Today the Schlossberg offers a series of gardens and shady terraces on which to stroll. Nearly tame squirrels rejoice the hearts of children and passers-by.

From the various terraces there are pleasant **views**★ of the town and the Mur Valley. Beyond the brown and red roofs of the houses, from which rise the bulbous church towers, can be seen to the southwest the outline of the Pre-Alps of Styria.

Make for the south end of the spur. The **clocktower** (Uhrturm), of which the four sides carry large dials and are surmounted by wooden galleries, rises from massed beds of flowers.

Come down from the Schlossberg on the opposite side of the funicular, avoiding the very steep paths on the right. Pleasant shady chestnut avenues bring you to St Paul's Gate.

St Paul's Gate (Paulustor). – This, together with the castle gate (Burgtor), is all that remains of the town's fortifications. The gate was built at the end of the 16C and the carved marble coats of arms of Ferdinand II of Austria and Mary-Ann of Bavaria may still be seen on its outside walls.

In the Sporgasse take the Färbergasse to the left. Go round the Färberplatz and for a moment follow the Prokopigasse, which runs through one of the oldest quarters in the town. Lively, picturesque alleys, sometimes covered, lead to the Herrengasse, which leads back to the Hauptplatz.

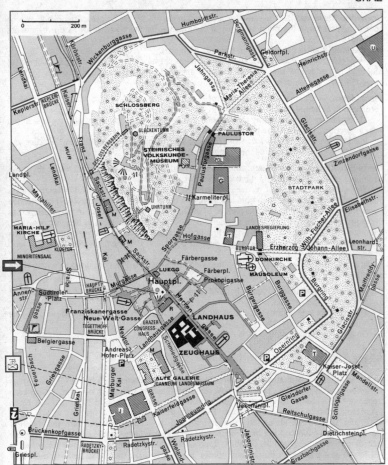

■ ADDITIONAL SIGHTS

Eggenberg Château★. – *3.5 km - 2 miles westwards.*

Since the Middle Ages the residence of the Eggenberg family, the building was transformed into this fine château between 1625 and 1635 by Italian architects. It consists of four buildings connected by corner towers and enclosing an elegant arcaded court.

An avenue, from which part of the park can be seen, leads to the main entrance, which is adorned with columns, statues, a carved balcony and the coat of arms of the Eggenberg family. The château contains Baroque apartments and two museums: a Hunting Museum and a Museum of Prehistory and Antiquity.

The **Baroque apartments** (Prunkräume) on the second floor *(guided tours – on request in English – (time: 1 hour) 1 April to 31 October 9am to 1pm and 2 to 5pm (last tour 4pm); 10S; brochure available in English)* are most interesting. The decoration of these rooms was done at the end of the 18C in the Baroque style, with a profusion of stucco and painting brightened by the light of crystal chandeliers. The large Festival Hall and the remaining saloons and bedrooms interspersed with Chinese rooms much in fashion at that time, are worth seeing more as an ensemble than for the artistic quality of each item independently.

The **Collection of Styrian Antiquities** (Abteilung für Vor- und Frühgeschichte) is displayed on the ground floor of the south wing. *Open 1 February to 30 November 9am to 5pm; 10S.* Note the small Strettweg votive chariot (8 BC) an example of work from the Hallstatt period.

The stairway, to the left after the entrance, hall, leads to the **Hunting Museum** (Jagdmuseum) on the first floor *(open February through November 9am to noon and 2 to 5pm; 10S; brochure available in English)* which contains complete records on the technical aspects of game shooting, numerous trophies and remarkable collections of old weapons.

Ancient Art Gallery (Alte Galerie) of the Joanneum Landesmuseum. – *Open Tuesdays to Fridays 9am to 4pm; Saturdays, Sundays and holidays 9am to noon; closed on certain holidays; 10S.*

The most interesting department, to the right of the entrance hall, is devoted to mediaeval art and contains a remarkable **collection of stained glass and altarpieces**★, the work of Styrian artists, from the end of the 12 to early 16C. You can see, among others, a small altarpiece made about 1320, whose four panels show St John, Mary Magdalene and two angels. It is similar to the altarpiece by Nicolas de Verdun, a masterpiece of goldsmith's art of the late 12C preserved in the Abbey of Klosterneuburg *(p 168)*. There are also an excellent portrait of Mary of Burgundy, the wife of the Emperor Maximilian, by a Dutch painter of the end of the 15C; two scenes from the life of St Thomas Becket – his death and his funeral – by Michael Pacher; a remarkable Head of Christ in wood, dating from the beginning of the 16C, and a Crucifixion done in 1467 by Conrad Laib. The museum also has a handicrafts section (Kunstgewerbe).

Cathedral (Domkirche). – The cathedral was built in the 15C by the Emperor Friedrich III, whose coat of arms adorns the main entrance. It is attractive for the elegance of its ogive network vaulting.

The long chancel has a beautiful Baroque high altar.

Two reliquary chests – formerly the marriage chests of Paula of Gonzaga, Duchess of Mantua – are shown at the entrance to the chancel. They are decorated with reliefs in ivory, carved in 1470, it is said, by Andrea Mantegna.

Mausoleum. – On the southeast side of the cathedral stands the tomb of the Emperor Ferdinand II, a domed structure dating from the first half of the 17C.

Guided tours (30 min) 1 May to 30 September 11am to noon and 2 to 3pm; the rest of the year 11am only; inquire at the presbytery; 10S.

Inside, the stucco and frescos were made to the designs of Johann-Bernhard Fischer von Erlach. A fine oval dome adorns the funerary crypt.

Maria-Hilf Kirche. – The church, which is dedicated to Our Lady of Succour, was built at the beginning of the 17C on the right bank of the Mur.

The good proportions of its twin towered Baroque façade and of its Renaissance style interior impart great unity. The Virgin, venerated on the high altar in a picture (1611) in a Rococo frame made of silver, is the patron saint of Graz. Go through the north door in the façade, cross the cloister, and you will come on a second court containing a pavilion in Renaissance style, although built at the end of the 17C. The first floor consists of a single room only, the **hall of the Minorite Brothers** (Minoritensaal). *Open 8am to noon and 2 to 6pm; closed Saturdays and Sundays.*

In this former ceremonial refectory, the walnut rostrum has been designed as a part of the door frame.

Styrian Folklore Museum (Steirisches Volkskundemuseum). – *Open 1 April to 31 October 9am to 4pm; closed Fridays; 10S.*

The museum is in a former Capuchin monastery. It has interesting reconstructions of rooms in Styrian houses.

On a rise beyond the museum is a *Heimatwerk (p 5).*

EXCURSIONS

Austrian Open Air Museum★★ (Österreichisches Freilichtmuseum). – *15 km - 9 1/2 miles – plus 1 1/2 hour tour.* Leave Graz by ⑤ *(Graz-Nordausfahrt)* towards Bruck an der Mur. At Gratkorn cross the Mur and after taking a right turn after the railway line continue 3 km - 2 miles. *Open 1 April to 31 October 9am to 4pm; closed Mondays; 25S.*

In the Mur Valley, about fifty rural homes and their dependencies, from the different provinces of the country, have been reconstructed. Dispersed among 40 hectares - 100 acres – according to their geographical situation, the dwellings blend beautifully with the landscape.

To the east a group of Burgenland homes characterize their traditional building method – thatched roofs.

From the eastern Alps, a typical 18C Styrian farm, where the smoke room with its twin hearth, is at the same time the kitchen, dining room and bedroom. Going farther along, a Carinthian farm is shown with its dependencies, forming an enclosed courtyard. Nearby is the usual Danube farm *(p 29).*

The Tyrolean chalets *(p 29)* are placed among an almost Alpine landscape. Continuing west is the Bregenzerwald farm *(p 29).*

A sawmill, smiths and mills combined with the farms – with their cribs, spinning wheels, decorated chests, fountains with running water, flowers and farm animals – create a true picture of the former rural community in Austria.

Katerloch★★. – *38 km – 24 miles. Temporarily closed.*

Leave Graz by the road No. 72 towards Weiz *(north of the plan p 74).* The road is a pleasant one, crossing an undulating countryside. At Weiz turn left into the road marked Katerloch further on at the top of a hill turn right *(signposted)* into a road which, at the square, brings you directly to the car park.

The highlights of the visit are the Phantasiehalle, containing a forest of stalagmites and stalactites (discovered in 1952), and the Seeparadies, an underground lake where stalagmites stand reflected in the water.

Alpine Flora

The name of "Alpine plants" is reserved for those which grow above the upper limits of the forests.

The early flowering of these species, which are usually small and lusty, is caused by the brevity of the growing season (June-August).

The disproportioned size of the bloom when compared with the plant as a whole and its bright colouring are directly connected with the large ultra-violet content of the light at high altitude.

Protection against draught often plays an important part in their structure. Among its features are downy coverings of the leaves, the water stored in small, lush plants, etc.

Walkers should refrain everywhere from wholesale harvesting of rare plants and should be content with picking a few flowers and avoid pulling up plants by the roots.

ALPINE ASTER
(July-August)

ALPINE PANSY
(May-August)

EDELWEISS
(July-September)

GENTIANELLA
(May-August)

Michelin map **426** folds 19 and 33

When the Grossglockner road *(1)* was opened in 1935, Austria inaugurated the age of the great modern Alpine highroads, both France and Switzerland have followed its example.

The commercial aim of those who built the road can be seen in the construction of two branch roads which spring from the main road: one leads to the summit of the Edelweiss-Spitze; the other to the terrace of the Franz-Josephs-Höhe with a view of the Grossglockner (alt 3 797 m - 12 457 ft), the highest point of the Austrian Alps, and the dazzling Pasterze glacier.

From Zell am See to Heiligenblut – *75 km - 47 miles – about 4 hours – Local map p 77*

The Grossglockner road is generally blocked by snow from early November to May (the Edelweiss-Spitze and Franz-Josephs-Höhe are often snowed in longer). A toll is payable (collected at Ferleiten or Heiligenblut): 220S for a car. There are tickets at 600S, additionally valid for the Gerlospass road (p 71), the Arlberg tunnel road (p 47), the Brenner pass road (p 56), the Felber Tauern road (p 67), the Tauern and the Pyhrn motorways (pp 146 and 143). Rtn trips from Ferleiten to the Franz-Josephs-Höhe and from Heiligenblut to the Franz-Josephs-Höhe are charged at the single rate (220S). Avoid arriving at the Franz-Josephs-Höhe at midday.

South of Zell am See *(p 173)*, the road to the Grossglockner properly speaking, begins at Bruck. It plunges into the Fuschertal, a valley whose austere setting and scanty sunshine have not encouraged people to settle there. In the east stand the dark foothills of the Schwarzkopf.

Between Fusch and Ferleiten the route, which is already more hilly, includes a short *corniche* section above a little wooded gorge, the Bärenschlucht. On emerging from this you begin to see the summits across the end of the valley, particularly the fine Sonnenwelleck group, rocky and jagged, and the Fuscherkarkopf, rounded and snow covered, standing to the right of the gap made by the Untere Pfandlscharte (alt 2 663 m - 8 737 ft).

Halt at a small dam on the right. A little farther upstream the Walcherbach falls tumble down the opposite slope.

From Ferleiten to the Fuscher Törl the route continues with several hairpin bends along the east side of the valley. Here it has to climb some 1 300 m - 4 200 ft – and flat sections are few. The first few miles (hairpin bends Nos. 1 to 4) are on the level of the Grosses Wiesbach-horn and the "3 000 m" - "10 000 ft" peaks nearby. Above the Piffkar ravine (alt 1 620 m - 5 315 ft) the **views**★★ are magnificent towards the Son-

nenwelleck group and the Fuscherkarkopf, at the foot of which lies the Käfertal amphitheatre. The last larches disappear and the road continues as a *corniche* as far as the bridges of Nassfeld. From here you climb to the pass across the basins of Nassfeld, and pass through the jumble known as the Witches' Kitchen (Hexenküche). Continue to the summit of the Edelweissspitze.

Edelweissspitze★★. – Alt 2 577 m - 8 455 ft. *Cars are forbidden.* From the observation tower erected on this belvedere-peak, the **panorama**★★ is made especially attractive by the heights enclosing the Fuschertal to the west, the Brennkogel across to the Grosses Wiesbachhorn. The peak of the Grossglockner can be seen just behind the Sonnenwelleck. To the east, the Goldberg group is more conspicuous for its covering of snow than for its height. Due north the Fuschertal gap opens up a view of the Zell Lake, the chalky massifs of the Loferer and the Leoganger Steinberge, and still farther to the right, the Steinernes Meer.

Fuscher Törl★. – Alt 2 428 m - 7 964 ft. The road builders had the idea of giving this "little gate" (Törlein) the form of a panoramic bend. Leave the car at the Fuscher Törl 2 car park.

The run from the Fuscher Törl to the Hochtor Tunnel through a somewhat sinister and stony landscape is a sort of interval. As they could not make the roadway pass directly from the Fusch to the Möll Valleys – the passes here being barred by glaciers – the engineers overcame the difficulty by making a *corniche* above the Seidelwinkl glade, one of the branches of the adjacent Rauris Valley. The views are impressive looking east towards the jagged heights of the Goldberg.

---

(1) For more detailed information consult the official map-guide Freytag "Grossglockner-Hochalpenstrassen" (in German) at a scale of 1/50 000 (scale: 1 inch = 0.8 miles).

The GROSSGLOCKNER Road★★★

Hochtor. – The road reaches its highest point 2 505 m - 8 218 ft - at the north end of the tunnel pierced under the pass (alt 2 575 m - 8 448 ft). From the south exit there is an open view of the Schober massif.

The winding descent from the Hochtor takes place among Alpine pastures within view of the Schober massif, which forms a crown round the Gössnitz Valley.

At the Tauerneck bend the sharp peak of the Grossglockner rises behind the Wasserradkopf foothills and you begin to look down into the Heiligenblut basin.

Emerging from the Guttal ravine, take the "Road of the Glaciers" (Gletscherstrasse).

Schöneck. – Alt 1 958 m - 6 424 ft. An excellent bird's-eye view of Heiligenblut.

As the Grossglockner gets nearer, the **view★★**, soon extending to the glaciary tongue of the Pasterze, becomes magnificent. But to reach the terrace of the Franz-Josephs-Höhe you must again tackle a series of hairpin bends in the Sturmalpe combe.

You then see Lake Margaritze artificially built below the tongue of the glacier by two dams bedded on a bolt. The reservoir is part of the equipment of Kaprun *(p 173)*.

Franz-Josephs-Höhe★★★. – On this spur is a large mountain mansion, the Kaiser Franz-Josephs Haus, to which the Heiligenblut mountaineering school is transferred in summer. This is an institution whose course of training for beginners ends with a climb up the Grossglockner. The "Road of the Glaciers" ends here in a long **panoramic terrace★★★**, partly hewn in the rock. Go along it, if possible, to the last platform, the Freiwandeck, at an altitude of 2 369 m - 7 772 ft. At the foot of the Grossglockner, buttressed by shining ice and sharp ridges, the magnificent 10 km - 6 mile flow of the Pasterze Glacier begins. Upstream, at the foot of the Johannisberg icecap, a spur has given the huge mass the effect of an eddy, producing an extraordinary air of fluidity.

Pasterze Glacier. – The descent from Freiwandeck to the glacier is made by funicular (Gletscherbahn). *Service from the beginning of May to the end of September, hourly, 8am to 4pm; 45S Rtn.*

Wasserfallwinkel★★. – Alt 2 548 m - 8 363 ft. *From Freiwandeck 1 1/2 hours Rtn; follow the signs "Zur Hofmanns– und Oberwalder Hütte".* The Gamsgrubenweg, a path, above the Pasterze, leads to the viewpoint.

Turn about and, at the Guttal fork, go down towards Heiligenblut, opposite the wooded opening of the Gössnitztal, which is cut by a cascade.

Kasereck★. – Alt 1 913 m - 6 276 ft. Halt on this grassy spur, which affords **views★** of the Grossglockner and the Heiligenblut basin.

Near the chalets are grain driers in the form of grilles *(illustration p 29)*. The 26th and last hairpin bend, curving above the Fleiss Valley, reveals the Sonnblick (alt 3 105 m - 10 187 ft). At last you see the well known picture of the Church of Heiligenblut *(p 81)* a stone spike standing in front of the Grossglockner.

(After A.N.T.O. photo)

Heiligenblut.

GURK ★ (Carinthia)

Michelin map 🔲🔲🔲 fold 36 – Pop 1 430 – Alt 662 m - 2 172 ft

The Cathedral of Gurk, in a cultivated valley in the north of Carinthia, was the seat of a chapter until the see of the province was transferred to Klagenfurt in 1787; it remained almost forgotten through the first half of the 19C. Then archaeologists and ecclesiastical authorities began to make every effort to make it well known and now have succeeded in drawing crowds to this church – the masterpiece of Romanesque architecture in Austria. The church furnishings are a revelation of Baroque inspired by the Counter-Reformation.

■ THE CATHEDRAL★★ *time: 1 hour*

Open 1 April to 1 November 7.30am (10.45am Saturdays, Sundays and holidays) to noon and 1 to 5pm (6pm depending on the season); the rest of the year 7.30am (10am Saturdays, Sundays and holidays) to noon and 1 to 4.30pm. The crypt and bishop's chapel (closed for restauration until late 1983) may only be visited on guided tours at 9.30 and 11am (11am only Sundays and holidays) and 2.30 and 4.15pm (in July and August only there is an extra tour at 1.30pm).

The onion domed cathedral, which was built from 1140 to 1200 by Prince-Bishop Roman I, Councillor to Frederick Barbarossa, is a symmetrical building with a triple nave and a non-protruding transept. It occupies the site of the first monastery at Gurk, founded in the 11C by the Countess Emma of Friesach-Zeltschach (died in 1045; canonized in 1938 – St Emma), who is still venerated in Carinthia.

After a general view of the façade, severe in style and with two towers, skirt the south side, going through the churchyard.

The careful setting of the stones, with their golden yellow patina, the elegant arched cornice, running along the wall, and the simple style of the chevet, with the shallow apses, are characteristic of the building.

Return to the front porch.

Porch. – The porch has had no exterior outlet since the Gothic period, when it was closed by a wall in which are stained glass windows (restored) dating from 1340. In the porch are Gothic mural paintings, of the Old and New Testaments, similar in style to the school of Giotto. The Romanesque doorway, with deep splaying, shows elaborate decorative foliage on the pilasters, vaulting and capitals. The panels themselves still have, in the upper third of their surface, medallions carved and painted in 1220.

Interior. – Some discord is noticeable between the Romanesque structure of the main building, its vaulting with Gothic network and the Baroque furnishings and adornments. The altarpieces of the altars enclose the main and smaller apses. Before examining the furniture and decoration of the church (of which the main features are illustrated on this page) turn and look at the architecture of the narrow vestibule (Innere Vorhalle): the semicircular engaged pilasters have fine Romanesque capitals with palm branches and foliage.

GURK CATHEDRAL
0   15 m

(1) Reliquary of St Emma: an elegant work, in the form of a tree, covered with precious stones.

(2) Samson doorway (Samson slaying the lion): the finest piece of Romanesque sculpture (1180) in Gurk.

(3 and 8) **Carved panels★** 16C, vividly depicting scenes from the life of St Emma.

(4) A gigantic picture – as tradition required – of St Christopher (1250).

(5) **High Altar★★** (1626-1632) with full size, strikingly realistic figures (72 statues, 82 angels' heads). During Lent the altar is shrouded by a **Fastentuch**. This is a curtain, intended to deprive believers of the view of the high altar during this time of penance. The curtain at Gurk is a rare example of one entirely decorated with paintings (scenes from the Old and New Testaments).

(6) Stalls (1680): these are the work of a local artisan. They are treated with the same happy inspiration as the "best" furniture in the peasants' houses.

(7) The 24 Old Men of the Apocalypse and the Conversion of St Paul: Gothic murals (1380).

(8) See (3) above.

(9) Altar of the Holy Cross (1741), with a pietà in lead by Georg Raphaël Donner.

(10) **Pulpit★** (Baroque, 1740), one of the most inspired works of the Counter-Reformation, on the triumph of the Church and of Truth (note especially the carvings of the sounding-board).

Crypt. – The crypt is supported by about 100 marble columns with plain square capitals. It was finished in 1174 and contains the tomb of St Emma.

Bishop's Chapel. – Closed for restauration until late 1983. The chapel is built into the tribune behind the façade and displays an impressive series of Romanesque **murals★★**. The general theme, which gives the key to the symbolic meaning of the various scenes, will be found in the Latin inscription over the altar niche: "Here shines in splendour the throne of the great King and of the Lamb." The throne of Solomon may be seen on the wall facing that with the Transfiguration of Christ. The vaults of the chapel, one depicting the Garden of Eden, the other a celestial Jerusalem, show an admirable adaptation of ornament to architecture.

Before leaving Gurk look at the large group of 15 and 17C priory buildings once occupied by the cathedral canons.

HALL, Bad (Upper Austria)

Michelin map **426** folds 21 and 22 – 19 km - 12 miles west of Steyr – Pop 4 060 – Alt 388 m - 1 273 ft – 🅸 ☎ 2031 and 2328 – Facilities p 39

Iodised springs which are among the strongest in Central Europe, and up-to-date equipment for the treatment of diseases of the eyes, heart, and circulation and glandular disorders, make Bad Hall (not to be confused with Hall in Tirol) a much sought after spa resort. The thermal park, with paths bordered with fine trees and lawns adorned with clumps of flowers, is well laid out, over 36 hectares - 89 acres.

Pfarrkirchen. – 1 km - 1/2 mile southwest. The **parish church★** is attractive for its interior decoration which was carried out in around 1744. The frescos on the vaulting, enhanced by delicate stuccowork, make a picture of great harmony glorifying the mystery of the Holy Blood. The pulpit, the organ-loft and the high altar are richly adorned with paintings of cherubs and statues. These are well proportioned and fit perfectly into an ensemble dominated by pastel shades. Sacred music concerts are given in summer.

For maximum information from town plans:
consult the conventional signs key, p 44.

Michelin map **426** fold 31 – *Local map p 90* – Pop 12 622 – Alt 581 m - 1 906 ft – 🛉 ☎ 6269
– *Facilities p 39*

Hall in Tirol, was the salt town of the Inn Valley. As such during the Middle Ages as the mining towns of the Salzkammergut did in Upper Austria or the archbishops in Salzburg, it played a leading part in the economic life of the country *(p 27)* and was especially cherished by the princes of the Tyrol. From 1303 onwards these granted it liberal constitutional rights, and by comparison with their austere court at Innsbruck, regarded it as a centre for pleasure and amusement.

The time is past when Hall marked the starting point of much river traffic on the Inn, and the end of their journey upstream for the rafts of logs which stoked the salt boilers. Today the sleepy little town is trying to replace its traditional industry with tourist traffic for which it has a large open air swimming pool. The old world look of its 15 and 16C quarter, the Obere Stadt, of which the centre is bounded by a girdle of boulevards – the Stadtgraben – helps to attract tourists.

General View★. – An excellent general view of the town may be had from the opposite bank of the Inn by going some way up the minor road to Tulfes, after having passed under the motorway. In front of the three belfries of the Upper Town can be recognized the remains of the former Hasegg castle (Burg) and its Münzerturm, or tower of the mint, with its curious polygonal crown. The building housed the mint of the princes of the Tyrol from 1567 to the time of the rebellion led by Andreas Hofer (1809).

■ **THE UPPER TOWN (Obere Stadt)** *time: 1 hour*

No traffic allowed in the Upper Town on Saturdays.

Start from the Unterer Stadtplatz, an open space formed by the road from Innsbruck to Vienna. Go up to the Oberer Stadtplatz by the Langer Graben.

Oberer Stadtplatz. – This irregular open space is bounded by interesting buildings. Several picturesque streets, lined with façades having oriels on several floors grouped together behind grilles, also radiate from the square.

The **Parish Church** (Stadtpfarrkirche), which was enlarged in the 15C, is surrounded by annexes like those of mediaeval churches, among them the Baroque Chapel of St Joseph, which is shaped like a pagoda.

The **Town Hall** (Rathaus) may be recognized by its large pavilion-like attic. On the 16C main building, set back, are delicate carved designs: the statue of a knight, named Roland, and to his right, the coats of arms of Austria and the Tyrol. Look into the Wallpachgasse, which affords a vista of the Bettelwurf (Karwendel massif).

Make for the Stiftsplatz by way of the Rosengasse.

Stiftsplatz. – Contrasting with the fantasy of the mediaeval town, the classical arrangement of this square is entirely harmonious, bounded as it is on the east by the sober façades of the former college and church of the Jesuits (transformed into a concert hall), and on the south by those of the former convent for Noble Ladies.

Ladies' Abbey (Damenstift). – The abbey was founded in 1567 by the Archduchess Magdalene, daughter of Ferdinand I, whose statue is on a fountain in the square. Its buildings, especially the façade of the church, show the transition between Renaissance art (church doorway) and the Baroque style. By the Eugenstrasse and the steps of the Schweighofstiege, to the left, return to the Unterer Stadtplatz.

Michelin map **426** fold 20 – *Local map p 128* – Pop 15 404 – Alt 461 m - 1 539 ft – 🛉 ☎ 2459

Hallein, with its streets hemmed in between tall 17 and 18C houses, was one of the most precious possessions of the Archbishops of Salzburg. It developed from the 13C onwards round the salt-pans laid out on an island in the Salzach to evaporate brine from the famous mines of the Dürrnberg, which have worked since Neolithic times. Today the chemical, paper and engineering industries share in the industrial activity of the town. Located in the upper town on the north side of the parish church are the home and tomb of **Franz-Xaver Gruber** (1787-1863), the composer of the famous carol *Stille Nacht, Heilige Nacht (Silent night, Holy night)*.

Dürrnberg Mines. – *Guided tours (1 1/2 hour) 1 May to 3 October 9am to 5pm. Cripples and children under six not admitted. Cable-cars to the mine (Salzbergbahn) leave every hour from 7.30am. 46S Rtn: admission to the mine: 75S, children 35S; brochure available in English.*

From the cable-car's upper station, make for the entrance to the mine, passing the large St Joseph "Kurhaus" and going to the right, down the main "street" of Dürrnberg. You can visit in passing, the fine pilgrims' church built in the local pink marble at the beginning of the 17C by Italian architects of the archiepiscopal court at Salzburg.

The tour entails a long walk through underground galleries, with a presentation in a cave showing the different techniques used in the extraction of salt and the descent of the Rutschen or Rollen (slides) which is limited to two toboggans used individually.

HALLSTATT ★★ (Upper Austria)

Michelin map **426** fold 21 – *Local map p 139* – Pop 1 131 – Alt 511 m - 1 677 ft – 🖼 ☎ 208 – *Facilities p 39*

The village of Hallstatt clings to the steep slope of a foothill of the Dachstein and takes its name from the **lake**★★, the Hallstätter See, into whose dark waters the slope dips. Hallstatt provides a picture of romantic Austria with streets so narrow and so steep that it has become customary to make the Corpus Christi procession, on the lake, in boats.

A Cradle of Civilization. – Human activity, stimulated by the mining of salt which, apart from a short interruption in the Middle Ages, has gone on in the sides of the nearby mountain since Neolithic times, has left so many traces in the environs of Hallstatt (1 000 tombs excavated) that the name of the locality has entered the language of science. To the **Hallstatt Period** (1000-500 BC) corresponds a form of civilization marked, by progress in iron-smelting and Celtic immigration into Gaul, of which valuable evidence may be seen in the **museum of prehistory** *(open 1 April to 31 October 10am to 5pm; 20S; brochure available English)* of the town, in the Château of Eggenberg at Graz (Collection of Styrian Antiques) and in the Natural History Museum in Vienna.

The salt-mines are still being worked in the hanging Valley of the Salzburg where archaeological excavations have been particularly fruitful and the galleries may be visited. *Guided tours 1 May to 30 September 9am to 6pm – last visit 4.30pm; the week of Easter and 1 to 17 October 9am to 4pm – last visit 2.30pm; wear sturdy shoes and warm clothing; children under 4 and the elderly are not admitted; 60S, children 30S. Allow 2 1/2 hours for the exursion, using the funicular (8am to 4pm; 45S Rtn) starting from Lahn.* The salt is taken in the form of brine by *Soleleitung* as far as Ebensee *(local map p 137)*.

■ **SIGHTS** *time: 1 hour*

Leave the car on one of the **belvedere-terraces**★. (The terraces running north-south are open, those south-north are covered.) Take some steps marked "Abgang zur Stadt" which will bring you out onto the picturesque rise of the church (Kirchenweg) and bear left.

Parish Church (Pfarrkirche). – Standing on a poetic **site**★★ in its churchyard bordering the lake, this massive building of the late 15C is flanked by a squat tower whose peculiar roof, with its overhanging eaves, suggests some Chinese building, in contrast with the pointed steeple of the Protestant church built on the lakeshore in the 19C.

Inside, the hall-type nave and chancel are double, with star vaulting, bearing witness to the taste for twin naves which became fashionable in the mountain districts of Austria at the end of the Gothic period. The large **altarpiece**★ on the high altar, presented by a rich *Salzfertiger* (salt merchant; *p 91*), represents, in its central panel, the Virgin between St Barbara and St Catherine. It was painted between 1505 and 1515. A certain liveliness of tone shows the growing influence of the Renaissance. In the only chapel on the north side of the church is another little altarpiece, older (pre-1500) and decorated entirely with paintings depicting the Crucifixion and, when the shutters are closed, scenes from the lives of St Anne and St Joachim.

Go right across the minute cemetery, to the north of the church.

Chapel of St Michael. – *Ask for the key at the grave-diggers cottage.*
The lower storey of this Gothic church houses the parish charnel-house, which has been in use since 1600, as the cemetery is so small. The transfer of the bones (about 1 200 skulls) 10 or 12 years after death is accompanied, here, with adornment. On certain skulls are painted the date of death and signs showing the age of the deceased (flowers for young girls) or what caused death (*e.g.* a snake).
Return and go down the Kirchenweg; turn right after the covered passage.

Local Museum (Heimatmuseum). – *Open 1 May to 30 September 9am to 6pm; 20S.*
The museum is in a picturesque house abutting on the rock and contains collections of folklore and history. Return to the lower town in order to take a walk along the lakeshore; and then to the car by way of the Kirchenweg and the stairs leading to the belvedere-terraces.

HEILIGENBLUT ★ (Carinthia)

Michelin map **426** fold 33 – *Local maps pp 77 and 110* – Pop 1 334 – Alt 1 288 m - 4 226 ft – 🖼 ☎ 2002 – *Facilities p 39*

Heiligenblut is at the bottom of the south slope of the Grossglockner. For the tourist who has just traversed the lonely upper mountains, Heiligenblut is a welcome return to civilization.

The **site**★ of the church, slim and upstanding, with its steeple in silhouette against the Grossglockner tempts many an amateur photographer *(illustration p 78)*. Due to the town's proximity to the Franz-Josephs-Höhe training school *(p 78)*, it has become a mountaineering centre. The Schareck chairlift attracts skiers in the late spring.

Church. – The church was built between 1430 and 1483 by the monks of Admont *(p 45)*, to perpetuate their prayers in the name of a relic of the Holy Blood (Heilig-Blut). The chancel stands on a twin-aisled crypt containing the tomb of Briccius, an officer of the Imperial Court of Byzantium, who is said to have brought the precious substance there in the 10C. This and the nave, whose pillars without capitals reveal its later building, are roofed, in the late Gothic tradition, with network and star vaulting. The side galleries of the nave were necessary to accommodate crowds of pilgrims. The great altarpiece on the high altar (1520), attributed to the school of Michael Pacher, and the Gothic canopy (1496) form the essential furnishings.

HERZOGENBURG Monastery (Lower Austria)

Michelin map **426** fold 11 – 12 km - 7 miles north of St. Pölten – *Local map p 62*

The Augustinian Canons' Monastery at Herzogenburg, founded at the beginning of the 12C by Bishop Ulrich of Passau, has enjoyed a prosperity to which the collections of works of art and manuscripts bear witness. The church and monastery buildings were virtually rebuilt in the Baroque style in the 18C.

Guided tours (1 hour) 1 April to 31 October 9am to noon and 1 to 5pm; 20S. Apply for tour in English: ☎ 2782 3435.

Church. – The paintings and stucco go well with the church's Baroque architecture. A series of domes rest on columns surmounted with Corinthian capitals. All the vaulting is painted with frescos as are the altarpieces on the side altars by Bartolomeo Altomonte. The pictures on the high altar, painted by Daniel Gran, show great skill in the art of composition: the Virgin and Child are flanked by the patron saints of the monastery, St George and St Stephen.

Monastic buildings (Stiftsgebäude). – The vaulting of the main hall (Festsaal) is adorned with a huge allegorical composition by Altomonte to the glory of the Prince-Bishops of Passau. Decorated with pictures, frescos, and in grisaille (grey monochrome), the library contains more than 80 000 works. One room, exposing Gothic art, contains a collection of 16C **paintings on wood★**, belonging to the Danubian School among which are four panels by Jörg Breu *(p 59)* representing scenes from the Passion on the outside and the Life of the Virgin inside.

HOCHOSTERWITZ Castle ★ (Carinthia)

Michelin map **426** fold 36 – 9 km - 6 miles east of St.Veit an der Glan – *Local map p 125*

The Castle of Hochosterwitz, standing on a height in the St.Veit basin on the edge of the Zollfeld, the cradle of Carinthia *(see Maria Saal p 106)*, has remained since 1571 the property of the Khevenhüller family. It is worth seeing chiefly for its eagle's aerie **site★★**. The ramp leading up to it, fortified with extraordinary care in view of the Turkish menace, which may still have seemed quite near when it was built, is no less interesting.

Castle★. – *About 1 hour on foot Rtn.* Drive through the hamlet of Hochosterwitz at the foot of the rock and on to the by-road where the climb to the battlemented castle begins. Leave the car at the supervised car park. The visitor goes up the approach ramp constructed between 1570 and 1586 by Georg Khevenhüller (1534-1587). Governor of Carinthia, this important official made his fortress a sort of refuge for Protestants.

Of the fourteen gateways on the road, advantage was taken of natural gaps in the ravine to form centres of resistance isolated behind drawbridges, the largest is the 7th gateway, known as the Khevenhüller Gate (1582), surmounted by a lion's head and a bust of Georg Khevenhüller. At the end of the climb, affording many **views** of the hilly St.Veit area, from which the Ulrichberg mound emerges, you pass the castle chapel and reach the **inner court** *(open Easter to the end of September 9am to 6pm; 25S)*, now a rustic café-restaurant.

Certain rooms of the castle are open to visitors. Exhibited are collections of arms and armour belonging to the Khevenhüller family.

HOFGASTEIN, Bad ★ (Salzburg)

Michelin map **426** fold 34 – 7 km - 4 miles north of Badgastein – *Local map p 51* – Pop 5 960 – Alt 860 m - 2 822 ft – ▯ ☎ 4810, 429, 482 – *Facilities p 39*

Bad Hofgastein is a lively and pretty resort. The numerous hotels or *Kurhäuser* can be used for the same cures as those at Badgastein since the waters were piped to them in 1828.

A swimming pool filled with spring water and 9 hectares - 23 acres of thermal grounds have brought to the city a less medical appearance. Skiing is also a popular sport especially on the Schlossalm slopes as high as 2 300 m - 7 546 ft.

Church. – The church was restored several times in the 15 and 16C. It bears witness to the long administrative history of the town, which was the capital of the most ancient parish in the valley. The Gothic building, with star or network vaulting, is impressively designed. All round the church, and especially in the bays on each side of the doorway, tombstones bear effigies of the rich gold- and silver-mine owners, reviving memories of the prosperous period (16 and 17C).

The HOHENTAUERN Pass Road ★ (Styria)

Michelin map **426** folds 22 and 36

The Hohentauern Pass (alt 1 265 m - 4 150 ft), known still as the Triebener Tauern or **Rottenmanner Tauern,** opens the way for a by-road locally called the **Tauernstrasse** (the Tauern Road). This was used long ago by the Romans as a link between Juvavum (Wels) and Virunum (near Klagenfurt). *See map of Roman provinces p 22.*

The Valley of the Pölstal is a rather difficult section, however, it is recommended because it is quiet and green, though dotted, near the Möderbrugg, with long, more or less dilapidated mining or industrial buildings, which are survivals, not without character, of a vanished industrial civilization based on silver mining and

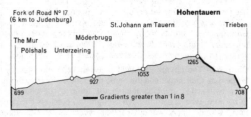

silver and metal working by artisans. The crossing of the Schoberpass by the main road from Trieben to Leoben is a mere formality compared with it.

From Judenburg to Liezen – *73 km - 45 miles – 2 1/2 hours – Local map p 83*

The gradients on the north slope of the pass call for great care. It is best to cross in the direction of Judenburg to Liezen, in order to take this section downhill.

Branching off from the Vienna-Klagenfurt road, 6 km - 4 miles from Judenburg, the Trieben road crosses to the left bank of the Mur. It climbs briefly on the last slopes of the Falkenberg – there are pretty views upstream of the wide valley overlooked by the Bocksruck – to enter the Pölsbach Valley over the slight shelf of the Pölshals. Looking back, on the right, the ruins of Reifenstein dominate the industrial settlement of Pöls (cellulose industry). Ahead, still far off, the jagged crests of the Hochschwung stand up on the horizon.

Unterzeiring. – The buildings of a former fortified priory attached to Admont *(p 45)* and the crumbling ruins of Hanfelden Castle lend distinction to this village.

Oberzeiring. – Pop 1 302. *At 1.5 km - 1 mile off the Hohentauern road (take the fork after Unterzeiring).* In this former mining village, one can visit a disused silver mine *(Schaubergwerk). Duration: 1 hour; 20S.*

Möderbrugg. – Several artificial falls in the torrent, here enclosed in old wooden troughs, recall the time when the noise of the little hammers used for iron-beating was heard in the village.

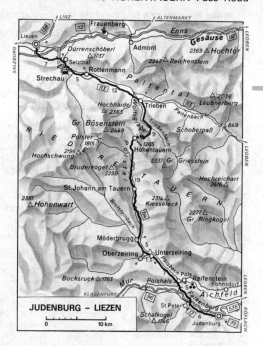

Huge barns can now be seen standing squat on the ground one above the other, on the slopes of the Pölstal. After the tiny resort of St. Johann am Tauern the climb becomes steeper. To the left rises the Grosser Bösenstein, from the foot of which the Polster pass rises in a smooth curve. At last you reach the upper combe of the pass, a quiet setting for the country resort of Hohentauern.

Hohentauern. – Pop 637. *Facilities p 43.*

On the north slope of the mountain the road plunges into the Wolfsgraben, a dark gorge of the Triebenbach, to emerge finally on the mountainside above Trieben.
The Paltental unfolds between Trieben and Selzthal. The valley is used by the main road from Graz to Salzburg.

Rottenmann. – Pop 5 425. This little town was once enriched by the traffic in salt. It still has its *Strassenplatz (p 28)*, its priory near the church, some traces of town walls (behind the church, on the mountainside), and makes a pleasant halt.

The high perched shape of Strechau Castle, formerly a refuge for Protestants in Upper Styria, lends attraction to the run from Rottenmann to Selzthal. At Liezen you will enjoy extensive views of the Enns gap. From the bridge over the torrent you can recognize, in the southwest, the Grosser Grimming (alt 2 351 m - 7 713 ft), an outcrop of the Dachstein.

The HÖLLENTAL ★★ (Lower Austria)
Michelin map **426** fold 24 – northwest of Gloggnitz – *Local map p 140*

The Höllental, or Hell's Valley, is the name which has been given to the gap made by the Schwarza River between the two chalky massifs of the Schneeberg and the Raxalpe.

From Schwarzau to Hirschwang – 18 km - 11 miles – about 1/2 hour

This is the most picturesque section of the valley. The road follows the course of the Schwarza, a torrent with green waters leaping over a shingle bed among rocks. A little after Schwarzau im Gebirge fine views open out on the left towards part of the Schneeberg massif. The valley gets deeper and deeper between high slopes, which are sometimes impressive. Fir trees cling to the greyish rocks; the road crosses from one bank of the river to the other. At Hirschwang the valley grows wider and its sides lower, marking the end of the "infernal" section.

INN Valley ★ (Tyrol)
Michelin map **426** folds 29 and 30

Since the southern frontier of Austria was brought back, in 1919, to the crest line of the Alps, the Inn Valley has become the main stem of the Tyrol. For 185 km - 115 miles – from the Finstermünz ravine to the Kufstein gap, the scenery is typical of the longitudinal furrows of the Alps, where the last phases of the Ice Age *(p 18)* made characteristic changes in the relief. Such is the **Mittelgebirge** (Pre-Alpine) area round Innsbruck, where spacious plateaux have become ideal sites for villages.

Downstream from Landeck, the Inn Valley emphasizes the meeting of the Limestone Alps, whose pale cliffs form a line on their north side, with the crystalline central massifs of the south. In the latter, dark coloured rocks of a heavier shape predominate. The Sellraintal, a tributary valley which opens from the right at the promontory of the Martinswand, between Zirl and Innsbruck, marks the traditional boundary between the Upper and Lower Valleys of the Inn (Oberinntal and Unterinntal).

The sheltered climate, sometimes oppressive in summer, which the valley enjoys, and the influence of the *Föhn (p 17)* brought by secondary valleys lying due south, make it possible to grow cereals and even maize, peaches and apricots.

The itinerary below describes, for the first 50 km - 31 miles the Upper Inn Valley (Oberinntal), majestically sunken and wooded.

From Nauders to Imst – *62 km - 39 miles – about 2 hours – Local map below*

By going up the Inn Valley you can reach Scuol (Schuls) and the Engadine directly without going up to Nauders. Branch off at the Kajetanbrücke to continue along the floor of the Finstermünz defile.

Nauders. – Pop 1 327. *Facilities p 43.*

Leaving the Nauders basin, where there are still crops at over 1 300 m - 4 000 ft, as in the nearby Valley of the Upper Adige (Val Venosta or Vintschgau), the road plunges into the Finstermünz defile.

Finstermünz Pass or Gorge* (Finstermünzpass). – This grim gorge forms the natural frontier between the Tyrolean Inn Valley the Lower Engadine and the Upper Adige.

Though the Engadine road follows the floor of the cleft throughout, the part which comes down from Nauders plunges into it through a rocky gap guarded by an old fort. You will see, at first only by glimpses, the narrowest section of the Inn gorge, and the fortified bridge of Alt-Finstermünz, which commanded this before the present road was made (1850-1854).

Downstream from the hamlet of Hochfinstermünz the road clings to the cliffs of the right bank. To halt on this **corniche*** choose the overhanging belvedere-terrace marked by a single pine, from which you can **look*** down on the valley, facing the tributary gorge, which marks the opening of the Romansh Samnaun Valley in Switzerland.

You will reach the floor of the valley at the Kajetanbrücke (St Gaëtano) Bridge.

Pfunds. – Pop 2 151. *Facilities see Pfunds p 42.* Near the "Dreiländereck" (the point where the Swiss, Italian and Austrian boundaries meet), the twinned towns of Pfunds-Stuben and Pfunds-Dorf, separated by the Inn typify the Engadine house – Rhaeto-Romansh, with oriels and deeply recessed little windows.

On leaving Stuben, bear left at the fork, onto the old Landeck road, passing through Birkach. From the end of the valley, below Stuben, you can recognize, looking back, the Schmalzkopf group, and particularly, on the opposite slope, the Piz Mundin (alt 3 146 m - 10 322 ft), which stands out better. Between Ried im Oberinntal and Prutz note, on the rock, the ruins of Laudeck, flanked by the little white bell tower of Ladis. As you arrive at Prutz the jagged skyline of the Kaunergrat rises above the end of the tributary valley of the Kaunertal.

Kaunertal*. – *22 km - 14 miles from Prutz.* The valley is deeply encased. At the height of the Gepatsch Dam (alt 1 767 m - 5 796 ft) is a wide, attractive view of the Weisseespitze mountain range.

The trip from Prutz to Landeck includes long sections of rocky *corniche* above the Inn, which is crossed by two bold, covered bridges.

Pontlatzerbrücke. – At the bridgehead on the left bank a memorial crowned with an eagle commemorates the battles in which the Tyrolese checked the Bavarians in 1703 (War of the Spanish Succession), and, in 1809, a French force marching on Finstermünz.

Landeck. – *Description p 101.*

From Landeck to Imst the valley is narrow and wooded. From the bridge at Zams there is a magnificent view of the slender ruins of Schrofenstein, clinging to the flank of the Brandkopf. In the forest, farther downstream, the tiny village of Zamserberg nestles below the ruins of the Kronburg.

At last you come out into the wide Imst basin, cut at either end by wooded gorges and, over to the east, in sight of the jagged crests of the Stubaier Alps.

Imst. – Pop 6 691. The Upper Town (Oberstadt), which is the more attractive with its houses with rounded window grilles and pretty fountains surmounted by old statues (St Sebastian), nestles round the imposing parish church (Pfarrkirche) of Gothic origin rebuilt after a fire in 1822, but preserving its Gothic doorways and, outside, the traditional gigantic statue of St Christopher *(p 30)*.

The well known Imst carnival, with its procession of *Schemenlaufen* (ghosts), takes place only every 4th or 5th year *(last time in 1981)*, but those who are interested may see the masks and dresses used on this occasion in the Tyrol Museum of Popular Art (Tiroler Volkskunstmuseum) in Innsbruck *(p 88)*.

Michelin map **426** fold 31 – *Local maps pp 90 and 143* – Pop 116 100 – Alt 574 m - 1 883 ft – ⓘ Burggraben 3 ☎ 25 715 – *Facilities pp 39 and 43*

Innsbruck (Bridge over the Inn) is at the junction of the Inn Valley and the Sill gap, on the road which runs, parallel with the railway, towards Italy. Several million cars a year are driven along it towards the Brenner Pass and the south. It is the cultural and tourist capital of the Tyrol and, besides Grenoble and Bolzano, the only town of more than 100 000 inhabitants inside the Alpine range.

The view along the Maria-Theresien-Strasse towards the steep slopes of the Nordkette (Karwendel mountain range) combines town-planning and landscape to form a **picture**★★ which has a leading place in the illustrations of tourist Europe. Many details show how closely man is linked with mountain life. At Innsbruck itself, though the altitude is less than 600 m - 2 000 ft – it is not unusual, in winter, to see employees and students devoting their midday break to the ski-runs starting from Seegrube, the halfway station of the Nordkette cablecar. The 1964 Winter Olympic Games marked a decisive development in the tourist amenities of Innsbruck: a ski-jump was constructed at Bergisel, an ice-stadium erected (indoor ice-rink) and an airport built. The superior quality of this equipment brought to the city the 1976 Winter Olympic Games – the already existing installations were improved and new equipment was built (speed skating track).

(After A.N.T.O. photo)

Innsbruck. - Maria-Theresien-Strasse.

The city, being only moderately industrialized, has kept its provincial character as soon as one leaves the main thoroughfares. The historical quarter is a pedestrian precinct as of 10.30am.

HISTORICAL NOTES

The Tyrol came into existence as a state in the 12C, on the southern slopes of the Alps. It is now part of Italy, but was then under the jurisdiction of the Counts of Tirol whose seat was above Merano.

In the 14C the Tyrol came under the Habsburgs. Power weighed in favour of the territories in the Inn Valley on the northern slopes of the mountain chain and Innsbruck, now the capital, knew a splendid development, particularly during the reign of Maximilian I.

"The Last Knight". – **Maximilian of Habsburg,** whose rich and stirring personality symbolizes the autumn of the Middle Ages for the Austrians, was invested with imperial rank in 1493. A great hunter, he believed that this sport was of prime importance for princes, since it enabled them to make contact with their more humble subjects.

"Max" married, as his first wife, Maria of Burgundy, the daughter of Charles the Bold, and by the increase of territorial power which their union brought him, justified the couplet so often applied to the Habsburg monarchy in later days:

> *"Bella gerant alii, tu, felix Austria, nube*
> *Nam quae Mars aliis, dat tibi regna Venus."*
> *i.e.* "Let others war, thou, happy Austria, wed;
> What some owe Mars, from Venus take instead."

It was in the parish Church of St James at Innsbruck that the second marriage of the Emperor with Bianca Maria Sforza took place in 1494.

Soon afterwards the Emperor had the famous Goldenes Dachl set up. This depicted him with his two wives and became the town's emblem. But his attachment went further than this; he chose Innsbruck as his burial-place and ordered the sumptuous Hofkirche to contain his mausoleum. However, this building was never to receive the remains of the Emperor, who, after seeing the town gates closed against him by its burghers, who were exasperated at the debts left there by the noblemen in his suite, died in 1519 at Wels, and was buried at Wiener Neustadt, his birthplace.

From Laughter to Tears (18C). – Innsbruck also knew a period of splendour under the reign of Maria Theresa. In 1750 the famous picture of the *Madonna* by Cranach – withdrawn from the former Church of St James which was badly damaged by an earthquake – was reinstalled in the rebuilt parish church. The Empress knelt in the state car which carried the picture. At the end of the procession was a boy of nine, proudly wearing Hungarian national dress. He was the future Josef II.

In 1765 the town was enlivened by new celebrations, dynastic this time. The imperial family was celebrating the marriage of Leopold, Grand Duke of Tuscany, with the Infanta of Spain, Maria Ludovica. A triumphal arch stood at the head of the present Maria-Theresien-Strasse. Suddenly consternation spread in the joyful city. The Emperor Franz had died suddenly. That is why the triumphal arch, which dates from these events, is devoted equally to earthly glories and to funeral trappings.

INNSBRUCK

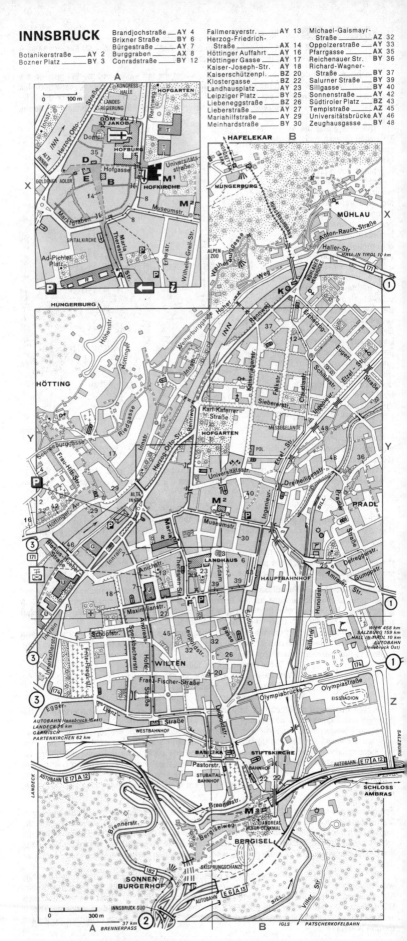

■ GENERAL VIEW

In the town itself the belfry (Stadtturm – *see below*) can be used as an observatory. To get a general view go up to the **Hungerburg★** (BX), either by car via the Alte Innbrücke (Old Bridge over the Inn), the Höttinger Gasse, the Hötting Church and the Höhenstrasse, or by funicular *(leaving the Mühlauer Innbrücke – the said Kettenbrücke – every 15 min from 9.10am to 7.55pm (inquire for early morning departure times) and every 1/2 hour from 8.10 to 10.40pm (11.10pm Fridays and Saturdays); 28S Rtn)*. From the belvedere-terrace you will see the town as a whole and the majestic peaks of the Serles and the Nockspitze which mark the entrance into the tranquil Stubaital Valley *(p 91)*, to the south.

Tourists coming down from the Brenner by car on road No. 182 should look out for a place called Sonnenburgerhof just before the last bends in the road; from the bend with the tram crossing, you will get an outstanding **general view★★** of Innsbruck.

■ MAIN SIGHTS *time: 2 hours*

Leave from St Anne's Column on the Maria-Theresien-Strasse.

Maria-Theresien-Strasse★ (AX). – This "street square" *(p 28)* affords an imposing **vista★★** of the Nordkette, whose rocky crown rises to an altitude of 2 334 m - 7 657 ft. Along this gap stand, in the foreground, the bulbous towers of the Spitalkirche and the belfry. St Anne's Column, white and standing against the greenish ochre background, is a traditional subject for amateur photographers.

St Anne's Column (Annasäule) (AX A). – This monument, set up in 1706, commemorates the 26 July 1703 – the birthday of St Anne – when the Bavarian invaders retreated during the War of the Spanish Succession (1703). The Virgin has the place of honour on the top of the slim column, St Anne appearing only on the base, beside St George, formerly the protector of the Tyrol (it is now St Joseph), and Sts Vigilius and Cassianus, who are the patron saints of Trent and Bressanone and whose dioceses formed the basis of the territorial unity of the region.

Prolonging the Maria-Theresien-Strasse is the Herzog Friedrich-Strasse, a busy street, whose arcades contain shops. In the centre of the street stands the Little Golden Roof.

Belfry (Stadtturm) (AX B). – The belfry stands beside the old town hall. The tower has a square base from which rises an octagonal Renaissance structure, bristling with turrets and crowned with a dome and a small lantern. *Open 1 April to 31 October 9am to 5pm (6pm in July and August); 15S; brochure available in English.*

Little Golden Roof★ (Goldenes Dachl) (AX D). – This charming structure, finished in 1500, is added to the styleless building which took the place of the former ducal palace. According to a tradition, which the most cultivated Tyrolese are sorry to see denied by irrefutable evidence, it was Friedrich the Penniless, Duke of the Tyrol (1406-1439), who, wishing to put an end to the jokes about his poverty, had this little roof, in full view of passers-by, covered with golden coins. As a matter of fact, the work dates from the reign of Maximilian and symbolizes the power of the Habsburgs. The whole thing, Gothic in style *(illustration p 33)* and with its decoration growing richer as it rises towards the roof, bears witness to the coming of the Renaissance.

The balustrade on the 1st floor is adorned with a frieze of delicately carved coats of arms, representing, from left to right, Styria (set back), Austria, Hungary, the Holy Roman Empire (a double-headed eagle), the kingdom of Germany (a single-headed eagle and a golden fleece), Philip the Fair (Maximilian's son), the Sforzas of Milan and the Tyrol (set back).

The 2nd storey looks like a lavishly decorated loggia. The designs on the balustrade, by the same hand as those on the 1st floor, include, in the centre, two pictures of Maximilian. On the left, the Emperor turns towards his second wife, Bianca Maria Sforza, who can be recognized by her long hair and her Italian headdress. The portrait of Maria, Maximilian's first wife, wearing the Burgundian headdress, completes the trio. On the right, Maximilian stands between his councillor (on the right) and his jester (on the left). The side panels each represent a couple of acrobatic dancers. The ensemble, the amusing work of a Swabian sculptor who was for a long time unknown, Niklas Türing the Elder, was used as the royal lodge during popular festivals and when tournaments were held. All of the original carvings, owing to their damaged condition, have had to give way to copies, but the originals can be inspected in the Tyrolean Museum known as the Ferdinandeum *(p 89)*.

Helblinghaus★ (AX E). – This house at the opposite corner of the Herzog Friedrich-Strasse was given, in the 18C, a Rococo facing, displaying lavishly decorated window frames and a highly decorated pediment. The arrangement of the windows in convex bows – a remedy for the lack of sunlight in the narrow streets of old cities – is still often seen in southern Germany. Farther to the left, towards the quays of the Inn, is the historic inn named the Golden Eagle (Goldener Adler). It is proud of the guests it has received since the 16C and displays their names on a marble plaque outside.

Return along the Maria-Theresien-Strasse, to take the narrow Pfarrgasse, which leads to the quiet Domplatz.

St James' Cathedral (Dom zu St. Jakob) (AX). – *Open 6am to noon and 2 to 5pm; closed Friday, Sunday and holiday mornings.*

The building, which was rebuilt at the beginning of the 18C, remains essentially the church of the Roman Catholic Old Tyrol.

The **interior★**, in the Baroque style, is roofed with domes – three on the nave and a dome with a lantern on the chancel – decorated in 1722 by a famous pair of artists from Munich, Cosmas Damian Asam (painter) and his brother Egid Quirin Asam (stucco worker); their compositions, with clever effects of perspective, glorify the intercessions of St James. Above the high altar the picture of *Our Lady of Succour* (Mariahilf), painted by Lucas Cranach the Elder and presented by the Elector of Saxony to the Archduke Leopold of the Tyrol, who took it with him on all his travels, is an object of deep devotion. In the north transept is the canopied tomb of the Archduke Maximilian (who must not be confused with the Emperor of Austria), a Grand Master of the Teutonic Order, who died in 1618. This tomb, which was restored to its original state in 1950, adds to the furnishings of the church a note of gravity which contrasts with the decorative exuberance of the pulpit and organ.

INNSBRUCK★★

Round the Cathedral of St James is the old town with its ancient, balconied houses. Their picturesque signs, reliefs, stuccos and frescos all make a most colourful picture.

Turn back. At the Little Golden Roof crossing, turn left into the narrow Hofgasse, then, after a covered alley, left again into the Rennweg, which skirts the Hofburg.

Hofburg★ (AX). – *Open 9am to 4pm; closed Sundays and holidays 16 October to 14 May; 15S; guided tours (35 min) in English; brochure available in English.*

Maria Theresa built the present palace, where her husband died during the fêtes of 1765, in place of a large building erected, little by little, on this site by the Habsburgs of the Tyrolean branch (Leopold III, the Penniless Friedrich IV, and Sigismund the Rich). The long and severe façade in "Maria Theresa yellow" *(p 163)* flanked by two domed towers, was finished in 1770 and is an example of the evolution of Baroque civil architecture in Innsbruck.

Inside, the state rooms, which may be visited, are devoted to the glories of the Tyrol and of the Habsburg monarchy, especially the **Giant's Hall**★★ (Riesensaal). This state room, lined with stucco panels with a porcelain finish, is about 31.5 m - 100 ft long. The ceiling was painted by Franz Anton Maulpertsch in 1776. The main theme is the triumph of the House of Habsburg-Lorraine, personified by two women holding their hands out to one another.

On the walls are full-length portraits of Maria Theresa's children following the imperial couple in procession. Above these portraits are places kept for kin and descendants. Among them is Louis XVI, shown as a young man above the picture of Marie-Antoinette.

Return to the Rennweg and enter the Hofkirche *(enter by the Tyrol Museum of Popular Art, left of the church)*.

Hofkirche (AX). – *Open 1 May to 30 September 9am to 5pm; 1 October to 30 April 9am to noon and 2 to 5pm; 15S; brochure available in English.*

This church was built by Ferdinand I *(see genealogical tree p 23)* who finally realized the projects of his grandfather Maximilian I. The nave and three aisles, all equal in size, built to contain Maximilian's mausoleum, is still Gothic in style, although masked in part by Renaissance (tower, entrance porch, capitals) and Baroque additions (stuccos).

On the gallery are placed the 23 statuettes of the protecting saints of the Habsburg family. The comparative grace of these effigies makes them more engaging than the sombre colossi who actually stand guard over the tomb.

Maximilian's Mausoleum★ (Grabmal Kaiser Maximilians I). – This tomb is the most important specimen left to us of German Renaissance sculpture. In the Emperor's mind it was intended to glorify the splendours of his reign, and also to record the flawless legitimacy of the Holy Roman Empire as the heir of the Caesars.

The original plan was grandiose but not illusory, for Innsbruck at that time enjoyed international renown for its bell founders and armour makers. The plan included, in particular, 40 large statues, 100 small bronzes of saints and 34 busts of Roman emperors. Inspite of a century of work this programme was not fully completed when, in 1584, the casting of the kneeling statue of Maximilian which crowns the structure marked the end of the work.

The 28 impressive statues of the "black fellows", as the people of Innsbruck call them, all in bronze save two which are in copper, and all more than life-size, stand on guard over the empty tomb. A torch could be set in the right hand of each during funeral services. The choice of figures is sometimes unexpected: it takes into account the ties of blood and marriage. Here are the royal families of Habsburg, Burgundy and Austria, but also the purely sentimental lineage of heroes of chivalry or precursors of mediaeval Christianity: King Arthur, Theodoric of Verona and Clovis. The contribution of Albrecht Dürer undoubtedly raises the artistic level of the group, with the statues of King Arthur – a British-looking type in armour! – and of Theodoric, a supple and vigorous work. These figures offer, to the admirer of old modes of dress, great pictorial value.

The tomb itself is surrounded with a splendid Renaissance grille in which, according to the Tyrolean taste of the period *(see Stams p 144)*, wrought iron and embossed sheet-metal are combined. It is surmounted by the kneeling statue of Maximilian and supported at the four corners by statues of the cardinal virtues, all carved by Alexandre Colin of Malines (Belgium – 1527–1612). Reliefs in marble, all except three panels, by this same Alexandre Colin, cover the sides of the structure, depicting great events of the reign (battles, weddings, etc.).

After going round the tomb do not neglect the Renaissance furnishings of the chancel and church, on the north side, the gallery known as the Princes' Chancel and the 1567 stalls.

The Hofkirche has also played the part of a national church of the Tyrol since the revolt of 1809. It contains the tomb and memorial of **Andreas Hofer** (1767-1810), hero of the Tyrolean uprising against Napoleon, which you will see as you go out.

Silver Chapel★★ (Silberne Kapelle). – This separate chapel, built by Archduke Ferdinand of Tyrol *(see genealogical tree p 23 and p 90)* so that he might rest beside his wife who was a commoner, was finished in 1587.

It owes its name to the large embossed silver Madonna, surrounded by designs representing the symbols of the Litanies, which are to be seen on the altarpiece of rare wood. The first bay, near the entrance on the left, contains the tomb of Philippine Welser, the beloved wife of Ferdinand, and is one of the most highly finished works of the Flemish master **Alexandre Colin** *(see above)* in his maturity. Nearer to the altar, the funeral statue of Ferdinand, by the same sculptor, depicts the deceased armed. His own armour is displayed separately on a console, in a kneeling position, facing the altar. A small 16C cedarwood organ, of Italian origin, completes the artistic reliquary formed by the chapel.

■ ADDITIONAL SIGHTS

Town Centre

Tyrol Museum of Popular Art★★ (Tiroler Volkskunstmuseum) (AX M¹). – *Open 9am to 5pm; 9am to noon Sundays and holidays; closed on certain holidays; 15S; brochure available in English.*

The ground floor displays a collection of Tyrolean mangers from their origins to the present.

The upper floors are devoted mainly to the showing of *Stuben* (best rooms). The panelling, ceilings and monumental stoves, taken from peasants' homes, are sometimes in the Gothic decorative style (1st floor) and sometimes in the Renaissance or Baroque periods (2nd floor).

On the 1st floor a collection of models of Tyrolean houses – in masonry, with the oriels (*Erker*) of the Upper Inn Valley, in wood from the Zillertal, where they resemble the classic Swiss chalet of the Bernese Oberland, etc. The exhibit illustrates clearly the position of the Tyrol as a melting pot of civilizations.

Equally presented are domestic utensils made of wood or leather and decorated with great ingenuity, tools, musical instruments and games.

Other rooms are reserved for ironwork, textiles and looms, glass and pottery.

Large collections of peasant costumes, religious objects, furniture, and folklore costumes, especially the adornments used at the Imst carnival *(p 85)*, are displayed in the rooms on the 2nd floor.

"Ferdinandeum" Tyrol Museum★ (Tiroler Landesmuseum "Ferdinandeum") (AX M²). – *Open 2 May to 30 September 9am to 5pm (noon Sundays and holidays); October through April 9am to noon and 2 to 4pm; closed Sunday and holiday afternoons and Mondays in winter only; 14S.*
This museum is devoted essentially to the development of the fine arts in the Tyrol. A large part of the museum is concerned with Tyrolean Gothic art and many works displayed also have historical value. This is the case with the 1370 chapel altar of Tirol Castle *(p 90)*, the original bas-reliefs of the Goldenes Dachl, etc. There is also a good collection of Dutch masters.

Hofgarten (BY). – This public garden with shady lakes and fine weeping willows offers the visitor to Innsbruck welcome relaxation. Evening concerts are held in the gardens in summer.

Landhaus (BY). – The Landhaus, which is an excellent specimen of Baroque civil architecture, was built from 1725 to 1728 by Georg Anton Gumpp to house the Diet and the provincial government. The grand staircase is adorned with stucco and displays statues and busts of antique gods. Note the ceiling design: the eagle of the Tyrol holding the map of the province.

Triumphal Arch (Triumphpforte) (AY F). – The arch commemorates the days of rejoicing and mourning which marked the year 1765 (marriage of Archduke Leopold) for the Tyrol *(p 96)*.
On the south side, the monument is crowned by the medallion of Franz I and Maria Theresa, while statues of the betrothed couple can be seen on the left side (on the right are the sisters of the Infanta). The north face of the monument bears symbols of mourning (medallion of Franz I being displayed by the Angel of Death, and a woman mourning the Emperor's death).

The Bergisel Panorama (Riesenrundgemälde) (BX K). – *Beside the Hungerburg funicular station. Open 1 April to 31 October 9am to 5pm; 16S; brochure available in English.*
This huge circular fresco depicting the Battle of Bergisel *(p 91)* was painted in honour of Andreas Hofer.

Innsbruck-Wilten, Bergisel and Ambras – plan p 86

The Wilten quarter is where the River Sill, running down from the Brenner, emerges from its final gorge to flow towards the cone built up by its alluvial soil. This was the site of the Roman town of Veldidena. To the south it abuts on Bergisel, a wooded eminence which became a sacred spot in the Tyrol after the battles on its slopes between Napoleon's troops and the Tyrolese insurgents under Andreas Hofer in 1809.

Wilten Abbey Church (Stiftskirche) (BZ). – The Abbey of Wilten, entrusted to the Premonstratensians in 1128, is the institution most closely connected with the origins of modern Innsbruck. The monks of St Norbert, in fact, owned all the land south of the Inn. It was only by an agreement made in 1180 between the Counts of Andech, who represented the civil power at the time, and their prior, that the primitive settlement on the left bank was moved to the present "old town" (the Hofburg quarter).
The church, which can be recognized from a distance by its red roughcast, is a Baroque building of the 17C, restored after damage in 1944. The façade, transformed in 1716 by the same architect who did the Landhaus *(see above)*, is deeply convex on each side of the doorway, which is guarded by two stone giants wearing the warrior costumes of classical tragedy. They represent Aymon, on the left, and Thyrsus, on the right.
In the narthex, enclosed by a magnificent **grille★** dating from 1707, with luxuriant adornments of foliage, is another statue, also in wood and more naïvely carved. This is the giant Aymon, sculpted in about 1500 who came from the Rhine Valley, and according to tradition founded the abbey as an act of expiation for the murder of the local giant, Thyrsus, he also rid the nearby Sill gorge of a tiresome dragon.
The building proper has a certain distinction with its series of altarpieces in black wood, relieved with gold, but many of the paintings and stuccos adorning the vaulting had to be restored. Above the high altar, note the work known as *Solomon's Throne,* a sort of gallery on a reduced scale, framed between columns and lions, which opens a vista towards a Christ seated on a throne.

Wilten Basilica★ (BZ). – In order to perpetuate devotion to Our Lady of the Four Columns, who had been the object of a popular pilgrimage at Innsbruck since the Middle Ages, the Premonstratensians of the nearby monastery had the parish church of Wilten completely restored between 1751 and 1756. The church was raised to the status of a basilica in 1957.
Inside, the building bears witness to the skill of the artists of the Rococo period, and especially of a team of decorators formed by a stucco-moulder, Franz-Xaver Feichtmayr, of the Wessobrunn School, and a painter from Augsburg, Matthäus Günther. Stuccos in the forms of flowers, scrolls and angels are arranged most successfully in the escutcheons. The excellent paintings on the vaulting depict, in the chancel, the Virgin as an advocate, and in the nave the Biblical figures, Esther and Judith. The statue of the Virgin which the pilgrims venerate stands at the high altar, under a baldachin with marble columns.

Bergisel (BZ). – *Reached by car via the Brenner road, the Bergiselweg and the avenue leading into the park.* This wooded hill has been pleasantly laid out for walks, and many city people come to it in search of rest or pleasure. The construction, in the background of a ski-jump recalls the 1964 and 1976 Winter Olympic Games. Several monuments, especially the statue of Andreas Hofer, commemorate the combats of 1809, but the "panorama" depicting the fighting is on the far side of the town *(see above)*.

The **Memorial to the Imperial Light Infantry** (Kaiserjägermuseum BZ M³) *(open 9am to 6pm (4pm in winter); closed Mondays; 10S; brochure available in English)* contains mementoes of the 1809 uprising and of the Tyrolean crack corps (arms, uniforms and paintings), which was disbanded in 1919.

From the various rooms, and especially from the moving 1914-1918 war memorial on the ground floor, there are open **views★** of the town of Innsbruck and the mountain barrier of the Nordkette.

Ambras Castle (Schloss Ambras). – *Open 1 May to 30 September 10am to 4pm; closed Tuesdays. 10S.*

Leave Innsbruck by the Olympiastrasse *(southeast of plan p 86)* turn off to the right *(leave the skating rink behind you)* and go under the motorway, then left onto the Aldrans Road then after about 500 m - 550 yds bear left towards the Ambras Castle.

The extensive rearrangements of the castle, have resulted, since the end of the 16C, in the castle being divided into two groups of buildings: the "lower castle", which includes the present entrance lodge, and the "upper castle", a former mediaeval fortress, much remodelled. This was the favourite residence of the Archduke Ferdinand (1529-1595), Regent of the Tyrol, and the beautiful Philippine Welser, his first and morganatic wife, whose memory the people of Innsbruck still revere in the Silver Chapel.

Ferdinand, a keen collector, had accumulated in the various rooms a huge and mixed quantity of *objets d'art* – especially armour and portraits.

During the years that followed parts of the collection were dismantled by the Habsburgs, and moved to their home in Vienna. In the lower castle is the gallery of **Arms and Armour★** with its exhibits of jousting equipment.

Also on display is a room (Kunst- und Wunderkammer) which includes rare objects – either by their value or interest (minerals, animals, robots, objects used in the celebration of bacchic ceremonies...) – which were collected at that time. On the way to the upper castle is the huge Spanish room with its valuable Renaissance inlaid ceiling.

Upper Castle. – *Guided tours only (1 1/4 hours - additional 10S)* at 10 and 11am, noon, 2, 3, and 3.30pm. There is a gallery of Habsburg portraits (15-18C). The furniture tapestries and frescos complete the Renaissance furnishings of the castle.

EXCURSIONS

Local map below

Hafelekar★★. – Alt 2 334 m - 7 657 ft – *You should allow 2 hours for this excursion by cable-car, which starts from the Hungerburg (access p 87). During the summer season the service operates at least hourly between 8.10am and 6pm; 158S Rtn.*

A magnificent belvedere overlooks the Inn Valley and the Stubai Alps, to the south, and to the north the chalky heights of the Karwendel.

Tour of the Mittelgebirge★★(Medium Mountains) via Hall in Tirol, Igls and the Ellbögen road. – *67 km - 42 miles – about 4 hours. The Ellbögen road is a narrow corniche road and with a gradient up to 1 in 7.*

Leave Innsbruck by ①, the road to Vienna.

Hall in Tirol. – *Description p 80.*

The road to Tulfes crosses the Inn goes under the motorway and, as it climbs, affords attractive open views of the town of Hall, its three church towers and the Bettelwurf range in the Karwendel massif. 2 km - 1 mile from the bridge, after a rotunda-chapel on the right, turn left into the downhill road leading to the isolated church of Volders.

Volders★. – *Description p 169.*

Turn back, and again take the road on the left to Tulfes, which soon emerges on the plateau where the attractive villages of Tulfes, Rinn, Sistrans and Lans appear, facing the Nordkette.

Igls★. – Pop 1 678. *Facilities see Innsbruck pp 39 and 43.* This resort, of long-established repute, has taken on new life since the 1976 Olympic Games, with the building of a rather daring toboggan and bobsled run. It enjoys a terrace setting and the resinous scents of the forest. Its sporting facilities indicate the proximity of a large town and the favour of a wealthy clientele. The Patscherkofel cable-car and the chairlift which continues to the summit, have made more summer and winter excursions possible on the nearby wooded slopes. These face north and make good snowfields.

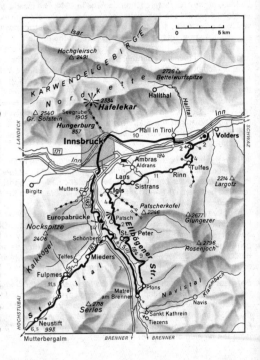

The **Ellbögen road★★**, which was once used for carting salt, runs above the Sill Valley, and is crossed, below, by the first stretch of the Brenner motorway which goes over the famous Europa Bridge. At the entrance to Patsch the road affords a **view★** along the length of the Stubaital, which opens out at the foot of the sharp pyramid of the Serles and the more clumsy snow-capped summit of the Habicht in the middle distance. After St. Peter, a village clinging to a promontory, the slope is steeper and the run becomes hilly. You join the road to the Brenner at Matrei, bearing right, towards Innsbruck. *See on p 56 for the sights on the Brenner road, between Matrei and Innsbruck.*

The Stubaital★. – *44 km - 27 miles as far as Mutterbergalm – about 2 hours – Local map p 90.* Leave Innsbruck by ② and take the Brennerstrasse; 15 km - 9 miles further bear right towards Schönberg. The Stubaital, a valley with long even slopes clothed with larches, forms a striking contrast in its deep calm with the valley from which it branches off, the Sill, where a constant stream of cars make for the Brenner Pass.

Mieders, situated on a sunny terrace, **Fulpmes** *(facilities p 39 and 43)*, which specializes in mountaineering gear, and **Neustift** the highest resort - alt 993 m - 3 258 ft *(facilities p 41 and 43)* are highly developed resorts.

In 1973 the glacial amphitheatre, which marks the valley's beginnings, was rearranged into an all year-round ski resort, **Hochstubai** (alt 3 200 m - 10 496 ft); access is by taking the Gletscherbahn cable-car at **Mutterbergalm** (alt 1 728 m - 5 669 ft).

ISCHL, Bad ★ (Upper Austria)

Michelin map **426** fold 21 – *Local maps pp 137 and 139* – Pop 13 027 – Alt 469 m - 1 539 ft – **⊞** **☎** 3520 – *Facilities p 39*

Bad Ischl is in the heart of the Salzkammergut and is the watering-place in Austria on which the reign of Franz-Josef has left the greatest marks of luxury, having been for seventy years one of the most brilliant centres of fashionable life in Europe. The therapeutic properties of its saline waters, brought to notice about 1820 by a Viennese practitioner, Dr Wirer, were confirmed by some historic cures like those which justified the nickname of "Princes of the Salt", given to the children of the Archduchess Sophia, and first of all to Franz-Josef.

Franz-Josef, by fixing his summer quarters here, near his favourite shooting-grounds, made it a country resort which attracted many crowned heads, actors, fashionable composers and painters. The list included Anton Bruckner, Johann Strauss, Brahms, Millöcker and Franz Lehar (whose villa has been arranged as a museum) for music, Ferdinand Waldmüller and Rudolf von Alt for painting, Lenau and Nestroy for poetry and the theatre. With the disappearance of court life, the spa has concentrated its efforts on the renewal of its thermal equipment, in rebuilding the medical establishment (Kurmittelhaus) and in modernizing the majestic Kurhaus or casino.

The resort. – The resort groups its *Biedermeier* style buildings *(p 34)* and parks in a setting of densely wooded mountains, on the inside of a loop formed by the rivers Traun and Ischl. The **Auböckplatz,** bordered by the drinking-hall *(Trinkhalle),* a former pumproom (1831), and the parish church reconstructed at the end of the reign of Maria Theresa, is the traditional centre of town life.

Joining the Auböckplatz with the Elizabeth Bridge (Elisabeth Brücke) spanning the Traun, the **Pfarrgasse,** which is the main shopping street of Ischl, still shows such survivals from the cure life of the 19C as the Zauner Café and pastry shop. The Pfarrgasse ends at the **Esplanade,** a shady walk beside the Traun, which was once the domain of the rich *Salzfertiger* (salt refiners). These men were allowed to store the salt on the Treasury account before it was embarked on the river. One of their dwellings, the Seeauer House (No. 10), with a Rococo façade, and triple gables, has kept its original character. Before it became the Hotel Aus-

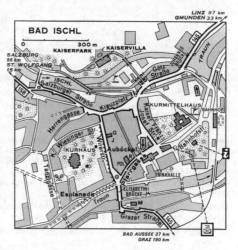

tria, the parents of Franz-Josef stayed there as guests from 1844 to 1877. The unfortunate Maximilian, Emperor of Mexico was born there in 1832.

■ **THE IMPERIAL VILLA★ (Kaiservilla)** time: 1 hour

Guided tours in English (30 min) 1 May to 15 October 9am to noon and 1 to 5pm (in winter weekends only noon to 4pm); 40S.

The villa stands to the north of the town, on the left bank of the Ischl, in a magnificent landscape garden, the **Kaiserpark.** It was given to the imperial couple as a wedding present by the Archduchess Sophia. Though it has colonnades in the ancient style, the house reveals the simple character of Franz-Josef by the importance given to hunting, of which he was an ardent devotee and the sovereign disregard of modern comfort and amenities to be found in his private apartments (the study and the bedroom). One of the more moving parts of the tour is the visit to the empress's Grey Saloon, off which lie the oratory and her private cabinet. This is exactly as it was left by "Sissi" on 16 July 1898 on the eve of her departure for Geneva – a journey from which she never returned.

Continue the tour with a walk in the park to the small marble château, the Marmorschlössel, a favourite retreat of the Empress Elizabeth, who made it in some degree her Trianon and which is, today, a Photography museum *(open 1 April to 31 October 9.30am to 5pm; 10S).*

The limestone massif of the Kaisergebirge is surrounded by the continuous depression in which Kufstein, Walchsee, Kössen, Griesenau, St. Johann in Tirol and Ellmau stand. It is well known for its mountaineering routes and is one of the most detached of the Northern Limestone Alps. This fact enables the motorist to easily distinguish the peaks of its outer limits.

In detail, the Kaiser has two crest lines: to the south, the highest, the **Wilder** (wild) **Kaiser** (alt 2 344 m - 7 690 ft) raises steep walls which can be seen from Kitzbühel and even better from Ellmau; to the north, the less jagged **Zahmer** (tame) **Kaiser** displays a more marked base of Alpine pasture. The Kaisertal, separating these two groups, runs between Kufstein and the Stripsenjoch (alt 1 577 m - 5 174 ft). On the opposite slope of the Stripsenjoch, lies the Kaiserbachtal, which cars climb from Griesenau. This has become the most convenient way into the massif.

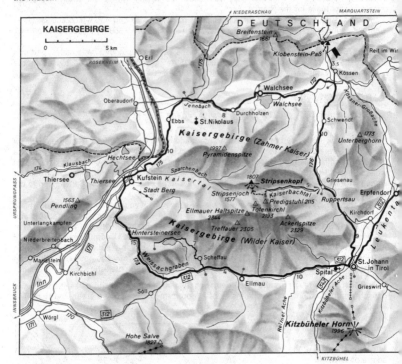

From Lofer to Kufstein – *54 km - 34 miles – about 1 1/2 hours – Local map above and opposite.*

The starting point of the trip is the Saalach Valley, at the foot of the Loferer Steinberge, a fine chalky massif. Before the Wilder Kaiser it affords pretty scenes of mountain life in the Strub Valley.

As soon as you leave Lofer *(p 106)* your eye is caught by the summits of the Loferer Steinberge. The valley narrows to the width only of the wooded ravine of the Pass Strub (memorial commemorating the fighting by Tyrolean rebels in 1800, 1805 and 1809), where the torrent rushes in a bubbling foam.

Beyond the Pass Strub the run through the Strub Valley affords a few more views of the Loferer Steinberge.

West of the Strub Pass the itinerary leaves the modern road, No. 312, to follow the old road serving the hamlet of Strub and the village of Waidring.

Strub. – Although decrepit, even the oldest houses have kept their Tyrolean character and style.

Waidring. – Pop 1 494. *Facilities p 42.* A group of houses with flower decked balconies, little belfries and shingle roofs, weighed down with stones, make a charming picture round a square with a fountain.

The arrival at Erpfendorf from the east is marked by the sight of the heart of the Leukental, a valley in which stand the church towers of Erpfendorf and Kirchdorf.

Erpfendorf. – Pop 840. The church, finished in 1957, is the work of Clemens Holzmeister, a master of contemporary religious architecture in Austria and author of the plans for the new building for the Salzburg Festival.

The belfry, entrance porch, and chapel containing oriel shaped fonts, wider at the top than at the foot, are brought together in a group which cleverly does away with the need for a façade.

The interior decoration which is progressing consists of stained glass windows (1971), mosaics in the chancel and woodwork (a rood beam depicting the Crucifixion).

From Erpfendorf to St. Johann, through the Leukental, the route enables you, when passing Kirchdorf and on arriving at St. Johann, to enjoy ideal views of the Wilder Kaiser.

St. Johann in Tirol. – *Description p 124.*

It is the section from St. Johann to Ellmau which affords the most distinct views of the south wall of the Wilder Kaiser, with the Treffauer as its outwork.

Spital. – This 13C hospice, surrounded by the buildings of an agricultural school and standing alone in the St. Johann basin, is marked by two century-old lime trees. It was decorated in 1744 by the painter Simon-Benedikt Faistenberger, a native of Kitzbühel. The window behind the high altar is the only authentic 15C specimen of stained glass still extant in the Tyrol.

Ellmau. – Pop 1 847. *Facilities p 39.* The village, slightly away from the main road, has a charming setting of which a little bulbous towered chapel, standing opposite the Kaisergebirge, is a feature.

Hintersteinersee. – *7 km - 3 miles by the road to Scheffau, which is prolonged by the lake road. This is fit for wheeled traffic, but narrow, steep and badly sited.*
The dark waters of this mountain lake reflect the Treffauer bastion.

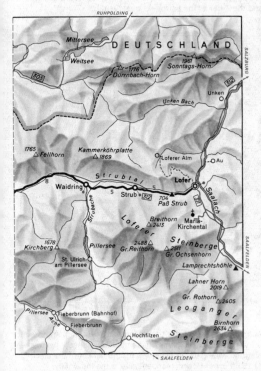

Leaving road No. 312, which goes on to Wörgl via the Söll shelf, the road plunges into the Weissach ravine, to cross the river on a bridge over a small gorge. Beyond this bottleneck, clouded up by the cement factory, may be seen the fortress at Kufstein (*p 99*).

From Kufstein to St. Johann in Tirol –
44 km - 27 miles – about 2 hours – Local map opposite.

Skirting the Kaisergebirge to the north, the road, marked with villages such as Ebbs and Walchsee whose comfortable houses show, by their style, the proximity of Bavaria, continues first at the foot of the slopes of the Zahmer Kaiser, and then through a more cruel landscape towards the Wilder Kaiser mountain walls.

North of Kufstein (*p 99*) the Kaisergebirge massif ends above the alluvial plain of the Inn in great precipices cut through by the terminal gorge of the Sparchenbach, a torrent whose valley – the Kaisertal – runs into the heart of the massif. Leaving the foot of these cliffs, the road affords an extensive view of the Ebbs plain, dominated by the pilgrims' Church of St Nikolaus, which is perched on a wooded foothill.

Between Durchholzen and the Walchsee, the corridor through which you run opens out into a harmonious combe, partly drowned by the lake but overlooked by a few peaks of the Zahmer Kaiser.

Walchsee. – Pop 1 321. *Facilities p 42.* The road runs along the north shore of this lake which is equipped for water sports. The village of the same name owes its tourist activity to this lake.

Klobenstein Pass. – *From the Kössen southern crossroads, 3.5 km - 2 miles, plus 1/4 hour on foot Rtn (Austrian customs control). Access and description p 98.*

South of Kössen, as you cross a hump, you will find a more extensive view, which now reaches, ahead, to the rocky Wilder Kaiser.

From a clearing containing the inn at Griesenau, one of the mountaineering centres of the massif, you can enjoy vistas of the Ackerlspitze cliffs.

Stripsenkopf*. – *From Griesenau, 5 km - 3 miles (toll: 24S per car) plus 4 hours on foot Rtn.* From the Griesener Alpe, terminus of the motor road, you climb to the Stripsenjoch Pass (mountain hotel) and then, turn northwards, to the summit of the Stripsenkopf (alt 1 807 m 5 928 ft). There is a closeup **view*** of the magnificent north walls of the Wilder Kaiser.

The last part of the trip encourages a halt. After the romantic Ruppertsau clearing, the horizon broadens. The road ends in a pretty **panoramic descent*** through the meadows above the Leukental and the St. Johann in Tirol (*p 124*) basin, facing the knolls of the Kitzbühel Alps.

The KARWENDEL ★ (Tyrol and Bavaria)
Michelin map **426** fold 17 – North of Innsbruck

The limestone massif of the Karwendel (highest point: the Birkkarspitze, 2 749 m - 9 019 ft) – whose first section, the Nordkette, lies north of Innsbruck, can also be seen as an impressive feature from Mittenwald or from the road to the Achensee (*p 94*). But only an excursion into the Rissbach Valley with a possible detour through Bavaria will enable the motorist to get near the greyish, pitted cliffs, the *Kar (p 12)* which give their character to these mountains.

Although you may not have time to do the "detour" leave the Inn Valley bottom and admire the Lake of Achensee, the largest in the Tyrol.

From the Inn Valley to the Sylvenstein Dam (Germany) – *39 km*
- 24 miles – about 1 1/2 hours – Local map below

This transverse route in the northern Alps links, by the Achenpass defile, the Inn Valley to the Upper Isar Valley or the Tegernsee (see Michelin Green Guide to Germany). The corniche section above the Achensee is the high point of the tour. Customs control on leaving Achenwald.
Beginning at the Inn Valley *(exit on motorway "Wiesing-Achensee"),* the panoramic ascent faces the mouth of the Zillertal.

Kanzelkehre★★. – An arranged belvedere-curve. The **view**★★ looks down on the Inn Valley and the Lower Zillertal, which is dotted with very sharp steeples (Wiesing in the foreground). The majestic Rofangebirge mountain peaks stand to the north.

Eben. – The church of this Lilliputian village contains the chalice of St Notburga, who is much venerated in Bavaria and the Tyrol as the patroness of servants.

Erfurter Hütte. – Alt 1 834 m - 6 033 ft. Allow 1 hour Rtn, including 20 minutes by cableway – the "Rofanbahn" – leaves (1 to 10 departures in an hour) during the season 9am to 5pm; 90S Rtn). This hut, the departure point for ascensions of the Rofangebirge massif, is set in a magnificent panorama above the Achensee and the Karwendel.

Achensee★★. – Facilities see at Maurach and Pertisau pp 41 and 42. Geographers will be interested in the local anomaly of the parting of the waters between the Isar (to the north) and Inn (to the south) basins. The lake empties, through the Achenbach, a tributary of the Isar, though

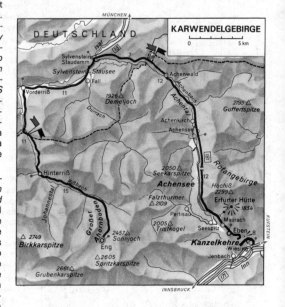

the sheet of water lies in a hanging valley over the trench formed by the Inn. A morainic barrier, created by the former Inn glacier, explains this phenomenon. Engineers have taken advantage of the site by tapping the waters of the Achensee for the benefit of the electrical power station about 350 m - 1 150 ft lower down, near Jenbach, in the Inn Valley.

The road, forming a corniche, offers the finest **view**★★ of the Karwendel summits, which rise massively round Pertisau on the opposite shore.

To drive along the edge of the lake, turn round at the village of Achensee and use the old road (one way: north–south).

The Sylvenstein Dam (Sylvenstein-Staudamm) is described in the Michelin Green Guide to Germany.

From the Sylvenstein Dam to Eng – *37 km - 23 miles – about 1 1/2 hours – Local map above*

The road, which is narrow and undulating cannot be used from December to May. Customs control between Vorderriss and Hinterriss. Leaving the banks to the artificial lake, once at Vorderriss, turn left into the deep Rissbach Valley.

Hinterriss. – Hinterriss, one of the holiday resorts of the Belgian Royal Family, groups its few houses near the hunting lodge built in the 19C for the Duke of Coburg-Gotha.
Scan through binoculars the slopes and steep cliffs overlooking the road, to see some of the 5 000 chamois which still live on the massif.

Eng. – The road ends here, in the **Grosser Ahornboden**★, a grassland where the maples glow with magnificent colours in the autumn to deck this otherwise severe landscape.
The walls of the Spritzkarspitze (alt 2 605 m - 8 547 ft) and the Grubenkarspitze (alt 2 661 m - 8 727 ft) mark the circular end to the valley.

The KATSCHBERG Road (Salzburg and Carinthia)
Michelin map **426** folds 34 and 35

Tourists anxious to arrive at the lakes of Carinthia, from Salzburg, will use the tunnel, instead of the Katschberg Pass, before descending into the Lieser Valley.

From St. Michael im Lungau to Spittal an der Drau – *43 km - 27 miles – about 1 1/2 hours – Profile of the road p 118*

A toll must be paid at the Katschberg tunnel April through September: 90S; October through March 50S.

Behind the tunnel, just before Rennweg, the view opens up onto the Upper Lieser Valley, with the village of St. Peter in the foreground. Below Rennweg, the road follows the Lieser River.

Gmünd. – Pop 2 607. Gmünd guarded, for the Archbishops of Salzburg, the old strategic and trading route from Nuremberg to Venice which went by way of the Radstädter Tauern and the Katschberg. The small town, which is still walled, has a fortified gateway at each end of its sunny and typical Strassenplatz *(p 28)*.

The most conspicuous buildings in Gmünd are two large châteaux. The older (15 to 17C), still decidedly military, rears above the roofs of the city. Its walls lost their crenellations in a fire in 1886. The New Château (Neues Schloss), which abuts on the town gate on the Katschberg side, was built in 1651 by Count Christoph Lodron, the brother of Pâris Lodron *(p 130)*. It presents on the side of the fine public gardens, a façade whose mass is relieved by two tall octagonal staircase-towers.

The valley, more and more winding, becomes a regular ravine. On this torrent-like section of the Lieser, kayak championships often take place.

The road, leaves the **Lake of Millstatt** to the east *(Millstatt – 6 km - 4 miles)* arriving at Spittal an der Drau *(p 144)* in the Drava Valley.

KEFERMARKT (Upper Austria)

Michelin map 426 fold 9 – 10 km - 6 miles south of Freistadt – *Local map p 105* – Pop 1 744 – Alt 512 m - 1 680 ft

Kefermarkt stands on the left bank of the Feldaist, in a restful, hilly landscape marking the transition between the Mühlviertel *(p 105)* and the Waldviertel, granite plateaux north of the Danube.

Church of St Wolfgang. – This Gothic church, contains a remarkable altarpiece of carved wood. *Ask the Sacristan at his house across from the church (No. 2) for the key.*

Altarpiece★★. – The altarpiece is in the chancel, behind the high altar. It is outstanding for its monumental size – it is more than 13 m - 40 ft high – the beauty of its proportions and the carved decoration, which show the exceptional skill of the artist. The altarpiece was made at the end of the 15C by an unknown sculptor and was probably painted, originally. Today all its carved portions, in high or low relief, are in the natural limewood.

Under richly carved canopies three figures – St Wolfgang, flanked by St Peter and St Christopher – occupy the central panel. The skill of the draping and expression of the faces recall the admirable composition of the altarpiece of St Wolfgang in the Salzkammergut, a masterpiece by Michael Pacher.

On the shutters flanking the central panel can be recognized, above: the Annunciation and the Birth of Christ; below, the Adoration of the Magi and the Dormition of the Virgin.

KITZBÜHEL ★★ (Tyrol)

Michelin map 426 folds 18 and 19 – Pop 7 872 – Alt 762 m - 2 500 ft – 🖪 ☎ 2155 and 2272 – *Facilities pp 39 and 43*

In spite of the tourist development, which is most evident in winter, Kitzbühel, the birthplace of Toni Sailer the triple Olympic champion in the 1956 games, has preserved the atmosphere of a little walled town. The original site – a terrace bounded by the beds of two streams flowing down from the Hahnenkamm – can still be discerned. The nucleus of the town, which is crossed by the "Vorderstadt" and "Hinterstadt" streets – pedestrian streets – still has sharp-ridged roofs on sturdily built houses with gables facing the street, in the Bavarian style *(illustration p 28)*.

Kitzbühel Alps (Kitzbüheler Alpen). – Between the Wörgl-Saalfelden gap and the Upper Valley of the Salzach, the Kitzbühel Alps, smoothly rounded in flinty soil, reach an altitude of 2 362 m - 7 749 ft – at the Grosser Rettenstein. Pleasant and restful "cow-pasture mountains" as they are known locally, *Grasberge* or turf mountains.

The contrasting shapes and colours of the surrounding massifs: the jagged walls of the Wilder Kaiser in the north and the enormous ridge of the High Tauern in the south, make the Kitzbühel Alps a massif much sought after for the quality of its views.

Winter sports at Kitzbühel. – Ski lifts, developed steadily since 1928, continue to spread. Today they serve some 56 ski-runs, to count only those that lead back to the Kitzbühel Valley. The division of the lines into various sections, following different directions, enables a wide variety of ski-runs to be combined without repeated journeys – this arrangement is known as the Kitzbühel Roundabout (Skizirkus). Skiers can make their base high up where conditions are most favourable, as for instance in the upper combe of the Ehrenbach (cable-car to the Hahnenkamm – *in summer departure every 1/2 hour; 60S Rtn)* or in the Trattalm amphitheatre at the foot of the Kitzbühler Horn.

The boldest skiers have many opportunities for runs down the reverse slopes of familiar heights to Kirchberg, Jochberg, and Grieswirt from which the train or the bus brings them back to Kitzbühel.

As regards competition skiing, the descent from the Hahnenkamm on the famous Streif run produces feats often attracting international attention.

KITZBÜHEL

0   300 m

Bichlstraße	2	J-Pirchl-Straße	7
Franz-Reisch-Straße	3	Klostergasse	8
Graggaugasse	4	Malinggasse	9
Hinterstadt	5	Sonnenhofweg	10
Jochberger Straße	6	Vorderstadt	12

KITZBÜHEL★★

■ **SIGHTS** *time: 45 min*

Parish Church (Pfarrkirche). – Like the neighbouring Liebfrauenkirche the church is set off by its raised site. The slender tower flanks a Gothic triple nave 15C, whose large overhanging roof, covered with shingles, gives it a distinctive mountain style.

The short nave is not without grace. A local family, the **Faistenbergers,** whose members were all well known artists of the 17 and 18C, is represented by the high altar, due to Benedikt Faistenberger (1621-1693) and by the painted ceiling of the Chapel of St Rosa of Lima, carried out by his grandson, Simon-Benedikt (1695-1759).

Church of Our Lady (Liebfrauenkirche). – A massive square tower distinguishes the church. The sanctuary in the upper storey is adorned with a Coronation of the Virgin painted on the vaulting by Simon-Benedikt Faistenberger in 1739 and a Rococo grille (1778).

A 17C painting of Our Lady of Succour (Maria Hilf) after Cranach the Elder reminds us of the important role this church played as a place of pilgrimage until the 19C.

Local Museum (Heimatmuseum) (M). – *Open 9am to noon; closed Sundays and holidays; 20S.* This collection will be instructive to tourists interested in the origins of the town, which was Bavarian for nearly 1 000 years.

EXCURSIONS

Kitzbüheler Horn★★. – Alt 1 996 m - 6 549 ft. *About 2 hours Rtn, including 35 minutes by cable-car (2 sections). Departure from Kitzbühel every 1/2 hour in summer; 90S Rtn.* A circular view of the jagged crests of the Kaisergebirge and the dazzling icy summits of the Grossglockner and Grossvenediger.

Black Lake (Schwarzsee). – *2 km - 1 mile by the Kirchberg road and the lake road to the right (level-crossing). It is, however, pleasanter to walk all the way by the Liebfrauenkirche and the Lebenberg road (northwest of the plan).* Bathing within view of the Kaisergebirge.

Pass Thurn. – *20 km - 12 miles.* Alt 1 273 m - 4 176 ft. Leave Kitzbühel by the road to Mittersill. The best-arranged **belvedere★** for cars to halt is about 1 800 m - 5 904 ft beyond the crest, on the Oberpinzgau slope, level with the "Tauernblick Buffet". From this point there is an end view of the Hollersbachtal, which runs south towards the main crest of the High Tauern range.
The slopes overlooking the pass are, in winter, the skiing fields of the resort of Mittersill.

*Good manners in mountain driving require
that you should give way to the ascending car*

KLAGENFURT ▣ (Carinthia) _____

Michelin map **426** fold 36 – *Local map p 172* – Pop 86 303 – Alt 446 m - 1 463 ft– ▣ ☎ 7961-223

Klagenfurt (60 km - 37 miles from Italy; 30 km - 18 1/2 miles from Yugoslavia) is the business, administrative and cultural centre of Carinthia. Its girdle of "rings" and many lovely gardens recalls its past as a stronghold, the walls of which were abolished by the French in 1809. Its checkerboard of wide streets cross at right angles. It has been the capital of the province, by grace of Maximilian, since 1518, and has developed its leather and light electrical industries remarkably in modern times. Summers are very hot in this interior basin of the Alps, which is one of those most cut off from the influence of the sea, but the water sports offered by Lake Wörther (Wörthersee), which lies in the western suburbs of the city, help to make a stay there very agreeable.

The fearful dragon (Lindwurm) which is the chief feature of the fountain in the Neuer Platz, the centre of life in modern Klagenfurt, is the city emblem.

■ **SIGHTS** *time: 1 1/2 hours*

Regional Museum★ (Landesmuseum) (M¹). – *Open May to October, 9am to 4pm; 10am to noon on Sundays and holidays; closed Mondays; 15S.*

The lawns framing the island of buildings are used for the display in the open air **(Parkmuseum)** of statues and Roman stonework from the different excavations which have occurred in Carinthia. Note especially the reconstruction of a Celtic fountain and a round basin encircled by fragments of funerary sculpture.

In the museum proper, which is devoted to the evolution of Carinthian arts and techniques through the ages, special displays have been made of mineralogy and prehistoric and Roman antiquity.

Note the diagrams of mines, a magnificent relief map of the Grossglockner massif and the glaciary basin of the Pasterze and a fossilized rhinoceros skull – the Lindwurmschädel – found in the Zollfeld in 1335 and said to have inspired the designer of the Lindwurm fountain *(see above).* A large mosaic with mythological designs is a reminder of the former Roman capital, Virunum. Numerous **works of religious art★**, notably the great altarpiece of St Veit, mark the contribution of the 15 and 16C.

Alter Platz. – This wide street and square which retains a certain nobility from the surrounding 16C mansions with their Baroque façades and flowered courtyards is in the heart of the old town. Round it, a few narrow, crooked streets afford vistas of the nearby towers and belfries. It is best to approach the courtyard of the Landhaus through the Alter Platz.

Landhaus. – Originally the arsenal, then the state headquarters of Carinthia, this building now serves to house the departments and assemblies of the regional government. Finished in 1590, it owes the design of its inner court – especially in the Renaissance group formed by the two-storey gallery and two staircases – largely to an architect from Lugano, Johann Antonio Verda.

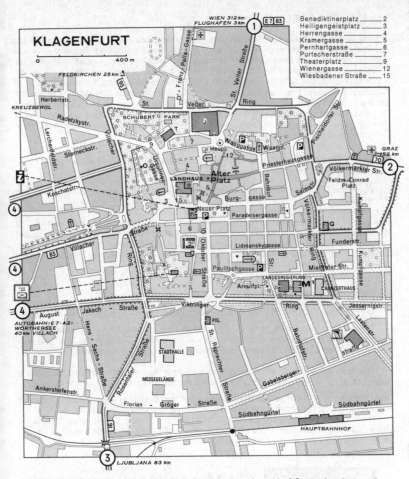

Benedktinerplatz ___ 2
Heiligengeistplatz ___ 3
Herrengasse ___ 4
Kramergasse ___ 5
Pernhartgasse ___ 6
Purtscherstraße ___ 7
Theaterplatz ___ 9
Wienergasse ___ 12
Wiesbadener Straße ___ 15

Great Blazon Hall (Grosser Wappensaal). – *Open April to the end of September 9am to 5pm; closed Sundays and Mondays; 6S; guided tours (1/2 hour) on request in English.*

The state hall on the 1st floor of the central block was decorated by Josef Ferdinand Fromiller (1693-1760). He depicted on the ceiling a scene showing Emperor Karl VI receiving hommage, in 1728, on the south wall the town, giving an offering to the members of the provincial states in 1518, and on the north wall an odd representation of a duke being crowned. The walls and window embrasures bear 665 heraldic shields representing the coats of arms of noblemen who sat in the States (Parliament) between 1590 and 1848.

The KLEINWALSERTAL ★ (Vorarlberg)

Michelin map 426 fold 15 – *Local map p 55* – Pop 4 600 – Alt of resorts: 1 084 m - 3 555 ft to 1 218 m - 3 995 ft – *Facilities p 39*

The Kleinwalsertal, which is forming a tiny mountain area of about 100 sq km - 38 sq miles

– is a region isolated from the rest of Austria by the peaks of the Allgäu Alps and is thus exclusively oriented towards Germany – whether it be economically or through tourism.

The Walser Colonization. – The Kleinwalsertal, a high valley of the Breitach, was settled in the 13C by emigrants of Germanic origin from the Upper Valais – the Walser. Like other regions of the Vorarlberg (Grosses Walsertal and Hochtannberg) cleared by these hardy workers, the small dark wood houses sprinkled about the slopes follow the traditions of their grim individualism. Until the modern road (1930) was built, the inhabitants were able to live their patriarchal way of life, and keep their curious costumes; today, however, these are worn mostly at weddings and in the Corpus Christi procession.

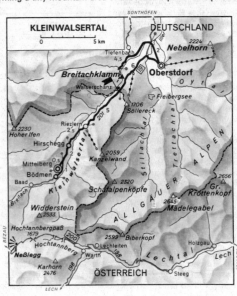

A Unique Administration. – By feudal ties, the Walsers, established here, passed under the sovereignty of the Habsburgs in 1453, so that they found themselves Austrian when the national frontiers were fixed. Cut off from the rest of Vorarlberg and oriented solely towards Germany in the commercial field, the district has had a special status since 1891.

Remaining under Austrian sovereignty, the Kleinwalsertal is today economically part of Germany. Because of this, there are only German customs officials on the road from Oberstdorf but the Austrian police maintains law and order. The postal vans which serve Mittelberg from Oberstdorf are German, but locally issued postage stamps are Austrian. (They can be paid for in Deutschmarks, the only means of payment for commercial transactions, including hotel bills and in the casino at Riezlern.)

From Oberstdorf (Germany) to Mittelberg – 16 km - 10 miles – about 1 hour
– Local map opposite

Oberstdorf★★ – *Description in Michelin Green Guide to Germany (West Germany and Berlin).*
Leave Oberstdorf by the Upper Breitach Valley road (No. 19).
The parish church steeples thrust themselves before the limestone Alps of Allgäu. The Widderstein *(for the legend attached to it p 55)* can be seen in the distance behind Hirschegg and the three rocky crests of the Schafalpenköpfe to the east of Mittelberg.
Go beyond **Mittelberg,** the valley's commercial centre to see an authentic Valaisian hamlet, **Bödmen,** with its traditional chalets.

KLOBENSTEIN Ravine (KLOBENSTEINPASS) (Tyrol)
Michelin map **426** fold 18 – On the Ache, north of Kitzbühel – *Local map p 92*

The Ache, a voluminous torrent flowing down from the Kitzbühel Alps, makes for the Chiemsee under various names (Kitzbüheler Ache, Kössener Ache, Tiroler Ache). It plunges after **Kössen** *(facilities p 39)* into a ravine, which forms a natural frontier between the Tyrol and Bavaria.

The road using this picturesque section runs from Kössen to Schleching (Bavaria); it overlooks, in the steep part of the ravine, two curious pilgrim's chapels clinging to the slope.

The Chapels. – *3/4 hour on foot Rtn by a downhill road branching off the route at the south entrance to the tunnel (the Austrian side) which marks the frontier with Bavaria.*
The two chapels, adjoining, are built between blocks of rock in a curious way. The larger chapel contains a black Virgin. The smaller one has a cleft like a sword-cut through the rocks, which had previously been its only entrance.

KREMS and STEIN (Lower Austria)
Michelin map **426** fold 11 – *Local maps pp 61 and 62* – Pop 23 123 – Alt 221 m - 725 ft – ⒤
☎ 2676

At the eastern end of the Wachau, **Krems** *(facilities p 39)* stands on the left bank of the Danube at the foot of terraced loess hills covered with famous vines.

This large settlement, really made up by Krems, Stein and their suburb, Und, is the subject of a joke among Austrians, who say: "Krems, Und (and) Stein are three towns."

■ **SIGHTS** *time: 1 hour*

Parish Church (Pfarrkirche) of Krems. – This church is very large but unfortunately overloaded with statues and gilding. The vaulting of the nave and chancel is adorned with frescos painted at the end of the 18C by Martin Johann Schmidt *(see below).*

Krems Historical Museum (Historisches Museum der Stadt Krems). – *Open Easter to mid-November 9am to noon and 2 to 5pm; Sundays and holidays 9am to noon; closed Mondays; 18S.*

The museum is located in the former Dominican monastery (restored). The influence of the friars on the 13 and 14C Gothic church is manifested by its austere appearance. It houses a gallery of paintings devoted to Martin Johann Schmidt (1718-1801), known in religious art history as **Kremser Schmidt.** The cloister is surrounded by conventual buildings. Its eastern gallery has Gothic

blind arcades shielded under small gables. A collection of historical and artistic documents can be found in the chapterhouse, calefactory and other rooms. There is also a **Wine Museum** (Weinbaumuseum) which displays everything connected with wine growing and wine, as well as the extent of vineyards in the Danube Valley.

Old Houses in Stein. – *Southwest - beyond the limits of the town plan.* The "Grosser Passauerhof", at No. 76 Steiner Landstrasse, is a curious Gothic building; an oriel adorns the tall façade, with its upper part decorated with intertwined designs, flanked at each end with turrets.

EXCURSION

Krems Valley★. – *16 km - 10 miles – Local maps pp 61 and 62.* Leave Krems by the Kremstalstrasse and the road to Zwettl (north of the plan). As soon as it leaves the town, the road joins the Krems River and runs along its left then right bank in a pleasant landscape of loess hills where vines and fruit trees – peaches, plums and apricots are grown on terraces.

You will soon see, on your left, the church and ruins of the Castle of **Rehberg** perched on a rocky spike, and, in the foreground, the Gothic tower of **Imbach** Church.

Soon after Imbach appears the proud shape of the ruined Fortress of **Senftenberg,** crowning a bluff. Beyond the attractive village of Senftenberg, the valley narrows between rock outcrops and becomes wild and solitary. Turn around at Untermeisling.

KREMSMÜNSTER Abbey (Upper Austria)

Michelin map **426** fold 21 – 8 km - 5 miles west of Bad Hall

The impressive Benedictine Abbey of Kremsmünster stands among the hills rising between the foothills of the Alps and the Danube, on a bluff which overlooks the Krems Valley. The tourist coming from the east suddenly sees the tall façade of the monastery buildings, from which emerge the two domed towers of the abbey church and, on its right, the "mathematical tower". Of all the buildings at least the monumental fish-pond should be visited.

The abbey was founded in the second half of the 8C and was the work of Tassilo III, Duke of Bavaria. According to legend, Gunther, the son of Tassilo, was mortally wounded by a wild boar when hunting in the forests which then covered the domain. Tassilo decided to create a religious community on this spot in order to perpetuate the memory of his son. The present appearance of the abbey church and its monastery buildings dates from the 17 and 18C. Great architects – Carlo Antonio Carlone, Jakob Prandtauer – and talented painters – Altomonte, Kremser Schmidt *(p 98)* – participated in the transformation of the abbey to the Baroque style.

TOUR   *allow 2 1/2 to 3 hours for a complete tour*

Park the car in the outer court of the abbey. Buy your tickets in the vestibule after the bridge leading to the great Prelates' Court (Prälatenhof). Guided tours in English (on request) Easter to 31 October 9 and 10.30 am and 2 and 3.30pm; 45S; brochure available in English.

Fish-pond (Fischbehälter). – The pond was built by Carlone and enlarged by Prandtauer between 1690 and 1717. It brings an unexpected note to the abbey group with its five basins, surrounded by arcades and adorned with statues spouting water. These last, which include Samson, David, Neptune, Triton, Jonas and St Peter suggest the elegance of the Italian Renaissance. It was restored in 1971, excepting the frescos on the vaults, damaged by the humidity.

Abbey Buildings (Stiftsgebäude). – The **Emperors' Hall** (Kaisersaal) owes its name to portraits of the Holy Roman Emperors (from Rudolf of Habsburg to Karl VI). The pictures were painted at the end of the 17C by Altomonte. Ceiling frescos and stucco mouldings of great delicacy adorn this state hall. On the 2nd floor are several rooms, containing collections of paintings. A *Crucifixion* in the second room, by Quentin Massys, attracts special attention.

Displayed with a great deal of pride is **Tassilo's chalice**, presented to the monks by the Duke at the end of the 8C. This piece of goldsmith's work, the oldest known in the Austro-Bavarian countries, is of gilded copper, inlaid with niellated silver plaques; the decorative designs and characters – Christ and saints – show the influence of the earliest Christian art – the Anglo-Irish.

Observatory or Mathematical Tower (Mathematischer Turm). – The tower is 60 m - 197 ft - high. It contains large collections connected with palaeontology, physics, mineralogy, zoology, anthropology and astronomy.

KRIMML Waterfalls ★★★ (KRIMMLER WASSERFÄLLE) (Salzburg)

Michelin map **426** fold 32 – *Local map p 72*

The Krimml Waterfalls, dropping some 380 m - 1 250 ft – spread their veils of foam and mist on the sides of the wooded amphitheatre which ends the Salzach Valley. Glowing with iridescence, they are among the finest falls in the Alps. The approach along an uphill road offers an excursion which is a favourite throughout the area between Innsbruck and Salzburg.

Tour. – *Allow 2 hours. The road (4S) is always open. Take a raincoat if you intend to linger.*

Leave the car in the car park at the bottom of the Krimml Valley on the Gerlospass road (if you do not want to use the Gerlospass toll road, go into Krimml and leave the car in the town). Go beneath the road to walk along the wide path which leads to the foot of the cascades and then climbs through the woods in hairpin bends. Minor paths branch off to belvederes over the lower and upper middle falls. After one hour you emerge on the level pastures where the Gasthof Schönangerl stands. If you are not making the full excursion by climbing to the Tauernhaus *(in that case allow 3 1/2 hours)*, which marks the origin of the Krimml Falls, at least go onto the Bergerblick belvedere, 20 minutes beyond the Gasthof Schönangerl. From there is a view of the upper falls, which are much bigger than those you have already seen.

KUFSTEIN (Tyrol)

Michelin map **426** fold 18 – *Local map p 92* – Pop 13 125 – Alt 597 m - 1 959 ft – **i** Münchner Strasse 2 ☎ 2 207

Kufstein is the last Austrian town in the Inn Valley. It is grouped at the foot of a rocky height and crowned with a fortress, which gives some idea of the unfriendly relations of Bavaria and Austria in past centuries. It was burnt down in 1703 by the fortress commander, who wished to have a clear field of fire when invested by the Bavarians. The grey, busy, little town now owes its tourist activity chiefly to the frontier station and the proximity of the Kaisergebirge (4 chairlifts make the approach shorter). *General information on the Kaisergebirge p 92.*

General View. – To appreciate the **site★** of the castle climb the Heroes' Bluff surmounted by a statue of Andreas Hofer, who fought here in 1809 against French and Bavarians.

- ## THE FORTRESS (Festung) *1/2 hour on foot Rtn*

Starting from the Unterer Stadtplatz, leave the church, and make for the Neuhof, on your left, which contains the auditorium for the Heroes' Organ. From this you pass through the walls by a covered stairway beneath the Burghers' Tower (Bürgerturm). *Other possible access: take the lift at the foot of the rock, along the quay of the Inn (Inn-Promenade).* Go straight ahead (the entrance to the buildings *(open) – see below –* is on the left) and by a new gateway and a bridge you reach the Wallachenbastion. This bastion, which overlooks the Inn, forms a **belvedere**★ facing the wooded Pendling, a small mountain range. To the left the Kitzbühel Alps may be seen, and in clear weather the snows of the Stubai Alps, southwest of Innsbruck.

- ## ADDITIONAL SIGHTS

Castle Interior Arrangements. – *Guided tours in English of the inside of the fortress (1 1/4 hours) 1 April to 26 October, starting from the cash-register 9.30 and 11am and 1.45, 3.15 and 4.45pm; (in July and August tours depart more frequently); closed Mondays in April, May, June, September and October; 17.50S.*

Local Museum (Heimatmuseum) (M). – The rooms devoted to illustrations of the fortress through the ages are the most interesting feature.

The Emperor's Tower★ (Kaiserturm) (A). – This colossal structure, completed in 1522, rears its walls, up to 4.50 m - 25 ft thick, on the highest point of the rock. Its inner arrangements are grouped round a huge central pillar, encircled by a vaulted gallery. The design can be clearly seen from the 2nd floor, as you begin the tour.

On the 3rd floor thirteen cells are reminders of the captives imprisoned at Kufstein, when the castle was a state prison from 1814 to 1867. The tour continues through bastions, casemates and cellars.

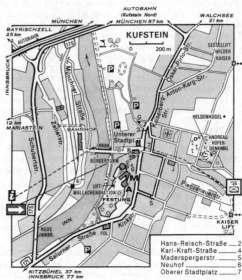

Hans-Reisch-Straße	2
Karl-Kraft-Straße	4
Maderspergerstr.	5
Neuhof	6
Oberer Stadtplatz	7

Deep Well (Tiefer Brunnen). – This was bored in the rock at the time of the Emperor Maximilian and is over 68 m - 200 ft deep.

Heroes' Organ (Heldenorgel). – *Recitals every day, at midday and, in summer, also at 6pm.*

This instrument, first played in public in 1931, was built in the top storey of the Burghers' Tower to commemorate the German and Austrian dead in the First World War. The recitals can be heard for several miles round the town in still weather. The organist's keyboard and the gallery for the audience are at the foot of the rock.

EXCURSION

The Ursprungpass Road★. – *26 km - 16 miles from Kufstein to Bayrischzell (Germany) – Local map p 92.*
This trip can be the beginning of a tour in the Bavarian Alps (customs formalities); description of the German section of this Alpine Road in Michelin Green Guide to Germany.
Leave Kufstein by the Bayrischzell Road, northwest of the plan. The road rises rapidly into the woods and as you leave the Inn Valley the sight of the fortress is lost.

Thiersee. – Pop 2 263. *Facilities p 42.* The Pendling spur dominates the scene of a small lake at the foot of a terraced village.

A succession of combes and gorges precede Ursprungpass (alt 849 m - 2 785 ft). After the pass, begin the final descent to Bayrischzell.

LAMBACH (Upper Austria)

Michelin map 🔟🔟🔟 fold 21 – 15 km - 9 miles southwest of Wels – Pop 3 165 – Alt 349 m - 1 145 ft

Its position on the left bank of the Traun River made Lambach, in the Middle Ages, when boats could not use the river beyond the Traunsee *(p 137)*, a transshipment point for salt which was brought from Hallstatt and embarked here for Vienna and Bohemia.

To this economic function were added the prestige and fame of a Benedictine abbey founded in the 11C.

Abbey (Stift). – *The frescos may be seen only with the guided tours (45 minutes) Mai through October 9 (10am Sundays and holidays) to 11am and 2 to 5pm; November through April 10am (11am Sundays and holidays) to noon and 3 to 4pm; 10S; brochure available in English.*

In the west front is a richly decorated **doorway,** built by Jakob Auer in 1693. Four marble columns support an entablature surmounted by statues: the Virgin, holding the Infant Jesus in her arms, between St Adalbero, the founder of the abbey, and St Kilian. The **abbey church** was remodelled in the Baroque style in the 17 and 18C. The 11C **Romanesque wall paintings** which adorn the west chancel and which were, at one time, hidden, were completely uncovered and restored in 1968 and now form a group unique in all Austria. On the vaulting may be seen the Adoration of the Magi and on the walls, scenes from the life of Christ.

Church of Stadl Paura. – *2 km - 1 mile. Leave Lambach, southwards.*

Cross the Traun River and 500 m – 547 yds further bear right as far as a mound on which stands the **Church of the Holy Trinity** (Dreifaltigkeitskirche), built from 1714 to 1724 by an architect from Linz, Johann Michael Prunner.

The plan is determined by the inscription of a circle within an equilateral triangle. The church holds 3 as its key number: 3 façades, 3 portals, 3 altars, 3 organ-lofts and 3 sacristies.

The frescos on the dome and the altarpieces are by Carlo Carlone, Martino Altomonte, and Domenico Parodi.

LANDECK (Tyrol)

Michelin map **426** fold 29 – *Local maps pp 49 and 84* – Pop 7 325 – Alt 816 m - 2 677 ft – ▣ Malser Strasse, ☎ 2344

This small industrial town at the junction of the Arlberg road and the Inn Valley is an important communications centre. Its massive fortified castle (13C) and a series of feudal strongpoints perched like eagles' nest in the near neighbourhood bear witness to the strategic importance of this section of the valley. The pretty Tyrolean villages in the neighbourhood, Stanz, Grins, Tobadill, Fliess, etc., which lie scattered over the plateaux, are worth visiting.

Parish Church (Pfarrkirche). – This church on a terrace at the foot of the castle is one of the most carefully planned Gothic buildings in the Tyrol. Inside, the Flamboyant fenestration and particularly the network vaulting indicate the later period, the end of the 15C.

Worthy of study is the said Schrofenstein altarpiece (from the high altar), representing the Adoration of the Magi. The work dates from the beginning of the 16C, except for the side panels and the crown, which are modern. The unusually high predella shows, in the centre, the sainted King Oswald, holding his sceptre and a sacred vase. The donors kneel on either side. These lifelike coloured statuettes reproduce the features of Oswald von Schrofenstein, whose ruined castle can still be seen nearby *(p 84)*, and of Praxedis von Wolkenstein.

LECH ★★ (Vorarlberg)

Michelin map **426** fold 29 – *Local maps pp 48 and 55* – Pop 1 270 – Alt 1 447 m - 4 747 ft – ▣ ☎ 217 – *Facilities p 39*

The resort of Lech has remained widely scattered in its setting of grassy slopes, divided by occasional curtains of fir trees or cut by deep escarpments *(Omeshorn)*.

The church, built on a spur, is the only ancient structure in the village, which was founded in the 14C by emigrants from the Valais *(on their colonization of the Vorarlberg, see p 54)*.

Its tourist development dates only from the opening of the road to the Flexenpass in 1896.

The adjoining resort of Oberlech (alt 1 700 m - 5 577 ft), which caters for skiers who seek even better snowfields and prolonged sunshine, is simply a group of hotels connected by cableway with the valley floor.

The latest developments in winter equipment have been the building of the Rüfikopf cable-car, which has connected the Lech snowfields and those of the neighbouring resort of Zürs, thus making possible a round trip from Lech to Rüfikopf, Zürs, Madlochjoch, Stierlochjoch, and back to Lech without having to climb a yard on foot; the Madloch cable-car also goes to the snowfields of Lech with the possibility of passing by Zug, Kriegerhorn and Mohnenfluh.

In summer, walkers will find it pleasant to make for the small Upper Lech Valley, where a heated swimming-pool and tennis courts are to be found in a pleasant setting. Farther up, the small road leads to the chalets of Zug which are dotted about a basin of Alpine pastures within sight of the imposing summit of the Rote Wand (2 706 m - 8 878 ft).

LECH, Upper Valley of the (Vorarlberg and Tyrol)

Michelin map **426** folds 15, 16 and 29

Upstream from Reutte the Lech Valley hollows out for 60 km - 37 miles between the Allgäu and Lechtal Alps, and parallel to the Inn Valley, a remarkably uniform furrow. The road which is not much used between Reutte and Warth, forms an interesting touring road. In the course of a journey through Austria it affords a peaceful interval which some will be glad to prolong.

From Reutte to Warth – *61 km - 38 miles – 1 1/2 hours – Local maps pp 48 and 49*

The road between Steeg and Warth can be closed (not more than 3 days) due to avalanches. However, it is not possible to make any connections between Warth and Lech in winter (p 48).

Upstream from Reutte *(p 70)*, the landscape hardly varies from an austerity due to the wanderings of the torrent, which has spread great beds of gravel – bare, or wooded with conifers – and shows no terraces or plateaux which could be repopulated. After Stanzach, nonetheless, the countryside is greener and more pastoral, and the frame of mountains gains in majesty with the apperance, to the northwest, of the magnificent steep crests of the Allgäu Alps.

Elbigenalp. – Pop 711. The prettiest painted houses in the village of Elbigenalp often belong to local people who emigrated to Holland and Germany and became wealthy in some prosperous business. A small professional school perpetuates the Tyrolean tradition of wood-carving. The church, rebuilt in the 17C, stands apart in the fields, in the churchyard enclosure, its sharp pointed spire attracts the visitor to the most remarkable building in the Upper Lech. Especially since the restoration of the Baroque interior (1969). Alongside the main church is the small 15C Chapel of St Martin, whose crypt once served as a charnel-house. The chapel is decorated with a series of painted panels representing a Dance of the Dead. This popular 19C work was done by Anton Falger (1791-1876) the valley's chronicler.

Holzgau. – Pop 398. *Facilities p 39.*

From Steeg and beyond Lech, the road climbs through a succession of narrow passes before suddenly rising through a broken scenery of rocks and woods and finally dominating the steep slopes below which runs the torrent. The road, then opens onto the Alpine pastures of Lechleiten, facing the Karhorn, before reaching Warth.

LEOBEN (Styria)

Michelin map **426** fold 23 – *Local map p 64* – Pop 32 006 – Alt 541 m - 1 775 ft

Leoben is known to historians for the peace treaty signed there by Bonaparte in 1797. Since the Middle Ages it has been a market town, and the centre of the Styrian metal industry. The proximity of the Eisenerz iron deposits *(p 64)* has encouraged the development of the metallurgical industry on the northwest side of Donawitz, and in the Mur Valley in the region of Bruck. Leoben also has a university.

War and Diplomacy. – After his lightning campaign of Italy in 1796, marked by the victories of Montenotte, Mondovi, Lodi, Castiglione, Arcola and Rivoli, Napoleon marched on Vienna. On 7 April 1797 the French Army entered Leoben. It was in this town that delegates sent by the Emperor of Austria came to ask for an armistice.

Exceeding his instructions from the Directory, Bonaparte dictated his conditions, making up for his inexperience of diplomacy by his certitude of military superiority: the troops of Archduke Karl had been routed, and he was only 20 leagues from Vienna. On the 18th, the preliminaries were signed. France obtained the Low Countries and a frontier on the Rhine. The Emperor of Austria also gave up Lombardy, but received Venetia, Illyria and Istria. On 16 October the 28 year old diplomat-general confirmed these preliminaries in a Peace Treaty at Campo-Formio.

A monument, erected near the church of St James (south of the town at the meander of the Mur), and a room in the local museum *(Kirchgasse 6)* commemorate these historical events.

Maria-Waasen Kirche. – West of the town, near the bridge over the Mur, the Gothic Church of Maria-Waasen has 15C stained glass windows in the chancel. Among them can be recognized the Apostles, the Coronation of the Virgin and scenes from the Life and Passion of Christ.

LERMOOS ★ (Tyrol)

Michelin map **426** fold 16 – *Local map p 69* – Pop 952 – Alt 995 m - 3 264 ft – ▣ ☎ 2401 – *Facilities pp 41 and 43*

With Ehrwald and Biberwier, the little resort of Lermoos marks the circumference of a basin of the Upper Loisach. It is a true road junction in the Northern Limestone Alps and enjoys an exceptional **site★★** facing the escarpments of the Zugspitze, which is separated from the bold pyramid of the Sonnenspitze (Mieminger Kette) by the Gaistal gap.

One can hardly find a better point, as regards distance, from which to admire this group of peaks. Lermoos is therefore one of the best country resorts for mountain views in Austria. It is also well equipped for winter sports (a chain of chairlifts goes up the side of the Grubigstein to an altitude of 2 000 m - 6 500 ft).

LIENZ (Tyrol)

Michelin map **426** fold 33 – *Local maps pp 67 and 110* – Pop 11 699 – Alt 678 m - 2 224 ft – ▣ ☎ 4747 – *Facilities pp 41 and 43*

Lienz lies in the shadow of the Dolomites, whose slopes, wrinkled with ravines and divided into many facets, thus justify their popular nickname of *Unholde* – the unfriendly. The town is the southern terminus of the road to the Grossglockner and the Felber Tauern. It is also the chief town in the eastern Tyrol (Osttirol) district of Austria, cut off, to all intents, from the central part of the province of Tyrol *(see map on p 3)* and Innsbruck, the provincial capital, since the transfer of the Pustertal (Val Pusteria) to Italy in 1919. Only in 1967 with the opening of the Felber Tauern Tunnel was the situation changed. About 15 km - 9 miles downstream, between Nikolsdorf and Oberdrauburg, the small ravine of the Drava known as the Tiroler Tor (gate of the Tyrol) has marked, since the 16C, the natural frontier with Carinthia.

■ **SIGHTS** *time: 1 hour*

Bruck Castle (Schloss Bruck) and the Museum of the East Tyrol (Osttiroler Heimatmuseum) (M). – *Open Palm Sunday through October 10am to 5pm; closed Mondays out of season; 24S.*

This castle is a former fortress of the Counts of Görz (now Gorizia) whose estates, extending from the Tauern to Istria, enabled the Habsburgs, who inherited them in 1500, to practise their policy of expansion towards the Adriatic. The castle now houses the museum of the East Tyrol. The latter is devoted among other things to local antiquities, folklore and handiwork. The Knights' Hall (Rittersaal) shows how the castle looked in mediaeval times with its bare beams and rafters, on which are traces of colouring. The two-storey chapel shelters, under its 15C Gothic vaulting, some mural paintings (1495) and, below, an altarpiece of Michael Pacher's school.

The large **Albin Egger-Lienz gallery** affords a comprehensive review of the work of this painter (1868-1926), who was often inspired by the Tyrol and its inhabitants. His violent and unadorned expressionism recalls the manner of the Swiss painter Ferdinand Hodler. The museum also exhibits, in another interesting gallery, the work of other contemporary artists.

The fragments of stonework collected in the section on Roman archaeology come mostly from the excavations at Aguntum and Lavant-Kirchbichl, which specialists may see east of the town, on either side of the Drava.

Albin-Egger-Straße	2
Andrä-Kranz-Gasse	3
Johannesplatz	4
Messinggasse	5
Rosengasse	6
Schweizer Gasse	7

St Andrew's Church (St. Andrä). – This church has a late Gothic nave and an 18C chance. During its restoration in 1968, mural paintings of the 14, 15 and 17C were discovered. Under the gallery are the magnificent 16C **tombstones**★, in Salzburg marble, of Count Leonard, the last of the Görz-Tirol line, and Michael von Wolkenstein (with his wife, Barbara von Thun), who succeeded him.

Within the graveyard precinct, once fortified, stands a monument to the war dead by Holzmeister. The memorial chapel contains the tomb of Albin Egger-Lienz, who helped to decorate the precinct.

EXCURSION

Tauerntal★★. – *45 km - 28 miles – plus 2 hours on foot Rtn – Local map p 67.*
Coming out of Lienz, follow the Felber Tauern road *(description p 67).* Make the excursion from the Matreier Tauernhaus towards the Grossvenediger.
By leaving Lienz early in the morning, you can have a full day in the high mountains – 205 km - 127 miles. Make for Mittersill, then, coming down the Salzach Valley, Bruck, the start of the Grossglockner road (description p 77) and your return route.

LINZ ★ ℙ (Upper Austria) _____

Michelin map **426** fold 9 – *Local maps p 60* – Pop 197 962 – Alt 266 m - 873 ft – ⓘ
Altstadt 17, ☎ 77484, 77483

Linz, the capital of Upper Austria, is built on both banks of the Danube, at a point where the valley opens out after a narrow section. Three modern bridges link the city with its suburb of Urfahr, on the left bank.

As a bridgehead, Linz owes a good deal of its prosperity to the Danube. It is today an industrial centre in a state of full development.

A Daughter of the Danube. – The Romans had already recognized the importance of this crossroads site, which commands both the Danube Valley and the former route for salt, which came down the Traun Valley from Hallstatt to reach Bohemia at its northerly end. From the Middle Ages onwards, shipping on the Danube contributed to the growth of the town, which was well fitted to take a leading role in river traffic, thanks to its wood and iron industries. Today, large scale engineering works have made the port of Linz the biggest on the middle Danube. It has the most modern equipment for transshipment and storage.

An Industrial Capital. – The coming of railways – the first train in Austria ran between Linz and Budweis (Ceské-Budejovice) in 1832 – facilitated the installation of the machine and textile industries between the old town and the confluence of the Danube and the Traun. This enabled Linz to expand and absorb Scharlinz, Bergern and Kleinmünchen, which are now part of its southern suburbs.

Moreover, a considerable programme of industrial equipment and concentration has been carried out since the end of the Second World War. Linz has specialized in the heavy and chemical industries.

The Austrian United Steelworks (VÖEST. Alpine. Montan AG) and the Chemical Factory production (Chemie Linz AG) between them employ more than 33 000 people. The equipment of these factories is among the most modern in Austria. The iron ore they use comes mostly from the Erzberg in Styria. The Danube is used to transport iron and coal. Fertilizers produced satisfy Austrian requirements and even allow a surplus for export.

■ **GENERAL VIEW**

Linz should be approached along the Danube, preferably from the west, but it is from the Pöstlingberg Hill 537 m - 1 762 ft – that the most interesting general view of the town is obtained.

Pöstlingberg★. – *4.5 km - 3 miles northwest.*
Take the Rudolfstrasse on the left bank of the Danube where the Nibelungen Bridge (Nibelungenbrücke) ends, then the Hagenstrasse to the right. After a levelcrossing the road climbs quickly. Turn right when you are on one level with an oratory. Leave the car in the car park below the church.

From a flower decked terrace below the pilgrims' church there is an extensive **view**★. You look down from nearly 300 m - 1 000 ft on the Danube Valley where you see Linz spread out along the right bank in a basin encircled by hills and closer, on the left river bank, the large suburb of Urfahr.

In Linz you can distinguish the business quarters, with their shopping avenues, and the large suburbs with their factory chimneys. Southwards, serving as a backcloth to this fine urban panorama, rise the foothills to the Alps.

■ **MAIN SIGHTS** *time: 1 1/2 hours*

Leave from the Hauptplatz. Follow the route marked on the map.

Hauptplatz. – This is more striking as a whole than for the beauty of the individual buildings round it.

In the centre stands the Trinity Column (Dreifaltigkeitssäule), erected in 1723 by order of the States of Upper Austria (provincial assembly) to commemorate the escape of the town from plague, fire and Turkish invasion. With its statues and cherubs in white marble, and the group representing the Holy Trinity at the top, it is a fine example of the Baroque columns which were set up in many towns of the Empire *(p 147)* at that period.

Leave the square by the Domgasse to the southeast, and passing the Alter Dom, the former cathedral, on your left, bear right through the Graben and the avenue to the Landhaus, which you go through.

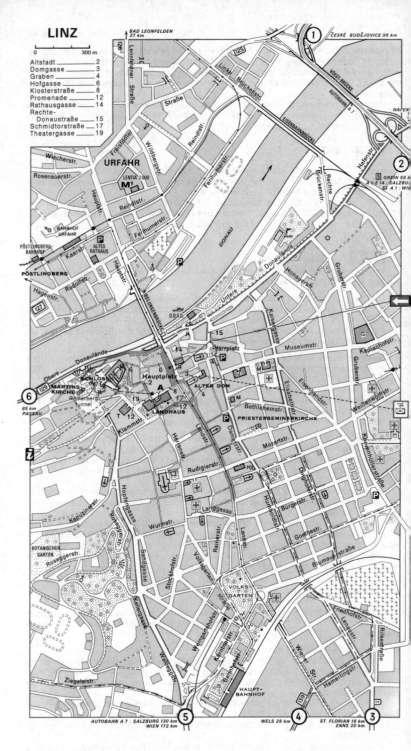

Landhaus. – This building, which is the headquarters of the provincial government, was erected in the second half of the 16C.

The inner court is lined on two sides with arcades.

On the base of the fountain seven figures representing the planets recall that the great astronomer and mathematician Kepler was from 1612 to 1626 a teacher at the Linz College, which was then in the Landhaus.

The north door, giving on the Klosterstrasse, is in the Renaissance style. The windows of the room over the passage are in harmony with the architecture of the doorway.

Church of the Minorite Brothers (Minoritenkirche) (A). – The Gothic church, founded in the 13C by the Minorite Brothers or Franciscans, was remodelled in the Rococo style in the 18C.

Interest lies in its decoration. The altarpiece on the high altar by Bartolomeo Altomonte represents the Annunciation; those on the six side altars were executed by Kremser Schmidt (p 98).

Château (Schloss). – The oldest part of the château, which was the residence of the Emperor Friedrich III, dates from the end of the 15C. It houses the historical collections of the Provincial Museum.

Provincial Museum of Upper Austria★ (Oberösterreichisches Landesmuseum). – *Open 10am to 1pm and 2 to 6pm; 9am to 1pm Sundays and holidays; closed Mondays, Tuesdays and second week in February; brochure available in English.*

The ground floor is devoted to prehistoric remains and the Roman period.

On the 1st floor, the history of art in Upper Austria is traced from the Middle Ages to the Rococo period. There is a large collection of weapons.

On the 2nd floor are to be found collections of popular art and folklore. Reconstitutions of Gothic and Renaissance interiors are also on view as well as a 19C painting gallery.

Cross the many courtyards in the castle to descend below the fortress to a terrace from which there is a pleasant view of the Danube and the Pöstlingberg Hill. Return to the Hauptplatz by way of the quay (Obere Donaulände).

■ ADDITIONAL SIGHTS

Former Cathedral (Alter Dom) or Jesuit Church. – *Closed noon to 3pm.*

The church was built for the Jesuits in the second half of the 17C and is the largest Baroque church in Linz. The plain, bare façade in contrast with the interior, where stucco, pink marble columns, an elaborately carved pulpit and stalls and a high altar adorned with marble statues make up a florid picture.

A medallion to the left of the entrance recalls that Anton Bruckner *(p 123)* was organist of this church for twelve years.

New Gallery (Neue Galerie der Stadt Linz-Wolfgang Gurlitt-Museum) (M¹).– *At Urfahr (left bank). – Open from 10am to 6pm (1pm Sundays; 10pm Thursdays); closed on Mondays and holidays; 10S.*

This museum is devoted to Austrian and German painting of the 19 and 20C (Kokoschka, Liebermann, Corinth, Klimt, Schiele, etc.).

Seminary Church (Priesterseminarkirche). – This little church, consecrated to the Holy Cross, was built at the beginning of the 18C for the Teutonic Order to the plans of the well known architect Johann Lukas von Hildebrandt. The exterior is highly ornate. The interior vaulting is adorned with light stucco, and over the high altar is a moving *Crucifixion* from the brush of Altomonte.

St Martin's Church (Martinskirche). – St Martin's is one of the oldest churches in Austria; it was built on Roman foundations by Charlemagne in the 8C.

EXCURSIONS

Abbey of St Florian★★. – *18 km - 11 miles – plus 1 1/2 hour sightseeing – Local map p 60. Leave Linz by ③, road No. 1, going towards Enns.* In Astern take the road to the right which crosses the motorway and leads to St Florian. The village is overlooked by its large abbey *(description p 123).*

The Mühlviertel. – *Round tour of 90 km - 56 miles – about 4 hours – Local map opposite.*
The Mühlviertel, or district of the Mühl, a small river which flows into the Danube above Linz, is formed of rather steep hills which develop between the Danube and the Czech frontier varying in height between 600 and 1 000 m - 2 000 to 3 000 ft. These are granite hills and they have been quarried extensively along the steep bank of the river, as at Mauthausen. The region beyond has wide valleys covered with a dark green carpet of forests contrasting, in its lonely melancholy, with the Danube Valley, where the towns are more frequent.
Leave Linz by the road to Bad Leonfelden to the north on the map. As soon as it leaves Linz, the road enters a little verdant gorge and begins to climb gently, sometimes among rocks, sometimes among orchards. Firs take the place of fruit and become denser after Glasau. The wild nature of the hills, where meadows alternate with fir forest, grows more marked as you approach Bad Leonfelden. About 500 m - 500 yds north of the town bear right towards Freistadt. The road is well laid and runs through a quiet countryside.

Freistadt★. – *Description p 70.*
Directly after leaving Freistadt, leave the Linz road and cross the Feldaist to follow its left bank. The road runs through woods before reaching Kefermarkt.

Kefermarkt. – *Description p 95.*
At the main crossroad of Kefermarkt turn right towards the railway station; cross the track and the Feldaist, 7 km - 4 miles further on you meet up with the main road, No. 125, connecting Freistadt and Linz.

Join us in our never ending task of keeping up to date.

Send us your comments and suggestions, please.

Michelin Tyre P.L.C.
Tourism Department
81 Fulham Road, LONDON SW3 6RD.

LOFER ★ (Salzburg)

Michelin map 426 fold 19 – *Local maps pp 93 and 122* – Pop 1 691 – Alt 625 m - 2 051 ft – 🅱 ☎ 322 – *Facilities pp 41 and 43*

The village of Lofer with the Loferer Steinberge, delicately chiselled and with snow-flecked walls, in the background, makes a delightful **picture**★★. The church tower stands out with its two onion roofs before an amphitheatre which, between the massive wooded foothills of the Ochsenhorn (2 511 m - 8 238 ft – at its highest point) and the Breithorn, opens on a view of the summit of the Grosses Reifhorn.

(After Lukas photo)

Lofer.

From one end to the other of the twisting village's main street, may be seen the comfortable and well wared for houses adorned with rounded oriel windows which recall Bavarian bourgeois architecture. The peasant houses on the outskirts of the village are often bedecked with a climbing pear – the local tree.

Lofer is the starting point for many excursions among the Alpine pastures: the most popular are to the Au meadows (Auerwiesen), the Loferer Alpe and the pilgrimage Church of Maria Kirchental.

MARIA SAAL ★ (Carinthia)

Michelin map 426 fold 36 – 7 km - 4 miles north of Klagenfurt – *Local map p 172* – Pop 3 215 – Alt 504 m - 1 654 ft

The pilgrims' Church of Maria Saal is the building nearest to the former Roman city of Virunum, capital of Norica *(map of Roman provinces p 22)*. This city, whose ruins are scattered over the Zollfeld plain, between Klagenfurt and St.Veit, was the first centre of reconversion in Carantania, as Carinthia was called in the 8 and 9C, after the Barbarian invasions.

■ THE CHURCH★ *time: 1/2 hour*

The present Gothic building is protected by a fortified enclosure, which once also included the churchyard and recalls how exposed the Zollfeld was to the Hungarian or Turkish hordes through the 16C. The existing church was built as a single project in the middle of the 15C. It has two towers of volcanic stone, decorated with delicate blind arcades forming a grille, and a vast roof of greenish stone slates. Many stone fragments are sealed into the south wall. Among the bas-reliefs of the Roman era, note especially that representing the triumph of Achilles, who is dragging the corpse of Hector, and a fragment representing a Roman mail waggon. The splendid tombstone of the Keutschach family, a work executed at Salzburg in 1510 for Archbishop Leonard von Keutschach, of whom you find many reminders at the Hohensalzburg *(p 132)*, has the Coronation of the Virgin as its central subject.

The interior of the church, remarkable for its unity, shows the design associated with late Gothic. In the main nave, the spaces in the network vaulting are decorated with figures emerging from chalices of flowers, representing the genealogy of Christ (1490).

The furnishings are of great value. In the north aisle, the altar to St Modestus combines a Carolingian table with a Romanesque sarcophagus, brought here some time ago to hold the sacred relics of the bishop. The chapel situated to the north contains the Arndorf altarpiece *(ca 1520)*, depicting the Coronation of Our Lady. The statue of the Virgin on the high altar (1425), with its serene and rather sleepy face, is an object of devotion to pilgrims. The chapel to the south is occupied by the altarpiece to St George (1526), a popular work.

Among the annexes to the church the most curious building is the octagonal charnel-house, which has two tiers of galleries. This romanesque building was rearranged in the 15C by a brotherhood of the Holy Sepulchre copying the Holy Sepulchre in Jerusalem. The galleries date from this period.

MARIASTEIN (Tyrol)

Michelin map 426 fold 18 – 10 km - 6 miles north of Wörgl and 13 km - 8 miles southwest of Kufstein – *Local map p 92* – Pop 170 – Alt 563 m — 1 847 ft.

The Castle of Mariastein draws pilgrims and tourists to a quiet little valley with fir covered slopes, which lies parallel to the Inn.

The Castle and its Chapels. – Leave the car below in the valley, before the final slope leading to the castle. The massive defensive tower of "Stein" was built on a huge eroded rock in the 14C. Its Lady Chapel later made it an object of Marian pilgrimage and ultimately the religious eclipsed the tower's military function.

Enter the castle court and climb the tower staircase. The **Knights' Hall** (Rittersaal) on the 2nd floor, houses the castle treasure – crown and sceptre of the Tyrolean counts. The upper storeys contain two chapels, one above the other. The lower or **Chapel of the Cross** (Kreuzkapelle) still has a Gothic interior dating from 1550. Above is the **Chapel of Miracles** (Gnadenkapelle) which has recovered its Baroque harmony and good lighting, thanks to the heightening of the windows and the removal of the second rate decoration which changed its character in the 19C. The Virgin is venerated in a gracefully draped statue dating from 1450.

Before leaving the little valley go up the slopes facing the castle to see the way it stands out before the crests of the Kaisergebirge on the horizon.

Michelin map **426** fold 23 – *Local maps pp 45 and 114* – Pop 1 927 – Alt 868 m - 2 848 ft – **▣ ☎** 2366 – *Facilities pp 41 and 43*

Mariazell is the most frequented pilgrims' city in Austria. Its **situation**★ on the gentle slopes of an escarpment, out of reach of morning mists (fine effects of sea clouds in still weather) and dipping towards a verdant Alpine basin, has charm. This extreme eastern end of the Alps, very jagged in outline, includes wild areas (massifs of the Hochschwab and the Ötscher, the Salza Valley, etc.) in spite of its modest altitude. You will get a good impression of the region by climbing to the **Bürgeralpe,** a belvedere to which there are frequent cable-cars from the centre of the town. *Departure 8.20am to 5pm (5.30pm July and August); 4pm in winter; 55S Rtn.*

The Pilgrimage. – The church celebrated its eighth centenary in 1957, thanks to the Habsburgs' cult of the Virgin of Mariazell and the continued devotion of the people.

It was in 1157 that the Benedictines founded a priory here. As early as the beginning of the 14C the first rescripts of indulgences appeared here, testifying to the attraction of the church for crowds of Christians. In 1365 Louis I of Anjou, King of Hungary, won a victory over the Turks which he attributed to the Virgin of Mariazell. From that time on, the worship of the Madonna of Mariazell more and more symbolized the spiritual forces which guaranteed the cohesion of the Austrian Empire and today even many Balkan refugees, who were formerly subjects of the Empire, make the pilgrimage in large groups. The most solemn ceremonies are on 15 August and 8 September.

For the rest of the summer the largest crowds assemble on Saturday evenings, when the great torchlight procession takes place.

■ THE BASILICA★ *time: 1/2 hour – brochure available in English*

In the 17C the growing number of pilgrims made it necessary to enlarge the original Gothic building which dated back to the 14C. The architect, **Domenico Sciassia** was given the task (1644 to 1704). He kept the nave but demolished the chancel to replace it by two vast bays, one of which was roofed by a dome. When he remade the façade, the architect left the Gothic porch intact between the two new and much squatter bulb-topped towers. This unusual architecture has become the emblem of this pilgrim city.

The main doorway still has its carved Gothic tympanum, whose lower register is devoted to the history of the pilgrimage.

Enter the church. The brilliant structure of the Chapel of Miracles marks the transition from the Baroquised Gothic main building to the after-nave, which is 17C.

West Nave. – This is nothing other than the former Gothic building, whose slim design can still be distinguished in spite of the Baroque shell and the width gained by including the former buttresses inside the building. Thanks to this last device, Sciassia found room along the aisles for a series of side-chapels, and on the first storey for a gallery whose large windows give an exceptional degree of lighting. To appreciate fully the details of the Baroque decoration – stucco and paintings – you must walk along these galleries.

Chapel of Miracles (Gnadenkapelle). – The chapel, built on a trapezoidal plan in the centre of the church, shelters a Romanesque statue, always in full regalia, of the Virgin of Mariazell. She is beneath a valuable silver baldachin on twelve columns designed by J.E. Fischer von Erlach the Younger. The enclosing grille, also of silver, was ordered by Maria Theresa from Viennese silversmiths in 1756.

East Nave. – This piece of Baroque architecture, superbly proportioned, is truly monumental. The inner nave thus formed is arranged, after a false transept, round a bay roofed with a dome. The oval plan of this lantern-dome is in harmony with the oblong shape of the church. In the last square bay, which ends the vista, stands the majestic high altar, completed in 1704, of J.B. Fischer von Erlach *(pp 34 and 165),* whose architecture is inspired by the triumphal arch of antiquity. The statues of the Crucifixion group, like those of the great angels guarding the Chapel of Miracles, are copies of the solid silver statues which were melted down to meet the needs of the Austrian treasury during the Napoleonic wars.

Treasury (Schatzkammer). – *Open 1 May to 31 October 10am to noon; 10S. Entrance by the staircase in the north tower and the gallery.*

On display are a remarkable brocade chasuble, (*ca* 1500) whose high relief embroidery represents saints under canopies and various robes for attiring the Virgin of Mariazell. Ex-votos can also be seen.

EXCURSION

Erlaufsee; Gemeindealpe★. – *Round tour of 20 km - 12 miles – about 2 1/2 hours – Local map p 114.* Leave Mariazell by the road to Bruck an der Mur. As soon as you reach the valley floor turn right into the Lunz road.

Marienwasserfall. – Go to the Marienwasserfall Inn. This small cascade flows like a shimmering veil in a rocky niche.

Go back to the car. At a junction of three roads, bear to the right. The road emerges from the woods and runs along the south shore of the **Erlaufsee** facing the Gemeindealpe. At the end of the lake, turn left towards Mitterbach and stop at the chairlift station (Alpensesselbahn) for the Gemeindealpe.

Gemeindealpe★. – *Alt 1 626 m - 5 335 ft – About 1 1/2 hours Rtn, including 1 hour by chairlift. Service from 8.50 to 11.30am and 1 to 4.50pm; Saturdays, Sundays and holidays only from Easter to 1 June and October; closed November to mid-December; 70S Rtn.*

From this height you can enjoy a general **view**★ of the Ötscher massif, overlooking a mountainous area cut across by the furrows of the Ötschergraben and the Törmauer. In the opposite direction the water of the Erlaufsee lies as a foreground to the Mariazell basin. In clear weather you can see the bastions of the Dachstein, in the southwest.

Return to the lower station and make for Mitterbach and from there to Mariazell by the direct road.

MAUTHAUSEN (Upper Austria)

Michelin map **426** fold 9 – 26 km - 16 miles east of Linz – *Local map p 60* – Pop 4 353 – Alt 250 m - 820 ft

Until 1938, when the Anschluss took place, Mauthausen was known only for its granite quarries, which supplied most of the paving-stones for Vienna. One of the quarries was used as a Nazi concentration camp, which made the name of Mauthausen one of the most sinister under their rule.

In 1949 the Austrian Government declared the camp to be an historic monument. By that time many of the hutments had been destroyed.

Tour of the Concentration Camp (Lager). – *Time: 1 1/2 to 2 hours; open 1 April to 14 October 8am to noon and 12.30 to 4pm (3pm 15 October to 31 March); closed 16 December to 31 January; 15S; tape and/or brochure available in English.*

Between 1938 and 1945 nearly 200 000 persons were exterminated within the boundaries or the annexes of the Mauthausen Camp. You can see the huts and the rooms in which the prisoners suffered and died.

Outside the massive and oppressive boundary are the memorials set up by countries whose people perished here. Below the plateau is the Staircase of Death, leading to the quarry.

MAYERLING (Lower Austria)

Michelin map **426** fold 25 – 36 km - 22 miles southwest of Vienna – *Local map p 169*

A Carmelite convent built by order of the Emperor Franz-Josef, marks the site of the hunting-lodge in which a drama that shook the world took place.

A Tragic Love Story. – The secrecy with which the imperial family surrounded the tragic affair gave rise to the most fanciful theories. Nonetheless, with the help of recently discovered documents, most of the drama can be recreated.

In 1888 the Archduke Rudolf, only son of the Emperor Franz-Josef and Empress Elizabeth and heir to the throne of Austria-Hungary, was thirty years old. His sympathy for the people opposed to the Hungarian parliament and his liberal ideas frightened the aristocracy. His lack of faith angered the Church; and his dissolute life, worsened by his unfortunate marital obligations created estranged relations with his family. His last "conquest" was made at a ball at the German Embassy, where he made the acquaintance of a girl of seventeen, Maria Vetsera. He fell in love with her, and his love was returned. Hearing of this liaison, the Emperor decided to put an end to the scandal. In the afternoon of 28 January 1889 he had a stormy interview with his son during which he told him of the refusal by Pope Leo XIII to annul his marriage; he also demanded him to reveal the names of the Hungarian conspirators. Refusing to betray his friends and weary of a situation full of unsolved problems, Rudolf, already depressed, decided to commit suicide with his loved one. The following day, he did not appear at dinner but isolated himself in the hunting lodge at Mayerling with Maria. On 30 January they were found dead. Maria was the first to die. Rudolf then wrote to his mother, his wife, and his very old friend Maria Casper (Mizzie), and at dawn shot himself.

MAYRHOFEN ★ (Tyrol)

Michelin map **426** fold 32 – *Local map p 72* – Pop 3 274 – Alt 630 m - 2 067 ft – ▣ ☎ 2305, 2635 – *Facilities pp 41 and 43*

Mayrhofen stands at the point where the Zillertal, one of the most open and most densely populated tributary valleys of the Inn in the Tyrol, springs from the high crystalline massif from which it takes its name (highest point: the Hochfeiler – alt 3 510 m - 11 516 ft). The town plays the part of a regional tourist capital and as a resort is a mountaneering and skiing centre. It has pleasant facilities for sport (tennis courts, swimming pool) in a shady setting and owes a great deal of its activity in summer to the international holiday courses of its university which keep up a lively atmosphere and help to maintain local folklore.

Mayrhofen is at the head of four mountain valleys or *Gründe,* which spread like a fan at the foot of glaciers of the Zillertal Alps. Motorists can follow the Tuxertal cul-de-sac, which is dotted with imposing chalets as far as **Hintertux** *(facilities pp 41 and 43)* a resort for summer skiing (at Gefrorne Wand).

The climb by cable-car from Mayrhofen to the Penken (alt 1 795 m - 5 889 ft) quickly affords a general panorama of the Zillertal Alps.

MELK ★★ (Lower Austria)

Michelin map **426** fold 10 – *Local map p 61* – Pop 5 074 – Alt 213 m - 699 ft – ▣ ☎ 2307

The Abbey of Melk crowns a rocky bluff overlooking the Danube from over 50 m - 150 ft – and is the apogee of Baroque architecture in Austria.

The Cradle of Lower Austria. – The princely family of Babenberg, who were natives of Bavaria, established their rule on the site of a Roman stronghold at Melk, fixing their seat there, at the end of the 10C. Recalling the fate of the Nibelungen – Melk is said to be the Medelike of the famous story – the Babenbergs followed the direction of the Danube Valley and established their court first at Tulln, then at Vienna.

At the end of the 11C, Leopold III von Babenberg handed over his castle to the Benedictines, who converted it into a fortified abbey. The spiritual and intellectual renown of Melk spread through the whole of Lower Austria.

Days of Storm and Days of Glory. – The spread of the Reformation hindered the development of monastic life. The Turkish invasion in 1683 sowed ruin and chaos beyond Vienna, many estates of the monastery were ravaged. It was gutted by fire but was entirely rebuilt from 1 702 onwards in the form it has kept. In 1805 and 1809, during his successful campaign against Austria, Napoleon I stayed at Melk and established his general headquarters there. The abbey has managed to preserve its artistic treasures. It still plays an important part in giving a good education to each generation of Austrians.

■ BENEDICTINE ABBEY★★ *time: 1 hour*

Above the high street of the town (Hauptstrasse) lined with fine middle class houses, stands the south façade of the abbey, extending for some 240 m - 787 ft.

The promontory on which the abbey is built, is approached from the east; follow the signs posted: P *Stift Melk.*

Guided tours (1 hour) in English (apply in advance) Palm Sunday to All Saint's Day 9 (9.30am Sundays and holidays) to 11.30am and 1 to 4pm (5pm 1 June to 31 August); the rest of the year 11 am to 2 pm; 30S; brochure available in English.

In 1702, Abbot Dietmayr laid the first stone in the rebuilding of the monastery. The architect, Prandtauer, managed to make the best of a trapeze shaped site which was hardly favourable, and to create a structure perfectly suited to the situation. After his death in 1726 the work was completed with the help of his plans by his pupil, Franz Munggenast.

The outer gateway, giving access to the first court, is framed by the statues of St Leopold and St Coloman, the abbey's patrons, and flanked by two bastions of the 17 and 18C. On the inner gate is the abbey coat of arms. Directly beyond a vestibule, with a painted ceiling depicting St Benedict, the founder of the Order, is the **Court of Prelates** (Prälatenhof), an admirable group of buildings with walls adorned with statues representing the prophets. The dome of the abbey church may be seen beyond the fountain.

Emperors' Gallery (Kaisergang). – The gallery, which is 196 m - 644 ft long, provided access to the chambers reserved for notable guests. It was decorated with paintings of the kings and regents of Austria, the place of honour being taken by the Empress Maria Theresa and her husband, François of Lorraine. Several rooms (west of the staircase) have been converted into museum galleries. The galleries contain old engravings of the abbey, a Gothic altarpiece (by Jorg Breu) from the former abbey and liturgical ornaments.

Marble Hall (Marmorsaal). – This hall, preceded by a vestibule adorned with portraits of the founder of the abbey and its architect, impresses the visitor less by the lavishness of its decoration than by the strength of its design which is dominated by a series of pilasters covered in a reddish brown marble stucco.

The allegorical painting on the ceiling – *Reason guiding Humanity from the darkness of obscurity towards the light of civilization and culture* – was done in 1732 by Paul Troger, whose blues are famous.

Terrace. – The terrace, lying along the tip of a rock spur, occupies the upper part of an elegant portico. This is used to link the symmetrical buildings which are, respectively, the Marble Hall and the Library. It affords a fine view of the Danube and the façade of the abbey church.

Library (Bibliothek). – Like the Marble Hall, the Library is two storeys high and has a fine ceiling painted by Troger. It contains 80 000 books and 2 000 manuscripts. The gilded wood statues at the entrances represent the four faculties; inside, the woodwork and the gilding gleam.

(After P. Ledermann photo)

Melk Abbey.

Abbey Church★★★ (Stiftskirche). – The church is surrounded by the abbey buildings but dominates the group with the symmetrical towers of its west front and its great octagonal dome.

The interior gives a great impression of lightness, due to many windows having been let into the walls, the sweep of great fluted pilasters and to a judicious use of colours, in which brownish-red, grey, orange and golden tones are mingled.

The lavish decoration includes frescos, gold ornaments and marble.

The vaulting of the nave, the dome and the altars are crowded with figures. In the dome, which is 65 m - 213 ft high, are enthroned God the Father, Christ, the Evangelists and the Doctors of the Church. On the vaulting of the nave you can recognize St Benedict, being triumphantly received in Heaven.

All these paintings are by Johann Michael Rottmayr, as well as those on the side altars depicting the Adoration of the Magi, St Michael and the Baptism of Christ. Paul Troger did the paintings on the other side altars, where you see St Nicholas and St Sebastian, while the Italian painter Gaetano Fanti was responsible for the wall paintings.

In the midst of these riches the eye is caught by the high altar. In the centre of the group of statues, the two Princes of the Apostles, St Peter and St Paul, to whom the church is consecrated, take leave of one another before their martyrdom.

Michelin main road maps

980 *Greece*
986 *Great Britain, Ireland*
987 *Germany, Austria, Benelux*
988 *Italy*
989 *France*
990 *Spain, Portugal*
991 *Yugoslavia*

MILLSTATT ★ (Carinthia)

Michelin map **426** folds 34 and 35 – Pop 3 149 – Alt 604 m - 1 903 ft – 🖪 ☎ 2021, 2022 – *Facilities p 41*

The **lake** reflects the distant peaks of the Kreuzeck and the Reisseck, outcrops of the Tauern. The lake has made the small town of Millstatt one of the favourite summer resorts of Carinthia.

An old abbey church with bulbous towers remains in the centre of the town – its main door and cloisters one of the glories of Romanesque art to be seen in Austria.

■ ABBEY (Stift) *time: 1/2 hour*

While making the tour you will find it interesting to see how the buildings and works of art are connected with the three stages in the history of the abbey, which was, successively: a Benedictine monastery of the congregation of Hirsau (1080-1469); a priory of the military Order of St George (1469-1598); and a house of the Jesuits (1598-1773). Since 1773 the monastery buildings have been, for the most part, used as an hotel.

From the car park in Millstatt's town centre go to the abbey through the archway beside the 15C Hôtel Lindenhof, former mansion of the Grand Master of the Knights of St George.

Abbey Courtyard★ (Stiftshof). – The 1 000 year old "Judgment" lime tree, and two tiers of galleries with Italian arches form a colourful scene. The elegance of this 16C architecture reveals the riches of the Order of St George, which was founded by the Emperor Friedrich III, to assist in the defence of Christianity against the Turks.

Cloister (Kreuzgang). – *Enter from the east side of the court.* The cloister was endowed with Gothic vaulting by the Knights of St George at the beginning of the 12C. It still possesses the Romanesque blind arcades with slim marble columns and the capitals decorated with animals or symbolic plants. In the east gallery, which is the most open, may be seen the design, often reproduced in tourist literature, of a gnome and a lion each supporting a slim column. In front of a former communicating door into the church are two detached columns, each resting on a sculptural group representing a woman (the Church) taming a monstrous male figure (the pagan world).

By way of the cloister you arrive at the small abbey museum (Stiftsmuseum).

Return to the abbey courtyard to go up to the church.

Church. – The porch contains a magnificent marble **Romanesque doorway★★**, whose decorative designs in the covings – rolls, braids – are preserved in all their delicacy. Masks and animals along the ends of the small columns represent the struggle between good and evil. The tympanum shows Abbot Heinrich II (1166-1177) paying homage to Christ in his abbey church.

The interior owes its network vaulting, with storied keystones, to the Knights of St George and its furnishings, as well as the statues in the main nave (saints of the Company), to the Jesuits. Two side chapels, facing one another, contain (on the left) the Tombstone of Grand Master Siebenhirter (d 1508), and (on the right) that of Grand Master Geumann (d 1533).

MÖLL, Upper Valley of the ★ (Carinthia)

Michelin map **426** fold 33

The winding Valley of the Möll, a tributary of the Drava, is an important means of passage. First of all, downstream from Heiligenblut (*see below*) it provides an exit for the Grossglockner road; in the lower section, between Winklern and Möllbrücke, a road has been built along it, diverting the large volume of traffic between the Dolomites, Lienz and the Carinthian Lakes from the more southerly Drava Valley.

From Heiligenblut to Lienz – *38 km – 24 miles – about 1 hour – Local map opposite*

As you leave Heiligenblut (p 81), the road passes through the gap made by the Möll in the Zlapp "bolt", then drops rapidly to a lower level in the valley. The peak of the Grossglockner is now out of sight.

The Valley of the Möll, quiet and green, is still dotted with houses of dark toned wood lending a touch of mountain scenery to this section. In the meadows are crop drying frames like grilles (*illustrated and explained p 29*).

Döllach im Mölltal. – Pop 1 556. *Facilities p 39*. The town was formerly a gold and silver mining centre.

Downstream from Mörtschach there is a first glimpse, to the south, of the cliffs and pinnacles of the Dolomites at Lienz.

At Winklern, **the road to the Iselsberg** – a pass at an alt of 1 204 m - 3 950 ft – (*facilities: see Lienz p 41*) emerges from the Möll Valley, which bends abruptly eastwards between wooded slopes. The **descent★★** from the Iselsberg to Lienz, of which the first two loops invite a halt (Gasthaus Dolomitenblick) is magnificently designed within view of the Lienz Dolomites. These have on their surface innumerable facets whose grey tone is warmed by the least ray of sunshine. Southwestwards, the Upper Drava Valley plunges, curving at Lienz (p 102).

HEILIGENBLUT – LIENZ

0   5   10 km

MONDSEE (Upper Austria)

Michelin map **426** fold 20 – *Local maps pp 136 and 137* – Pop 2 140 – Alt 493 m - 1 617 ft –
🏛 ☎ 2270 – *Facilities p 41*

Up to 1791 the history of Mondsee is intermingled with that of its Benedictine abbey. Today, many tourists are attracted to this township, which bears the same name as the nearby lake whose shady banks are approached from the town along an avenue of lime trees. The **Mondsee★**, a lake shaped like a crescent at the foot of the cliffs of the Drachenwand and the Schafberg, is the most temperate in the Salzkammergut. The lake is becoming even better known since the opening of the **sector★** of the Salzburg-Vienna motorway, going along its north shore. The neighbouring region still produces one of the rare Austrian cheeses with an excellent flavour known as Mondsee.

■ **SIGHTS** *time: 1 hour*

Parish Church (Pfarrkirche). – This former, late 15C abbey church stands on the square – formerly the monastery cemetery – which borders, on the left, the bygone buildings of the abbey. The present façade, with its Baroque helmeted towers, was remodelled in 1740.

The interior escaped the Baroque influences of the 17C and has preserved its Gothic network vaulting as the monastery ran into financial difficulties.

Meinrad Guggenbichler (1649-1723) who is known in Austria's art history as the Sculptor of Mondsee, endowed the different halls with furnishings (7 of the 13 altars) which give a great unity of style. The altar of the Holy Sacrament, on the lower left hand side, with its twisted columns supported by cherubs is one of his most representative works. The altar to St Sebastian (facing the other altar) is well known with its statue of St Roch. In the choir can be seen the gate to the sacristy in lustrous metal leaf. The seven charming little statues surmounting the arch are, like this masterpiece of ironwork, late 15C.

Local Museum (Heimatmuseum). – *Open 1 May to the end of October 9am to 6pm. 15S.*

Installed in different chapels of the former abbey, the museum contains local antiquities and traditions.

A photographic sequence illustrates the making of *Einbaum* boats, cut from a single tree of which some are still in use. In the upstairs part of the church, under the Gothic arches of the monks' library, the history of the abbey and the showing of manuscripts (reproductions) is featured. Also exhibited are works of Meinrad Guggenbichler.

Smoking House (Mondseer Rauchhaus). – *Access by the motorway direction Salzburg-Vienna (the second car park after the Mondsee exit). Open April to the end of October 8am to 6pm; closed November to April; 15S, children 7S.*

The house is a primitive wooden chalet built in the local style and surrounded by outhouses. The most noticeable feature is the old fashioned but logical placing of the vaulted hearth which lacks a chimney. The escaping smoke formed a rising cloud which spread out to dry the farm crops in the attics without inconveniencing the inhabitants.

Maria-Hilf Chapel. – *For access see above.* A 15C building which has been Baroquised; well situated on a bluff overlooking the lake.

MÖRBISCH ★★ (Burgenland)

Michelin map **426** fold 26 – 20 km - 12 miles southeast of Eisenstadt – *Local map p 112* –
Pop 2 362 – Alt 118 m - 387 ft – *Facilities p 41*

Mörbisch is the last village on the western shore of Neusiedler Lake before the Hungarian frontier. In the neighbourhood is produced a well known white wine. The village is charming, with colourful and picturesque alleys at right angles to either side of the main street. *(See tourist calendar of events p 31.)*

The houses are whitewashed and nearly all have an outdoor staircase, surmounted by a porch. Doors and shutters painted in bright colours, bunches of maize hanging on the walls and generously flower decked balconies and windows strike a cheerful note and form a delightful picture.

A road east of the village leads across marshes and reed-beds to a small bathing centre *(access is payable)* on Neusiedlers Lake, from which you can see the no man's land between Austria and Hungary.

A Street in Mörbisch.

South of Mörbisch, about 1.5 km - 1 mile away, you come to the end of the road (barred) marking the Hungarian frontier. A double row of barbed wire, look-out towers and defensive works mark the Iron Curtain.

When visiting the Continent

use Michelin Red Guides

 – **Benelux - Deutschland - España Portugal - France - Italia**
  (hotels and restaurants)

and the Michelin Green Guides

 – **Austria - Germany - Italy - Portugal - Spain - Switzerland**
  (sights and tourist routes)

MUR Valley ★ (Styria)

Michelin map **426** folds 23, 37 and 38

The route we propose from Graz to Leoben runs up the darkly wooded Mur Valley for 70 km - 43 miles. This is only about one-seventh of the course of the river, which rises in the Radstädter Tauern, in the Salzburg district, and ends in Hungary, 483 km - 300 miles away, where it throws itself into the Drava, a tributary of the Danube.

An Industrial Corridor. – In a mountainous and wooded region like Styria, valleys are of first class economic importance. Work in the forests has led to the installation in the Mur Valley of many saw and papermills. The mining of magnesite, which is exported to all parts of the world and is used on the spot to make firebricks for furnaces, has also contributed to the prosperity of the region.

Between Graz and Bruck an der Mur, three power stations use the waters of the river to produce electricity.

From Graz to Leoben – *70 km - 43 miles – about 2 1/2 hours – not including the Lurgrotte.*

Leave Graz *(p 73)* by ⑤, the road to Bruck an der Mur. Directly after crossing the river, whose left bank you will follow upstream, wooded hills appear and, soon, rock outcrops.

As you come out of Peggau, a large industrial town covered in dust from its cement factories, you will see to the right of the road an impressive limestone cliff. In the mountain behind lies the Lurgrotte, the network of galleries which links the Valley of the Mur with the small Valley of the Semriach to the east.

Lurgrotte (Peggau entrance). – *Open in summer 9am to 4pm; closed Mondays; 30S; brochure available in English.* The walk beside the underground river enables you to see several concretions such as the Prince, which stands at the end of the walk. *It is possible to continue to Blocksberg (time: 2 hours - 40S).*

The valley, often bordered by rocky slopes, becomes greener and more picturesque.

There is an attractive view from the bridge by-passing the town of Frohnleiten, whose houses cluster at the foot of the church on the steep bank of the River Mur. The long leats which, farther downstream, supply the Laufnitzdorf and Pernegg power stations, have created new stretches of water parallel to the river.

Bruck an der Mur★. – *Description p 56.*

Beyond Bruck the road follows the right bank of the Mur, which runs in a west-to-east direction. To the left you see the summit of the Brucker Hochalpe, a limestone massif which reaches an altitude of 1 643 m - 5 390 ft. The valley now widens and becomes more and more industrial until it reaches Leoben *(p 102)*.

NEUSIEDLER Lake ★ (NEUSIEDLER SEE) (Burgenland)

Michelin map **426** fold 26

The Neusiedler See is the only example in Central Europe of a steppe-type lake. It has a melancholy aspect and is one of the great curiosities of the Burgenland *(general information on this federal district p 13)*.

A Capricious Lake. – The lake has an area of 320 km² – 124 sq miles – of which most belongs to Austria, though Hungary holds the southern basin (1/5 of the total surface). Its waters are warm and salty, and it is almost completely surrounded by a thick belt of reeds. It is nowhere more than about 2 m - 7 ft deep and is fed from underground lakes. The only tributary of any size, the Wulka, is an almost negligible factor when you consider that the bulk of normal evaporation is four times the quantity of water that flows in. There is no permanent outflow. When a strong wind blows for some time in the same direction, the waters are driven towards one shore, while the level on the near shore drops perceptibly. When the wind drops, the lake returns to its normal level and appearance.

A Bone of Contention. – It even happens that the waters disappear altogether (the last time was 1868-1872). This, for the lakeside dwellers, is a wonderful chance to enlarge their estates. Each refers to documents used by his family in similar circumstances; disputes break out and lawsuits are begun until such time as the lake reappears as mysteriously as it vanished.

A Paradise for Birds. – In the inextricable thickets formed by the reeds, an extraordinary aquatic fauna lives. More than 250 varieties of wildfowl have settled there: herons, waterhens, wild duck and geese, gulls, teals, storks, bustards, egrets, etc.

Fishing, shooting and aquatic sports. – Every village near the lake has a little bathing-beach, normally reached by a roadway between two hedges of reeds. Owing to its proximity to Vienna (50 km - 31 miles) it attracts all those who care for aquatic sports and in winter those who are keen on ice sports. Many skilled anglers and wildfowlers use flat-bottomed boats to make their way along the canals among the reed-beds.

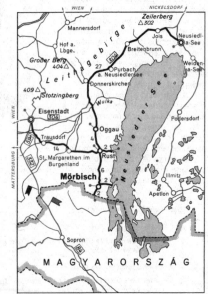

The Landscape. – The lakeshores, to the east, are less fertile, appearing as a steppe-like countryside divided by pools and ponds, whereas to the west, the shores are limited by a range of hills, the Leithagebirge, overlooking the lake from about 300 m - 1 000 ft. Vines, maize and fruit trees – even almonds – as well as vegetables, flourish at the foot of these heights.

The vineyards, terraced on the slopes or lying in the plain, enjoy plenty of sunshine and produce famous vintages: the red and white wines of Rust, Mörbisch and Oggau, being the most famous for their bouquet. Thus, the winegrowers of Rust saw the quality of their vines recognized by royal privilege in 1364, and by virtue of this privilege they enjoy the right to adorn the huge vats in their vaulted cellars with the coat of arms of the town.

From Neusiedl to Eisenstadt – *69 km - 43 miles – 2 hours – Local map p 112*

Leave Neusiedl northwestwards (if you have come from Vienna by road No. 10, make straight for Jois without passing through Neusiedl) and follow the road towards Eisenstadt, bear left 2.4 km - 1 1/2 miles after Donnerskirchen to Rust.

Rust. – Pop 1 702. Rust is famous for its storks' nests, to which the birds return faithfully every year. It is a rich winegrowing village: huge carved doorways give access to the arcaded inner courtyards of the winegrowing owners. From the village, you can drive by a causeway through the rushes to a landing-stage and to the bathing resort *(must pay for car park and access to beach)* which is worth seeing for its lakeside dwellings. *Excursions on the lake are organized in season.*

Mörbisch★★. – *Description p 111.*

Return to Rust where you bear left for St. Margarethen and Eisenstadt. Before reaching Eisenstadt *(p 65)*, the small capital of the Burgenland, one drives through a hilly district with alternating vineyards and orchards.

OBERNBERG AM INN (Upper Austria)

Michelin map 426 fold 7 – 37 km - 23 miles south of Passau – Pop 1 682 – Alt 352 m - 1 155 ft

Obernberg, built on the right bank of the Inn, marks the frontier of Austria and Germany.

Marktplatz. – This street-square *(Strassenplatz – p 28)*, which is spacious and has in its centre a carved stone fountain, is framed by elegant houses with brightly coloured façades, some of which are decorated with stucco. From the middle of the square the fretted gables, and the silhouette of the bulbous belfry of the church, make a pleasant picture.

OSSIACH, Lake of ★ (OSSIACHER SEE) (Carinthia)

Michelin map 426 fold 35

A little apart from the Villach basin, the Lake of Ossiach, which is as yet largely unknown to tourists, is distinguished from other large lakes in Carinthia by its uniform, rather wild setting of steep, wooded slopes. These afford green country scenery. The road along the north shore forms a part of the rapid route from Villach to Vienna by-passing Klagenfurt.

Tour of the Lake, starting from Villach – *39 km - 24 miles – about 1 1/2 hours – Local map p 172*

Leaving Villach *(p 169)* the road from Vienna (No. 94) leads into the alluvial plain. Ahead and to the right the ruins of Landskron stand on a spur. Skirt the north shore of the lake, at the foot of the steep Gerlitzen slopes.

Gerlitzen★★. – *From Tschöran, 12 km - 7 miles on a toll road – plus 1 hour on foot Rtn. Access and description p 71.*

Going round the lake by the east, the road takes the southern shore, which is slightly steeper and more countrified with its hamlets of old wooden houses (at Altossiach)

Ossiach. – Pop 568. *Facilities p 42.* The Benedictine Abbey of Ossiach (now transformed into a hotel) was the centre of the re-evangelisation and Germanisation of Carinthia and Slovenia from the 11C. In the 16 and 17C, it had periods of splendour, as in the summer of 1552, during which the Abbot, when receiving Charles V, sailed a fleet of galleys on the lake for his imperial visitor. The monastery **church**★ suffers a little from having so large a mass for its single clock-tower, built at the crossing of the transept. Inside, the upper parts were greatly modified by Baroque influences between 1741 and 1749. This is particularly noticeable in the raised **stuccos**★ coloured according to the technique of the Wessobrunn School *(p 34).* The less brilliant decorative painting is the work of the local artist, Joseph Ferdinand Fromiller, who also worked in the Landhaus at Klagenfurt. The ancient Gothic chapel, with its baptismal fonts on the left of the entrance, preserves one of the most precious of the sixty altarpieces dating from the end of the Gothic era, to be found in Carinthia. This masterpiece, wich dates from the beginning of the 16C is attributed to one of the St. Veit studios. It represents the Virgin between St Margaret and St Catherine, with the apostles, in groups of three, on the panels.

As the tour of the Lake of Ossiach ends, the ruins of Landskron appear once more against the distant crests of the Villacher Alpe.

Landskron Castle. – *1.5 km - 1 mile from St Andrä by a steep road.* The castle, which in the Middle Ages was one of the strongholds of the Habsburgs in Carinthia, passed in the middle of the 16C to the Khevenhüller family who rebuilt it. Bartholomew Khevenhüller, who owned the castle of Velden *(p 171)*, displayed during his stay there a brilliance which was chronicled at the time. But becoming an object of endless appropriations and appeals, started by the measures taken against Protestants at the time of the Thirty Years War – for the Khevenhüller family supported the Reformation – the fortress was no longer maintained after the 17C. A café-restaurant now occupies its ruins. From the esplanade there is a wide **view**★ of the Villach basin, the Karawanken and the Lake of Ossiach.

Return to Villach along the lake's effluent.

Michelin map **426** folds 11, 23 and 24

The mountainous area south of St.Pölten, between the Wienerwald and the Eisenerz Alps, is part of the limestone Pre-Alps. The first foothills, which are wooded and 600 m to 800 m - 2 000 ft to 2 600 ft high – give way to a succession of minor ranges, reaching an altitude of 1 893 m - 6 211 ft – at the massive peak of the Ötscher. This can be seen at a great distance, especially when approached from the north.

From St.Pölten to Mariazell – *81 km - 51 miles – about 2 1/2 hours – Local map below*

Starting from St. Pölten, take road No. 20 southwards. The first height appears a little after St. Georgen. The road runs up the left bank of the Traisen and climbs gently among dales where the meadows are enclosed by fences of plaited laths.

Lilienfeld. – Pop 3 030. The Gothic church of this Cistercian Abbey is of astonishing size and architectural purity.

Beyond the quiet country resort of Lilienfeld you leave, at Freiland, the road to St. Aegyd, from which you will finally emerge on your return from Mariazell. The road, which is pleasant and picturesque, becomes more and more enclosed, first between wooded slopes, then in a rocky gorge where there are outcrops of schist. Reservoirs supply small factories, including papermills at Dickenau.

Beyond Türnitz, the well laid road climbs steadily affording wider and wider views of limestone ridges of 1 200 m to 1 400 m - 4 000 ft to 4 600 ft. A series of hairpin bends leads to the village of Annaberg, built on a pass at an altitude of 973 m - 3 192 ft – and facing the summit of the Ötscher.

Annaberg. — Pop 1 058. Annaberg has a curious site at the top of a pass, facing a range of mountains from which emerges the Ötscher (1 892 m - 6 207 ft).

The pilgrims' church, well known to the faithful on their way to Mariazell, is 14 and 15C. It is dedicated to St Anne, as the Holy Family (15C) at the high altar shows ; and still has fine ogive vaulting but was decorated in the Baroque style in the 17 and 18C. The ceiling of the small south chapel is adorned with frescos and stucco; cherubs and statues overload the high altar and side altars, and there is a mass of gilding and carving on the pulpit and the organ-loft.

During the hairpin bend descent, the Ötscher, towering 1 000 m - 3 280 ft above, stands out clearly to the west. Josefsberg is the start of a pleasant run downhill among fir woods, affording fine vistas towards the Gemeindealpe (1 626 m - 5 335 ft) on the right.

All this region lives on cattle raising and forestry. In the valleys there were once many little forges, working on the Styrian iron ore from the nearby Eisenerz. Today they have disappeared. You leave on the right of the road the artificial Erlaufstausee lake, barring the upper course of the Erlauf.

Mitterbach. – Pop 693. *Facilities p 41.*

On leaving Mitterbach take a right turn and drive along a second lake, this one being natural, the Erlaufsee, before reaching Mariazell *(p 107).*

Alternative Return Route via St. Aegyd. – *4 km - 2 miles – less drive.* Leave Mariazell eastwards, by the road to Mürzzuschlag which runs steeply downhill, enters the Salza Valley and follows the stream closely. After Terz the road, which is picturesque, plunges into a gorge with rocky sides to which conifers cling.

At St. Aegyd you are in the Unrecht Traisen Valley, which is lined whith factories and sawmills. Beyond Hohenberg the limestone cliffs are broken, here and there, by amphitheatres. At Freiland you return back to road No. 20, on which you started out.

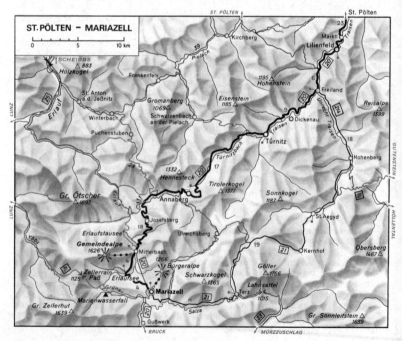

The Ötztal, which is remembered by moutaineers as a series of shining glaciers – total surface area: 173 km² - 67 sq miles – is a deep valley running into the Inn and consisting for 50 km – 31 miles of ravines separated by isolated basins, where the patriarchal traditions of Old Tyrol have long been observed.

When mountains unite more than they divide. – The Ötztal Alps include the highest point in the northern Tyrol, the Wildspitze (3 774 m - 12 382 ft). Schoolboys also learn that the highest parish in Austria, Obergurgl (1 927 m - 6 321 ft) and the highest permanent human habitation in the country, **Rofen,** near Vent (2 104 m - 6 608 ft) are in the upper basin of the Ötztal.

Until the First World War these places were more closely connected with the Upper Adige, to the south, from which these people originally came, than with the Inn Valley. For long the inhabitants preferred to trudge through snowfields on wide passes like the Hochjoch or Niederjoch, at an altitude of nearly 3 000 m - 10 000 ft – rather than make their way along the floors of the gorges of the Ötztaler Ache, on unsafe roads exposed to floods, falling stones and avalanches.

When the Timmelsjoch road was completed, in 1969, the Ötztal stopped, at least in full summer, being inaccessible.

From the Inn Valley to San Leonardo – *88 km - 55 miles – about 4 hours – Local map below*

On the Italian side the road is generally snow-free from mid-June to mid-October. The route is impressive (no barriers) with an irregular surface, especially in the tunnels. Trailers, caravans, buses and trucks are forbidden.

On the Austrian side, however, the road is generally open all year round, at least to Hochgurgl.

Above Hochgurgl, a toll of 80S is exacted (a car with 6 passengers) 120S Rtn. Customs offices are closed 8pm to 7am.

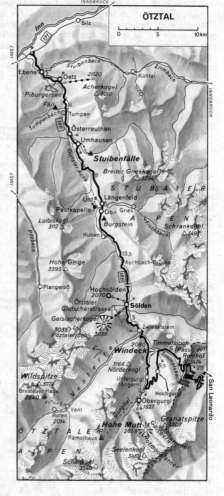

Starting from the main road along the Inn Valley, the Ötztal road runs through pleasant pine woods among piles of debris brought down from the Ötztaler Ache which has been deeply furrowed by the torrent. This flows beneath the picturesque covered bridge at Ebene to enter the Ötz basin, which is dominated by the rocky tooth of the Acherkogel. Chestnuts, fields of maize and peach and apricot orchards show that the Ötztal corridor, running due south, acts as a warm air vent, thanks to the Föhn (p 17).

Ötz (Oetz). – Pop 1 999. *Facilities p 42.* The town is well sited on the last levels of the sunny slope on which the large church is built. Several buildings have a traditional air, for example, the Gasthof Stern (Star Inn) with its flower decked oriel and painted façade.

The walk to the romantic Lake Piburger (Piburgersee) nearby is popular.

The road climbs over a first shelf, crossed by the torrent in a muddy stream. It reaches Tumpen in another basin into which the Tumpenbach, on the right, pours in a series of cascades.

Österreuthen. – This hamlet is one of the most harmonious architectural groups in the valley. Note the overhanging upper storeys sheltering a veranda, a detail which is found also in the Cortina Dolomites.

Umhausen. – Pop 2 301. A typical large inn (the Gasthaus Krone) is characteristic of this pleasant village. Customers may ask to see the room with a balcony still furnished in 17C style.

Stuiben Falls★★ (Stuibenfälle). – *About 2 hours on foot Rtn along a signposted track which begins at* the Tourist Office pavilion (Verkehrsverein). The road leads first to a restaurant-chalet. Here, cross the torrent and walk up the left bank to the foot of the cascade.

You must go down to reach a second wooded ravine, near the swiftly flowing Ötztaler Ache. The valley widens again to form the Längenfeld basin.

Längenfeld. – Pop 3 149. This resort is divided into two separate settlements by the Fischbach torrent.

The town nestles in an angle of the valley made by the steep promontory of the Burgstein. Its nearby larch woods have been well prepared for walkers.

The ÖTZTAL★

The scene has a harsh beauty, for the inner plain of Längenfeld, which still carries a few crops at 1 200 m - 4 000 ft altitude, is hemmed in between peaks approaching 3 000 m - 9 840 ft but many details of the landscape are charming. Among these is the shape of the 17C Pestkapelle, a votive chapel for the plague, in the woods on the opposite slope.

Beyond Huben begins a long ravine which, after the bridge at Aschbach (Aschbach-Brücke), narrows to a **gorge**★ covered with larches.

Sölden★. – Pop 1 668. *Facilities p 42*. Sölden lives on two levels. A chairlift links the old Tyrolean village (1 377 m - 4 158 ft) with its mountain annexe of Hochsölden (2 070 m - 6 791 ft), a magnificent sloping site.

Sölden is the departure point for the cable-car to the **Geislacherkogel**★★ whose upper station at 3 058 m - 10 033 ft serves as a viewpoint for the entire Ötztal Alps. It is also the place from where the **Ötztal Glacier Road** begins (Ötztaler Gletscherstrasse - toll: 150S and 45S per person *after the 4th passenger*). This road is one of the highest in the Alps (highest point 2 822 m - 9 258 ft). It serves an area of 20 km² - 8 sq miles open to ski in winter as well as in the summer. The Rettenbachferner and Tiefenbachferner glaciers are connected by a tunnel and have ski lifts. At Zwieselstein the valley divides: on the right, the Ventertal provides access to the formerly much used Hochjoch (2 875 m - 9 433 ft) and Niederjoch Passes (3 019 m - 9 905 ft). Take the valley on the left, the Gurgltal, into which pour the last of the Timmelsbach Falls.

Obergurgl. – Pop 356. *Facilities p 42. 4 km - 2 miles upstream from Untergurgl*.

This small resort (alt 1 927 m - 6 321 ft) has grown up in the combe at the end of the valley, within **view**★ of some of the ice covered peaks of the Schalfkogel group. A wider **panorama**★★, including among others the glaciary amphitheatres of the Rotmoosferner and the Gaisbergferner, can be seen from the top of the **Hohe Mutt**★★ spur (2 659 m - 8 724 ft).

Hochgurgl. – *Facilities see at Obergurgl p 42.*

After a steep climb the Timmelsjoch road drops briefly to reach the **Windeck belvedere**★★ (alt 2 080 m - 6 824 ft) from which there is a view of the Gurgl Valley and the Great Gurgl Glacier and, to the north, the cleft of the Ötztal. The road begins to climb once more through an austere landscape up to the Timmelsjoch (2 509 m - 8 032 ft). On the southern slope of the *col* the road, often cut out of the living rock, passes through a tunnel 700 m - nearly half a mile long – before plunging into the Val Passiria and affording impressive views of the crest marking the frontier, particularly the Monte dei Granati (Granatenkogl) to the south *(belvedere-terrace Gasthaus "Saltnuss" at an altitude of 1 630 m - 5 346 ft)*. The road does not descend to the river level but continues along the mountainsides, which are often steep, as far as Moso. The journey then becomes easier as the valley opens out.

At San Leonardo you can join the road which leads from Merano to the Brenner by way of the Monte Giovo or Jaufenpass.

The PACKSATTEL and STUBALPE Roads ★ (Styria and Carinthia)
Michelin map 426 folds 36 and 37

Between the valleys of the Mur and Lavant Rivers and the Graz basin, the Pannonian Pre-Alps raise wooded heights. These mountains, known as the Koralpe, the Packalpe, the Stubalpe and the Gleinalpe, form a barrier less by their height, which hardly exceeds 2 000 m - 6 500 ft than by their solitude. The road from Graz to Klagenfurt passes over the Packsattel as an inter-regional route, while the Stubalpe is crossed by the road which cuts across the wide bend of the River Mur between Judenburg, Köflach and Graz.

THE STUBALPE★
From Judenburg to Köflach – 44 km - 27 miles – about 2 hours – Local map opposite

Beware of the downhill gradient of the east slope of the pass (maximum 1 in 5) between Puffing and Salla Valley. The road reveals, from the start, the town of Judenburg, closely built on its spur, at the foot of the tall tower which has become a sign of its municipal dignity.

The mountainous stretch of the "Gaberlstrasse" begins at the village of Weisskirchen. The tortuous road rises in stages under the pines to the crest-line which it will follow nearly to the Gaberl-Sattel. There are many attractive vistas both to the north and to the south, through woods of the nearby valleys. Behind the Aichfeld plain (in the Judenberg-Knittelfeld region) lies at the foot of the bare crests of the Lower Tauern, which are stretching northwest. The main crest of the Stubalpe is crossed at the Gaberl-Sattel (alt 1 547 m - 5 075 ft – inn).

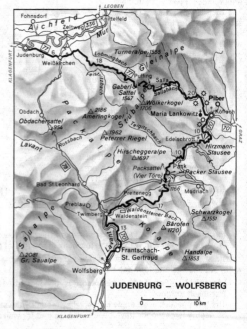

JUDENBURG — WOLFSBERG

On the east slope of the pass, the road drops suddenly into the wild and narrow wooded **Salla** Valley, reaching its floor at a tiny village of the same name. Here and there a large chalet or an old mill stand by the torrent. The sawmills and scythe factories *(Sensenwerk)* which introduced industry to the valley, may still be seen, though some are now in ruins. (Styrian scythes have a worldwide reputation.)

The valley widens again.

Köflach. – Pop 12 009. An industrial (metallurgy, glass ware, shoes, and textiles) and mining centre surrounded by outcrops where lignite is dug on a large scale.

THE PACKSATTEL*
From Köflach to Wolfsberg – *52 km - 32 miles – about 1 1/2 hours – Local map p 116*

As you pass through Köflach, remember that you can easily visit the Piber stud (3 km - 2 miles northeast), a centre for the breeding of Lippizaner horses. See at Piber below.

To reach the heights on leaving Köflach *(see above)*, the road to the Packsattel, after skirting the outcrops where lignite is dug on a large scale (the Köflach deposits are the richest in Austria), first runs, bandolier-fashion, up a detached foothill on the main Packalpe crest. Soon the curves of its layout and especially the straight section after Edelschrott afford views of the industrial basin of Köflach, where you will see the white pilgrims' Church of Maria Länkowitz.

After a sunken section in the Teigitschbach you reach the last climb, within view of the village of Pack. The horizon extends.

Pack. – Pop 531. A peaceful **panorama★** of the last wooded hills of the Pannonian Pre-Alps and the Graz plain, and the proximity of the **Packer Stausee,** a lake equipped for bathing and boating, bring holidaymakers with simple tastes to this country resort.

In gentle pastoral surroundings the road reaches the Packsattel, which is also known still as the Packhöhe or the Pass of the Vier Tore (four gates – alt 1 166 m - 3 825 ft).

The road passes into an even quieter and more thickly wooded zone. A series of hairpin bends below the Preitenegg ridge lends a little variety to this descent of the Carinthian slope, during which you will see, in the distance, the crests of the Saualpe, rising in series to the west. If the weather is clear, the rocky barrier of the Karawanken can be seen, to the south, through the Lavanttal gap. The run ends at the foot of the dark Castle of Waldenstein. From now on the road follows the floor of the Waldensteiner Bach ravine, to meet, at Twimberg, the equally enclosed Valley of the Lavant.

The countless tree trunks in the stacks of timber outside the papermills at Frantschach are symbolic of the Austrian economy which is so largely based on its forests *(p 25)*.

Wolfsberg. – Pop 28 182. The old, upper town, was built at the foot of the château of the Counts Henckel von Donnersmarck, which was reconstructed in the 19C in the Tudor style. It has as its centre the Hoher Platz, a square adorned with a column to the Virgin (1718) and surrounded by houses in the Biedermeier style. The lower town is modern, with wide streets and pleasant walks beside the Lavant.

PIBER ★ (Styria)

Michelin map 🗺 fold 37 – 3 km - 2 miles northeast of Köflach – *Local map p 116* – Pop 600 – Alt 503 m - 1 650 ft.

The entire Styrian village of Piber lives on horses. The Lippizaner stallions, who may be admired at their training in the Spanish Riding School in Vienna *(p 154)*, are bred here.

Stud Farm★ (Gestüt). – *Guided tours (about 1 hour) Easter to the end of October at 2 and 3pm (minimum 20 persons); Sundays and holidays 3 and 4pm; 20S, 10S children.*

Leave the car at the car park at the foot of the hill and walk to the castle of Piber (court with two tiers of arches), which houses the management of the stud and the general services.

A visit to the stables and a walk in the fields nearby will give a close view of the famous Lippizaners. Foundation of the breed dates back as far as 1580. They were brought in 1920 from the Austrian imperial stud at Lipiza, near Trieste, formerly a part of the Austro-Hungarian Empire and is now in Yugoslavian territory. Their ancestry is Spanish, Arabian and Berber and the six strains (Pluto, Conversano, Neapolitano, Favory, Maestoso and Siglavy) are named after their foundation sires.

Originally of all colours, the Lippizaners are largely grey with an exceptional bay and brown, they do not get their white coats until they are between four and ten years old. In appearance they are of comparatively short stature with a long back, a short thick neck and powerful conformation. They average 15.3 hands (approximately 155 cm - 61 in) high. Intelligence and sweetness of disposition, perhaps accentuated by their attractive expressive eyes, as well as gracefulness have destined it for academic horsemanship as practised in Vienna.

The object of dressage is the harmonious development of the physique and ability of the horse. *Haute école* is an elaborate and specialized form of dressage: some characteristic airs are the pirouette, the piaffe (the horse trots without moving forwards, backwards or sideways), the passage (high stepping trot), the levade (the horse stands balanced on its hindlegs its forelegs drawn in), the courvet (a jump forward in the levade position), the croupade, ballotade and capriole, movements where the horse jumps and lands again in the same spot.

PÖRTSCHACH ★★ (Carinthia)

Michelin map 🗺 folds 35 and 36 – *Local map p 172* – Pop 2 499 – Alt 458 m - 1 503 ft – ▣ ☎ 2354, 2810-15 or 16 – *Facilities p 42*

A peninsula jutting into Wörther Lake decided the tourist future of the resort of Pörtschach whose opulent villas and hotels nestle among foliage. The existence of this tongue of land prompted the construction of a long, flower decked promenade beside the lake.

The little structure known as the "Gloriette", a belvedere overlooking the lake and the Karawanken, is the favourite goal of walks and drives from Pörtschach. It is situated beside the Castle of Leonstein, which stands on a rock to the southwest of the town.

PULKAU (Lower Austria)

Michelin map **426** fold 11 – 8 km - 5 miles northeast of Eggenburg – Pop 1 738 – Alt 291 m - 955 ft

Pulkau is a large winegrowing township not far from the Czech frontier, in a hilly area which lends itself to the cultivation of vines. The highest ridges are marked by dark woods of spruces and the town itself has the added interest of two unusual churches.

Parish Church (Pfarrkirche). – The church crowns a hill to the north of the town. It is flanked on the east by a Romanesque tower and is noteworthy for the simplicity of the main building. The north chapel has a few traces of early 14C frescos; the south chapel has foliated capitals.

In the middle of the churchyard stands a curious **charnel-house** *(Karner)*. This is a 13C twelve sided building, entered through a Romanesque doorway adorned with statues.

Chapel of the Holy Blood (Heilig-Blut-Kapelle). – The chapel is an unfinished Gothic building which contains, above the high altar, a fine carved and painted wooden **altarpiece★** made by artists of the Danubian school at the beginning of the 16C. Christ, St Sebastian and St Bartholomew occupy a central position; the painted panels are decorated with scenes of the Passion.

RADKERSBURG, Bad (Styria)

Michelin map **426** fold 39 – 32 km - 20 miles south of Bad Gleichenberg – Pop 1 846 – Alt 208 m - 682 ft

The fate of Bad Radkersburg, for a long time a bastion and Styrian outpost, controlled one of the entrances to Croatia and has always been connected with the part it plays as a military town. The town was built on the left bank of the Mur and guarded by the Castle of Ober-Radkersberg, erected by the Dukes of Styria on a hill on the right bank. Hardly anything is left of the 13C fortifications which were attacked by the Hungarians and the Turks. The castle and that part of the town which lies on the right bank of the Mur have been Yugoslav possessions since 1918.

The town is also a resort. Its spring with bicarbonate bearing waters remedies kidney disorders; and its spa cures rhumatism and does physical therapy.

■ **SIGHTS** *time: 1/2 hour*

Leave the car in the **Hauptplatz**, which is lined with a few arcaded houses and in the centre of which is a **column** (Pest- und Mariensäule) dedicated to the Virgin. It is adorned with statues and commemorates the escape of the town from the plague and the Turks.

Go round the **town hall** (Rathaus), flanked by a tall octagonal tower surmounted by an amusing bulbous belfry, and, a little way along the main street, to the right. Bear left, to the **Parish Church** (Stadtpfarrkirche) which is in the Gothic style. The network vaulting in the aisles contrast with barrel-vaulting in the nave.

Turn left to follow the main street again before bearing right towards the **former arsenal** (ehemaliges Zeughaus). A covered alley leads to a fine rectangular courtyard with arcades.

Turning right at once, return to the Hauptplatz, which you must cross to enter the **Frauenplatz★**, a shady square near the Frauenkirche. The square tower of the church, adorned with pilasters and surmounted by a bulbous dome, and the court planted with trees and lined with small, low houses, make a charming picture.

Return to the Hauptplatz.

The RADSTÄDTER TAUERN Road ★ (Salzburg)

Michelin map **426** folds 20, 34 and 35

This road was much used in the Roman era, and is still marked by military milestones which have been recently set up again *(M - local map p 119)*. The road, which crosses the summit of the Lower Tauern (Niedere Tauern) at 1 700 m - 5 577 ft – connects the Upper Valleys of the Enns and the Mur and was, in the Middle Ages, one of the lines of expansion towards the south pursued by the Archbishops of Salzburg.

The last witness of these ambitions, the Lungau (basin of the Upper Mur), is one of the most secluded areas in the Alps and the most subject to ancient traditions. It is still linked politically, with the Salzach region, now facilitated by the motorway.

On arriving at St. Michael, motorists climb the Katschberg, either by the pass or by the tunnel of the same name *(toll at tunnel p 94)*, to reach the lakes of Carinthia or the Cortina Dolomites.

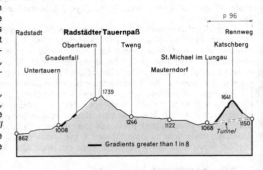

From Radstadt to St. Michael im Lungau – *49 km - 30 miles – about 2 hours – Local map p 119*

15 km - 9 miles of narrow, hilly road out from Radstadt.

Radstadt. – Pop 3 994. Radstadt, built at the end of the 13C by the Archbishops of Salzburg, is on a regular plan and surrounded with ramparts which still dip, on the west side, into the old moat. A charming landscape, dotted with country houses (Tandalier and Mauer Châteaux) built in the style of Salzburg with wide, overhanging roofs, corner turrets or watch towers, adorns the approaches to the little town.

The run from Radstadt to Untertauern unfolds above magnificent meadows, dotted here
and there with big farms. On
the horizon, the crests of the
Radstädter Tauern stretch in an
almost unbroken line. Radstadt
remains in sight for a time as
you look downstream.

Above Untertauern a series of
hills and ravines cooled by the
shade of maples and the Taurach cascades gives access to
the upper combe.

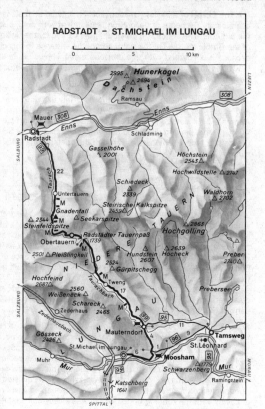

RADSTADT – ST. MICHAEL IM LUNGAU

Gnadenfall. – This pretty
cascade of the Taurach
leaps a wooded shelf in
two light falls.

The depression in the pass is
fringed with larch and fir trees
and has been occupied by the
hotels of Obertauern which are
dotted about near the pass (alt
1 739 m - 5 705 ft). About 800 m
- 2 624 ft before the highest
point in the road over the pass,
at the head of a bridge, stands
a modern statue (1951) of a
Roman legionary.

Obertauern. – Pop 177. *Facilities p 43.* This winter
sports centre, which was
created out of nothing, provides ski lifts for the large
basin whose hilly and treeless slopes converge on
the threshold of the Rad-
städter Tauernpass.

The descent of the south slope involves, at first, a forbidding section, but between Tweng and
Mauterndorf pleasant clearings appear on the banks of the calmer torrent. Soon the roofs of the
Castle of Mauterndorf emerge from the trees.

*Inside the castle the galleries, the keep, and the local museum (Landschaftsmuseum) can be
visited 1 June to 30 September 10am to noon and 4 to 6pm; Christmas to Easter 5 to 7pm;
closed Tuesdays and Fridays; 20S.*

Mauterndorf. – Pop 1 685. *Facilities p 41.* This little town, like that of St. Michael im Lungau,
derives great dignity from its large blocks of dwellings, sometimes surmounted with
stepped gables and pierced, in the façade, with arched windows.

A broad corridor links Mauterndorf and the Mur Valley, the road descends to the valley floor
down the mountainside leaving the Château of Moosham *(1 km - 3/4 mile)* eastwards *(see
below).*

Recommended alternative route* via Tamsweg. – *Extra distance: 17 km - 11 miles. Allow
1 hour longer for the trip.*

Tamsweg*. – *Description p 145.*

Moosham Castle*. – *Open 1 June to 1 September 10am to 4pm; the rest of the year 10am to
3pm; closed Mondays in June and September; 30S.*
This former fortress of the Archbishops of Salzburg was restored and refurnished last
century. In the arolla (pine) panelled rooms on the 2nd floor and in the vaulted chancellery
there are considerable collections of furniture and art objects. Ask for the comical picture of
nationals classified by their characteristic features to be explained when you see it in the
bedroom on the 2nd floor.

The castle's **lower courtyard*** provides a lasting and picturesque memory: the stillness, the
grass and the surrounding wooden galleries. The old well is 64 m - 210 ft deep.

RANKWEIL (Vorarlberg)

Michelin map 426 fold 28 – *Local map p 55* – Pop 9 929 – Alt 463 m - 1 519 ft – 🄸 ☎ 42141

The pilgrims' church at Rankweil rises above the Rhine Valley in Austria, overlooking a wide
plain covered with orchards (huge pear trees).

This part of the Vorarlberg, known as Paradise, displays, along the road coming from Götzis,
via Klaus, landscapes which, like the fertile fields on the Swiss bank of the river, resemble parts
of England in their greenness.

Church of Our Lady or Castle Church (Liebfrauenkirche or Burgkirche). – *Time: 1/2 hour.*

The church is reached by car up a ramp beginning to the northeast, at the ring-road round
the castle. It grew up from the 14C on a steep-sided rock within the walls of the former fortified
castle of the Counts of Montfort from which it evolved in arrangement and character. It owes its
lofty air to these origins, as can still be seen from the existing fortifications including a cylindrical
keep and parapet walk. The old castle court has become a churchyard.

The body of the church takes the place of a knights' hall; the present chancel, as can be
seen, is the castle's original chapel. The whole has recently been renovated.

The **Chapel of Miracles** (Gnadenkapelle), created in 1658, is a continuation of the aisle, and contains, in a scheme of decoration resplendent with gold, a statue of the Virgin venerated by the pilgrims. The statue is a graceful figure carved by the Swabian school in the 15C at the end of the Gothic period. On the right, before the entrance to this chapel, a "silver" cross, so called because it is covered with this precious metal, shows on its exposed surface a Roman Christ (13C) and three medallions representing the Entry into Jerusalem, the Annunciation and the Resurrection.

By a door under the gallery in the nave you reach the castle's **parapet walk**★ (Wehrgang). This gallery, being almost circular, affords a fully extended **panorama**★ of the Rhine. To the west and southwest is the barrier of the Alpstein (Appenzell Alps), including the 2 436 m - 7 992 ft Altmann. Next come the Wildhaus shelf, the jagged Churfirsten and the Alvier group. On the Austrian side, beyond the III gap marking Feldkirch, the Drei Schwestern (Three Sisters) indicate the frontier with Liechtenstein. Through the opening of a small valley appears the Schesaplana summit (Rätikon massif alt 2 965 m - 9 728 ft).

RATTENBERG (Tyrol)

Michelin map 426 fold 18 – Pop 591 – Alt 514 m - 1 686 ft

This tiny frontier town was a subject of dispute between the Tyrol and Bavaria until 1504, when Maximilian of Austria annexed the Lower Inn Valley as far as Kufstein. Rattenberg took advantage of a bottleneck in the alluvial plain of the Inn which enabled it to control traffic on the road and on the river. Never having been able to revive its economy once the mines were exhausted in the 17C, the town has retained the appearance of an Inn Valley town of the early Renaissance *(illustration p 28)*. Thanks to the motorway built in 1972, the main street has been freed of traffic.

As well as Tyrolean handicrafts, Rattenberg is known for its engraved and finely modelled glassware *(p 12)* which is made in the Rattenberg and Kramsach workshops (on the opposite bank of the Inn).

Main Street★ **(Hauptstrasse).** – *Time: 1/2 hour.* The most characteristic houses have plain façades under dull coloured roughcast, adorned with some stucco, with window and door frames in pink marble and crowned with a horizontal pediment *(illustration and comment p 28)*. As one can see from the castle *(for access see below)*, the pediment does not conceal a flat roof, which would be unsuitable to the Alpine climate, but the saw-teeth of a ridge roof *(Grabendach)* anticipating the trussed roofing of 19C workshops. This division of the roof into several ridges at right angles to the street made for a better protection against fire than a single, gabled roof, and did away with the running gutter, which was a cause of trouble between neighbours.

Parish Church (Pfarrkirche). – This Gothic church, constructed in 1473 to abut the bluff on which the castle stands, is remarkable externally for the disposition of its blocks of pink marble. The two naves, of unequal size, remodelled in the Baroque style in about 1740, were decorated with large compositions, mostly by Matthäus Günther, the painter of the parish church of Innsbruck-Wilten *(p 89)*, who has painted here a masterly *Last Supper*.

The shorter south nave and the stalls against the windowless façade wall are called "those of the miners". They are a reminder of the former silver-one workings which once flourished here, as at Schwaz *(p 141)*. The altar is the work of Guggenbichler.

The unusual number of altars shows the generosity of notables and guilds in the 14 and 15C, a period of economic prosperity.

Fortified Castle (Burg). – *1/2 hour on foot Rtn.* Go beneath the railway bridge behind the church and on emerging from the covered way, bear right and start the climb up the path to the castle. When you come to a green open space turn right to reach the edge of the terrace at the foot of the tower.

From this vantage point there is a good **general view** of the town, hemmed in between the Inn and the mountain with the belfry of the Servites' Church (13-18C) rising above the ridge roofs. Downstream may be seen the Kaisergebirge rising in the line of the Valley of the Inn.

RETZ (Lower Austria)

Michelin map 426 fold 11 – Pop 4 373 – Alt 252 m - 827 ft

Retz, near the Thaya Valley, is an important winegrowing and farming centre, in a hilly region which forms part of the Bohemian massif. The old town still has its chessboard plan, ramparts and defensive towers. *Guided tours of the wine cellars (45 min) during the week at 1.30pm, Sundays and holidays 10 and 11am, 2 and 3pm. 20S. Apply to Karl MRVKA, A 2070 Retz, Lehengasse 10, ☎ (02942) 2379.*

Hauptplatz. – This is the heart of the old town. It is rectangular, very large, and looks fine with its column to the Holy Trinity and is surrounded by a few houses which are remarkable for their architecture and decoration. To the north is the **Verderberhaus**, crowned with a gallery and having its ground floor pierced by an arched passage. No. 15, opposite, is the **Sgraffitohaus**, a handsome building with a carved doorway and a façade covered with inscribed maxims.

The **Rathaus** was rebuilt in the 16C from a Gothic church, which is still there. The Lady Chapel is on the ground floor.

Michelin road map 426 Austria
*   at a scale of 1/400 000 (1 in: 6.30 miles)*

*   – Road network with their characteristics: snowbound, gradients, hilly roads...*
*   – A wide variety of tourist information: scenic routes, ski-lifts, viewpoints, refuge
       huts...*
*   – A detailed inset of Vienna and suburbs*
*   – An index with map co-ordinates.*

The perfect companion to this guide.

Michelin map **426** folds 38 and 39 – 10 km - 6 miles north of Feldbach – Pop 2 553 – Alt 450 m - 1 476 ft

Riegersburg, proudly standing on the top of a basalt height nearly 200 m - 650 ft above the Grazbach Valley, is one of the most imposing strongholds which have guarded the eastern frontiers of Austria through the ages. First the Celts, then the Romans, saw the value of this defensive position and dug in there several times. The castle, built in the 13C, successfully withstood the attacks of the Hungarians and the Turks. In 1945 violent fighting took place here between the Russians and the Germans, the latter defending Riegersburg to the last gasp.

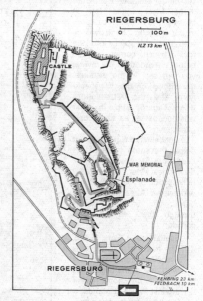

■ THE CASTLE★ *time: 1 hour*

From whatever direction you approach it, the **site**★ and boldness of Riegersburg are a surprise. On the south side, the village clings halfway up the slope, 100 m - 330 ft below the castle.

By a steep path, you pass through the first line of ramparts and reach a large esplanade, on which stands a memorial to the numerous victims of the last phase of the War in 1945 from the Riegersburg district.

The upper castle is open 15 March to 30 April and 1 October to 15 November 9am to 4pm; 1 May to 30 September 8am to 5pm; closed Mondays; 25S; brochure available in English.

Enter through a gateway bearing the coat of arms of the Radkersburgs.

This castle is of interest more for the fine **views**★ it affords of the Styrian countryside than for its architecture and internal arrangements. There are a collection of arms and armour and, in the inner courtyard, a well surrounded by a graceful wrought iron grille. On the north side, the fortress commands the valley from the top of a dizzy precipice.

SAALACH Valley ★ Salzburg and Bavaria (Germany)
Michelin map **426** fold 19

The Valley of the Saalach, making a gap in the Northern Limestone Alps, is served by an excellent road. It establishes quick communication between Salzburg, Zell am See and the Grossglockner and would be even more frequented as a transalpine route if the delimitation of the frontier did not compel one at the outset of the trip to cross the salient Berchtesgaden (German territory).

Owing to the clearance made by enormous masses of glacier ice coming down northwards from the Tauern, the most open scenery is to be found near Saalfelden and Zell am See, that is near the source of the Saalach. Below Saalfelden, on the other hand, the river rushes through a rock cleft which is considered to be one of the most impressive transverse defiles in the Alps. After Lofer the cleft is replaced by a less striking series of basins and small wooded gorges.

From Salzburg to Zell am See – *83 km - 52 miles – about 2 hours – Local map p 122*

Customs control at the entrance into Germany – Schwarzbacher Landstrasse – and at the entrance into Austria – Steinpass.
Leaving from Salzburg *(p 129)* by ③ of the plan and route No. 1, arrive first at Bad Reichenhall.

Bad Reichenhall★★ (Germany). – *Description in Michelin Green Guide to Germany.*

Branching off at Schneizlreuth from the German Alpine Road the Lofer road, laid within view of the typical peaks of the Drei Brüder (Three Brothers), in the middle distance southwards, turns away temporarily from the Saalach, whose course is too deeply sunken, and slips into a side valley ending at Melleck. Soon afterwards the Steinbach ravine marks the Austrian frontier. This is the Steinpass.
Beetween Unken and Lofer several bottlenecks, especially the Kniepass, where the Saalach foams close beside the road, lend the run a touch of excitement. The arrival at Lofer from the north affords glimpses, directly after the Hallenstein, of the central group of the Loferer Steinberge (Ochsenhorn, Grosses Reifhorn, Breithorn) at a distance from which can be seen even farther away and even more finely fretted, the Leoganger Steinberge.

Lofer★. – *Description p 106.*

Making a contrast with these scenes, the **enclosed section**★ from Lofer to Saalfelden, in a former glaciary gorge, is strikingly uniform. The Leoganger Steinberge (Lahner Horn, Grosses Rothorn) are particularly close at a point where the road passes for a time to the right bank of the Saalach.

Lamprechtshöhle. – *Open 1 May to 30 September 8am to 6pm; 15S.*
An interesting series of illuminated chambers and galleries leading to an underground cataract.

Seisenbergklamm. – *From the road it is a 500 m - 1 640 ft run via the Weissbach church and the marked road leading to the car park (open May through October 8.30am to 6.30pm; 14S).* Galleries and stairways, hidden by overhanging foliage, enable you to walk up the floor of this fissure where the Weissbach roars.

SAALACH Valley*

South of Weissbach this massif disappears, and the road then runs along the floor of a long canyon, whose steeper and steeper sides form part of the Leoganger Steinberge and Steinernes Meer ranges. Note, in passing, the Diesbach cascade. In the Brandlhof bend (village with a chapel built into the rock), which comes a little before the mouth of the ravine, you can see, in the distance, the snows of the Wiesbachhorn and the Kitzsteinhorn (High Tauern) and, in clear weather, as far as the Grossglockner.

The Saalfelden basin opens out below the south walls of the Leoganger Steinberge and the Steinernes Meer. This slightly hilly section of the road affords wide views. Ahead, the Tauern barrier can be seen clearly through the Zell am See corridor.

Saalfelden. – Pop 11 436. The name of Saalfelden is associated administratively with that of the Steinernes Meer, a limestone massif against which it stands. It is a large market town enlivened by the trade in Noric horses, which are much liked in the Austrian countryside, and in Pinzgau beef cattle. The cliffs of this Sea of Rocks, striped with reddish iron bearing layers, produce a surprising effect on the landscape when the sun strikes fully upon them. In the opposite direction, the snows of the High Tauern which can be seen through the gap formed by Lake Zeller, heighten the panorama.

Maria Alm. – Pop 1 741. *6 km - 4 miles southeast of Saalfelden. Facilities pp 41 and 43.* The pilgrims' church, whose sharp spire rises to 84 m - 276 ft above the ground, makes a choice foreground for the crests of the Steinernes Meer.

At the end of the run the road skirts the steeper shore of Lake Zeller before arriving at Zell am See *(p 173).*

ST. ANTON AM ARLBERG ★★ (Tyrol)

Michelin map 426 fold 29 – *Local map p 48* – Pop 2 174 – Alt 1 287 m - 4 222 ft – 🏨 ☎ 2269 and 2463 – *Facilities pp 42 and 43*

St. Anton, with its abundance of quality snow and total lack of trees, occupies a special place in the world of skiing. It was on the nearby slopes that Hannes Schneider, the pioneer of the Arlberg method *(p 19)*, gave the first lessons to tourists in 1907. Since then, the exceptionally easy access to the town – it offers, with Kitzbühel, a rare example of a skiing metropolis, served by the great international express trains – has helped to ensure its growing popularity and brilliant animation.

The ski-fields, extending for nearly 15 km² - 6 sq miles which St. Anton manages in common with St. Christoph *(p 47)* its mountain annexe, were for long without lifts. But mechanical equipment has been installed since the Second World War. The 50 ski-runs' highest point is at an altitude of 2 650 m - 8 684 ft (Vallugagrat).

Many, even among those most faithful to St. Anton, do not know how the resort looks in summer, and this is a pity, because few Alpine resorts at an altitude of 1 287 m - 4 222 ft have such a tranquil and gracious pastoral setting. What a delight it is to walk amidst the green pastures sprinkled with wild flowers.

If in doubt where to find a place name or historic reference look in the index at the end of the guide.

The Abbey of St. Florian, the largest abbey in Upper Austria and an eminent cultural centre, has been occupied, since the 11C, by Canons of St Augustine. The present buildings are in the purest Baroque style, since it was from 1686 to 1751 that the monastery was entirely rebuilt under the direction, first of Carlo Antonio Carlone, then of Jakob Prandtauer.

HISTORICAL NOTES

St Florian and His Legend. – Florian was head of the Roman administration in the Noric province *(map p 22)*. He was converted to Christianity, martyred in 304, near the camp of Lauriacum, and thrown into the Enns. It was on the site of his grave that the monastery which bears his name was later built. This death by drowning caused him to be invoked against flooding and also against fire, often with the naïve prayer, "Good St Florian, spare my house and rather burn my neighbour's." There is, therefore, hardly a church in Austria without a statue of this saintly protector, in which he figures as a Roman legionary holding a sprinkler or a pail to put out the flames.

Anton Bruckner at St. Florian. – Anton Bruckner, recognized as the greatest composer of church music in Austria in the 19C, was born in 1824 at Ansfelden, near St. Florian. At the age of thirteen he lost his father, a local schoolmaster, and was taken into the choir school at the monastery, where he came to know the masterpieces of sacred music. As an assistant teacher, he led for some years a wandering life, far from the abbey where is real ties were. In 1845 he managed to be appointed a teacher at the monastery and, to his great joy, its organist. He composed a number of masterpieces: masses and symphonies. When, in later years, he was called to Linz as cathedral organist and then to Vienna as a teacher at the Conservatory, he became famous; but his thoughts kept returning to the abbey and it was there that he said he wished to be buried, under the organ which had seen his greatest successes as a composer and artist.

TOUR *about 1 1/2 hours*

Guided tours (minimum 10 people) April to October at 10 and 11am and 1.45, 3 and 4pm; the rest of the year apply in advance to: Stift St. Florian, A 4490; ☎ 07224/503; 25S; brochure available in English.

The west façade, which is 214 m - 702 ft long, is surmounted by three towers. The doorway (Stiftstor) leading to the inner court (Stiftshof) is elegant, with two superimposed balconies, carved columns and statues.

A remarkable sculptured fountain, the Eagle's Fountain (Adlerbrunnen), and a wrought iron well-head dating from 1603, adorn the inner court.

Library★ (Bibliothek). – The fine allegorical paintings on the ceiling, by Bartolomeo Altomonte, represent the union of religion and science. Marquetry in walnut, encrusted with gold, sets off the valuable early texts, manuscripts and over 130 000 books.

Marble Hall (Marmorsaal). – This hall was dedicated to Prince Eugene of Savoy as a tribute to the leading part he played, as a captain, in the defence of the Austrian Empire from the Turks. It was used as a concert-hall and is adorned with frescos and pictures. The paintings on the ceiling *(Victory over the Turks)* are by Martino Altomonte.

Altdorfer Gallery★★★ (Altdorfer Galerie). – The most valuable pictures in the abbey collection are by Albrecht Altdorfer (1480-1538), master of the Danubian school *(p 59)*, who distinguished himself not only as a painter, but as a steel and wood engraver and architect.

The fourteen pictures on the altar to St Sebastian, painted in 1518 for the Gothic church of the abbey, form the world's most important collection of Altdorfer's work.

The panels depicting the martyrdom of St Sebastian, and the eight pictures evoking scenes of the Passion, are striking for the feeling in the characters of Christ, the Virgin, Judas and Caiaphas. The background of foliage in shadow lends power to the dramatic scenes.

In his devotion to landscape, Altdorfer resembled his contemporary, Dürer, and was by several centuries a forerunner of the Romantics. But what is most attractive, in his work is the balanced composition and rich, warm colour.

Imperial Apartments★★ (Kaiserzimmer). – The apartments are reached by the magnificent grand staircase, which extends for two storeys; the balustrades are adorned with statues and the walls and ceilings embellished with stucco and frescos. Until 1782 the apartments received such illustrious visitors as Pope Pius VI, emperors and princes.

Amidst a succession of halls and state rooms note the Faistenberger room, the bedrooms of the Emperor and Empress, the reception room and a room known as the "Gobelins" room; they contain rich furniture and interesting stuccos, frescos and pictures.

Church★ (Stiftskirche). – In designing its interior decoration, Carlone's imaginative exuberance enjoyed free rein. One can only regret the clumsy stuccos and the harsh dominant tones (yellow and violet) of the wall paintings in the nave. The high altar is adorned with a painted altarpiece framed between pink Salzburg marble columns. A fine black marble pulpit, choir-stalls ornamented with gilding and carved designs, and altarpieces in each of the side chapels complete this sumptuous display. In the crypt, is the coffin of Anton Bruckner.

ST. GILGEN ★ (Salzburg)

Michelin map 426 fold 20 – *Local map p 136* – Pop 3 070 – Alt 548 m - 1 798 ft – ⓘ ☎ 348 – *Facilities p 42*

St. Gilgen, at the end of the Lake of St.Wolfgang and now affording one of the best known landscapes of the Salzkammergut, was formerly an eastern outpost of the prince-archbishops of Salzburg.

It is worth while to remember the family connection of Mozart with this favoured land: his mother, Anna Maria Pertl, was born here in 1720, and his sister, Nannerl, settled here after her marriage to Baron Berchtold zu Sonnenburg, the governor of the district. A plaque on the law courts (Bezirksgericht) recalls this memory, while a Mozart Fountain (Mozart brunnen) was erected in 1927 on the central square, in front of the Rathaus.

(After A. Gründler photo)

St. Gilgen.

St. Gilgen is a delightful sight for anyone coming from Salzburg, or more especially from Scharfling *(route ① described p 136)*. Its equipment for water sports appeals to adepts.

ST. JOHANN IN TIROL (Tyrol)

Michelin map 426 fold 19 – *Local map p 92* – Pop 6 495 – Alt 660 m - 2 165 ft – ⓘ ☎ 2218 – *Facilities pp 42 and 43*

St. Johann has easy communications with all the northeast Tyrol thanks to the valleys round its basin, which make it a road junction. It has a good tourist situation near the Kaisergebirge, a domain of mountaineers *(p 92)*, and the peaceful heights of the Kitzbühel Alps *(p 95)*. The town, which is the local market town and, therefore, always lively, has pretty, spotlessly clean Tyrolean houses and large inns decorated with outside paintings.

St. Johann is able to play the part of a satellite resort to Kitzbühel in winter, since the Angerer Alm funicular, supplemented by a chairlift goes up to an altitude of 1 600 m - 5 250 ft. This has made it possible to downhill ski on the Kitzbüheler Horn.

ST. PAUL IM LAVANTTAL (Carinthia)

Michelin map 426 fold 37 – Pop 5 770 – Alt 400 m - 1 312 ft

The Abbey of St. Paul, half hidden in the trees and slightly above the wide Lower Lavant Valley, has always been occupied by Benedictines. Its church is one of the finest examples of Romanesque architecture to be seen in Austria.

Abbey Church (Stiftskirche). – To reach the church by car, come out of St. Paul by the Lavamünd road. At the top of the climb enter within the walls through a monumental doorway. The church, which was consecrated in 1264, ends in a flat chevet from which three rounded apses jut out, their great blind arcades, chequered friezes and cornices above blind arcades, composing a very pure Romanesque decoration. The south doorway (the Adoration of the Magi) and the west door (Christ in Majesty) have been heavily restored.

Inside, the nave with Romanesque capitals, of which some have been restored, is covered with a Gothic network vaulting. The transept and chancel are the most interesting parts of the building by virtue of the position of the apses and the mural paintings. In the main apse note the 13C effigies of St Peter and St Paul and on the north wall of the north transept the 15C paintings of the church donors and the saints.

ST. VEIT AN DER GLAN (Carinthia)

Michelin map 426 fold 36 – Pop 12 021 – Alt 476 m - 1 562 ft – ⓘ ☎ 2326 – *Facilities p 42*

St. Veit was the seat of the Dukes of Carinthia until 1518, when it left the role of regional capital to Klagenfurt. Suburbs brought into existence by the timber and cloth industries have grown up round the mediaeval nucleus of the city, the rectangular plan of which can still be clearly discerned from traces of the walls on the northwest side of the town.

On the hills round St. Veit are an unusually large number of castles – no less than fifteen in a radius of about 10 km - 6 miles. These provide many excursions and walks for tourists.

From St. Veit road No. 94, skirting the Lake of Ossiach *(local map p 172; text p 113)*, makes it possible to go quickly to Villach and Italy, avoiding Klagenfurt.

Main Square (Hauptplatz). – *Time: 1/2 hour.* This rectangular space, whose longer sides are only infrequently broken by alleys, is the centre of town life. The regular architecture of the houses enhances its design.

Of the three structures which distinguish the square, the most interesting, apart from the traditional memorial column to the plague, erected in 1715 *(general information p 148)*, is the fountain called the **Schüsselbrunnen** whose basin, it is believed, came from the forum of the Roman city of Virunum *(p 106)*. The small bronze statue (1566) surmounting it, the Schüsselbrunnbartele, representing a grotesque figure in 16C miner's costume, is the town mascot. Level with this fountain, at the corner of the street leading to the church, is a 15C statue of St Veit (St Guy), the patron saint of the city.

The most carefully designed buildings in the square are the **Military Headquarters** (Bezirks-hauptmannschaft), in the Classical style (1780) which adorns the short west side of the quadrangle, and, more especially, the **town hall.**

Town Hall (Rathaus). – This graceful municipal building was given its Baroque stucco in 1754. On the pediment is the double-headed eagle of the Holy Roman Empire, embossed, in the centre, with the statue of St Veit. Through the gateway, which has a Gothic arch and a vaulted passage, also Gothic, you reach the inner court with three tiers of arcades, on which the decoration of sgraffiti (1) can plainly be seen. The **Great Hall** (Rathaussaal – guided tours (1 hour) in English 8am to noon and 1 to 4pm; closed Wednesday afternoons, Saturday and Sundays November to April) is on the 1st floor, under a low Gothic vault to which an 18C decorator has added stuccos of scroll ornaments.

EXCURSIONS

Frauenstein Castle★. – 5 km - 3 miles plus 1/2 hour on foot Rtn. Local map below; narrow country roads (passing impossible). Leave St. Veit via Obermühlbach (northwest) and then about 1 500 m – 1 1/2 miles beyond this village take the second road on the right.

This 16C castle presents a picturesque ensemble with its towers, turrets and roofs of unequal height. Before walking round the outside of the castle note the arched courtyard.

Hochosterwitz Castle★; **Launsdorf; St. Georgen.** – Round tour of 25 km - 16 miles – about 2 hours – Local map below. Leave St. Veit by the road to Brückl. Soon Hochosterwitz will be seen, on the right, on the top of a rock, round which winds a fortified access ramp. At a point about 400 m - 450 yds beyond a level-crossing, turn right. In the hamlet, at the foot of the rock, turn left up the road to the castle and the car park.

Hochosterwitz Castle★. – Description p 82.

Turn back, but follow the direct road to Launsdorf, straight ahead.

Launsdorf. – The country church has a touching effect with its mixed architecture, in which all the schools since the Romanesque period have left traces. In the tiny Gothic chancel is a gentle Virgin with a Pomegranate of the 15C.

Return towards St. Veit, but bear right to St. Georgen. About 1 300 m - 1 mile farther on leave on your left the by-pass; enter St. Georgen.

St. Georgen am Längsee. – Pop 3 093. The former abbey for Benedictine noble ladies has kept its original design. A large quadrilateral of buildings encloses a church transformed into the Baroque style about 1720. The inner court is imposing, with large façades pierced by rounded arches. Facing the main door of the church is the Renaissance north gallery topped with graceful arcatures.

Skirting the Längsee, you soon find the main road, which takes you back to St. Veit, to the left.

Magdalensberg★. – 15 km - 9 miles – about 2 hours – Local map above.

Leave St. Veit by the road to Klagenfurt. After 7 km - 4 miles turn left on to a uphill road on the flank of the Magdalensberg, within view of the Klagenfurt basin and the Karawanken mountain barrier. The road ends at the **Magdalensberg excavations** (Ausgrabungen) which have exposed traces of a Noric town inhabited by the first Roman settlers who came as traders in 1 BC (guided tour (1 1/2 hours) in English May to October 8am to 6pm; 15S; brochure available in English).

Walk (45 min Rtn) up to the top of the mountain (1 058 m - 3 470 ft), where there is a Gothic pilgrims' chapel dedicated to St Helen and St Mary Magdalene.

There is a majestic **panorama**★ of the wooded Saualpe range, the Klagenfurt basin, the Karawanken and the great semi-mountainous area known as the Nockgebiet, to the northwest. Among the nearest heights, the Ulrichsberg with Celtic temple ruins may be seen.

ST. WOLFGANG ★★ (Upper Austria)

Michelin map 426 fold 20 – Local map p 136 – Pop 2 479 – Alt 549 m - 1 801 ft – 🔋 ☎ 239 – Facilities p 42

An invasion of visitors is no novelty for St. Wolfgang which stands beside a lake of the same name and since the 12C has been a place of pilgrimage and thus the church has been enriched by magnificent works of art. This tradition explains, perhaps, why local life has not been upset by the rush of tourists, for the town has now become the country of the "White Horse Inn", with operetta-like landscape and **lake**★★ to match. The charm of St. Wolfgang is most strongly felt in the less busy periods of the summer season and at the early and late hours of the day.

Access. – Leave your car in one of two car parks at the entrance of the village, or at the Schafberg station, about 1 km - 1/2 mile beyond the church. In times of dense traffic a pleasant alternative is to arrive by boat. To do this from the main road from Salzburg to Bad Ischl, make for the Gschwendt landing-stage on the south shore of the lake, where you leave the car. Departures, on the average, every hour 9 May to 10 October; 30S Rtn. The boat calls in succession at Schafberg station and the centre of St. Wolfgang.

---

(1) The "sgraffito" owes its decorative effect to a layer of roughcast limewashed in grey and then scraped.

125

ST. WOLFGANG★★

■ CHURCH *time: 1 hour*

Open May to September 9 am to 5pm (noon to 6pm Sundays and holidays); the rest of the year 10am (11am Sundays and holidays) to 4pm; 5S; brochure available in English. This church was the successor to the chapel of a hermitage built, according to tradition, by St Wolfgang, Bishop of Regensburg (canonized 1052), who came to seek solitude on the shores of the "Abersee". The present structure dates from the second half of the 15C. It is sited on a rocky spur, which explains, given the need to accommodate as many pilgrims as possible, its irregular plan. It abuts on to the elegant structure of the 16C priory, which at one time was served by the Benedictines of Mondsee *(p 111)*. The outer cloister, lined with arcades which yields bird's-eye views of the lake, complete the character of the **site★★**. Enter the church by the south door.

Michael Pacher Altar★★★. – This masterpiece (1481), showing rare unity in composition and considered to be an outstanding example of Gothic art, was commissioned for the high altar by an abbot of Mondsee and made at Bruneck (Brunico) in South Tyrol, in the master's studio. Subjects for the various scenes were supplied to Pacher by the local bishop, Cardinal Nikolaus Cusanus, famous theologian and humanist of his time. It is certain that the carving of the central panel (Coronation of the Virgin) and the paintings on gilded backgrounds of the shutters, which match it, are by Michael Pacher himself. It will be explained to you how the various positions of the shutters were arranged to follow the liturgy.

When the Baroque style became fashionable the altarpiece was nearly removed to make way for a work in the taste of the day. But Thomas Schwanthaler (1634-1707), the artist who had been commissioned to do a new altarpiece, had fallen under the spell of Pacher's work and persuaded the abbot of Mondsee to give up this plan. It is even said that he deliberately prevented the operation by making his own work the wrong size. Schwanthaler's altarpiece (1676), with its unusual design in two symmetrical sections, was installed in the middle of the nave.

After visiting the church, the tourist may stroll along the lakeshore to the famous White Horse Inn (Weisses Rössl – *open mid-December to early November*).

EXCURSION

Schafberg★★. – *About 4 hours Rtn, including 2 hours by rack railway and 1/2 hour on foot. Departures about every hour: 9 May to 11 June 8.35am to 4.45pm; 12 June to 12 September 7.05 am to 6.25pm; 13 September to 10 October 8.35am to 6.25pm; 130S Rtn. If possible sit on the left for the ascent.*
From the terminus, make for the hotel on the summit (1 783 m - 5 850 ft), a few yards from the impressive precipice of the north face. Of Salzkammergut's thirteen lakes that it is said you can count from here, those best seen are the lakes of Mondsee, Attersee and St. Wolfgang. In the background, in succession, are the Höllengebirge, the Totes Gebirge, the Dachstein with its glaciers, the Tennengebirge, the Hochkönig, which can be recognized by its large patch of snow, the Steinernes Meer, the Berchtesgaden Alps and the Loferer Steinberge.

SALZA Valley ★★ (Styria)

Michelin map **426** folds 22 and 23

The Salza is a tributary of the Upper Enns. Among the last eastern massifs of the limestone High Alps, and at the feet of the jagged cliffs of the Hochschwab (highest point 2 277 m - 7 470 ft) it traces a furrow which for 70 km - 45 miles is almost uninhabited, except for the tiny villages of Wildalpen and Weichselboden. It offers nature lovers opportunities for delightful expeditions through the woods and along the rapids and pools of the torrent.

From Hieflau to Mariazell – *80 km - 50 miles – about 3 hours – Local map below*

The road, although surfaced in some parts, should be taken slowly on account of its uneven nature and its steep sections (gradients of 1 in 6). There is a difficult stretch between Grossreifling and Palfau where the road is narrow and the surface poor.
Between Hieflau and Grossreifling two dams in part drown the Enns defile. The setting created by these constructions, parallel to the road bridge and the Wandau Dam, is impressive.

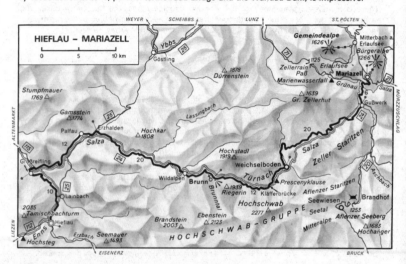

On the section between Grossreifling and Palfau the road is steeply uphill and follows a winding, hillside course under fir trees or the light shade of beeches. There are several glimpses of the smooth sheet of water below and, later, of the once more swirling torrent.

From Erzhalden to Wildalpen the Salza ravines are clothed in darker forest.

Upstream from Wildalpen the river draws near the Hochschwab cliffs. The sides of the Riegerin, eroded into needles are a strange sight.

Brunn★. – From this oratory there is a **view**★ as far as the end of the Brunntal combe, in the heart of the Hochschwab.

After passing the oratory at Brunn, the **view**★★ opens out all along the north slope of the massif, whose rocks are still fantastically shaped by erosion. The cliffs of the Türnach, opposite, are no less curious.

Near the Kläfferbrücke you will see a small guardhouse on the conduit which collects the underground waters of the area and supplies Vienna with drinking water.

Prescenyklause. – You go through this rock gateway built in the form of a tunnel. The dam constructed here made it possible to release a mass of water at will and float down logs but it has been out of use since the Salza raftsmen ceased to carry on their dangerous trade.

Weichselboden. – The church, in its clump of limes, and an hotel, make up almost all the village. To the southeast lies the steep sided valley known as "In der Höll" (In Hell).

Between Weichselboden and Mariazell the road, passing for a moment out of sight of the Hochschwab, again climbs above the valley, which is now wider but entirely given over to the forest. The landscape becomes gradually less mountainous.

Saw and papermills at Gusswerk mark the return to civilization. The road does not follow the floor of the Mariazell basin but climbs in wide bends to the centre of pilgrimage *(p 108)*.

SALZACH Valley ★ (Salzburg)

Michelin map **426** fold 20

The Alpine Valley of Salzach is an artery of the province of Salzburg, whose hooked shape conforms with the bent course of the torrent. Strung out between the Krimml Falls and Salzburg is a series of basins, separated by ravines. Therefore, until the coming of the railway, life was much isolated in these areas, each of which kept its traditional placename and was for a long time regarded as under-developed.

GEOGRAPHICAL NOTES

The Pinzgau. – The roads to the Gerlospass and Pass Thurn *(described pp 71 and 96)* afford views of the Upper Pinzgau Valley (Oberpinzgau), which the growth of tourism and the hydro-electrical undertakings *(see under Kaprun p 173)* have withdrawn from isolation. The region of Zell am See and Saalfelden – the Mittelpinzgau – is more lively. It lies at the foot of the Steinernes Meer Dam, which here indicates the Bavarian frontier.

The Pongau. – The bottlenecks of the valley between Taxenbach and Lend, upstream, and between Werfen and Golling, downstream, clearly define the Pongau basin. To the east, the Fritztal and Wagrainer Höhe sections, on the other hand, open easy communications with the Upper Enns Valley, which explain the attachment of the Radstadt district to the province of Salzburg. Tourist traffic in the Pongau is most intense in the tributary Valley of Gastein *(p 51)*.

The Tennengau. – Downstream from the Pass Lueg, as far as Hallein, a less mountainous area unfolds. It is densely wooded and rich in running water (Golling Falls). Here the Salzach receives a contribution from the waters of the Lammer, flowing down from the pastoral heights of Abtenau and the Salzburg Dolomites. The fine villages of the Tennengau (Abtenau, Golling, Kuchl, etc.), spreading the accordion folds of their ridge roofs above painted and flowering gables, already have many features in common with Bavaria *(see p 28)*.

The Flachgau. – Beyond Hallein the Salzach enters the flat land of Salzburg and brings a note of wild liberty to the dignified city of the prince-archbishops. After receiving the waters of the Saalach, the river becomes a natural frontier, dividing Styria from Bavaria, then washes the Bavarian cities of Tittmoning and Burghausen before joining the Inn.

From Lend to Salzburg – *75 km - 47 miles – about 2 hours – Local map opposite*

The Valley of the Salzach remains enclosed until it reaches Lend – an industrial town with aluminium factories where the Gasteiner Ache ends in a series of waterfalls – then opens out beyond Schwarzach to form the Pongau basin.

Liechtensteinklamm. – *From the fork leading to St. Johann im Pongau, road No. 159, 5 km - 3 miles by the road to Grossarl and that to the gorges, to the right – plus 1 hour on foot Rtn. Open 10 May to the first Sunday in October 8am to 5pm; 16S; brochure available in English.* The interest of this gorge lies in its high, sometimes overhanging sides, the play of light and the structure of the slaty rocks, polished and fancifully streaked with white.

Excursion to Radstadt *(p 118)* **via Wagrainer Höhe**★. – *From St. Johann im Pongau to Radstadt, 25 km - 15 miles – about 3/4 hour.*

The direct run from St. Johann im Pongau to the Enns Valley affords many charming scenes which are specially attractive as you pass through **Wagrain** (pop 2 569 - *facilities p 42*).

The panorama opens up – after Wagrainer Höhe – to the northeast, onto the Dachstein summit (2 995 m - 9 826 ft) edged with snow; and to the south onto the peaks of the Radstädter Tauern. One arrives at Radstadt.

Little by little the walls of the Tennengebirge begin to appear to the north. The details of the landscape become clearer as you approach Bischofshofen. While to the west notice the prow of the Mandlwand, a height in the Hochkönig Range.

For the continuation of the itinerary along the Salzach see Bischofshofen p 52.

Alternative route* between Lend and Bischofshofen by the Hochkönig Road (Hochkönig-Strasse). – *Extra distance: 10 km - 6 miles – count 1 hour longer. The road from Dienten to Mühlbach am Hochkönig is a mere country by-way (gradients up to 1 in 6 on the east slope, surface often loose). The road is usually closed due to snow from December to March.*

Upstream from Lend, leave road No. 311 for the by-road to Dienten, crossing the Salzach. The perched church of Dienten soon stands out in front of the Hochkönig crests. The road then runs along a pastoral combe. The highest point of the road is reached at the Dientner Sattel at 1 357 m - 4 452 ft at the foot of the rocky Hochkönig chain.

The much steeper descent to Mühlbach, affords another view of the Hochkönig, with a few glimpses of the jagged terminal crest of the Mandlwand to the east. Mühlbach is the starting point of several mountain expeditions facilitated by isolated refuges or hotels in the neighbourhood (Rupertihaus, Arthurhaus). Since the Bronze Age it has been a copper mining centre.

Bischofshofen. – *Description p 52.*

In the vicinity of Werfen, there suddenly arises on a wooded hump, the **outline*** of the massive Fortress of Hohenwerfen.

Eisriesenwelt Caves**. – *Description p 66.*

At this section comes the impressive Werfen-Golling cleft, one of the deepest transverse cuts in the Alps (more than 1 000 m - 3 280 ft) of which the Pass Lueg forms the outlet.

Pass Lueg. – As you come out of the Werfen, the valley forms a pronounced bend. Take either the road with a distinct hump, which is forced away from the banks of the inaccessible Salzach, or take the Tauern motorway which avoids the pass by means of tunnels.

In summer, a halt at the Pass Lueg may be prolonged to include a descent into the **Salzachöfen.** A steep path *(3/4 hour on foot Rtn; toll: 5.50S),* slippery in rainy weather, leads to a jumble of rocks which form a natural bridge over the Salzach, flowing along the bottom of the gorge. Notices – "Dom" – invite you to walk with some difficulty through dark alleyways to reach a spot under the rocky arch.

Lammeröfen. – *9 km - 5 miles from Golling (south) to Abtenau. Open (tour: about 1/2 hour) from 1 May to 31 October; 11S.* A walk along the floor of this cleft made by the Lammer, which overhanging sides and trees keep in a state of semi-darkness, might provide a welcome break.

Golling. – *Pop 3 409. Facilities p 39.*

Golling Waterfalls** (Gollinger Wasserfall). – *From Golling, 3 km - 2 miles, plus about 3/4 hour on foot Rtn.* Outside of Golling bear left and cross the level-crossing at the station and the bridge over the Salzach. Drive under the motorway and follow the "Wasserfall" sign posts. Leave the car at the Gasthof Brennerwirt car park. *(Entrance pavilion – 8S.)* A path leads first to the foot of the lower cascade, which, as it falls, prettily resembles a fountain flowing into a series of basins. The path then climbs to the curious upper cascade, which falls into a natural well made by a landslide.

From Golling to Hallein the road crosses the most vivid part of the Tennengau, a smiling basin with wooded, hilly slopes. The hills themselves gradually decline.

Hallein. – *Description p 80.*

The Anif water-tower (Wasserschloss), reminiscent of an English manor house, in the middle of a pond, stands unexpectedly in the Salzburg suburbs.

SALZBURG ★★★ P

Michelin map **426** folds 19 and 20 – *Local maps pp 128 and 136* – Pop 138 213 – Alt 424 m - 1 391 ft – *Facilities p 42*

Reception and Tourist Bureaux: ⊞ central tourist bureau: Auerspergstrasse 7, ☎ 71511, 74620 and 73866; other tourist bureaux: Mozartplatz and the main railway station (Hauptbahnhof); automobile information centres at motorway exits: Salzburg-Mitte (Münchner Bundesstrasse 1), Salzburg-west (at the airport – *1 April to 31 October*) and Salzburg-south (Alpenstrasse 67).

Festival information: Festspielhaus ☎ 42451.

Salzburg, Mozart's birthplace, is a delight from the first sight of the outline of the Hohensalzburg, the symbol of the power of the prince-archbishops. The fortress rises over the roofs and belfries of the town, through which flow the waters of the Salzach as the river bends in its course.

A soft light bathes the shapes of its towers and churches in a wonderful setting. It enjoys the attraction of the nearby Salzkammergut, and it has the prestige of the festival drawing lovers of classical music each year.

Its picturesque streets, with their wrought iron signs, its spacious squares, with sculptured fountains and the noble architecture of its buildings inspired by bishops with a passion for construction, leave memories which linger for years.

HISTORICAL NOTES

The Heritage of the Prince-Archbishops. – The See of Salzburg was founded shortly before 700 by St Rupert and was raised in the following century to an archbishopric. In the 13C the bishops were given the title of Princes of the Holy Roman Empire. Their temporal power extended to Italy, while much of their large revenue came from the mining of salt in the Salzkammergut *(details p 27)*. Three of these overlords, while cleverly governing their states, showed a taste for building. In a little more than half a century they converted the little town, with its maze of streets, into something resembling an Italian town, with palaces and open spaces.

Wolf Dietrich von Raitenau was elected Archbishop in 1587. He was a figure typical of the Renaissance: brought up in Rome and closely connected with the Medicis, he longed to make his capital the Rome of the North. When the former cathedral and the quarter round it were conveniently destroyed by fire, he turned to the Italian architect Scamozzi and asked him to build a cathedral larger than St Peter's in Rome. Raitenau's private life was not above criticism: by a Jewess of great beauty, Salome Alt, he had fifteen children; he had the château of Mirabell, on the right bank of the Salzach, built for her. He was drawn into an unfortunate conflict with the Dukes of Bavaria, over the salt trade *(p 27)* – he lost. The archbishop was condemned by the Court of Rome, and imprisoned in Hohensalzburg Castle in 1612, where he died after five years of captivity. His only project to be completed was his last, his mausoleum in the St Sebastian cemetery.

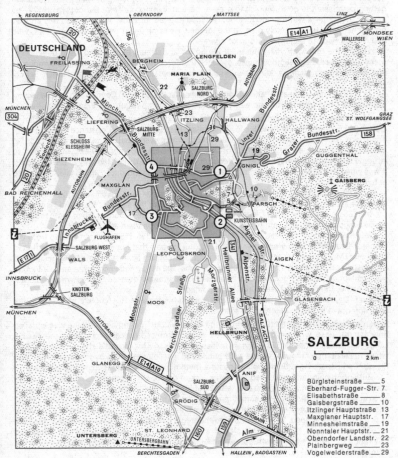

SALZBURG

0   2 km

Bürglsteinstraße	5
Eberhard-Fugger-Str.	7
Elisabethstraße	8
Gaisbergstraße	10
Itzlinger Hauptstraße	13
Maxglaner Hauptstr.	17
Minnesheimstraße	19
Nonntaler Hauptstr.	21
Oberndorfer Landstr.	22
Plainbergweg	23
Vogelweiderstraße	29

His successor, **Marcus Sitticus,** undertook to build the cathedral on a more modest scale and entrusted the work to another Italian architect, Santino Solari. To the south of Salzburg he had the mansion of Hellbrunn built as a country house, and the park laid out with fountains.

Pâris Lodron (1619-1653) took advantage of his long episcopate to complete the work begun by his predecessors. He finished the cathedral, and it was solemnly dedicated in 1628. On this occasion a mass written by the Italian choir-master, Horatio Benevoli, was sung. It had fifty-three parts; eight two-part choruses, two string orchestras and two ensembles for the brass, woodwind, drums and organ of the cathedral. This remarkable achievement opened for Salzburg a musical tradition which was to blossom in the following century.

Pâris Lodron also completed the Residence, near the cathedral, a less austere building than Hohensalzburg Castle. He opened new streets in the town, creating the face of Salzburg for generations to come.

Wolfgang Amadeus Mozart (1756-1791). – It was in this bishops' city, which owed as much to German as to Italian influences, that Mozart was born on 27 January 1756.

A Child Prodigy. – Leopold, a composer and violinist in the archbishop's service, soon understood what he could gain from the exceptional gifts displayed by his son Wolfgang and his daughter, Nannerl, who was four years older. Leopold encouraged the development of these natural gifts – Wolfgang could improvise on the piano at the age of five and played the violin without ever having been taught. The father began to give his son a serious musical education and Mozart also undertook what was to be a memorable tour of Europe. Between 1762 and 1766, Munich, Vienna, Augsburg, Frankfurt, Paris, London and The Hague, received Leopold and his children with enthusiasm. At Schönbrunn, the Empress Maria Theresa embraced little Wolfgang. Paris published four sonatas for piano and violin by the eight-year-old composer, whose talent continued to develop, being strongly influenced in London by Johann Christian Bach, the youngest son of Johann Sebastian Bach.

Returning to Salzburg, Mozart stayed there for three years, leaving the town only to go, at the command of the Emperor Josef II, to Vienna. There he gave his first comic opera, *La Finta Semplice*, and a pastoral opera in the German tradition, *Bastien and Bastienne*. Mozart was appointed conductor of the archbishop's orchestra. He composed both church and court music.

Dedication. – In 1770, at the age of fourteen, Mozart already had behind him a career and volumes of music that more than one composer might envy. But to his father a visit to Italy was necessary to complete a musician's education. This was where Wolfgang would learn to compose an opera.

Triumph followed him all over the peninsula. In Rome, after hearing it only once in the Sistine Chapel, the young master could re-write the nine-part chorus of the famous *Miserere* of Gregorio Allegri. On his return to Salzburg, he composed steadily.

First Disappointment. – Until 1777 Mozart lived most of the time at Salzburg. But Archbishop Jerome Colloredo, who had succeeded Archbishop Sigismund in 1772, took a poor view of Leopold's and his son's constant journeys abroad. Thus, in 1775, Wolfgang had some trouble in getting permission to go to Munich to present his comic opera, *La Finta Giardiniera*. In 1777 he had his first quarrel with the archbishop, resigned and left for Paris, accompanied this time by his mother, who unfortunately died on the journey. He came under the influence of Gluck, who had chosen Paris to begin his reform of opera.

During the following years the quiet life he led at Salzburg encouraged the production of many works including religious music, of which the *Coronation Mass* is an example, symphonic and lyrical pieces such as *Idomeneo*, and opera where the influence of the French School appears.

In 1781, after a heated altercation between Wolfgang and Count Arco, representing Archbishop Colloredo, the breach was complete. Mozart left Salzburg for Vienna.

The Lean Years. – Life now drew him into a fearful whirl, where disappointment and suffering disturbed his peace of mind and his joy in creation. His marriage with Constance Weber did not bring him the moral support he needed. These years were marked by the production of innumerable works, all, or nearly all, of which were successes; nonetheless, Mozart had to struggle all the time against harassing creditors, and he usually composed only to pay his debts. It was when the future seemed darkest that his best works were produced an his talent appeared in full maturity.

In 1782 he produced the comic opera *Die Entführung aus dem Serail* and some admirable violin sonatas. In the *Mass in E minor* (1783), he assimilated the styles of Bach and Handel.

In 1785 he dedicated to his friend Haydn six remarkable string quartets. Then came the great works associated with his name: *The Marriage of Figaro, Don Juan* and *Cosi fan Tutte.*

Much affected by the death of his father, which occurred in 1787, and not getting from the Emperor Leopold II, who was crowned in 1790, the support that his predecessor, Josef II, had given him, Mozart used up the last of his strength in struggling against an unfriendly destiny. He composed and presented *The Clemency of Titus* and *The Magic Flute* and wrote an *Ave Verum*. His swansong was the *Requiem*, commissioned by a stranger dressed in grey who would not give a name. Death did not leave him time to finish it.

On 6 December 1791, a pauper's hearse carried his remains to complete obscurity in the common grave at the cemetery of St Mark's, in Vienna.

Mozart's Music. – The fecundity shown by "the divine Mozart" during his short life was equalled only by the ease with which he mastered every form of musical expression: the Köchel catalogue, which contains 626 items, is evidence of this. As for Mozart's style, it has a charm which makes him a favourite with a wide public and is recognized even by the unpractised ear. Pleasant and sparkling motifs ripple beneath a rhythmic counterpoint of charming liveliness.

But spontaneity and *brio* need not mean lack of depth, and Mozart is no buffoon or mere comic-opera musician. Though he may attract, at first, simply by easy writing, the listener finds an exquisitely pure melodic line, sometimes tinged with melancholy. Towards the end of his life this vague sadness turns into despair, which gives their full meaning to the Fortieth Symphony in G minor, to *Don Juan*, to the quartets, to the tragic quintet in G (K 516) and to the *Requiem* (K 626) that Chopin wished to be played at his funeral. In it are reflected the emotional frustration of Mozart's life, his struggle against illness and poverty and from it was to evolve the Romantic Movement.

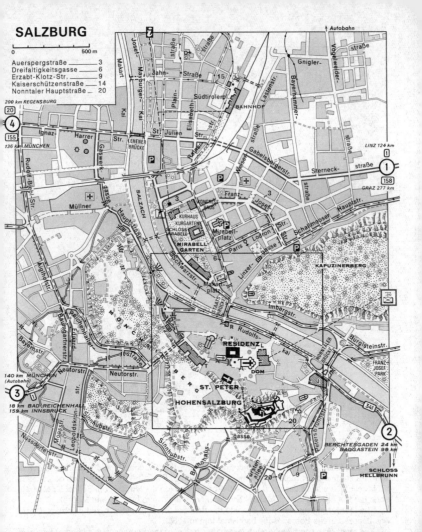

The Salzburg Festival. – In 1842 Salzburg put up a statue to Mozart; later it founded the musical academy named the **Mozarteum.** In 1917, the poet Hugo von Hofmannsthal, the composer Richard Strauss and the producer Max Reinhardt conceived the idea of a Mozart festival. The first of these now annual festivals was held in 1920. In August about thirty lyric and dramatic performances and about fifty concerts are given at the **Festival Hall** (Festspielhaus), the **Mozarteum, Landestheater** and the **Mirabell Château** *(see town plans).* The Festival Hall (1960) designed by Holzmeister is alongside the original theatre organized in the former Winter Riding School, its mass built into the rock wall of the Mönchsberg (theatre to seat 2 300). The open-air performances are held in the Summer Riding School (capacity: 1 500 seats). Mozart is the centre of attraction, but Hofmannsthal's play, *Jedermann* (Everyman) acted each year on the cathedral forecourt, is also a traditional feature. The best symphony orchestra, under the most esteemed conductors, and the most famous lyric artists, interpret classical and modern works – each festival sees the world *première* of an opera.

■ **GENERAL VIEW★★**

You should go up the Mönchsberg Hill, whose rocky mass hems in the old town from the banks of the Salzach to the Hohensalzburg Castle, to see the setting of the town.

From the Gstättengasse a lift *(Rtn fare: 12S)* leads to a terrace laid out just below the Winkler Café, from which there is a fine **general view★★** of Salzburg. The modern town spreads widely along the right bank of the Salzach, while old Salzburg, bristling with domes and church towers, lies crowded between the river and the Hohensalzburg Fortress. Southwards, on the horizon, are the Salzburg Alps, while eastwards the Kapuzinerberg (Mount of the Capuchins) and, in the background, the Gaisberg, indicate the city boundaries.

■ **THE OLD TOWN** *time: 4 hours*

Leave the car in the modern part of the town, on the right bank of the Salzach, outside the blue restricted parking zone. The old town is for pedestrians, we suggest you use one of the underground car parks of the Mönchsberg. Walk to the Domplatz.

Domplatz. – Three porticos link the buildings surrounding this square, the cathedral and the former ecclesiastical palaces. In the centre is the Virgin's Column (1771).

Cathedral (Dom). – The cathedral, which was built from 1614 to 1655, is a huge construction in which the Baroque style shows through the last features of the Italian Renaissance.

The west front, flanked by two symmetrical towers, is of light coloured Salzburg marble. The pediment between the two towers, dominated by the statue of Christ, is adorned with the coats of arms of Archbishops Marcus Sitticus and Pâris Lodron, flanked by statues of

131

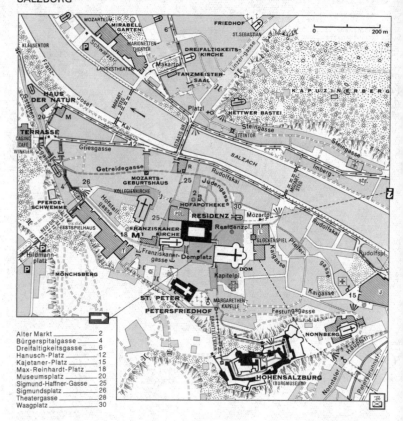

Moses and Elijah. Below them are the figures of the four Evangelists and in front of the main door are statues of St Rupert, St Virgil, St Peter and St Paul. The modern bronze doors (1957-58) in relief have been designed on the theme of Faith (on the left, by Toni Schneider-Manzell), Hope (on the right by Ewald Mataré) and Charity (in the centre by Giacomo Manzù).

The interior impresses by its size and the richness of marble, stucco and paintings. Mozart was baptized in the Romanesque baptismal font in 1756.

The **crypt** was completely remodelled after traces of the Romanesque cathedral had been uncovered (look at the plan of the succession of different buildings on the same spot on the pavement beneath the central rotunda, from the episcopacy of St Virgil in the 8C). The tombs of the prince-archbishops and a Romanesque Crucifix may be seen in the crypt.

Museum (Dom-Museum). – *Open 15 May to 26 October 9am to 6pm; 35S.*

Featured here is the cathedral treasure and the Archbishops' gallery of "art and wonders" (Kunst- und Wunderkammer) presented as it was in the 17C.

In the Kapitelplatz is the Kapitelschwemme, a drinking-trough for the horses of members of the chapter. The trough, built in 1732 by Archbishop Leopold Anton Firmian, is in the form of a monumental fountain. An uphill street out of the square takes you to the station of the Hohensalzburg funicular. *(Fare for the ascent – take a single ticket only: 9S.)*

Hohensalzburg★★. – The former stronghold of the prince-archbishops stands on a block of Dolomite rock, about 120 m - 400 ft above the Salzach. The castle was begun in 1077 by Archbishop Gebhard, who was an ally of the pope and wished to secure a safe retreat from the threats of the princes of South Germany who were supporting the emperor in the war between Church and Empire. The castle was frequently enlarged and remodelled, becoming a comfortable residence by the addition of state rooms. The archbishops often resided there until the end of the 15C, reinforcing it considerably by the addition of towers, bastions for cannon and barbicans and the construction of magazines and arms depots.

At the exit to the upper station, turn left for the panoramic terrace through which one goes to enter the fortress by way of some stairs and a postern. Go past the visitors' ticket office, to descend gradually, bearing right, along the lists and circling the fortified nucleus of the inner castle. One comes out in a square opposite the south wall of the **Church of St George,** decorated with a bas-relief of the Crucifixion and, higher up in a niche, a group of statuary in red Salzburg marble, of Archbishop Leonhard von Keutschach (1495-1519) between two priests.

Go through the door to the right of the church to the terrace of the **Great Kuenburg Bastion** where there is a good **view★★** of the old town, particularly its domes and belfries.

Return to the square (the steps "Abgang zur Stadt" at the east end should be descended at the end of your tour to bring you back into town) and, bearing straight ahead once more towards the inner castle, cross the square by the vaulted Fire Passage, a gallery containing the cannons.

The Castle and the museum. – *Guided tours (1/2 hour) Mai to September 9am to 5.30pm; October to April 9am to 4.30pm; closed 1 November and 24 December; 20S; brochure available in English.*

From the Reck watch-tower there is a **panorama★★**, which is particularly interesting in a southerly direction towards the Tennengebirge and the Salzburg Alps.

In the castle is a hand-operated barrel-organ dating from 1502. It plays melodies by Mozart and Haydn as well as the original 1502 chorale.

The state rooms, formerly the archbishops' apartments, were arranged by Leonhard von Keutschach and have kept their original decorations of walls adorned with Gothic wood carvings, doors fitted with complicated ironwork and coffered ceilings with gilded studs. In the Gilded Room is a monumental porcelain stove, dating from 1501, the work of a local potter. It is decorated with flowers and fruit, scenes from the Bible and the coats of arms and portraits of sovereigns of the period.

The Hall of Justice has a coffered ceiling whose beams are adorned with shields bearing the arms of the province and the dioceses or abbeys under the archbishop and those of the dignitaries of his court. The hall also has four red marble columns whose twisted barrels bear the coat of arms (a turnip) of Leonhard von Keutschach.

An interesting **museum**★ (Burgmuseum) may also be visited. Apart from records – plans and prints – showing the development of the town throughout the history of the Salzburg archbishopric, this museum contains a remarkable series of mediaeval works of art (arms, armorial bearings, etc.).

Descend to the town by the ramps, with occasional steps, which pierce the fortress walls. Follow the Festungsgasse to the left. This brings you to the lower funicular station, where you enter St Peter's churchyard, immediately on your left.

St Peter's Churchyard★★ **(Petersfriedhof).** – This touching cemetery, which evokes the past history of the town, abuts on the vertical rock wall of the Mönchsberg, in which catacombs were hollowed out. Wrought iron grilles under Baroque arcades enclose the chapels where several generations of the patrician families of Salzburg lie.

The 15C St Margaret's Chapel (Margarethen Kapelle) is a delicate construction dating from the end of the Gothic period.

St Peter's Church★★ **(Stiftskirche St. Peter).** – *Enter by the south transept. Under restoration.*
This former triple aisled Romanesque basilica was drastically remodelled in the 17 and 18C and was, at one time, decorated with stuccos and frescos.

To enjoy the best overall view of the main building, stand near the gilded and elaborate wrought iron grille between the porch and the nave. The simplicity of the architecture, heightened by the white walls, emphasizes the elegance of the Baroque decoration, which is made attractive by its restraint, the quality of its paintings and the freshness of the pastel shades, especially pale green, used to bring out the delicate stuccos on the vaulting, the cornices and the capitals.

Frescos on the vaulting in the nave depict scenes in the life of St Peter. On either wall, over the great arches, note, among other compositions, an Ascent to Calvary and a Crucifixion. Under the upper windows is a series of paintings representing, on the south side, the life of St Bénedict, and on the north side the life of St Rupert.

The altarpiece on the high altar and those in the nave, with their red marble columns, gilded statues and pictures, make a rich ensemble.

Only the south aisle has chapels. In the chapel farthest from the chancel there is a fine marble tomb built by Archbishop Wolf Dietrich for his father, Werner von Raitenau.

Leave the church by the west door, which has a Romanesque doorway in the white and red Salzburg marble. Romanesque arches (laid bare in 1957), on either side, are the only traces left of the 12C church.

Cross the abbey courtyard, turn right into the covered passage and go straight ahead into the Franciscans' Church by the Romanesque side door.

Franciscans' Church★ **(Franziskanerkirche).** – The church was consecrated in 1223 but has been remodelled several times. It offers a comparison of the Romanesque and Gothic styles.

The plain Romanesque nave, divided from the side aisles by massive pillars with capitals adorned with foliage and stylized animals, makes a striking contrast with the well lit chancel which dates from the final Gothic period, the 15C. The high star vaulting is supported by palm shaped cylindrical columns.

The finely modelled statue of the Virgin which adorns the Baroque altarpiece of the high altar was formerly part of a Gothic altarpiece made by Michael Pacher at the end of the 15C.

Go out by the main door and, leaving on your right the Sigmund-Haffner-Gasse, at the end of which stands the outline of the town hall belfry, bear left and follow the Franziskanergasse westwards.

Directly after the Max-Reinhardt-Platz, leave on your right, the massive Baroque University Church (Kollegienkirche), the work of Johann-Bernhard Fischer von Erlach to skirt, on your left, the Festival Hall (Festspielhaus).

From the Sigmundsplatz where, on the left, there is a tunnel (the Neutor), about 135 m - 150 yds long which was made in 1767 under the Mönchsberg hill. Look back for a fine view of the Hohensalzburg fortress and the St Peter's Church.

Horse Trough (Pferdeschwemme). – This monumental trough was built about 1 700. It was reserved for the horses in the archbishops' stables, and is adorned with a sculptured group, the *Horsebreaker* by Mandl, and frescos depicting fiery steeds.

Getreidegasse★. – This is one of the main streets of old Salzburg. Like the rest of the Old Town, which, being crowded between the Mönchsberg and the Salzach, could expand only vertically, it is narrow and lined with five and six storey houses.

A lively shopping street, it is adorned with many wrought iron signs which provide a picturesque touch, while the houses with their carved window frames lend a note of distinction.

Salzburg. - The Getreidegasse.

Mozart's Birthplace (Mozarts-Geburtshaus). – *9 Getreidegasse. Open 9am to 6pm (July and August 8.30am to 7.30pm); closed Christmas; 25S; guided tours in English apply in advance; brochure available in English.* Leopold Mozart lived on the 3rd floor from 1747 to 1773. It was there that Wolfgang was born on 27 January 1756.

In this flat, where Mozart composed nearly all the works of his youth, can be seen moving mementoes of his life (in particular from 1773-80) such as his violins, including the little violin he used as a child. His spinet and musical manuscripts are shown, as well as a selection of portraits and letters. *One may also visit the Tanzmeistersaal (see below).*

Continuing along the Getreidegasse, you leave the town hall (Rathaus) on your left, then, on your right, the Alter Markt or Old Market Square, on which stands a fountain to St Florian (opposite the fountain, note the curious **Hofapotheke,** a chemist's shop which still retains its complete Rococo interior).

Judengasse. – This street is in the middle of the former Jewish Ghetto. It is narrow and picturesque and, like the Getreidegasse, adorned with wrought iron signs. At No. 4, note a curious sculptured group in stone representing the Virgin of Maria Plain *(p 135).*

Through the Waagplatz make for the Mozartplatz, where you will see on the north side, instead of the roofs and belfries you might expect, the wooded spur of the Kapuzinerberg.

Residenzplatz. – Until the 16C there was a cemetery on the site. Archbishop Wolf Dietrich created the present square when he had his cathedral built. It was adorned in the 17C with a fine fountain (group of horses, a Triton and an Atlas). The square is bounded on the south by the cathedral and the west by the palace of the Residenz. On the east side is the **Glockenspiel,** a carillon of thirty-five bells cast at Antwerp at the end of the 17C and set up at Salzburg in 1705.

Residenz★★. – The present buildings, which were begun in 1595, on the initiative of Archbishop Wolf Dietrich, took the place of a building which had been the residence of the prince-archbishops since the 12C. The northwest wing is late 18C.

It was in this palace that the Emperor Franz-Josef received Napoleon III in 1867, and the German Emperor, Kaiser Wilhelm I, in 1871.

The gallery of paintings (**Residenzgalerie** – *open 10am to 5pm; closed mid-November to mid-December; 15S; guided tours in English (40 min) apply the day before; brochure available in English)* established by the prince-archbishops houses mostly 17 and 18C works. It also contains art from the interesting Czernin and Schönborn-Buchheim collections.

The fifteen state rooms are decorated with frescos and stuccos and adorned with pictures, tapestries, and statues. In the Conference Hall the young Mozart conducted many concerts before the guests of the prince-archbishop. A door in an antechamber gives an unexpected view down into the Franciscans' Church.

In 1983 the Moderne Galerie und graphische Sammlung Rupertinum will exhibit contemporary art (as of 1918).

Mirabell Gardens★. – Little is left of the luxurious mansion built at the beginning of the 17C by Wolf Dietrich. It was remodelled by the architect Johann-Lukas von Hildebrandt in the following century but destroyed by fire in 1818, and only its grand staircase is now of interest.

The gardens, laid out at the beginning of the 18C by Fischer von Erlach, have many statues, and the pools are adorned with groups of sculpture and many flowers, providing an excellent place in which to linger. From a terrace-belvedere there is a fine end view of the gardens, the rose-gardens, the former bastions and the Fortress of Hohensalzburg.

■ ADDITIONAL SIGHTS

Natural History Museum★★ (Haus der Natur). – *Guided tours in English (1 1/2 hours – apply in advance) 9am to 5pm; 20S, children 10S.* A modern display (dioramas) makes the most of remarkable collections on the history of the earth – geology, mineralogy, zoology, ethnology, etc. – tracing man's relationship with nature. On the 3rd floor, which is devoted to animals, is shown the mummified body of a rhinoceros of the Ice Age, discovered in 1929.

Hettwer Bastei★. – To reach the terrace of this bastion on the flank of the Kapuzinerberg take the Steingasse from the "Platzl", at the end of Staatsbrücke bridge on the right bank. The Steingasse is so narrow that horse vehicles using it have made marks on the walls of its houses. Go as far as the Steintor, a picturesque town gate of the 17C pausing on the way to look at the fine carved doorway of No. 18. Come back to No. 7 and climb, on the right, the stairs leading to the Capuchin monastery.

From the Hettwer Bastei terrace there is a pleasant **view★** of the left bank of the Salzach and the episcopal city. From left to right may be seen the Nonnberg convent, the Hohensalzburg, the cathedral and other churches of the Mönchsberg spur.

Tanzmeistersaal. – *Makartplatz 8. Open 1 June to 30 September 10am to 4pm; closed Sundays; 20S.*

This was the Mozart family home from 1773-1787 (rebuilt after 1944). The music room, transformed into a museum displays instruments and memorabilia of this period. *Chamber music recitals are held in July and August.*

St Sebastian Cemetery (Friedhof St. Sebastian). – Only the doorway in the Rococo style (1752), surmounted by a bust of the patron saint, remains of the former Church of St Sebastian, which was destroyed by fire in 1818 and subsequently rebuilt. Cross the church. Behind a grille is the tomb of **Paracelsus,** a doctor and philosopher of the Renaissance who died at Salzburg in 1541.

Adjacent to the north side of the church is a cloister whose arches shelter funerary monuments and surrounds a shaded cemetery which in about 1600 was made into the likeness of an Italian *campo santo.* In the centre stands the curious tomb of Wolf Dietrich; the interior is lined with porcelain in many colours. In the central lane of the cemetery are the tombs of Mozart's wife and father.

Church of the Trinity (Dreifaltigkeitskirche). – *Illustration p 34.* The church was built from 1694 to 1699 by the great architect Fischer von Erlach *(p 33).* The oval dome and the interior are in the Baroque style. As at the St Charles Church in Vienna, the originality and daring of this dome show off the frescos by Rottmayr.

Nonnberg Convent. – This Benedictine convent was founded at the beginning of the 8C by St Rupert. St Ehrentrude, his niece, was the first abbess.

The convent church *(closed 11.30am to 1.30pm and 6pm in the evening (4pm in winter)* enclosed in its churchyard, is late Gothic in style and dates from the end of the 15C. The high altar is adorned with a fine carved and gilded altarpiece. In the central section a Virgin and Child are between St Rupert and St Virgil. On the wings are scenes of the Passion. The crypt contains the tomb of St Ehrentrude.

In the Chapel of St John *(open 8am to 4pm)* is a Gothic altarpiece (1498) said to be by Veit Stoss. The central section depicts a Nativity.

EXCURSIONS

See local map p 130

Road to the Gaisberg★★. – *16 km - 10 miles.* Leave Salzburg by ① and bear right along the road to Graz, which you leave at Guggenthal to turn right onto the Gaisberg road. This is well laid (maximum gradient, 1 in 8), sometimes through woods, sometimes hewn out of the rock.

From the end of the road, you go first westwards, to the edge of the steep slope dropping towards Salzburg (**view★** of the town, the Salzach gap and the Salzburg Alps); then northeastwards, to the Cross on the highest point, at an altitude of 1 288 m - 4 226 ft from where there is a **panorama★** of the mountains of the Salzkammergut and the Dachstein massif.

Untersberg★. – *12 km - 7 miles plus 1 hour Rtn, including 1/4 hour by cablecar. (Open 1 July to 15 September 9am to 5.30pm (4.45pm 1 March to 31 October); 24 December to 28 February 10am to 4pm; closed 1 November to 23 December; 105S Rtn.* Leave Salzburg by ② and go towards Berchtesgaden. Directly after the major St Leonhard crossroads, bear to the right along the road leading to the lower cable-car station.

At a height of 1 853 m - 6 079 ft, there is a panorama of the Salzburg basin, the Salzburg Alps (Watzmann, Steinernes Meer, Staufen), the Wilder Kaiser and the Dachstein.

Maria Plain. – *4 km - 2 1/2 miles.* Leave Salzburg by the Plainstrasse *(north of plan p 131)* and the Itzlinger Hauptstrasse. At the exit from a bridge, turn right into Plainbergweg, the road which ends at the Maria Plain Church. This crowns a bluff, to whose slopes oratories cling.

The church, built from 1671 to 1674, has a squat façade framed by two towers. The interior is ornate: the altar in the chancel and the side chapels are adorned with altarpieces, and the pulpit, organ, confessionals and chancel screen were made in the late 17C in an exuberant Rococo style.

Hellbrunn Castle. – *5 km - 3 miles.* Leave Salzburg by ②. At a point about 600 m - 1/4 mile from the Rudolfsplatz bear to the right along the Hellbrunner Strasse which leads to the castle. *Open May through August 8am to 5.30pm; 1 to 15 September and 16 to 30 April 9am to 5pm (4.30pm 1 to 15 April); 16 to 30 September 9am to noon and 1 to 4.30pm (4pm in October); 30S; children 17S: guided tours and brochure available in English. The zoo (Tiergarten) is open November through March 8.30am to 4pm (6pm April through October); 25S; children 5S.* The castle was the summer residence of Archbishop Marcus Sitticus (1615).

The interior decoration of the rooms dates from the 18C. The banquet hall, with its *trompe-l'œil* painting and the high, domed Octagon or music-room are the most interesting. A tour of the gardens and fountains is both pleasant and full of surprises: fountains and caves are adorned with human figures, a "mechanical theatre" has 113 figures which are set in motion by a clockwork movement to the music of an organ and fountains suddenly shower the unwary visitor.

Mattsee. – *23 km - 14 miles.* Leave Salzburg by the Plainstrasse *(north of plan p 131)* and the Itzlinger Hauptstrasse. Then, to reach Mattsee, follow the route through the townships of Bergheim, Lengfelden and Elixhausen.

Because of its site on the shores of the nearby Obertrumer See, Niedertrumer See and Grabensee (lakes) this resort (pop 2 097 – *facilities p 41*) offers relaxation to the people of Salzburg. There is also an interesting selection of tombstones (more than 120, dating from the 14C) in the cloister of the 13C collegiate church, founded in 777 by Duke Tassilo of Bavaria; and modified in the Baroque style in the 18C.

The SALZKAMMERGUT ★★★ (Upper Austria, Salzburg and Styria) ⸺

Michelin map **426** folds 20 and 21

Salt, a traditional emblem of good health and a source of riches, has given the Salzkammergut its name, and, until recently, exceptional economic importance *(read Salt and Spas p 27)*. Tourism today tends to restore the prosperity of this former salt area of which the old resort of Bad Ischl is the centre.

With Salzburg as starting point it is possible to tour the Salzkammergut in 3 days following, in succession, the 1st day itineraries ①, ②, ③ and 2nd and 3rd day itinerary ④.

Round the Schafberg. – The circular view from the Schafberg embraces a landscape of lakes and peaks which, when split into small pictures like the setting of St. Gilgen, seem to transpose the exquisite urbanity of Salzburg into an Alpine setting. Yet, when you consider the various elements of the landscape there are only modest sheets of water and, apart from the north slope of the Schafberg, unpretentious mountains. But the delicate balance of these scenes, the light in which they are bathed is worthy of all the publicity put out, including that on the lake of St. Wolfgang.

Along the Traun. – From Gmunden to Bad Ischl and Bad Aussee, you will find less restrained and more romantic scenery. The Hallstättersee and Gosausee, the Grundlsee and the Altaussee fill steep-sided hollows. The peaks of the Dachstein and the Totes Gebirge remain mostly out of sight. Your surprise, therefore, is great when you discover, at the end of some cable-car in the region, and especially from the Krippenstein, the rounded shapes of the upper surfaces of these massifs, regular limestone plateaus riddled with basins and caverns, where only a few sharp peaks locate the highest points (2 995 m - 9 826 ft – at the Hoher Dachstein). The appearance of glaciers in this petrified world – the Dachstein is the most easterly massif in the Alps that boasts eternal snow – is no less strange.

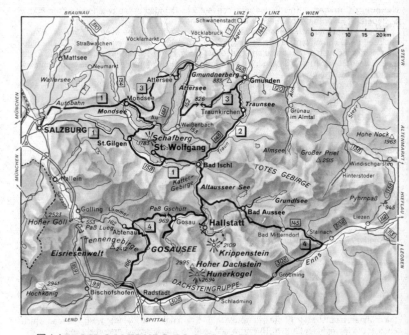

1 ★★FROM SALZBURG TO BAD ISCHL via St. Wolfgang

84 km - 52 miles – about 4 hours – Local map pp 136-137

Because of a small pass (alt 608 m - 2 000 ft) in the wooded crest between Scharfling and St. Gilgen, this itinerary connects the shores of the Mondsee and the St. Wolfgang.

Between Salzburg (p 129) and Mondsee the motorway, above the little Thalgau Valley, is slightly raised and affords open views of the Drachenwand cliffs beyond which, in the middle distance, stands the Schafberg spur. The **Lake of Mondsee★** at last appears below the Schafberg.

Mondsee. – *Description p 111.*

The north shore of the Mondsee, which is calm and smiling at first, becomes a little more severe beyond the Pichl promontory, cut by the road in a pronounced hump.

> **Burggrabenklamm.** – *From Au 5 km - 3 miles along the road beside the Attersee at the foot of the Schafberg slopes. Leave the car at the Gasthaus Zum Jägerwirth car park and then 1/2 hour on foot Rtn.*
> *Unprotected walk on rocks which are slippery after rain.*
> Exploration of a ravine as far as a waterfall.

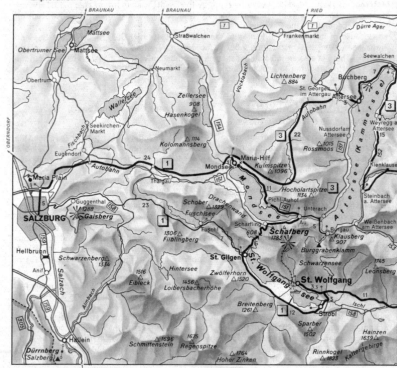

The south shore of the lake of Mondsee, along which you run between See and Scharfling is framed by the lower cliffs of the Schafberg; the road can get through only by means of bracketed sections under the overhanging rock and by short tunnels.

The crossing of the little pass connecting Scharfling and St. Gilgen is remarkable for the **panoramic section**★★ which bends in a curve above St. Gilgen *(car park)*. Beyond the slender bulbous-domed village bell-tower, the **Lake of St Wolfgang**★★ stretches towards the Rinnkogel massif of which a characteristic peak, the Sparber, seems to form an advanced bastion *(illustration p 124)*.

Short cut by the direct road (No. 158) **from Salzburg to St. Gilgen.** – This road, though less varied, saves 21 km - 13 miles – (not including the trip along the Lake of Mondsee) and pleasantly overlooks the small lake of Fuschl *(facilities: see Fuschl am See p 39)*.

St. Gilgen★. – *Description p 124.*

Soon the road from Salzburg to Bad Ischl draws away from the lake. The Schafberg, smiling on this southern slope, is crowned with an hotel, served by a rack railway. To the left a road branches off which leads to the Gschwendt landing stage from which you could reach St. Wolfgang by boat *(p 125)*. Leave the main road at Strobl to make the detour to St. Wolfgang.

Strobl. – Pop 2 767. *Facilities p 42.* The main square of the village, the church and the lakeshore with its flower gardens form a quietly graceful scene.

St. Wolfgang★★. – *Description p 125.*

Turn back to Bad Ischl *(p 91)* on the direct road, avoiding Strobl.

② FROM BAD ISCHL TO GMUNDEN via Traunkirchen

34 km - 21 miles – about 1 hour – Local map p 137

This run is marked by a corniche section along the shore of the Traunsee, the deepest lake in Austria (191 m - 527 ft). Cliffs rise from the lake waters in tortured shapes.

Below Bad Ischl *(p 91)* the Traun corridor, which was one of the great European salt routes, unwinds evenly between the Höllengebirge and Totes Gebirge foothills. Beside the road, at the foot of the west slope, a track follows the course of the *Soleleitung* (saltwater conduit – *p 27*), which since the 17C has brought the salt waters from Hallstatt to the refinery at Ebensee, whence the salt was at one time sent by boat across the Traunsee. From Gmunden the boats continued on the Lower Traun, using a reach which since 1552 has enabled them to avoid the last falls of the river (Traunfall). Glassmaking and chemical factories have set an industrial stamp on Ebensee today.

The **corniche**★ from Ebensee to Traunkirchen is spectacular. From the road, which is hewn in the rock above the **Traunsee**★, you can see the gold peak of the Rötelspitze standing out from the Erlakogel, and then, farther north, beyond a slope pitted with quarries, the huge and lonely Traunstein.

Traunkirchen. – *Description p 146.*

During the last part of the trip across a smiling landscape, those who enjoy solving puzzles can pass the time trying to pick out the Sleeping Greek *(p 72)*.

Altmünster. – Pop 8 583. *Facilities p 39.*

The charming Ort Castle welcomes you to Gmunden *(description p 72)*.

③ ★FROM GMUNDEN TO SALZBURG by the Grossalm road and the Lake of Attersee

103 km - 64 miles – about 3 hours – Local map above

The route which links the three lakes, the Traunsee, the Attersee and the Mondsee crosses a sometimes bucolic countryside as in the Upper Aurach Valley or a sometimes open countryside as in the Mondsee hollow.

From Gmunden *(p 73)* take the Bad Ischl road to Altmünster.

Altmünster. – Pop 8 583. *Facilities p 39.*

Gmundnerberg★. – *6 km - 4 miles from Altmünster. Description p 72.*

The road leaves the banks of the Traunsee to enter a tranquil valleyed region dotted with brilliantly white-washed farmhouses and clumps of huge lime trees. After passing on its right the hamlet to Grossalm the road burrows into the forest which lies within sight of the northern escarpments of the Höllengebirge to reach a pass at an altitude of 826 m - 2 710 ft.

The descent down the Attersee slope, which is at first very steep, becomes interesting only on reaching the panoramic **run**★, from Kienklause to Steinbach, where it runs along a bare slope which plunges directly into the lake.

Steinbach am Attersee. – Pop 956. *Facilities p 42.*

137

The SALZKAMMERGUT***

The road stretches like a quay beside the **Lake of Attersee*** (or Kammersee), the largest lake in the Austrian Alps (fishing, boating) which bathes, to the south, the last cliff-like slopes of the Schafberg. The west bank of the lake, between the villages of Seewalchen and Attersee, unfolds through a region of smilling sunbathed hills where orchards flourish. Only the cliffs of the Höllengebirge, rising up on the far bank bring a note of harshness to the scene. To get a good view of the whole lake, stop at the viewpoint (bench) beside the Buchberg Chapel.

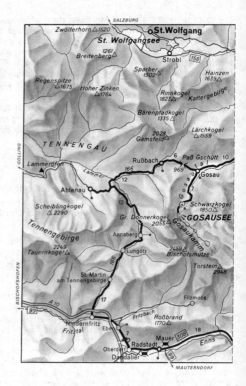

> **Attersee.** – Pop 1 352. *Facilities p 39.*

Leave the banks of the lake at Attersee and take the motorway towards Salzburg (entrance "St. Georgen").

The road down towards Mondsee offers a **panorama*** of the mountains which enframe the lake (Drachenwand, Schafberg) and the Salzkammergut Alps.

> **Mondsee.** – *1 km - 1/2 mile – from the "Mondsee" exit. Description p 111.*

Continue on the motorway to Salzburg *(p 129).*

---

④ ***TOUR AROUND THE DACHSTEIN
leaving from Bad Ischl – *210 km - 130 miles – allow one or two days – Local map pp 138-139.*

This tour can start from the Salzach Valley (Golling) or from the Enns Valley (Radstadt, Schladming, Steinach, etc.) where you will discover the two faces of the Dachstein massif *(p 57).*

Branching off from the Pötschenhöhe route south of Bad Goisern, the road to Bad Ischl *(p 91)* at Hallstatt follows the floor or the Traun Valley, which is planted with orchards. At Steeg, the road along the **Lake of Hallstatt*** (Hallstätter See) begins – it is a deep blue and boats with lofty prows sail upon it. At the Gosaumühle fork, turn towards Hallstatt and follow this lakeside route at the foot of a slope which is still steep, facing the Sechser Kogel promontory, a spur of the Sarstein. The **view*** opens out onto the town of Hallstatt grouped below its church; the amphitheatre of Obertraun also appears.

Enter the tunnel to bypass Hallstatt, leave the car at the terrace-belvedere which at one point breaks the tunnels and walk into town.

> **Hallstatt**. – *Description p 81.*

> **Ascent to the Krippenstein**. – *From Hallstatt – 6 km - 4 miles – and ascent: 2 1/2 hours (belvedere only) to 4 hours (belvedere and caves) of cable-car and walking (p 57).*

After visiting Hallstatt, continue through the tunnel and on emerging turn round to take the tunnel for south-north traffic only. Return to Gosaumühle and passing below the Soleleitung *(p 27)* aqueduct, enter the mountains along the Gosaubach.

When the valley widens again the magnificent crest of the Gosaukamm bristling with peaks unfolds on the left above the Gosau basin. Here two almost identical churches are a reminder that Protestant communities have been able to survive in this part of Upper Austria.

Turn towards the lake of Gosau and leave the car at the car parks at the end of the road.

> **Lake of Gosau*** (Gosausee). – From the **lower lake of Gosau** there is a **view*** of the limestone group of the Hoher Dachstein (alt 2 995 m - 9 826 ft) and its small plateau glaciers. The early and late hours of the day, when the glaciers and mountain walls are bathed in light and deep shadows reign on the floor of the valley, provide the best light.

Turn round; at Gosau take the Pass Gschütt road.

On the west slope of the pass, the road drops among parklands to the Russbach hollow, where you find large peasants' houses with little belfries recalling those of the Tyrol *(illustration p 29)*; it then crosses the Abtenau depression at the foot of the Tennengebirge.

> **Abtenau.** – Pop 5 043. *Facilities p 39.* This little town (Abtenau - the abbey meadow) at the foot of the enormous Kogel is a centre for several popular country resorts. The Gothic church, a former pilgrimage stop with its twin aisles, is interesting as much for its graceful outline as for its furnishings (statues of St George and St Florian). The carefully built priest's house is worthy of the patronage of St Peter's Abbey at Salzburg.

Turn round and bear right towards the Annaberg, the "Salzburg Dolomite" road. The furrow of the Upper Lammer separating the Tennengebirge and Dachstein massifs, begins by a romantic gorge. The most remarkable views of the journey are oriented to the east, especially in the Annaberg-Lungötz section. This is in the direction of the Gosaukamm which is distinguished here by the cleaved peak aptly named Bischofsmütze – a bishop's mitre. The pass at St. Martin leads into the Fritztal, a tributary valley of the Salzach (views westwards towards Hochkönig).

> **Radstadt.** – *Description p 118.*

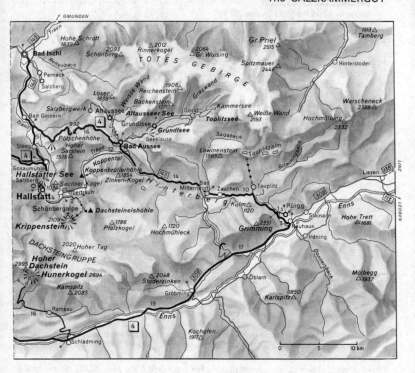

The road now runs through the Enns gap at the foot of the south wall of the Dachstein; the Hunerkogel cable-car rises above Ramsau.

Schladming. – Pop 3 930. *Facilities pp 42 and 43.*

Ascent to the Hunerkogel★★. – *From Schladming, 16 km - 10 miles plus about 1 hour Rtn of cable-car. See p 149.*

At the Neuhaus crossroads, leave the Enns Valley and take a left turn on road No. 145 – a main road of the Styrian Salzkammergut massif, which rises quickly into a ravine carved by the Grimming at the foot of the scaly cliffs of Gross Grimming. To the right the white village of Pürgg dominates the Enns Valley, which you now leave.

Pürgg. – Pop 1 034. *1.5 km - 1 mile from the tour road.* Leave the car at the entrance of the village. Art lovers should go up to the bluff on which stands the Chapel of St John (Johanneskapelle) – *to visit ask for the key from Herr Spöckmoser at the house nearest to the chapel.* The church decoration is typical of a country church of about the year 1200. The Romanesque frescos uncovered and restored (the last time in 1959) depict, in the nave, the Annunciation, the Birth of Christ and its Announcement to the Shepherds, a fabulous fight between cats and mice and the Wise and Foolish Virgins. Figures seen on the triumphal arch are Christ Giving His Blessing, Cain and Abel and the church donors. On the chancel dome the Mystic Lamb is surrounded by the four Apostles, who are symbolically supported by the four sections of the world (on the pendentives). The crucifix on the altar is also Romanesque. The parish church, also ancient, is curiously built on the mountainside. You enter it either at ground floor level through the façade or at gallery level.

The road goes through an enclosed depression known as the Hinterberg Plateau. In the foreground the magnificent chiselled walls of the Grimming face the slab-like shapes of the Lawinenstein. This crest masks the Alpine combe pastures of the **Tauplitzalm** *(facilities see at Mitterndorf p 41 and at Tauplitzalm p 43)* which is popular with skiers in winter thanks to the mountain road beginning at Zauchen and a cable-car which travels up from the village of Tauplitz.

Mitterndorf. – Pop 2 854. *Facilities p 41.*

Through a ravine of the Traun, arrive at Bad Aussee.

Bad Aussee★. – *Description p 50.*

Grundlsee★. – *From Bad Aussee 5 km - 3 miles. Description of the lake p 50.*

The Pötschenhöhe (alt 992 m - 3 255 ft) road enables you to cross the great loop of the Traun, partly drowned by the lake of Hallstatt. The east slope of the pass from Bad Aussee forms a small **crest★★** with a panoramic view. The pincer-shaped precipitous promontories of the Loser and the Trisselwand jut out from the petrified surface of the Totes Gebirge. Opposite stands the Sarstein. The west slope of the Pötschenhöhe begins in the smiling Bad Goisern basin. The last bend, which has been arranged for stopping, makes a **belvedere★** overlooking the waters of the lake of Hallstatt. The lake turns to penetrate the amphitheatre hollowed out by the Traun at the foot of the Dachstein Massif.

At Bad Goisern join up with the road No. 145 to Bad Ischl.

If you intend to combine your tour of Austria
with journeys through Germany, Switzerland or Northern Italy,
*remember to take the **Michelin Green Guides***
Germany, Switzerland, Italy.

The limestone bastions of the Raxalpe and the Schneeberg *(read pp 16-18, The Alps in Austria)* are separated by the deep Valley of the Schwarza, called the Höllental. The mountains are much frequented by the Viennese in summer and as soon as the first snows whiten the ski-runs of their summits in winter.

Without climbing these heights, motorists can at least skirt their wooded foothills, cut by wild ravines. The route below invites them to do so.

*TOUR OF THE SCHNEEBERG

From Neunkirchen to Semmering – *114 km - 71 miles – about 4 hours (excluding the climb to the Schneeberg) – Local map opposite*

Leave from Neunkirchen.

Ternitz. – Pop 16 154. The modern church is adorned in the chancel, behind the high altar, with a large mosaic representing the Crucifixion. Architecturally, the chancel is the most important part.

The pleasant road, sometimes under trees, runs up the smiling Sierningbach Valley from Ternitz onwards. The Schneeberg can be recognized from afar by its bare slopes. A little before Puchberg rocky shelves become numerous on either side of the road.

Puchberg am Schneeberg. – Pop 3 190. *Facilities p 42.* A pleasant resort at the foot of the Schneeberg. In this village are an old castle and a ruined keep.

From Puchberg you are advised to go up the Schneeberg by the mountain railway.

Schneeberg★. – *From the station at Puchberg you must allow a whole day for the ascent, as the cog railway trains run only at long intervals. In summer there are only two daily departures at 9 and 11.40am, returning to Puchberg at about 2.35 and 5.35 pm; 92S Rtn.* After climbing for 1 1/4 hours you reach the Hochschneeberg terminus (alt 1 795 m - 5 889 ft). Nearby, clinging to the mountainside, in a fine position above the Puchberg basin, is a hotel. End the excursion by going up *(about 2 1/2 hours on foot Rtn)* to the **Kaiserstein** (alt 2 061 m - 6 762 ft – **panorama★** of the Pre-Alps) and to the **Klosterwappen** spur (**view★** of the Raxalpe, beyond the Höllental). This, with an altitude of 2 076 m - 6 811 ft – is the highest point of the massif.

After Puchberg the road, still picturesque, winds among fir trees and follows the courses of torrents dotted with many sawmills.

The route goes round the north of the Schneeberg massif and joins the fine Schwarza Valley, which soon narrows, forming the Höllental.

Höllental★★. – *Description p 83.*

Raxalpe★. – This steep sided limestone massif has become, owing to its proximity to Vienna, a regular climbing centre. Its walls contain several hundred named and numbered tunnels. A much used cable-car, starting above Hirschwang, reaches the edge of the upper plateau at 1 547 m - 5 075 ft. The upper plateau is a typical limestone shelf, affording various **views★**: onto the Semmering Massif to the south, and the Kaiserstein and the Höllental to the north. Several hotels and refuges are ready to receive tourists.

NEUNKIRCHEN-SEMMERING

South of Hirschwang the road you are following leaves the Schwarza Valley, and with many bends cuts across a picturesque, rugged region of wooded spurs and ravines. The difficulties of the ground did not daunt the builders of the Semmering railway, who have accomplished monumental engineering feats.

Raxblick*. – As you go up from Hirschwang to Orthof, leave the route for a moment to go to this spur below an isolated hotel. It stands out well and forms a belvedere overlooking the Raxalpe.

Semmering*. – Pop 840. *Facilities pp 42 and 43*. This mountain cure and winter sports centre, built on terraces between 985 m and 1 291 m - 3 231 ft and 4 235 ft – enjoys a privileged position. It does not suffer from the cold fogs of the valleys and has an exceptionally sunny atmosphere, which helps to make it one of the greatest centres of attraction in Lower Austria. Hotels and villas nestle in greenery on the sheltered slopes of the Semmering pass.

The road leading to the pass was relaid in 1842 on the Gloggnitz slope with a maximum gradient of 1 in 17. It and the railway constructed in 1854, the first main line in the high mountains in Europe, do honour to the engineers of Imperial Austria.

SCHWAZ ★ (Tyrol)

Michelin map **426** fold 17 – Pop 10 936 – Alt 538 m - 1 765 ft – 🔋 ☎ 3240

From the 15 to 16C when its silver and copper mines were in full production, Schwaz was the most densely populated town in the Tyrol, after Innsbruck. The town was well cared for by the emperor and the financial powers of the period, especially the Fugger family of Augsburg. The degree of prosperity it enjoyed is attested today by the unusual size and the decoration of its most representative buildings, all erected between 1450 and 1520.

This extravagant period also survives in popular tradition according to which the miners of in the past could make the paving of Schwaz ring with the silver nails in their boots.

■ PARISH CHURCH* (Pfarrkirche)

time: 1/2 hour

The church rears its cold façade, bristling with pinnacles in the Swabian style, in line with the Franz-Josef-Strasse. Under a huge roof, covered with 15 000 copper plates, it shelters four aisles and two parallel chancels, restored in 1912 to their Gothic style of the 15C, with network vaulting. The main south aisle and its side aisle, on the right, were reserved for the miners' corporation, as certain tombs indicate.

The organ-loft shows particularly elaborate Gothic decoration in the vaulting supporting it and in its balustrade. The Baroque organ-case is gorgeous. As you go along the main part of the church, you will see a few traces of the Gothic furnishings: the octagonal font of 1470 and, against the pillar separating the two chancels, a Christ with a very intense expression. But the finest piece of religious sculpture is the **altar of St Anne** in the south side aisle. Its Baroque altarpiece (1733), honouring the patron saints of Austria, St George and St Florian, frames a fine group of the early 16C: the Holy Family *(illustration p 28)* between St Elizabeth on the right and St Ursula on the left.

■ ADDITIONAL SIGHT

The Franciscan Church (Franziskanerkirche). – The Gothic church was finished in 1515. In the strict arrangement of its three naves it was in accordance with the building rules imposed upon by the Order. Its Baroquisation in 1736 destroyed neither its pleasant proportions nor its good lighting. The capitals on the tall marble columns, reduced to simple rings, have a decorative function. The Renaissance **stalls*** (1618) are the work of a local artisan.

Cloister (Kreuzgang). – *Entrance by the door of the monastery on the south side of the church.*
The cloister is pure Gothic in style. It contains important remains of wall paintings representing scenes from the Passion (1512-1526), attributed to a brother who came from Swabia. Charming designs of foliage and birds have adorned the vaulting since the beginning of the 17C. The community of Schwaz is symbolized by various shields: craftsmen and miners' guilds and, as well, wealthy shareholders are shown. The Emperor Maximilian is represented by the arms of his hereditary states.

SECKAU Abbey (Styria)

Michelin map **426** south of fold 22 – 11 km - 7 miles north of Knittelfeld

The Benedictine Seckau Abbey was the centre of the diocese of Styria from 1218 to 1782, and the prelate residing at Graz bears the title of Bishop of Graz and Seckau. This monumental group, which has a military air with its corner towers, stands majestically at the foot of the Lower Tauern.

■ BASILICA* *time: 1/2 hour*

The body of the church, which is mid-12C, was built with alternating piles and columns topped with huge square capitals with little decoration, in accordance with an antique Romanesque German tradition. Since the end of the 15C the internal unity has been broken by the rich network vaulting of the main nave – originally roofed with timber – by the 19C transept and by the changes in the chancel, which the Benedictines, installed in the abbey since 1883, ordered in the taste of the period.

Three chapels, of differing periods and arrangements, spring from the north aisle. They are interesting for their works of art. The first in order, the **Angels' Chapel** (Engelkapelle), contains a huge composition, inspired by the Apocalypse, by Herbert Boeckl (1960).

Chapel of the Blessed Sacrament (Sakramentskapelle). – Over the tabernacle is a 12C alabaster of Venetian origin, representing the Virgin and Child. This is the jewel of the Seckau Treasury and the oldest Marian likeness venerated in Austria.

Episcopal Chapel (Bischofskapelle). – The **altarpiece★★** of the high altar (1489), celebrates the Coronation of the Virgin. In a circular framework, which is itself most unusual, the artist has represented the three persons of the Holy Trinity with identical features, in strict conformity with the orthodox definition, three Persons in one God. Stand back a little to see with what talent the sculptor has mastered so difficult a subject, for the slightest error of taste in this group of three heads on one body would have been fatal.

Mausoleum of Karl II. – The Mausoleum of Archduke Karl II stands in the chapel which forms a prolongation of the north side aisle. Together with that, it forms a decorative scheme which is regarded as a specimen of the transition from late Renaissance to Baroque art. As it was carried out by two Italians between 1587 and 1612, it also marks the beginning of the penetration of transalpine taste into Austria. This influence, which appeared in a dazzling fashion rather later in the mausoleum of Ferdinand II (the son of Archduke Karl) at Graz *(p 73)*, was naturally felt first in Styria.

SEEFELD IN TIROL ★★ (Tyrol)

Michelin map **426** fold 16 – *Local map p 143* – Pop 2 484 – Alt 1 180 m - 3 871 ft – 🏢
🕿 2313 and 2316 – *Facilities pp 42 and 43*

Seefeld, an elegant country resort, has an especially high reputation as a ski resort, due to the Olympic games which were held here twice. To the advantages of its altitude, Seefeld also adds those of a situation on a broad site looking out towards the rocky crests of the Hohe Munde, the Wetterstein and the Karwendel.

Parish Church (Pfarrkirche). – This Gothic building was erected, with the generosity of the Princes of the Tyrol, in the 15C, to perpetuate the worship of a miraculous host which had been an object of pilgrimage since 1384 and was kept until 1949 in the high chapel of the Holy Blood. The tympanum of the south door represents, on the right, the martyrdom of St Oswald of England, the patron saint of the church, and on the left the miracle of the host: a knight who, from pride of rank, has insisted on consuming a large host, like the celebrant, finds himself half buried. Inside, the network vaulting, characteristic of the late Gothic style *(p 33)*, displays thorny groins. In the chancel, the mural paintings of the 15C (legend of St Oswald, the Passion, legend of St Mary Magdalene) have been restored. On the right, a picture (1502), of the late Gothic period, depicts the miracle of the host.

SEEFELDER SATTEL, Roads of the ★★ (Tyrol and Bavaria)

Michelin map **426** folds 16, 17, 30 and 31

The Seefelder Sattel or Seefeld Saddle, raised above the Inn Valley, and the Scharnitz ravine, make a gap through the Northern Limestone Alps along the Munich-Innsbruck axis. Nonetheless, this section, though of great tourist interest, does not take the place, for international traffic, of the less direct but less mountainous route of the Inn Valley.

THE ZIRLERBERG★

From Innsbruck to Mittenwald – *37 km - 23 miles – about 1 hour – Local map p 143*

Austrian and German customs controls at Scharnitz.
Between Innsbruck *(p 85)* and Zirl the road, following the floor of the Inn Valley, runs beneath the steep slopes of the Martinswand opposite the tributary valley of Sellrain. This promontory marks the traditional boundary between the Upper and Lower Inn Valley and provided the setting for an episode dear to the hearts of the Tyrolese: Emperor Maximilian *(p 85)*, in the excitement of the hunt, is said to have fallen down this cliff and been saved from a perilous plight by an angel, appearing in the guise of a peasant.

The well known **Zirlerberg★** slope covers the 500 m - 1 640 ft difference in altitude between Zirl and Reith bei Seefeld. It was as steep as 1 in 4 in places, before improvement – it now being 1 in 7 – and it is said that every weekend spectators posted themselves at vantage points on the lookout for accidents. The only hairpin bend in this section is now an organized **belvedere★**, with a car park and bar, affording a view of the sawteeth of the Kalkkögel opposite and in the middle distance. Higher up in this ascent you see in line with the road, to the northwest, the surprisingly smooth hump of the Hohe Munde. Leave the modern for the old road which goes through the centre of Reith.

Reith bei Seefeld★. – Pop 787. The church stands in a charming **setting★** facing the small Rosskogel range and the jagged crests of the Kalkkögel, which lie south of the Inn Valley.

Seefeld in Tirol★★. – *Description above.*

Coming out of Seefeld to the north the **view★** becomes extensive and embraces, from left to right, the summit of the Hohe Munde, the Wetterstein ridge (except for the Zugspitze), the Arnspitze and the first peaks of the Karwendel. The road drops quickly to the floor of a valley leading to the Isar and reaches the mouth of the Scharnitz ravine, gateway to Bavaria; then 6 km - 4 miles from the border you arrive at Mittenwald *(see Michelin Green Guide to Germany)*.

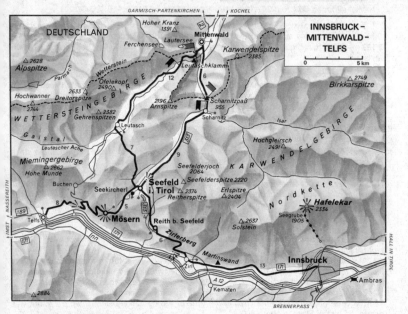

THE LEUTASCH VALLEY★★
From Mittenwald to Telfs – *32 km - 20 miles – about 1 1/2 hours – Local map above*

This route combines a run through the secluded Leutasch Valley and a visit to Mösern, one of the most attractive belvederes of the Upper Inn Valley.

The road is often narrow. German and Austrian customs controls between Mittenwald and Leutasch.

The road comes out of the Isar Valley as this emerges from the Mittenwald and immediately climbs above the Leutasch Gorge (Leutaschklamm), within view of the Karwendel Massif (Viererspitze).

Over a bridge across the Leutascher Ache it debouches into the grassy combe of Unterleutasch, majestically bounded on the left by the Arnspitze, on the right by the rock walls of the Wettersteinwand, from which spring the promontories of the Ofelekopf and the Gehrenspitzen. A few roofed crosses and occasional houses with roofs weighed down with big stones are dotted about this lonely valley, preserving its primitive air. Ahead, the Hohe Munde rises in line with the road.

Leutasch. – Pop 1 674. *Facilities pp 41 and 43.*

From Leutasch onwards the road runs through a jumbled, wooded landscape to Seefeld.

Seefeld in Tirol★★. – *Description p 142.*

A little Valley, whose beginning is marked by a charming rotunda chapel (Seekircherl), soon brings you 600 m - 2 000 ft above the Inn Valley.

Mösern★★. – Pop 134. *Facilities p 41.* This splendidly sited village is the very place for a halt. The **belvedere★★** easiest to reach – benches on a grassy spur below the church – belongs to the Gasthof Inntal. From there you can see, upstream, the Inn winding along the floor of the Telfs furrow and then slipping into a tangle of crests among which, on the horizon, the Hoher Riffler (alt 3 168 m - 10 394 ft) stands flecked with snow. Farther to the right, the green terrace of the Meiming Plateau (Meiminger Hochland) can be seen at the foot of the Mieming range, which ends at the great dome of the Hohe Munde. South of the valley rise the Sellrain mountains, and, in the middle distance, the jagged crests of the Kalkkögel.

The quick descent, mostly through woods, from Mösern to Telfs is of interest for the panorama in the bend after the Buchen fork (views of the Mieminger Kette).

SPITAL AM PYHRN (Upper Austria)

Michelin map **426** fold 22 – Pop 2 290 – Alt 647 m - 2 123 ft – *Facilities p 42*

Spital is the halting place, as its name suggests, on the ancient road over the Pyhrn Pass (alt 945 m - 3 100 ft) which connects the Steyr and Enns Valleys, and, through them, Linz and Graz. It has a former collegiate church in the Baroque style of unusual unity.

Collegiate Church★ (Stiftskirche). – *If the grilles inside the church are closed ask the sacristan to open them (bell to the right of the entrance).*

The church, built from 1714 to 1730, has a harmonious façade framed between two towers, of which three projecting cornices balance the height.

The interior of the main building gives an impression of fullness enhanced by the addition to the architecture of decorations which were diminished by a fire in 1841. When Master Schmidt of Krems (Kremser Schmidt) had finished the paintings on the altarpieces of the side altars, about 1780, no further embellishment in the taste of that time was given to the church. In the chancel, Bartolomeo Altomonte (1693-1783) painted a remarkable decoration of colonnades in *trompe-l'œil*, opening at the centre on the scene of the Assumption of the Virgin. This composition (1 740) ends at the dome with a representation of the celestial Court.

Michelin map **426** fold 34 – Pop 14 769 – Alt 554 m - 1 818 ft – ⓘ ☎ 3420

The pleasant city of Spittal an der Drau is a commercial and cultural centre of Upper Carinthia. It occupies an extensive site at the foot of the belvedere-peak of the Goldeck (alt 2 139 m - 7 018 ft, cablecar) at the confluence of the Lieser and the Drava (Drau) near the Lake of Millstatt.

Porcia Château. – This cube shaped structure was begun in 1527; it is framed by corner turrets and is one of the rare specimens of an Italian palace on Austrian soil. The château is now communal property and its park, which has become public, is a pleasant place to relax.

The **courtyard★**, lined on three sides with Italianate galleries, shows perfect unity of style in its Renaissance decoration, antique medallions, balustrade pillars, door-frames, etc. Dramatic performances are held in the courtyard in summer. Splendid 16C wrought iron grilles separate the stairs from the upper galleries.

Regional Museum (Bezirksheimatmuseum). – *In the castle on the second floor and in the attics. Open 15 May to 30 September 9am to 6pm; 18S.*

A detailed and evocative display of the dynastic history and the traditions of the Spittal area. Note the reconstruction of a primary schoolroom of the 1900s. Also presented is an important collection of agricultural equipment and local crafts.

EXCURSION

Teurnia Excavations (Teurnia-Ausgrabungen). – *5 km - 3 miles to the northwest, plus 1/2 hour sightseeing.*

At a point 4.5 km - 2.5 miles from Spittal at St. Peter im Holz, turn off left from the road to Lienz to reach, at a bend in the former roadway, the two isolated buildings which house the museum of the Teurnia excavations *(open May to October 9am to noon and 1 to 5pm; 10S).*

Between 1910 and 1914 the foundations of an early 5C cemetery church of the city of Teurnia were unearthed. It flourished at the time of the Roman Noricum *(map p 22),* but was destroyed by the Slavs in about 590.

In the chancel is a semicircular stone bench where priests sat. The south side chapel contains a large mosaic (500 AD) with certain designs representing animals, possibly pagan or early Christian symbols.

The end of the season
(October, early November)
is the time of the year
when you get the most brilliant views of the Alps.

Michelin map **426** fold 30 – Between Silz and Telfs – *Local map p 69*

The Cistercian Abbey of Stams was founded in 1273, in the Upper Inn Valley, by Elizabeth of Bavaria, married, for the second time, to Count Meinhard II – the first builder of Tyrolean unity – in memory of her son by her first marriage. The son, Conradin Hohenstaufen, was tortured at Naples by order of Charles of Anjou. The majestic pile of architecture, made conspicuous since the end of the 17C by the two church towers, is purely Baroque in style. Since 1968 a conventual building houses a ski school where the young Tyrolean hopefuls study and ski at the same time.

Leave the car on the shady esplanade at the foot of the pretty 14C village church, with Rococo decoration. Pass through the abbey gateway, which opens in line with the abbey church, and apply at the porter's lodge of the monastery *(first door on the right of the pedimented forepart of the main façade).*

Guided tours (30 min) 9 to 11.45am and 1.30 to 5.30pm; 15S; brochure available in English.

Abbey Church★★ (Stiftskirche). – The present building results from the Baroquisation, in 1732, of a Romanesque nave without a transept, which was vaulted only in the 17C. The small apses behind the high altar have kept their original appearance, but the aisles have given way to six side chapels.

Directly on entering you will see, on the right, the famous **Rose Grille.** This screen, a masterpiece in ironwork dating from 1716, closes the passage leading to the outer Chapel of the Holy Blood (Heiligen Blut).

A balustrade in the nave bounds the crypt, where twelve naïve gilded wood statues of the Princes of the Tyrol are reminders that Stams is the burial-place of this dynasty.

The showpiece of the furnishings is the high altar (1613), whose altarpiece represents the Tree of Life in the form of interlacing boughs supporting eighty-four carved figures of saints surrounding the Virgin. On either side of the altar, Adam and Eve, representing the beginnings of man while at the crown Christ on the Cross represents the mystery of the supernatural. In the monks' chancel a grille marks the tomb of Duke Friedrich the Penniless *(p 87).*

Hall of Princes★ (Fürstensaal). – The hall is reached from the porter's lodge by an oval shaped **grand staircase★** with a fine wrought iron balustrade. The hall of state, whose ceiling opens onto a balustraded gallery, is decorated with paintings (1722) recalling outstanding episodes in the life of St Bernard.

Michelin map **426** fold 22 – Pop 38 967 – Alt 310 m - 1 017 ft – ⓘ ☎ 23229

Steyr had a glorious past, giving its name to the province of Styria and becoming, for a time, a rival to Vienna. It still plays the part of an industrial capital in Upper Austria. To the east of the town, whose old quarter is huddled at the foot of a bluff at the confluence of the Enns and the Steyr, industrial suburbs have developed. In spite of these industries, Steyr has preserved in its old quarter the charm of a bygone but attractive past.

■ **SIGHTS** *time: 1 hour*

Stadtplatz*. – The Stadtplatz, which is a street in the form of a square, is lined with fine late Gothic and Renaissance houses with balconies, supported on corbels, and with projecting first floors. In the middle is a graceful 17C fountain, the **Leopoldibrunnen.**

No. 27, the **town hall** (Rathaus), and No. 32, the **Bummerlhaus (B)**, are of outstanding interest. The Rathaus, built in the Rococo style from 1765 to 1771 has a narrow façade surmounted by a belfry; the Bummerlhaus is a fine mansion in the Gothic style, with a gable and the characteristic first floor overhang.

Many of these houses have remarkable courts: No. 9 has a Renaissance one, with fine pillars supporting two tiers of arcades on which Virginia creeper grows; No. 12 has one with baskethandle arches and large pillars supporting wrought iron balconies; No. 14, of the late Gothic period, with two tiers of balconies and pillars which are sometimes turned or carved, and No. 39 (Dunklhof) one which has two tiers of arcades, of the Renaissance, adorned with a wooden lean-to roof and *sgraffiti* decorations *(see note p 125).*

Dominican Church (Dominikanerkirche). – The church is flanked on the north side by the **Eisengasse,** a picturesque alley going down to the Enns.

The interior Baroque decoration includes a high altar overloaded with gilding, a Virgin and Child of 1704, pictures framed in stucco and a Rococo pulpit.

South of the Stadtplatz is the **Innerbergerstadl (M)**, a 17C granary turned into a local museum. Together with a town gate (the Neutor) and a house flanked with a turret built on brackets, it forms a charming picture.

Go round the Innerbergstadl to the right and make for the parish church along an alley ending in a stairway.

Parish Church (Stadtpfarrkirche) (A). – The church was built in the mid-15C, in the Gothic style, by the architect of St Stephen's Cathedral in Vienna, with which it has many resemblances both in plan and elevation. The font is adorned with 16C bas-reliefs.

Go back to the Stadtplatz by the Pfarrgasse, a pedestrian street.

TAMSWEG ★ (Salzburg) _____

Michelin map **426** fold 35 – *Local map p 119* – Pop 5 256 – Alt 1 021 m - 3 350 ft – *Facilities p 42*

Arriving at Tamsweg by the Mauterndorf road you get a flattering view of the town, which appears to be dominated by the great Church of St Leonard, standing alone in the forest on the sloping valley wall.

Tamsweg is the capital of the Lungau and is still a centre of folklore: according to a custom reminiscent of that of Flanders, processions take place every summer *(see tourist calendar of events p 31),* headed by a gigantic dummy representing Samson, accompanied by two grotesque dwarfs.

■ **SIGHTS** *time: 1 1/2 hours*

Marktplatz. – The regular design of this square, lined with pretty inns, lends distinction to Tamsweg. Characteristic are the Lungau peasants' houses, which have here become middle class, because of the typical arrangement of attics where a small triangular section of roof shelters the façade on the gable side. By contrast the **Rathaus** (town hall) in a house dating from the 16C displays corner turrets and closely resembles the style of country mansions commonly found in the Salzburg region.

Church of St Leonard (St. Leonhardkirche). – Leave Tamsweg by the bridge over the River Mur (the Murau road) to the south of the town. Cross the railway and leave the car at the start of the road, on the right, which climbs directly up to the Church of St Leonard. Bearing right, take the less steep of the rises, which soon affords a good view of Tamsweg and of the deeply jagged ridges of the Tauern.

The 15C Church of St Leonard has kept its early Gothic plan and design – tall light windows, network vaulting, etc. Some of its **stained glass,** which dates from the period when the building was erected, is among the most precious in Austria. Note also, immediately to the left on entering (near the gallery), the window of the Tree of Life in which the Virgin of the Annunciation is presented at the foot of the tree which spreads out on either side and at its tip forms the arms of the Cross. The "gold window" – Goldfenster (recently restored), on the right of the chancel, is very well known: in a flamboyant architectural setting, it depicts, upwards from the base, the arms of Salzburg borne by two cherubs, St Virgil and St Rupert standing on either side of the donor prelate, the Holy Trinity figuratively represented as the Throne of Grace – the Holy Father presenting Christ – between St Peter and St Paul. South of the high altar, the small altar to St Leonard is surmounted by a statuette of the saint held in the branches of a juniper tree. The discovery of the statuette is the basis of the pilgrimage.

STEYR

0   300 m

Eisengasse _____ 2
Grünmarkt _____ 3
Kirchengasse ____ 4
Pachergasse _____ 5
Pfarrgasse _____ 6
Schuhbodengasse __ 7

TAUERN Tunnel (TAUERNTUNNEL)

Michelin map ▨▨▨ folds 20 and 34 – between Mallnitz and Böckstein

The railway tunnel through the Tauern mountains with an underground gallery – 8 551 m - 5 5/16 miles long was until the opening of the Felber Tauern road tunnel the only way through the Eastern Alps which allowed traffic to flow at all seasons through this particularly impenetrable region of the Tauern mountains east of the Brenner. A car-ferry train system has kept the route popular with motorists.

The route described below begins, in the south, at Spittal an der Drau. It therefore includes, between Spittal and Obervellach, a first section along the warm and well-tilled Lower Möll Valley, to the Gastein Alpine Valley.

In summer: from Mallnitz – open every 1/2 hour 7am to 6pm; hourly 1 to 7am and 6 to 11pm – from Böckstein – open every 1/2 hour 7.30am to 6.30pm; hourly 1.30 to 7.30am and 6.30 to 11.30pm. In winter hourly – from Mallnitz 6am to 10pm and from Böckstein 5.30am to 9.30pm. Duration: 10 min; 160S per car (240S Rtn valid for a month).

From Spittal an der Drau to Lend – *67 km - 42 miles – about 2 1/2 hours not including the railway journey*

Kolbnitz. – Pop 1 519. The electrical power station is fed, from both sides of the valley, by pressure conduits collecting water from the Reisseck and Kreuzeck Massifs. This equipment, which was completed in 1959, required the tapping, on the Reisseck slope, of four mountain lakes. The maximum drop is 1 772 m - 5 812 ft. The funicular and the railway of the station, available to the public, have opened the Upper Reisseck region to mountaineers and skiers.

Obervellach. – Pop 2 523. The church★ is a massive building of the late Gothic period (beginning of the 16C). It contains valuable works of art, outstanding being the 1520 **altarpiece**★ of the Dutch Master Jan van Scorel, on the north side altar, depicting the Holy Family between St Christopher and St Appoline. Among the wall paintings which remain, look in the chancel at the "auxiliary saints" of 1509 (from whom the Christian people used to expect cures for the most diverse ills). Also in the chancel is a bas-relief of the Garden of Olives, and various statues forming an excellent Gothic ensemble of the 16C.

Mallnitz. – Pop 1 019. *Facilities pp 41 and 43.* A mountain resort (alt 1 190 m - 8 904 ft) within reach of the last eastern 3 000 m - 10 000 ft peaks of the High Tauern (Goldberg and Ankogel groups), where large ice-caps persist. Mallnitz affords good facilities for mountain expeditions and ski excursions.

Böckstein. – The rotunda church of 1765 forms an exquisite example of the beginnings of Neo-Classical architecture in the Salzburg region.

Badgastein★★. – *Description p 51.*

Bad Hofgastein★. – *Description p 82.*

Klammpass. – The tower at Klammstein, under which the road passes in a tunnel, marks, upstream, the beginning of this section. By taking the second tunnel, the tourist avoids the former road (maximum gradient 1 in 7) which follows the torrent through the gorge joining the Gastein Valley with the main Salzach Valley.

TRAUNKIRCHEN (Upper Austria)

Michelin map ▨▨▨ fold 21 – *Local map p 137* – Pop 1 608 – Alt 430 m - 1 411 ft – *Facilities p 42*

The **position**★ of Traunkirchen, jutting out on its promontory, affords varied views of the Traunsee and especially the south basin of the lake, in its steep and wild setting.

Parish Church (Pfarrkirche). – The church stands on the north flank of the rock within view of the Erlakogel and the dome of the Traunstein. It originally formed part of a Benedictine abbey founded in the 11C and occupied by the Jesuits in the 17C. After a fire the Jesuit Fathers in 1632 rebuilt the church as it is today, in accordance with the precepts of their Order. The Baroque furnishings are dazzling, especially the **Fisherman's Pulpit**★, the drum of which, in the form of a boat, represents the apostles' ship with its dripping nets. On the sounding-board overhead is depicted a picturesque episode of the mission of St Francis Xavier: a lobster returning to the saint, who converted Japan, a crucifix which he had lost when shipwrecked. The good St François-Régis, is in a place of honour on the extreme right of the high altar.

TULLN (Lower Austria)

Michelin map ▨▨▨ fold 11 – *Local map p 62* – Pop 11 287 – Alt 180 m - 591 ft

Tulln grew up on the site of the Roman camp of Comagena *(see map p 22)*. Considerably later it became one of the seats of the Babenbergs, who preceded the Habsburgs.

Parish Church (Pfarrkirche). – This former Romanesque basilica of the 12C, dedicated to St Stephen, was transformed about 1500 into the Gothic style only to be Baroquised in the 18C.

The Romanesque west doorway, framed between two Baroque towers, is adorned with busts of twelve Apostles and surmounted by a double-headed eagle, the symbol of the Holy Roman Empire, holding two Turks' heads in its talons. These represent the terrible danger of invasion which threatened Austria in the 16 and 17C.

The nave and chancel have ogive vaulting and are strikingly spacious. The high altar, in marble, is ornamented with a 1786 altarpiece representing the martyrdom of St Stephen.

Funerary Chapel★★ (Karner). – Level with the chevet of the parish church stands one of the finest funerary chapels in Austria. It is known as that of the Three Kings and was built about 1250. Its outside shape is that of a polygon, to which an oven-vaulted apsidal is attached. Each panel of the polygon is adorned with arches and capitals; under one of the arches is a statue of the donor. The doorway is decorated with palm leaf capitals and geometric designs. The interior is roofed with a dome and painted with Romanesque frescos, among which can be recognized: Judgement, Redemption, Damnation.

Michelin map **426** folds 3, 4 and 12 – *Local map p 62* – Pop 1 515 666 – Alt 156 m - 512 ft –

Tourist and Reception Bureaux *See table p 150* – Dialing code: 0222

Vienna was the residence of the imperial court for six centuries and is deeply marked with the seal of the Habsburgs. The chances of history make it now the seat of a Federal Government whose influence extends only over a mutilated state, but being neutral since 1955, it enjoys considerable prestige.

Metternich's famous remark, "Asia begins at the Landstrasse", is all the more apt when one remembers that "Landstrasse", the 3rd district of Vienna, is only separated from the centre of the city by the width of a single street. The statesman's dictum has been illustrated many times in the course of history. Vienna was an outpost of the Roman Empire, and a stronghold of Christianity in spite of the Turkish assaults. It is now only about 70 km - 44 miles from the Iron Curtain.

In 1979 Vienna became the third UN capital (after New York City and Geneva) with the opening of the International Centre – UN City – in Donaupark. The centre includes the UN Industrial Development Organization, the International Atomic Energy Agency and some lesser UN bodies.

The Austrian capital revolves round St Stephen's Cathedral. For many, Vienna suggests the rhythm of the waltz or the shape of the Prater's Big Wheel. Its prestige, however, is due above all to its buildings, to memories of the Habsburgs, to the treasures in its museums, to the musical tradition preserved by the Opera and its famous choirs, orchestras *(p 35)* and to the elegance of the shops which line its great avenues.

HISTORICAL NOTES

From Attila to the Babenbergs. – In the saga of the Nibelungen *(p 58)* it is at Vindobona, a town on the site of the Roman camp where Marcus Aurelius died, that Attila and Kriemhild celebrated their wedding. Later, when the Babenberg family assumed the destinies of the Eastern Marches, its representatives adopted in succession, as residences, Pöchlarn, Melk, Tulln and Leopoldsberg before settling in Vienna. In 1155, Heinrich II Jasomirgott installed his ducal court in the city at a place called Am Hof. The eminence arising from its official function enabled Vienna also to expand as a market town.

Under one of his successors, Leopold the Glorious, Vienna became the capital of the Duchy and was guarded by massive walls with six fortified gateways and nineteen towers. In the centre stood the Romanesque Church of St Stephen (it became the bishop's seat only in 1469). By the time Frederick the Warrior, last of the Babenbergs, died in 1246, Vienna had become, after Cologne, the most important German-speaking town. Its growth, from then on, was linked with the fortunes of the Habsburgs, who reigned over Austria from 1273 to 1918.

The Plague and the Turks. – In many Austrian towns columns dedicated to the Virgin or the Holy Trinity were set up at the end of the 17C to recall that the Austrian Empire had escaped two scourges: the plague and the Turks.

In 1678, just after the celebrations in Vienna for the birth of a son to the Emperor Leopold I, a terrifying sickness made its appearance. Corpses lay in heaps in the streets or were thrown into the Danube. All who could, fled the capital. Only a few notables, headed by Prince Schwarzenberg, decided to fight the plague. Drastic measures of hygiene enabled them to stop the epidemic, which only ceased a year after having begun.

In 1682 the column to commemorate the deliverance from this plague was erected in the Graben, but another threat, exceptionally grave, loomed on the frontiers of the Empire. An army 300 000 strong, under the command of Grand Vizier Kara-Mustapha, crossed the Danube at Belgrade, marching on Vienna, Prague and the Rhine. Following the green standard of the Prophet, was a motley horde in which Turks, Slavs, Bosnians, Tartars, and even Hungarian rebels jostled one another.

To this fateful march, when the fate of the Empire and the Christian world was at stake, Leopold had much trouble in organizing resistance. He could not count on the support of Louis XIV, who was pursuing a policy of weakening the Austrian royal house and playing the Turkish card. Of all the monarchs of Western Europe, only Sobieski, the King of Poland, who felt himself to be directly threatened, concluded a pact of mutual assistance with the Emperor.

On 14 July 1683 the Grand Vizier began to invest Vienna (it had previously been besieged by the Turks in 1529). The town was abandoned by the Emperor and the court and defended only by 24 000 men under **Starhemberg**. For nearly two months the beleaguered city resisted all attacks. Duke Charles of Lorraine was urged by the Emperor to organize a relief force. King John III Sobieski crossed the river at Tulln and Krems at the head of 80 000 Austrians, Poles, Saxons, Bavarians, Swabians and Franconians on 10 September. The following night he camped on the hill at Kahlenberg, and on the 11th deployed his army in the Wienerwald. On 12 September the Turks, caught between two forces took to flight in a general panic.

The victory of the Kahlenberg became famous throughout Europe. From that time on, the western sovereigns recognized the pre-eminence of the Emperor, who had saved Christendom. The Turkish menace disappeared, broken by Prince Eugene, one of the most famous generals of his time. There followed for the Austrian Empire a long period of prosperity, distinguished by the reign of Maria Theresa.

The "Great" Maria Theresa (1740-1780). – Throughout her long reign the daughter of Karl VI established herself in Europe by a strength of character and steadiness in political action *(p 22)* which made her famous during the Age of Enlightenment.

In Vienna the Empress lived very simply in the Hofburg and at Schönbrunn, where she carefully brought up the survivors of the sixteen children she had by François of Lorraine, who was elected Holy Roman Emperor in 1745 after the death of Emperor Charles VII, until his own death in 1765. There she arranged the marriages of her daughters, Marie-Antoinette, the future Queen of France, Maria Carolina, Queen of Naples, and Maria Amalia and Maria Christina, who became respectively Duchess of Parma and Regent of the Netherlands. Meanwhile, the four fair-haired archduchesses led carefree lives, for the sweetness of which Marie-Antoinette was to pine later at Versailles. An anecdote illustrates this happy time: when Mozart, at the age of six, came to Schönbrunn he slipped in a corridor and fell. Marie-Antoinette consoled him and the child declared: "I'll marry you when I'm grown up!"

Maria Theresa, too, kindly welcomed the child prodigy. As a protector of artists, steeped in French culture, she founded in Vienna the Collegium Theresianum, an astronomical observatory and a library.

The Force of Destiny. – Born at Bonn in 1770, **Ludwig van Beethoven** was, like Mozart, inescapably drawn to Vienna, the capital of music, where he arrived in 1792 with his pianist's talent for his only luggage. This was where he had unfortunate love affairs with Giulietta Guicciardi, for whom he wrote the *Moonlight Sonata* (1801), and then with "the immortal beloved", Teresa Brunswick. Here, too, at thirty years of age, he felt the first attacks of that deafness which filled him with despair and brought about the *Testament of Heiligenstadt* (p 168).

In Vienna and in the pastoral villages, now more or less taken over by the suburbs were created the works which revolutionized musical expression: the *Eroica Symphony,* originally dedicated to Napoleon; the opera *Fidelio*, played to an audience of French officers (1805), the *Fifth Symphony*, a drama of Beethoven's soul fighting against an adverse destiny; the *Pastoral Symphony* (1808) and, ending in the beautiful Hymn to Joy, the gigantic *Ninth Symphony,* which the master conducted himself though he could not hear a note and the orchestra was really conducted by an improvised leader.

In his last years Beethoven retired to Baden *(p 51)*, near Vienna, where he went for long walks, often by moonlight, in the romantic countryside of the Vienna Woods. At the end of a life full of disappointments he died in Vienna on 26 March 1827, saying to his friend Hümmel: "I had a certain talent, hadn't I?"

His tomb is near that of Schubert in the musicians' enclosure of the city's Central Cemetery (Zentralfriedhof – *p 168*).

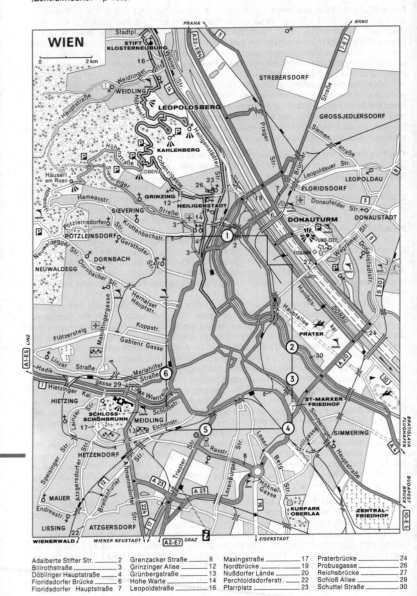

Adalberte Stifter Str.	2	Grenzacker Straße	8	Maxingstraße	17	Praterbrücke	24
Billrothstraße	3	Grinzinger Allee	12	Nordbrücke	19	Probusgasse	26
Döblinger Hauptstraße	4	Grünbergstraße	13	Nußdorfer Lände	20	Reichsbrücke	27
Floridsdorfer Brücke	6	Hohe Warte	14	Perchtoldsdorferstr.	22	Schloß Allee	29
Floridsdorfer Hauptstraße	7	Leopoldstraße	16	Pfarrplatz	23	Schuttel Straße	30

The Congress of Vienna. – When Napoleon's empire collapsed in March 1814, Vienna supplanted Paris as the centre of Europe. It became the scene of the international congress which was to settle the fates of victors and vanquished. For a year the Congress of Vienna, apart from the working sessions of its committees, furnished a pretext for splendid festivities, which are still remembered. Here the crowned heads – the Emperor of Austria, Franz I, the young and handsome Czar Alexander I, the King of Prussia, Friedrich-Wilhelm, the King of Württemberg, and many princes and archdukes – composed a brilliant court. Diplomats came, with their prestige: for Great Britain, Lord Castlereagh; for Russia, Nesselrode; for Prussia, Wilhelm Humboldt; for France, Talleyrand; for Austria, Metternich.

Receptions and balls were held in the embassies, in the state rooms at the Hofburg, and in the Great Gallery at the palace of Schönbrunn. "The Congress doesn't advance; it dances," said the old Prince de Ligne maliciously. The remark became famous. More than any other city Vienna could offer choice entertainment to its guests: art collections of rare quality, concerts of chamber music.

Ludwig van Beethoven himself conducted a gala concert, and his opera *Fidelio* was received with enthusiasm.

Although the Czar Alexander I made himself conspicuous by the brilliance of his receptions and by his libertinism, and though Prince Talleyrand succeeded, by his cleverness and a long experience of European affairs, in making for himself a privileged position among the participation states while defending the rights of minorities, the central figure of the Congress remained **Prince Metternich.**

The career of Clement Lothair Wenzel, Prince of Metternich-Winneburg, begins in 1806, when he was appointed Ambassador in Paris and had every opportunity to observe Napoleon I. In 1809 Metternich was given the heavy burden of directing the foreign policy of his country. It was then that he proposed a *rapprochement* with France and succeeded in making this alliance a reality by negotiating the marriage of Napoleon and the Archduchess Marie-Louise. With remarkable diplomatic insight he made Austria buffer state between the Russian and French Empires, a third force which might restore the balance of Europe.

This policy enabled Metternich, at the Congress of Vienna, to act as mediator and to have a moderating influence which made Austria, till 1848, defender of order in Europe.

A "Fine Epoch". – After the Napoleonic Wars, the Congress of Vienna began a carefree period that the Austrians call *Vormärz*, Before March, because it ended with the revolutionary days of March 1848. Wine, women and song – also dancing – seem to have been the chief interests of the Viennese, who lived at that time in a fever of pleasure.

Under the benign dictatorship of Metternich, the idyllic Vienna of the Biedermeier *(p 35)* consumed moka, chocolate and pastries at cafés like Hugelmann's, near the Danube, on the road to the Prater.

On holidays the Viennese went out among the *Heurigen,* the wine shops of the Danube and Vienna Woods, where they would relax over pitchers of young wine, listening to impromptu poets, violinists and zither players.

Everything was an excuse for idling: the parade of beasts being led to the slaughter, the menageries, the boatmen, the changing of the guard to Schubert's dreamy music. People would also meet to hear Schubert's *Lieder (see Music p 36),* which were in the repertory of every woman singer in Vienna.

The violins sobbed in the Schottenfeld quarter *(town plan p 150* AVX). At the Apollo, a dancehall which could hold 4 000 people and had the biggest floor in Europe, 28 meeting rooms, and 13 kitchens formed annexes to the establishment.

At the Prater, the waltz was born.

The Waltz. – Besides the minuet, the galop and the polka, which originated in Styria, a dance developed from the Tyrolean 3-time *Ländler,* appearing around 1820. This was the giddy Viennese waltz.

It was introduced to Vienna by Josef Lanner and Johann Strauss, senior, and reached its greatest popularity under his son Johann Strauss, junior (1825-1899), whom the Viennese called "Jean" because of his great success in Paris.

The Blue Danube – ordered in 1867 for one of the Carnival balls – *The Artist's Life, Tales from the Vienna Woods* and *The Emperor Waltz* made Strauss the "king of the waltz". He employed 300 musicians who distributed themselves in the ballrooms and whom he conducted there in turn. Strauss created the Viennese operetta as typified by *Die Fledermaus* (The Bat) and *The Gypsy Baron.*

Fashion at the Prater. – The Prater *(p 167)* was the rendezvous of rank, fashion and smart carriages.

Not only the pale, fair-haired Duke of Reichstadt appeared wearing his tight fitting white uniform, but also the Emperor Ferdinand would stroll, unescorted, returning the salutes of passers-by.

The Comte de St-Aulaire, French Ambassador in Vienna, noted in his memoirs: "At five o'clock in the afternoon, carriages begin to cross the little bridge over the Danube ... the procession breaks up only at the entrance to the Prater. Until then they have gone slowly in single file; no one must leave his place. There is no privilege. I have seen the Emperor and Empress obey this rule and, after waiting for a long time, give up hope of reaching the Prater before nightfall, abandon their outing and turn back to the Burg."

Franz-Josef and the Growth of Vienna. – Already, after the disappearance of the Turkish peril, a new face had been given to the capital, marked by the influence of Baroque architecture *(p 33).*

Princely palaces, winter residences and churches had sprung up; the Schwarzenberg Palace (Prince Eugene's mansion), for instance, on the Belvedere Hill and the Church of St Charles, overflowed the narrow limits of the 17C city walls. New quarters developed and extensive suburbs were established without a definite plan.

Death took Josef II, "the enlightened despot", by surprise, while he was preparing to transform the whole of Vienna. The difficult period of the Napoleonic Wars did not facilitate the realization. With the reign of Franz-Josef (1848-1916) and Josef II's large scale projects, Vienna was transformed into the city it is today.

VIENNA★★★

USEFUL INFORMATION

Tourist and reception bureaux

Central Office of Information: Opernpassage (shopping mall under the Opera Square); open daily 9am to 7pm, ☎ 43-16-08, *does not make hotel reservations.*

Automobile Information Centres: west (open all year round), at the exit of the motorway coming from Salzburg, ☎ 97-12-71; south (open April to October) at route No. 17, ☎ 67-41-51. *Does make hotel reservations. See local map p 148.*

Other Information Centres: at the West Train Station – Westbahnhof ☎ 83-51-85 or 83-51-88, at the South Train Station – Südbahnhof – ☎ 62-21-68, at the Wien-Schwechat airport, ☎ 77-70. Open daily.

Österreich Information (Vienna branch office of the Austrian Tourist Information Centre), Margaretenstr. 1, ☎ 57-57-14.

Parking: Parking is forbidden on roads where there are tramways.

VIENNA IN 3 DAYS

Relevant during tourist season

As complicated opening times make it difficult to visit the chief buildings in Vienna, we advise tourists to conform strictly with the itinerary below.

If the visit to Vienna begins on a:

- Monday see in order of days **A.C.B**;
- Tuesday see in order of days **A.B.C**;
- Wednesday see in order of days **B.C.A**;
- Thursday see in order of days **C.B.A**;
- Friday see in order of days **A.B.C**;
- Saturday see in order of days **B.C.A**;
- Sunday see in order of days **B.A.C**.

Day **A.** **Morning:** Tour of the exterior and Imperial Apartments in the Hofburg, Capuchins' Crypt
Afternoon: Palace and park of Schönbrunn.
Evening: dine in the hills (Cobenzl, Kahlenberg).

Day **B.** **Morning:** Walk in the Prater and visit (as of 10am) of the Museum of Fine Arts.
Afternoon: St Stephen's Cathedral and the Old Quarter.
Dine: in the Old Quarter.

Day **C.** **Morning:** Belvedere: Gallery of the 19 and 20C Art, Baroque Art Museum.
Afternoon: Imperial Treasury, Church of St Charles, Donaupark with Danube Tower.
Dine: near the Graben.
Evening: at Grinzing in a "Heuriger".

From April to June and from September to December, an extra morning or evening should be left to the Indoor Riding School.

The Museum of Fine Arts, the Imperial Treasury and the Belvedere are closed during Easter and Whitsun (1):
Good Friday: all museums closed.
Holy Saturday: Imperial Treasury closed.
Easter Sunday: all museums open.
Easter Monday: Belvedere closed.
Tuesday after Easter: Museum of Fine Arts and Imperial Treasury closed.
Ascension Day: all museums open (holiday opening times).
May Day (1 May): all museums closed.
Whitsuntide: same opening times as Easter (see above).
Corpus Christi (2nd Thursday after Whit Sunday): all museums closed.

---

(1) Inquire before leaving.

WIEN

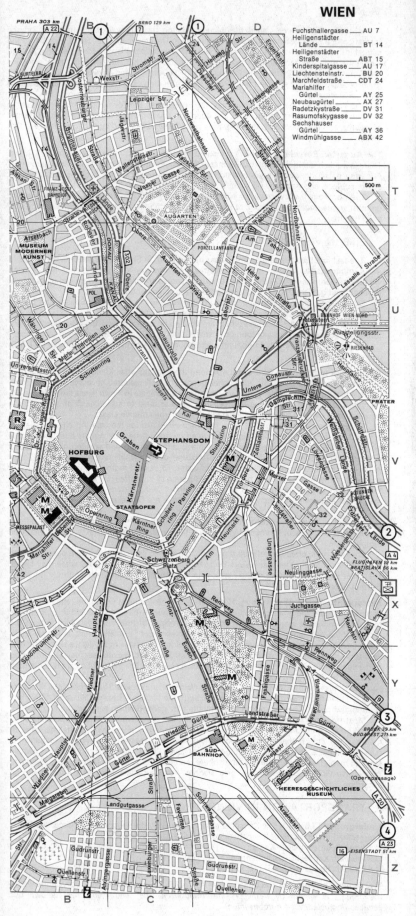

151

VIENNA★★★

In 1857 the Emperor signed the decree ordering the removal of the bastions and the formation of a belt of boulevards round the old town. The creation of the "Ring" was to turn the capital into a huge building site; it was 57 m - 187 ft wide and 4 km - 2 1/2 miles long, planted with four rows of trees and embellished with parks and gardens among which were set monumental buildings. Famous architects and artists, Austrian and foreign, contributed to this great project, which is equalled only by the transformation of Paris under the magic wand of Baron Haussmann.

The Votive Church, the New University, the Burgtheater, the Town Hall, Parliament *(open to the public)*, the Academy of Fine Arts, the buildings housing the Fine Arts and Natural History Museums, and the Opera lined the Ring, which was further beautified by public gardens and fine vistas.

The Augarten Porcelains. – The first Viennese porcelain factory was founded in 1717. Maria Theresa made it a national pottery, like that at Sèvres, and installed it in the imperial gardens at Augarten (CTU). Its voluminous productions, under the mark of the Beehive, specialized in flower subjects and decorative gilding.

The porcelain factory made for Napoleon the famous Schönbrunn service. It reached its greatest vogue under the direction of the miniaturist Daffinger, when the Biedermeier style was at its height.

LIFE IN VIENNA

The fashionable shopping centre is near the Hofburg, St Stephen's Cathedral, the Opera, in the Kärntnerstrasse, Graben and nearby streets *(all open only to pedestrians)*. It is a living witness to Viennese taste, with couture and dress shops, porcelain, chinaware and glass stores, jewellers and goldsmiths, as well as bookshops, music and antique shops.

Cutting through from the Ring to the West Station is the Mariahilfer Strasse, the busiest street in the city where all the department stores are to be found.

The kindness of the Viennese, their amiability and courtesy and their consideration for foreign visitors can only incline tourists to share more closely in the way of life of their hosts.

To do this you have only to go, in the afternoon, to one of the cafés which keep up a 300-year-old tradition.

A Viennese Institution – The Café. – Among the baggage abandoned by the Turks in their flight in 1683 were large quantities of coffee beans. The dark coloured beverage was to become increasingly popular even giving its name to the establishments in which it was drunk. In the 19C the café became the rendezvous of those who liked to meet to enjoy the drink and read the newspapers – café life became essential to the prosperous middle class.

Today, when offices empty at 5pm, the Viennese make for the café. An almost religious atmosphere reigns in these establishments ruled by good taste. The waiters busy themselves discreetly, the customer orders his coffee: black coffee, strong and scented, moka, with or without cream, coffee with whipped cream, "mixture" or "capuchin" *(see A Few Culinary Terms p 32)*, accompanied by the traditional glass of water. To enjoy it more there is a large choice of pastries, from simple rolls to the richest cakes. As soon as the coffee is drunk, the waiter collects the cup and brings another glass of water; without being asked, he renews newspapers, magazines and reviews. Among the best-known cafés are Demel's, Lehmann's, Heiner's and Sacher's.

It is not unusual for a customer to sit for hours without repeating his order; the gift for appreciating the present moment and enjoying the sweetness of life makes up the Viennese temperament.

Crescent rolls, often served with the coffee, are said to have originated in a patent granted by Ferdinand I to the Viennese bakers because they gave the alarm in 1683 when they heard, near their ovens, the tapping of the Turks, who were trying to enter the town through tunnels driven under the ramparts.

Restaurants, Keller, Weinstuben, Heurigen. – The restaurants, where the refinements of a great capital and the smiling good-nature of the Viennese may be observed in turn, enable tourists to make the acquaintance of the original recipes of the countries which formed the empire of the Habsburgs. Most of them afford the pleasures of a small orchestra. The cellars or *Keller* have a convivial atmosphere. They often provide a cold table or set dishes which one eats with a glass of either beer or white wine. The Gasthäuser and Weinhäuser (café, bistro) serve home cooking. In Vienna they are popularly known as Beisel. The *Weinstuben* are the Viennese equivalent of the English "pub".

The wineshops or wine gardens known as *Heurigen*, are crowded in the evenings. Most are to be found in the winegrowing villages which surround Vienna – Grinzing, Nussdorf, Sievering, Gumpoldskirchen... They are recognizable by the pine garland which hangs at the entrance.

Most *Heurigen* are owned by the vinegrowers themselves who hold no café licence but by special privilege are allowed to sell their new wine *(Heuriger)* in their own courtyards, beneath the trees and vines in their gardens and in the ground floor rooms of their houses. In many it is possible to get a cold plate, and some, which have turned into restaurants, offer a simple evening meal. The totally Viennese atmosphere is completed by a musical group, a *Schrammel-musik* (two violins, an accordion – or a clarinet – and a guitar) or at least a violin and an accordion.

TRANSPORTATION IN VIENNA

Underground (U-Bahn). – The Karlsplatz station (access by the shopping mall under the Opera intersection) is the centre of this network of new lines:

U 1 (red): Reumannplatz – Kagran
U 2 (purple): Karlsplatz – Schottenring
U 4 (green): Heiligenstadt – Hütteldorf.

Tramways (Strassenbahn) and buses. – The entire built-up area, excluding the city centre within the "Ring", is served by tramways and mini-buses. The central area has its own bus services *(Innerstädtische Autobuslinien)*.

Practical Information. – We suggest you buy the 3-day tourist ticket *(3-Tage-Wien-Netzkarte)*, with unlimited journeys on the underground, tramways, buses and mini-buses.

The ticket becomes valid at the start of your first trip when you insert it into the slot of the blue turnstile (*Entwerter* – found at the entrance to the underground, or inside the tramway or bus). Those under 15 years of age (passport or identity card may be requested for verification) travel free on Sundays and holidays as well as during the Austrian school holidays (especially July and August).

Ticket booths. – Tickets may be obtained at the shopping mall under the Opera intersection (subway booths indicated: *Vorverkauf*) and at the tourist information centres indicated p 150.

City Transportation maps. – These maps can be bought at the Vienna Transportation Information Centre *(Wiener Verkehrsbetriebe – Kundendienst)* located in the shopping mall cited above.

■ GENERAL VIEW OF VIENNA

The **Kahlenberg**★ and the **Leopoldsberg**★★ *(p 168),* among the hills encircling the city of the northwest and commanding the course of the Danube, provide remarkable viewpoints.

The **Danube Tower**★★ or Donauturm – a 252 m - 827 ft television tower (including the antennae) – erected in the new Donaupark affords, from its platform 150 m - 500 ft from the ground *(lift: 28S)* or its two revolving restaurants, an aerial **view**★ of the whole of Vienna massed on the far bank of the Danube. The **Giant Wheel** of the Prater *(p 167)* offers, equally, a **panoramic view**★ of the capital and its surrounding area.

① THE HOFBURG★★★

The Hofburg is a town within a town. It was the imperial palace and the favourite residence of the Habsburgs, and was progressively enlarged during the centuries. The nucleus, built about 1220, was a quadrilateral bristling with towers round a courtyard which later came to be known as the Swiss Court.

Successive additions by sovereigns anxious to enlarge and beautify their residence explain the juxtaposition of different styles which impairs the unity of the whole, but bears witness to the moving continuity of this building.

The castle chapel (Hofburgkapelle) was erected in the mid-15C; the Amalienhof and the Stallburg in the 16C; Leopold's apartments (Leopoldinischer Trakt) in the 17C, those named Maria Theresa's apartments are used by the President, the Imperial Chancellery (Reichskanzlei-trakt), the Spanish Riding School (Spanische Hofreitschule) where the "Spanish" riding takes place, the Albertina and National Library in the 18C, and, in the 19 and 20C, the Neue Burg, whose completion just before 1914 marked the close of the monumental building in the palace.

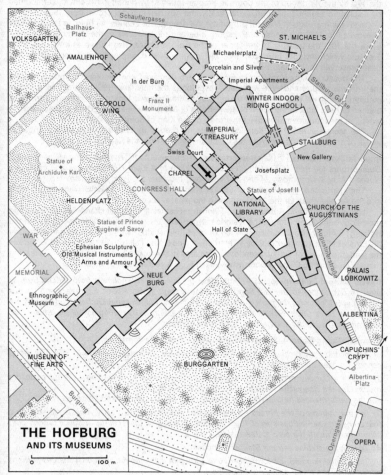

THE HOFBURG
AND ITS MUSEUMS

0   100 m

Exterior

The structure, which is severe and full of majesty, affords remarkable vistas of the courts opening between the various parts of the palace or the monuments round it.

The semicircular façade giving on to the **Michaelerplatz** is decorated with two monumental fountains, adorned with statues; above this façade rises the dome which roofs the rotunda. The main arches are closed by bronze gilded grilles. It is an inspiration to stand beside the rotunda and through a wrought iron lattice see the steeple of the Church of St Michael in the distance. The square known as "In der Burg", in the centre of which stands the monument to the Emperor Franz II, is reached through this rotunda. From the court a fine Renaissance doorway, bearing coats of arms and inscriptions, leads to the **Swiss Court** (Schweizerhof); bordering the court, on the right, are stairs leading up to the Burgkapelle.

Through arched passageways one arrives at the elegant **Josefsplatz** which owes its name to the fine equestrian statue of Josef II the base of which is adorned with bas-reliefs in bronze. The pediments of the buildings round it are surmounted by groups of sculpture.

Behind this square, the early 18C **Austrian National Library** (Österreichische Nationalbibliothek) by Fischer von Erlach can be seen. Return to the Heldenplatz.

The **Neue Burg** or New Château, which was erected between 1881 and 1908 in the Italian Renaissance style, was intended by the architects to have, as its pendant, a similar wing on the northwest side, but this was never constructed.

This building presents a concave façade to the view of the Heldenplatz which is bounded on the northwest beyond the shady Volksgarten by the steeple of the Neues Rathaus. Here stand the memorials, in the form of equestrian statues, of Prince Eugene of Savoy and Archduke Karl, by the sculptor Fernkorn.

On the southwest side is the monumental gateway, the Äusseres Burgtor, which leads to the Ring (1824). It is now (as of 1934) a war memorial (Heldendenkmal).

Interior (Souvenirs of the Habsburgs)

Imperial Treasury★★★ (Schatzkammer). – *Open Mondays, Wednesdays and Fridays 10am to 3pm; Tuesdays and Thursdays 1 to 5pm; Sundays and holidays 9am to 1pm; closed Saturdays; 20S; brochure available in English. The Imperial Treasury may close; the collection's more exceptional objects will be exhibited at the Museum of Fine Arts (p 158).*

The treasures displayed here recall the long history of the Habsburg dynasty, whose sovereigns amused themselves by collecting these symbols of the power of their family.

The **secular treasure** *(to the right on entering)* rich in items of religious significance, contains some dazzling pieces.

The symbols of the reign of the House of Habsburg – crown, sceptre, orb – were produced in the 17C by the Workshop of the Court, in Prague, founded by Rudolf II. His crown, surmounted by a splendid sapphire, became, symbolically, the Austrian Imperial Crown from 1804 to 1918.

With the marriage of Mary of Burgundy, the daughter of Charles the Bold, to the Archduke Maximilian in 1477 the House of Habsburg inherited the treasures of the Duchy of Burgundy. Since the 18C, the treasure of the Order of the Golden Fleece, also known as the Burgundian Treasure which includes liturgical relics and insignia used during enthroning ceremonies, has been preserved in Vienna.

The treasure of the Holy Roman Empire is also displayed: the famous 10C imperial crown, the imperial sceptre and even more awe-inspiring is the holy lance (9C) regarded as a sacred emblem of imperial power – which during the Middle Ages was looked on as the weapon which pierced Christ's side. In the room of mementoes of Marie-Louise and the Duke of Reichstadt, is exhibited the monumental cradle, in vermeil, of the King of Rome.

The **sacred** or rather the **liturgical treasure** *(to the left on entering)* includes a number of works of art (12 - 19C) taken from the castle chapel and from the Capuchins' crypt.

Imperial Apartments★★ (Kaiserappartements). – *Entrance by the rotunda of the Michaelerplatz. Guided tours (30 min) in English (in season) 8.30am to 4.30pm (1pm Sundays and holidays); closed 1 May, 2 November, 24 and 31 December; brochure available in English; 15S.*

The apartments occupy parts of the 1st floor of the Chancellery (Reichskanzleitrakt) wing and the Amalientrakt. Of the 2 600 rooms in the palace, about 20 are open to visitors.

Luxurious furniture, Aubusson and Flemish tapestries and crystal chandeliers (in the large reception room) do not forget the historic memories of the people who lived in this part of the Hofburg: L'Aiglon (Napoleon I's son, the Duke of Reichstadt), Karl I, Franz-Josef and especially the Empress Elizabeth (portraits by Winterhalter). The dining hall with its table laid for 20 evokes the sumptuousness of family receptions in the time of the Austro-Hungarian Empire. On leaving there is an amusing Chinese clock, where each hour is represented by an animal.

Castle Chapel (Hofburgkapelle). – *High Mass on Sundays and holidays from the 1st Sunday after 15 September to the last Sunday in June (except 26 December, 6 January and Corpus Christi) at 9.15am with the male members of the Vienna Philharmonic Orchestra and the Opera and Vienna Boys' Choir. Tickets available on Fridays at 5pm or by writing 8 weeks in advance to: Verwaltung der Hofmusikkapelle. A 1010 Wien-Hofburg.*

Spanish Riding School (Spanische Reitschule). – *Practical information:*

1) Ask for the annual calendar from the Austrian tourist information centre (p 150). The riding school is closed July and August.

2) To see a Sunday performance reserve as soon as possible by writing (without enclosing money) to: the Spanische Reitschule, Hofburg, A 1010 Wien.
For the performances held during the week contact travel agencies and box offices.

3) For the training of the horses no reservations are accepted. Go early. Tickets are sold on a first come first served basis as of 10am (Tuesdays through Fridays) at the entrance to the riding school underneath the arch at Josefsplatz, Door 3.

4) To visit the stables see the Stallburg opposite.

5) Tickets: training 35S; performances 70 to 330S (not including the additional charges perhaps added on by the travel agency or box office).

The all white, **indoor riding school,** is the work of Josef Fischer von Erlach; it is lined with two galleries supported on columns. It is in this interesting creation of Baroque art built in the early 18C by Karl VI, the father of Maria Theresa, that you see performed the feats of *haute école* that date back to the second half of the 16C.

The **parades**★★ (Vorführungen) make a fine spectacle – it is usual for men, who are in full dress, to take off their hats during the equerries' parade. The riders wear brown tail coats with black silk facings, white buckskin breeches, riding boots and cocked hats. The Lippizaner horses *(p 117)* are white, with gleaming coats, their tails and manes are plaited with gold ribbons, and they dance the quadrille, the gavotte, the polka and the slow waltz *(p 118).*

The **training** (Morgenarbeit) although less spectacular (without music or chandeliers) shows the horse performing difficult jumps, steps and other movements.

Stallburg. – *Entrance: Reitschulgasse, 2.* Separated from the indoor riding school, by a glassed in passageway, the Stallburg is composed of three floors of galleries, surrounding a Renaissance courtyard, decorated with a wrought iron well. The ground floor was transformed by Maximilian II into stables for the horses of his guard. It is still used as a stable by the Spanish Riding School. *Open Wednesdays and Saturdays 2 to 4pm; Sundays and holidays without performances 10am to noon and with performances from 12.15 to 12.45pm; in July and August every day of the week 2 to 4pm, Sundays and holidays 10am to noon; 5S, children 1S.*

Austrian National Library (Österreichische Nationalbibliothek). – *Josefsplatz. Open May to September 10am to 4pm; the rest of the year 11am to noon; 15S; closed Sundays and holidays; brochure available in English.*

The royal library was established in the 14C. The **Great Hall**★, a masterpiece of architecture and Baroque decoration (frescos by Daniel Gran in the oval dome; statues by the Strudel brothers), holds Prince Eugene's magnificent library.

Capuchins' Crypt (Kaisergruft). – *Open 10am to 4pm; 15S.*

For more than three centuries the Kaisergruft has been the burial place of the imperial family. The church was built from 1619 to 1632. A statue on the façade represents the Capuchin Marco d'Aviano, who was the Papal Legate with the army of Charles of Lorraine. It was he who celebrated mass at the summit of the Kahlenberg on the morning of the battle *(p 168).*

12 emperors, 16 empresses and more than a 100 archdukes are buried in this crypt, but their hearts are in the Church of the Augustinians and their entrails in the catacombs of St Stephen's Cathedral. Here lay the bronze coffin of the King of Rome, Duke of Reichstadt, the son of Napoleon I and Marie-Louise, before it was transferred to Paris in December 1940. Of the 138 coffins here, only one does not belong to the Habsburg family: it is that of Countess Fuchs, who brought up Maria Theresa, and whom the latter held in such esteem that she granted her this signal honour.

The Empress Maria Theresa and her husband, François of Lorraine, lie in a double sarcophagus, the work of Balthasar Moll (as is the sarcophagus of Karl VI, father of Maria Theresa) adorned with the busts of the deceased placed symbolically opposite each other and the statue of an angel, ready to sound a trumpet on the day of judgment. In the new crypt (Neue Krypta) note the sarcophagi of Marie-Louise, Empress of the French, of the Emperor Franz-Josef and his wife, the Empress Elizabeth, who was assassinated at Geneva in 1898, and of their son, Archduke Rudolf, who died at Mayerling *(p 108).*

The members of the imperial family who are not in the crypt are Archduke Franz Ferdinand and his wife, victims at Sarajevo and Karl I the last Habsburg emperor.

Church of the Augustinians (Augustinerkirche). – Built during the first half of the 14C in the enclosure of the Hofburg, this was the church of the court. In 1784 the Baroque interior decoration was removed and the building thus regained its original Gothic aspect.

Many court marriages were celebrated in this church: in 1736, that of Maria Theresa and François of Lorraine; the marriages by proxy of the Archduchess Marie-Antoinette (1770) of Marie Louise (1810) and of Franz-Josef and Elizabeth of Bavaria (1854).

Facing the entrance is the **tomb**★ of the Archduchess Marie Christine, favourite daughter of Maria Theresa. This mausoleum of white marble is considered one of the masterpieces of the Italian sculptor Canova, who worked in Vienna from 1805 to 1809. Under a medallion, a portrait of the Archduchess, a number of figures symbolizing Virtue and Christian Love are depicted advancing towards the tomb. The Chapel of Our Lady of Loreto (Loretokapelle) near the Chapel of St George *(access by the right side aisle)* protects, in its crypt (Herzgruft – *open Easter to the end of September Mondays 2 to 2.30pm, Tuesdays through Fridays 10am to 12.30pm; closed Saturdays, Sundays and holidays)* fifty-four urns containing the hearts of the Habsburg.

Art Collections and Museums

Collection of Court Porcelain and Silver★★ (Schausammlung der Ehemaligen Hoftafel- und Silberkammer). – *Entrance by the rotunda of the Michaelerplatz. Open Tuesdays, Fridays, Sundays and holidays from 9am to 1pm; 5S; brochure available in English.*

The magnificent pieces displayed were used, until the fall of the monarchy in 1918, for the service of the court. Chinese and Japanese 18C porcelain, silver-gilt chased cups and bowls and a large silver-gilt service may be seen with gold plate of Maria Theresa's time, several Sèvres services – a fine green set dating from 1776 and a gold-and-white Empire set – and admirable sets of glasses.

Collection of Arms and Armour★★ (Waffensammlung). – *Neue Burg, main entrance, 2nd floor. Open Tuesdays through Fridays 10am to 3pm; Saturdays and Sundays 9am to 1pm; closed 1 January, Good Friday, Tuesday after Easter and Whitsun, 10 June, All Saints' Day, 24 and 25 December; 20S; brochure available in English.*

A display of sabres, swords, helmets, cross-bows, cuirasses, pistols, guns and full-dress harnesses made up the armoury of the Habsburgs during the reigns of Maximilian and Charles V (15 and 16C). They were made by the best arms guilds of Milan, Innsbruck and Augsburg for the royal family, and are enamelled, beautifully engraved and delicately carved. Also on display are the hunting arms of the imperial family and the loot taken from the Turks (end of the 17C) – saddles and scimitars.

Collection of Old Musical Instruments★ (Musikinstrumentensammlung). – *Same entrance, tickets, and conditions of visits as the Collection of Arms and Armour.*

Retrospective exhibitions of old instruments (16-19C): wind instruments, percussion or string, played by such famous musicians as Haydn, Beethoven, Schubert, Schumann, Brahms, Liszt, Mahler and various princes of the Habsburg family.

New Gallery (Neue Galerie). – *Entrance under the Stallburg arches, 2nd floor. Open Tuesdays, Wednesdays and 2pm Fridays); Saturdays and Sundays 10am to 1pm; closed holidays, 24 to closed 1 January, Good Friday, Tuesday after Easter and Whitsun, 10 June, All Saints' Day, 24 and 25 December; 10S; brochure available in English.*

The juxtaposition of French and German-Austrian painters from 1800 to 1920 offers an interesting comparison of schools and artists: the Romanticism of Delacroix and C.D. Friedrich, the landscapes of Courbet and W. Trübner, the Impressionism of Monet and Max Slevogt and the nudes of Renoir and Lovis Corinth. Remarkable colour effects are evoked in the last room with Van Gogh *(Self-portrait, The Plain of Auvers)*, Cézanne and Edvard Munch.

Albertina. – *Temporary exhibits: Monday, Tuesday and Thursday 10am to 4pm (6pm Wednesdays and 2pm Fridays); Saturdays and Sundays 10am to 1pm; closed holidays 24 to 31 December and on Sundays in July and August; 10S.*

The Albertina collection of graphic art owes its name to its founder, Duke Albert of Saxony-Teschen (1738-1822), a son in law of the Empress Maria Theresa, through his marriage to Marie Christine *(see p 155)*. To his personal collection was added, in 1920, the engravings of the former imperial library assembled by Prince Eugene of Savoy, some of which date from the early 16C. More than 1 000 000 sheets – engravings, old masters' drawings and architectural designs – illustrate the development of the graphic arts since the 14C. The **Dürer collection★**, belonging to Rudolf II, particularly, contains such drawings and engravings as the *Praying Hands*, and the *Hare*. These are now displayed as facsimiles, the originals only being shown in a special exhibition. In such occasional exhibitions one may also see drawings and watercolours by Rubens, Rembrandt, Poussin, Burgkmair, Fragonard and others.

Museum of Ephesian Sculpture (Ephesos-Museum). – *Neue Burg; same entrance, tickets and conditions of visit as the Arms and Armour and Musical Instrument Collections.*

In the large entrance hall among the sculpture and reliefs are the eleven marble **Reliefs of Ephesus★★**. These belonged formerly to the mausoleum of Lucius Verus, co-regent with the Emperor Marcus from 161 to 169 AD. The reliefs show the adoption of Marcus Aurelius and Lucius Verus, battle scenes from the wars with the Parthians, and the deification of Lucius Verus Note also the large model of the town of Ephesus.

Ethnographic Museum (Museum für Völkerkunde). – *Neue Burg, side entrance. Open 10am (9am Sundays and holidays) to 1pm (5pm Wednesdays); closed Tuesdays; 10S; guided tour in English (1 hour) at 10.30am – apply in advance.*

African art is well represented on the ground floor. On the 1st floor are objects brought back by Captain Cook from his voyages to Australasia and, in the Mexican department, famous throughout Europe, **Montezuma's treasure,** consisting of three robes made from multicoloured plumage and, according to tradition, given to Cortes by the ruler, Montezuma.

② THE OLD TOWN★

time: 4 hours, museums not included

Leave from the Stephansplatz *(plan below)*.

Between the cathedral and the Danube Canal lies the centre of Old Vienna – its houses, hôtels and long narrow streets, which in spite of reconstruction still evoke a special atmosphere.

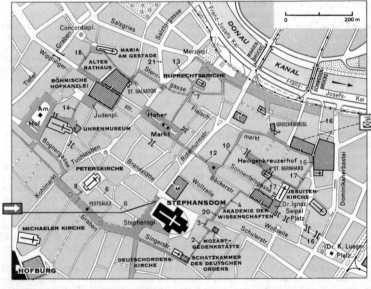

St Stephen's Cathedral★★ (Stephansdom). – On the site of the present building, stood a Romanesque sanctuary built towards the middle of the 12C. Another basilica followed it, built in the late Romanesque style; this was very badly damaged in the fire that ravaged Vienna in 1258 and only the Giants' Doorway (Riesentor) and the Towers of the Pagans in the west façade remain today.

At the beginning of the 14C the Romanesque building was gradually replaced by a Gothic edifice whose nave received its vaults about 1450. Damaged during the Turkish siege of the city in 1683, the cathedral fared even worse in 1945. It was almost completely destroyed by first Russian then German bombardments. A complete restoration has given the cathedral its old aspect.

Exterior. – The Stephansplatz, centre of the mediaeval city, accentuates by its smallness the great size of the cathedral, whose steeple rises like an arrow to the height of 137 m - 450 ft (Salisbury Cathedral 123 m - 404 ft).

The Romanesque west door or the Giants' Doorway is crowded with statues: Christ in Majesty on the tympanum, the Apostles at the base of the recessed arches. The decoration is intricately carved.

Go round the cathedral by the right; at its southwest corner stands the copy of a Gothic lantern of the dead, from the cemetery of St Stephen (now the Stephansplatz). On the square tiles outline the plan of the Chapel of St Mary-Magdalene which served as a charnel house. As you continue along the south side of the cathedral note the tombstones (recalling the former cemetery) and sculptures, unfortunately half-hidden by dirt; on the south side of the chancel scenes depicting the Visitation, Christ in the Garden of Olives and, on the wall outside the axial chapel, an early 15C bust popularly known as the Christ with Toothache and on the north wall a Last Judgement.

Enter the cathedral by the Giants' Doorway.

Interior. – *Open 6am to 10pm; guided tours (30 min) in English 10.30am and 3pm (Sundays 3pm only) – apply in advance; 20S; brochure available in English.*

The cathedral interests more by its furnishings than by its architecture – a slender nave flanked by side aisles and a chancel divided into three sub-naves of equal height.

The carved stone **pulpit** dates from the early 16C and is the masterpiece of Anton Pilgram, who has portrayed himself, under the ramp, holding his sculptor's tools and looking out of a half-open window. All round are busts of the four Fathers of the Church: Saint Augustine, Saint Ambrose, Saint Gregory and Saint Jerome.

The left apsidal chapel, the Virgin's Choir, contains an altar decorated with an **altarpiece★★** in carved wood, painted and gilded, known as the Wiener Neustadt altarpiece. Carried out in the first half of the 15C, it shows a group of figures sculptured in the round on the wooden base; on the central panel are the Virgin and Child flanked by St Barbara and St Catherine and, up above, the Crowning of the Virgin.

In the chancel the altarpiece on the high altar represents the stoning of St Stephen.

The right apsidal chapel, the Apostles' Choir, preserves a remarkable **tomb★★** of the Emperor Friedrich III, made of red Salzburg marble by Nikolaus Gerhart of Leyden at the end of the 15C. The artist has illustrated the struggle between Good and Evil, symbolizing the evil spirits in the form of noxious animals trying to enter the tomb to trouble the sleep of the Emperor, while the good spirits, represented by local personages, stop them.

Catacombs. – *Guided tours (30 min) in English (apply in advance) 10am to 4.30pm; 20S.*

In the catacombs are urns containing the organs of the emperors of Austria; chapels established since 1945 and traces of the former Romanesque basilica destroyed by fire in 1258.

Ascent of the Towers. – *The main tower is open and can be ascended to a height of 73 m - 240 ft – by means of a stairway of 344 steps: 6 March to 15 November and 19 December to 6 January 9am to 3.30pm (5.30pm 1 April to 30 September); 12S; brochure available in English (entrance Aufgang-Hochturm on the south side of the cathedral). The north tower can be ascended to where the tenor bell hangs (Pummerin) and a platform 60 m - 197 ft above ground by a lift (gate inside the cathedral in the north transept) between 8am and 5pm; 20S.*

Interesting **panorama** of the city and the Kahlenberg peaks.

By the Stephansplatz, arrive at Singerstrasse.

Church of the Teutonic Order (Deutschordenskirche). – This church was built by the Order of the Teutonic Knights, a German hospitaller order founded in the Holy Land in 1190 for German pilgrims (became military order in 1198 and was consecrated in 1395).

The church has a beautiful 16C Flemish **altarpiece★** at the high altar, which is made of gilded and carved wood, with painted panels. On the altarpiece may be seen St Andrew and St Peter, St John, St James and among the carved scenes a Flagellation, an *Ecce Homo* and a Crucifixion.

Treasure of the Teutonic Order★ (Schatzkammer des Deutschen Ordens). – *Singerstrasse 7. 2nd floor, open 10am to noon and 3 to 5pm; closed Monday, Thursday and Sunday and holiday afternoons. 12S; brochure available in English.*

History of the Order (seals and coins) and accumulated wealth during the centuries: sacred vases in gold covered in enamel; silver arms decorated in gold and precious stones, crystal, clocks, and portraits of Heads of the Order are also on display.

Take a left turn on Blutgasse.

Mozart Memorial (Mozart-Gedenkstätte oder **Figarohaus)**. – *Domgasse 5. Open Tuesdays to Fridays 10am to 4pm; Saturdays 2 to 6pm; Sundays and holidays 9am to 1pm; closed 1 January, Good Friday, 1 May, 1 November and 25 December; brochure available in English.*

Mozart lived in this house from 1784 to 1787 and composed *The Marriage of Figaro*.

From the Domgasse and Strobelgasse, one arrives at Wollzeile, a busy commercial street of old Vienna. Take Essiggasse straight ahead then right on Bäckerstrasse (Baker's Street) where there are elegant 16 and 17C houses.

Skirt round the **Academy of Sciences** (Akademie der Wissenschaften) the former university built in the middle of the 18C to plans by Jean-Nicolas Jadot, the French architect attracted to Vienna by François of Lorraine. The Church of the Jesuits, stands on Dr.-Ignaz-Seipel-Platz, surrounded by quiet houses and little covered passageways.

Church of the Jesuits (Jesuitenkirche). – The richness of the Baroque decoration shows the success of the Counter-Reformation: the church, built from 1627 to 1631, was renovated inside in the early 18C by the Jesuit Andrea Pozzo. Note the pulpit inlaid with mother of pearl, the wreathed columns, the altarpiece of the high altar and the *trompe-l'œil* frescos of the dome.

Behind the Academy of Sciences, take the Sonnenfelsgasse and then the Schönlaterngasse; both streets are flanked by picturesque 16C houses.

Heiligenkreuzerhof. – A former dependence of the Heiligenkreuz Abbey *(p 169)*; this courtyard framed by 18C ochre coloured façades and St Bernard's Chapel (St. Bernhard) is a retreat for artists and writers, seeking a peaceful atmosphere.

Take the Postgasse to the Fleischmarkt (Meat Market), just on the right is the narrow Griechengasse, where one of the oldest inns in Vienna, the Griechenbeisl, is located.

Hoher Markt. – In the middle of a rectangular square is the Fountain of the Virgin's Wedding (Vermählungsbrunnen, 1732) which marks the centre of the Roman camp – Vindobona where Vienna began. (At No. 3 legionaries' homes are still standing.) During the Middle Ages the square was used not only on market day but also for public executions. At No. 10, the Ankeruhr (1913), a jacquemart clock presents, at noon, a procession of historic characters.

Take the Judengasse (area where second hand clothes are sold) to the Church of St Rupert.

Church of St Rupert (Ruprechtskirche). – Built in the 11C on the ruins of one of the gates of the Roman city, this is Vienna's oldest church, but it has been restored several times. The Romanesque clock tower and great roof give it unusual character.

Return to Sterngasse, a narrow street cut by a stairway. At the end of the street, take the Fischerstiege, on the left, then a right turn on Salvatorgasse (at No. 5 there is the handsome Renaissance doorway of the Salvatorkapelle).

Church of Our Lady of the River Bank (Maria am Gestade). – In the heart of Vienna, on a terrace which used to dominate the main branch of the Danube, a sanctuary called Our Lady of the River Bank or Our Lady of the Steps was started in the 12C on the site of a Gothic edifice of which the general outline is still to be seen.

The western façade, of Flamboyant Gothic style, is ornamented with sculptures and the portal is preceded by a canopy. The seven-sided Gothic tower is surmounted by a beautiful pierced dome.

In the interior, the chancel has interesting stained glass windows, and elegant statues on the pillars of the nave. The Chapel of St Clement (on the right) contains an altarpiece (1460) with two remarkable **panels**★: the Annunciation and the Coronation of the Virgin where the beauty of the faces – that of the Virgin is of a remarkable serenity – is heightened by the vividness of the reds and the gold, revealing Flemish influence.

Follow the Schwertgasse (interesting Baroque doorway at No. 3).

Along the Wipplingerstrasse, facing each other, are two handsome Baroque buildings: on the left **(Altes Rathaus)**, the former town hall of Vienna from 14 to 19C – in the courtyard is the fountain of Andromeda (1741) by Donner – on the right is the old **Chancellery of Bohemia** (Böhmische Hofkanzlei) with its outstanding façade by Johann-Bernhard Fischer von Erlach (1714). Skirt the Chancellery to the Judenplatz, the heart of the Viennese ghetto in the Middle Ages, then follow the narrow Parisergasse to the Am Hof church (Church of the Nine Angels Choirs).

Clock Museum★ **(Uhrenmuseum der Stadt Wien).** – *Schulhof 2. Open Tuesdays through Fridays 10am to 4pm; Saturdays 2 to 6pm; Sundays and holidays 9am to 1pm; closed 1 January, Good Friday, 1 May, 1 November and 25 December; brochure available in English.*

A remarkable collection of watches and clocks from the primitive clocks to the electronic ones; miniature clocks to the wheel works of St Stephen's Cathedral; as well as jacquemarts and cuckoo clocks. Note the amazing astronomical clock (18C) by Rutschmann.

Square Am Hof. – This square is decorated by a bronze column to the Virgin (Mariensäule, 1667). It was here that Franz II, on August 6, 1806, announced the renunciation of the German Imperial Crown, thus ending the Holy Roman Empire.

The Bognergasse takes you to the Graben.

Church of St Peter (Peterskirche). – This beautiful church, which is acclaimed as the most sumptuous of all the Baroque churches of the capital, with its frescos and gilded stuccos, was built from 1702 to 1708 by Johann-Lukas von Hildebrandt to replace a Carolingian sanctuary (the first place of worship in Vienna). The very short nave is topped by a cupola ornamented with a fresco attributed to Michael Rottmayr and representing the Assumption.

The altarpieces of the side chapels were executed by the most eminent artists of the time, among others Martin Altomonte *(Vision of St Anthony – The Holy Family)* and Rottmayr *(St François de Sales)*.

Column of the Pest (Pestsäule). – The column, dominating the elegant Graben Avenue, that gives onto the Church of St Peter, was constructed in the Baroque style (end of 17C). Depicted are a mass of figures in upheaval, aptly symbolizing the end of the epidemic.

Return to the Stephansplatz.

③ MUSEUM OF FINE ARTS★★★ (Kunsthistorisches Museum)

Framing the Maria-Theresien-Platz (BV) are two symmetrically domed buildings, erected from 1872 to 1891 in the official style laid down for buildings in the Ring (Ringstrassenstil).

The building on the northwest side of the square houses the Natural History Museum (p 167); that on the southeast, the Museum of Fine Arts.

Maria-Theresien-Platz. – The square owes its name to the memorial built in 1888 to the glory of the great empress. Seated on a throne, she holds her sceptre; at her feet are equestrian statues of her famous generals, Daun, Laudon, Traun, Khevenhüller; among her most eminent servants are shown Chancellor Kaunitz, the Comte de Mercy-Argenteau, the Prince of Liechtenstein and also the great composers of her reign – Gluck, Haydn, Mozart.

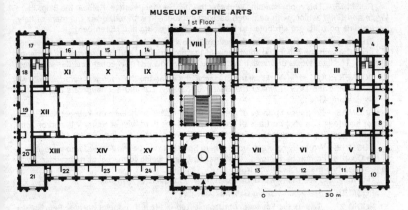

MUSEUM OF FINE ARTS
1st Floor

Open from 10am to 3pm Tuesdays through Fridays; 9am to 1pm on Saturdays, Sundays and holidays; 20S; brochure available in English. A tour of this museum takes at least 3 hours. We note below the most remarkable works, which you should see.

The collections of art in this museum, patiently assembled by the Habsburgs, are among the most important in the world. The whole 1st floor is devoted to paintings – the left wing is reserved for the Flemish, Dutch and German schools; the right wing for the Italian, Spanish, and French schools.

On the 2nd floor, assembled in the annexe (Sekundärgalerie) are many Flemish, German and Italian works of art of the 16 and 17C. The 19C collection of art (Neue Galerie) is presented at the Stallburg *(p 155)*.

Facing the entrance hall, the monumental staircase adorned with a marble group by Canova – *Theseus and the Centaur* – leads to the 1st floor.

Flemish, Dutch and German Schools

GALLERY VIII. – By **Jan Van Eyck,** an admirable portrait of *Cardinal Albergati;* by **Roger Van der Weyden,** of Tournai, a triptych representing the Crucifixion, with remarkably expressive faces; by **Memling,** a small altarpiece of St John; by Van der Goes, a diptych of *The First Sin* and *Redemption;* by Patinir, *The Baptism of Christ.*

GALLERY IX. – Dutch and Flemish Mannerists: M. de Vos, Pieter Aertsen, Reymerswaele *(St Jerome),* Valckenborch (landscape series).

GALLERY X. – Entirely devoted to **Pieter Bruegel the Elder,** a master artist of the Flemish Renaissance; he was a truculent realist and excelled in popular scenes. *The Village Wedding;* the *Massacre of the Innocents,* transposed to a Dutch village under snow; the famous *Return of the Hunters* (on the left), painted in black and white; the *Suicide of Saul* and the *Tower of Babel,* of remarkably detailed execution; the *Meeting of Lent and Carnival* (on the right on entering) in which the artist gives free rein to his fancy, are noteworthy.

GALLERY XI. – Rubens' contemporaries: *The Fish Market* (people done by Van Dyck) by Snyders and *Twelfth Night, the Bean King's Feast,* by Jordaens.

GALLERY XII. – Devoted to **Van Dyck:** *Portrait of a Young General, Venus in Vulcan's Forge,* as well as large religious paintings destined as altarpieces.

GALLERIES XIII and XIV and ROOM 20. – These are devoted to **Rubens.** A fine *Self-portrait; Woman with a Cloak,* in which the features of Helen Fourment, his second wife, can be recognized; the Altarpiece of Ildefonse, a solemn composition whose value lies in the perfection of faces and poses, the beauty of drapery and richness of colour; and the *Château Garden* – which can be compared to the impetuous *Festivities of Venus* – a charming pastoral scene (in Room 20) which seems like a foretaste of Watteau. In Gallery XIV one can admire an *Annunciation* and compare the works of the apprentices (altarpieces) placed side by side with the Master's sketches.

GALLERY XV. – Dutch landscapes and portraits (17C) are exhibited: Jacob van Ruysdael's *The Vast Forest;* Van Goyen's *View of Dordrecht;* and Rembrandt's *Paul the Apostle.*

After touring the galleries, visit the smaller rooms, passing through Gallery VIII, which you have already seen.

ROOM 14. – By Geertgen tot Sint Jans; the *Lamentation for the Dead Christ.*

ROOM 15. – This is one of the highlights of the tour. **Albrecht Dürer** was a man of the Renaissance and one of the most complete artists of his time, who in the most varied domains – architecture, engineering, anatomy and humanism – bore comparison whith his contemporary, Leonardo da Vinci.

In this room he is magnificently represented by the charming *Virgin and Child* (the picture is known as the Blue Madonna) of Venetian inspiration; the *Martyrdom of 10 000 Christians,* where the landscape in the background is a picture in itself; an altarpiece *All-The-Saints* done in brilliant colour.

Dürer possessed to a supreme degree: knowledge of portraiture, perfection of modelling and brilliance and harmony of colour. These are seen, in his *Portrait of Johann Kleberger,* that of a *Young Woman of Venice,* with her enigmatic gaze, and in the completely successful portrait of the *Emperor Maximilian I,* whose face expresses majesty, perfect self-control and knowledge of power.

The *Holy Family* by **Martin Schongauer** exemplifies the style of Dürer's contemporaries in Germany, as shown in the following rooms.

ROOM 16. – This room contains works by the 16C German masters. Holbein the Elder has a *Virgin and Child,* which, with its gilded background touched with red, bears the mark of Italy. Several fine portraits are attributed to the masters of Augsburg and Nuremberg.

The early works of the **Danubian School** *(p 59)* show great dramatic intensity: the Crucifixions of Lucas Cranach the Elder and the panels of the *Entombment* and *Resurrection of Christ* by Altdorfer. The later works of Cranach in the next room show just how ephemeral this style was.

CORNER ROOM 17. – Works by the Cranachs, the Elder and the Younger: *Paradise,* the two works showing the *Deer Hunts of the Elector of Saxony. Lot and his daughters* by Altdorfer recalls Baldung Grien.

ROOM 18. – Portraits of princes of the first half of the 16C by **Holbein the Younger,** who spent part of his life in England, portraits of *Jane Seymour,* the third wife of Henry VIII, and of *John Chambers,* the king's physician; by **François Clouet,** two portraits of *King Charles IX.*

ROOM 19. – Works by painters, among them Spranger *(Venus and Adonis)* who were invited to the Court of Prague by Rudolf II. In *Winter-Fire,* **Arcimboldo** forms hallucinatory faces with vegetables, inanimate objects and fruit.

One may also see many works by Jan Bruegel *(Bouquets of Flowers).*

ROOM 20. – *See when visiting Galleries XIII–XIV.*

ROOM 21. – **Teniers the Younger,** who specialized in Flemish popular scenes, here shows another aspect of his art with a picture of *Archduke Wilhelm in his Picture Gallery.*

ROOM 22. – Beginning of the Dutch collection: 4 portraits by **Frans Hals** (1580-1666).

ROOM 23. – **Rembrandt** is represented in Vienna by portraits only: but these are among his most famous – two *Self-Portraits, His Mother* showing moving realism, and one of his son, Titus *(Young Man Reading).*

ROOM 24. – Paintings by Terborch, Jan Steen. The *Painter in his Studio,* one of the famous pictures of **Vermeer of Delft,** is distinguished by its harmonious composition, softness and smoothness of colouring and the study of light shining on the model's face and the painter's easel.

Italian, Spanish and French Schools

GALLERY I. – By **Titian** (1490-1576), a wonderful colourist, *Ecce Homo,* portraits of the *Margravine of Mantua, A Girl with a Cloak, Jacopo di Strada* and the *Elector Johann-Friedrich of Saxony.*

GALLERY II. – **Tintoretto** (1518-1594), given to Mannerism, in *Susanna in the Bath,* and much knowledge of portraiture in *Lorenzo Soranzo; Portrait of Women* by Bordone.

GALLERY III. – **Veronese** (1528-1588), a virtuoso in colour – his green is famous – excels in compositions where grace of movement continues in the draping of silk and velvet, as in his *Adoration of the Magi* and *Lucretia.*

GALLERY IV. – Examples of the Italian Baroque School (Bolognese, Florentine and Milanese masters of the first half of the 17C): **Guido Reni** *(Baptism of Christ),* Caracci *(Venus and Adonis)* and Cagnacci *(Suicide of Cleopatra).*

GALLERY V. – The innovative **Caravaggio** (1573-1610): the large altarpiece *The Virgin of the Rosary* and *David Holding Goliath's Head,* with marvellous chiaroscuro.

GALLERY VI. – Continuation of the Italian Baroque School (works by Giordano, Solimena, Strozzi, Tiepolo).

GALLERY VII. – 18C Italian School: views of Vienna by Belloto.

Return to Gallery I to see the Rooms.

ROOM 1. – Among the representative 15C Italian masters are: an excellent *St Sebastian* by **Mantegna** (1431-1506), a series by **Giorgione** (1478-1510): *The Three Philosophers, Portrait of Laura* and the altarpiece (in fragments) of San Cassiano by Antonello da Messina.

ROOM 2. – Works by the young **Titian:** *Virgin of the Bohemians.* A fine *Portrait of a Woman* and a *Portrait of a Young Man in front of a White Curtain* by Lorenzo Lotto.

ROOM 3. – This completes the collection in Galleries II and III: Tintoretto, Veronese and Bassano.

ROOM 4. – Works from the Brescian School *St Justina* by Moretto da Brescia.

ROOM 5. – Early Florentine and Perugian works: paintings by Perugino (1445-1523).

ROOM 6. – *A Madonna in a Rural Setting* by **Raphael** (1483-1520).

ROOM 7. – *A Presentation in the Temple* by Fra Bartolomeo and a *Pietà* by Andrea del Sarto.

ROOM 8. – The importance of the Mannerist period is reflected in the Habsburg collections. The famous *Self-Portrait* by **Parmigianino** (1503-1540); his compatriot Antonio Allegri, known as **Corregio** (1494-1554) shows the influence of Leonardo da Vinci, in the alluring compositions, the *Kidnapping of Ganymede* and *Jupiter and Io.*

ROOM 9. – *The Holy Family* by Bronzino; *Landscapes* by Caracci; the *Destruction of the Temple of Jerusalem* by Poussin.

ROOM 11. – Works by the Italian Feti (early 17C) and portraits of the Spanish Habsburg Princes (16C).

ROOM 12. – A remarkable series of works by **Velazquez** (1599-1660). The painter, attached to the Court of Philip IV of Spain, portrays the sovereign and his children with great care for truth, scrupulously detailing the court costumes. Note his portraits of *Philip IV* and the *Infanta Margarita Teresa,* standing stiffly in her wide blue and silver dress, with fine highlights.

ROOM 13. – Venetian School of the 18C. Views of Venice by Antonio Canaletto and Francesco Guardi. Several portraits by the 17 and 18C French painters: Rigaud (1659-1743) *Portrait of Count Sinzendorf;* Largillière (1656-1746) *Portrait of Boucher d'Orsay;* and Duplessis, *Portrait of Gluck.*

Ancient Egyptian, Greek and Roman Art (Antikensammlung)

At the mezzanine, first staircase on the right of the hallway. Galleries I–XVIII.
Among the statues, pottery and other minor arts, there is a small Egyptian hippopotamus in blue faience of the Middle Period, the elegant athlete of Helenenberg, discovered in Carinthia and Greek and Italic helmets in perfect condition. (Galleries XII–XIII).

There is the exceptional collection of cameos in onyx (Galleries XIV–XV), of which certain belonged to Emperor Augustus (Gemma Augustea), numerous other works in gold and silver (Galleries XVII–XVIII) demonstrate the goldsmith trade of the Lower Roman Empire.

Sculpture and Minor Arts (Plastik und Kunstgewerbe)

At the mezzanine, first staircase at the left of the hallway. Follow in reverse the Galleries XXXVI–XIX.
Fascinated by the minor and decorative arts of daily life, the Habsburgs collected curiosities and precious objects, often made by the great craftsmen of Europe.

As one walks through the galleries hung with tapestries from the Early Middle Ages to the Age of Enlightenment one can admire: 9C ivory horns, 12C drinking cups, the *Virgin and Child* by the Franconian sculptor Riemenschneider (Gallery XXXIV), Nuremberg and Italian Renaissance bronzes (Leone Leoni, Giovanni Da Bologna) and the famous salt-shaker by **Benvenuto Cellini** (Gallery XXVII) for François I – a masterpiece of Renaissance goldwork.

Horns, jaspers, onyx, rock crystal and enamel decorate the goblets, ewers and other tableware during the reign of Charles V; there are as well delicately carved platters and vases of the Baroque period (Gallery XXIV) and the delicate Rococo breakfast service of the Empress Maria Theresa (Gallery XX).

Coins (Münzkabinett)

2nd floor. A collection of coins and currency dating from Antiquity; and Austro-Hungarian medals.

④ THE BELVEDERE★★

Open 10am to 4pm (1pm Fridays); Sundays and holidays 9am to noon; closed Mondays, 1 January, Good Friday, Easter Monday, 1 May, Whit Monday, Corpus Christi, 1 and 2 November, 24 and 25 December; 10S; guided tours (1 hour) in English apply in advance; brochure available in English.

The two Palaces of the Belvedere (DXY) were built by the architect Lukas von Hildebrandt as a summer residence for Prince Eugene of Savoy (1663-1736) – a remarkable military strategist and teacher of Frederick the Great – who defeated the Turks in 1683, and with his great friend the Duke of Marlborough, the French Army of Louis XIV at Blenheim in 1704 (during the War of the Spanish Succession).

It was a battle of great historical significance because it saved Vienna from the Franco-Bavarian Army, preserved the alliance of England, Austria and the United Provinces and won Bavaria (thus all of Germany).

While the Lower Belvedere and Orangery were being built from 1714-1716 as a summer residence and the Upper Belvedere from 1721-1723 for the festivities given by the Prince, the Duke of Marlborough was enjoying Blenheim Palace (northwest of Oxford) (1705), a national gift of the English Parliament for his victory at Blenheim.

Beautiful Baroque terraced gardens from which there is a pleasant **view**★ of Vienna, link the two buildings and the orangery which contain works by Austrian artists or artists who painted in Austria.

Upper Belvedere (Oberes Belvedere). – In 1954 this became the Austrian Gallery for 19 and 20C Art (Österreichische Galerie des 19. und 20. Jahrhunderts).
The collections on the ground floor: Neo-classical and contemporary (after 1945) may be closed.

Gallery of the 19 and 20C★. – *Go straight to the 1st floor.* In the large red marble room, the State Treaty, ending the occupation of Austria by the Allies, was signed, on May 15, 1955. On the ceiling a fresco by Carlo Carlone – *The Apotheosis of Prince Eugene.*

The east wing, which opens onto the marble room, contains paintings of the Biedermeier period *(p 34)* as illustrated by Waldmüller (1793-1865) with his genre scenes, landscapes and, especially, portraits. In the 3rd gallery in a glass cabinet is a miniature of the Duke of Reichstadt (1831). Through the glass door of the tribune the palace chapel can be seen: altarpiece by Solimena and ceiling by Carlo Carlone.

The west wing is reserved entirely to the art during the reign of Franz-Josef, known as the Ringstrassenzeit period.

Hans Makart's (1840-1884) historical painting *The Entry of Charles V into Antwerp* is a colourful, lively work. Facing it is the *Cycle of Life* by Hans Canon (1829-1895), an allegorical painting depicted with warm tones reminiscent of Rubens.

Anton Romako (1832-1889) with his battle scenes *(Tegethoff at the Naval Battle of Lissa)* intimate scenes *(Two Friends)* and psychological portraits *(Empress Elizabeth – located in the large gallery)* exemplify a style quite individualistic. The large gallery is largely devoted to the works of Makart: his grandiose *Triumph of Ariadne,* two portraits and the lovely *Senses.*

In the rooms overlooking the city and gardens are the works of the landscapists, contemporaries of the French Impressionists. Among them two atmospheric works by Emil-Jakob Schindler (1842-1892) are worth noting: *Forest Scene (February), Impression of Mars.*

The 2nd floor is devoted to 20C Austrian representational art.

Makart had considerable influence on **Gustav Klimt** (1862-1918). Klimt was one of the founders of the movement called Secession, in 1897, which gave great emphasis to symbolism. Klimt was essentially a decorative and mural painter. In his works, he tended to combine extreme realism in such details as the face and hands with intricate decorative patterns for the clothing. These characteristics can be noted in *Judith, The Kiss,* two portraits of women, *Adam and Eve,* and five landscapes, along the Attersee.

Egon Schiele (1890-1918), was a pupil of Klimt's. His work expresses an important linear quality *(The Wife of the Artist)*, sometimes combined with a cruel vision of people *(The Artist's Family)* or a morbid attraction *(Death and Girl)*. Works by **Oskar Kokoschka** (1886-1980) are also found on this floor. Kokoschka was the most representative and influential artist in Austria during half a century. His work shows a restless energy and vivid colours: *Still Life with a Dead Ram, Prague Harbour, Herodotos,* and *Tigon.* With Herbert Boeckl (1894-1966) art becomes geometric and is inspired by religion.

By way of the gardens (right alley) go to the Lower Belvedere.

Lower Belvedere (Unteres Belvedere). – The long façade is soberly decorated.

Museum of Baroque Art★ (Österreichisches Barockmuseum). – The former summer apartments of the prince with its marble tiles, and paintings form a nice ensemble.

The same subject matter enables you to compare the technique of two famous fresco painters, who can be considered the founders of Baroque religious art in Austria: Michael Rottmayr and Martin Altomonte *(Susannah and the Elders).* Martin Johann Schmidt, known as Kremser Schmidt *(p 98)* masters equally well mythological *(Venus in Vulcan's Forge)* and religious themes.

The large room in the central pavilion displays the original **sculptures★** from the Neuer Markt *(p 166)* fountain by **Raphaël Donner** (1693-1741).

The works of **Franz-Anton Maulbertsch** (1724-1796), the major 18C Austrian painter and one of the most prolific (an entire room is devoted to him), are vibrant in colour and pervade with luminosity. In the corner room, known as the "grotesques" because of its wall decoration (subjects inspired from the first excavations of the Palatine Hill in Rome), note Messerschmidts' four studies of heads: the clever, the sad and the lustful...

At the end of the gallery the visitor is held by the beauty of the **Gold Room★** with its brilliant woodwork and mirrors reflecting the *Apotheosis of Prince Eugene,* in marble, by Balthazar Permoser – the artist represents himself at the feet of the prince.

Museum of Austrian Mediaeval Art★ (Museum mittelalterlicher österreichischer Kunst). – This museum is located in the Orangery. The works displayed are mostly from the Gothic period.

In the 1st room there is a Tyrolean crucifix, still Romanesque in style, carved in the late 12C and delicate statues by the master of **Grosslobming** (14 and 15C). Exhibited in the 2nd room are a Crucifixion painted by Conrad Laib (1449) and a seated statue of St Peter as pope.

The central room displays, across from the Vienna altarpiece, 7 panels by **Rueland Frueauf the Elder** representing scenes from the *Life of the Virgin* and *Passion.* On the sides is an excellent selection of **Michael Pacher's** work.

The 4th room contains the *Adoration of the Magi* by the Master of the Scottish Altarpiece in Vienna and a *Flight into Egypt* by the Master of the Mondsee School.

The last room marks the end of the Gothic period (early 16C) shown by a concern for detail and a faithful depiction of landscape (instead of the traditional gold background) – the Danube School altarpiece. Admire the two works by **Marx Reichlich** *The Visitation* and the *Virgin Walking up to the Temple (ca.* 1515).

⑤ SCHÖNBRUNN PALACE★★

Underground – U-4 (green line): Schönbrunn or Hietzing stop.

The Emperor Mathias is credited with the discovery, at the beginning of the 17C, of the Beautiful Fountain (Schöner Brunnen) which has given its name to this area of the city **(AY)**. The quarter has a fine view over most of Vienna and, beyond it, to the vine-clad hills and the Kahlenberg.

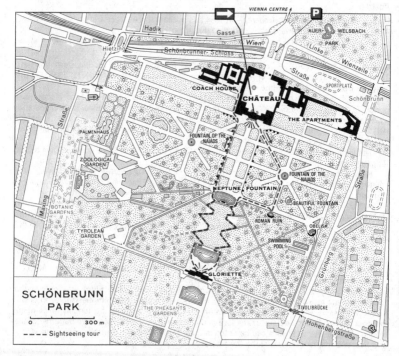

SCHÖNBRUNN PARK

0   300 m

- - - - Sightseeing tour

A hunting lodge, which was built in place of a mill, was destroyed by the Turks in 1683.

Once the danger of invasion had passed, it was in 1695, that the Emperor Leopold I asked Johann-Bernhard Fischer von Erlach, one of the great architects of the time, to draw up plans for a huge palace for his son Josef I.

The Emperor wanted Fischer von Erlach to create a summer residence that would surpass in splendour all other royal residences and even eclipse Versailles itself. These grandiose plans were never realized. Every kind of difficulty beset the monarchy, thus more modest building was carried out from 1695 to 1700. After Karl VI, who was not particularly interested in Schönbrunn, his daughter Maria Theresa modified the château to its present form, after the plans of Nikolas Pacassi from 1743 to 1749, and the park was made by Ferdinand of Hohenberg. Schönbrunn is, nevertheless, an architectural success, particularly when it is viewed in the setting of its famous park.

A Short History. – Many historical memories are linked with the palace and the park. During the reign of Maria Theresa, Schönbrunn was the summer residence of the court. Marie-Antoinette, the future Queen of France, spent her childhood there. It was in the concert room that Mozart, at the age of six, astonished the empress and her courtiers with his amazing talents and, later, in the castle's little theatre, the prodigy directed his opera *Der Schauspieldirektor (Impressario)* in 1786. Later his work *Don Juan* was played there. In 1805 and 1809 Napoleon I set up his headquarters in Schönbrunn.

In 1815, during the Congress of Vienna, the Great Gallery was the scene of many magnificent receptions.

After the fall of the French Empire, Schönbrunn served as residence for Napoleon's son, the King of Rome. The boy was placed under the guardianship of his grandfather, the Emperor Franz, who forbade him all contacts with France. In this gilded cage he lived a life of exile, was given the title of Duke of Reichstadt and was immortalized by the French poet and playwright, Edmond Rostand, in his play entitled *L'Aiglon* (The Young Eagle).

It was at Schönbrunn that the Emperor Franz-Josef was born and where he died and it was in this castle that Karl I, last of the Habsburgs, signed the Act of Abdication on 11 November 1918.

Tour. – The main part of the building lies behind a façade of 180 m – 550 ft long. The wings and steps which form part of this façade do nothing to give it the flow of line which was a characteristic of Viennese Baroque at its height in the time of Fischer von Erlach. The harmony of the whole construction is maintained by the ochre colour of the buildings, known as Maria Theresa Yellow, which is heightened by the green of the window frames.

From the façade, giving on to the park, there is a fine **view**★★ of the Gloriette, an elegant arcaded gallery, topped by a canopy of stone and surmounted by the imperial eagle.

The apartments★★★. – *Obtain your tickets on the right as you enter the hall; waiting-room on the first floor. Guided tours (40 min) in English 1 May to 30 September 9am to noon and from 1 to 5pm (4pm the rest of the year); closed 2 November, 24 and 31 December; 30S; brochure available in English.*

A total of 45 rooms out of the 1 200 that make up the palace are open to visitors.

The palace is a triumph of the Rococo style of the 18C – red, white and gold. The detailed elegance of the stuccos, framing ceilings and frescos with their scrolled whorls, the crystal chandeliers, the richly ornamented faïence stoves, and the priceless tapestries and furniture make these apartments a luxurious and moving link with the past.

The **apartments occupied by the Emperor Franz-Josef and the Empress Elizabeth** are followed by the **ceremonial rooms** consisting of three rooms decorated by the Austrian painter Josef Rosa, two Chinese chambers, one adorned with lacquer work, the other with porcelain. These chambers lie on either side of the Little Gallery, which communicates through an arcade to the Great Gallery and the Great Ceremonial Hall with its beautiful portrait of Maria Theresa by Meytens.

The **guest apartments** are among the most luxurious of the palace. These include the Blue Salon, hung with Chinese tapestry, the Old Lacquer Room, with black panelling framing remarkable miniatures, the Napoleon Room, decorated with Brussels tapestry, which was the Emperor's study and where, on 22 July 1832, his son, the Duke of Reichstadt, died at the age of twenty-one and the Room of a Million with its fine Chinese rosewood panelling framing Persian miniatures painted upon parchment.

After crossing a last suite of apartments where one of the rooms has been arranged as a memorial to the Duke of Reichstadt (marble bust carved after the death mask) one reaches the Great Gallery, adorned with gilded stuccos and paintings.

The Park★★. – *Open until sunset.* Designed by the Viennese, Ferdinand of Hohenberg, the park is a remarkable creation of Baroque art, where the Rococo is mixed with the Antique style. Arbours, veritable cradles of greenery, and vast formal beds of flowers serve as settings for charming groups of allegorical statues and gracious fountains.

Shaded walks lead to the fountain of Neptune (Neptunbrunnen) and the Roman ruin (Römische Ruine), to the zoological gardens (Tierpark) and, to the Gloriette, from which there is a fine view of Vienna.

Coach Room★ (Wagenburg). – *Open 10am to 5pm (4pm in winter); closed Mondays; 10S; brochure available in English.*

Here one can see a very interesting collection of coaches dating from the 17, 18 and 19C, which belonged to the court.

Included are those of Maria-Louise, Napoleon, Franz-Josef and Elizabeth, the phaeton of Napoleon's son, sumptuous harnesses and trappings, and the gilded and ornate **coronation coach** of Karl VI, which was pulled by 8 white horses.

For reservations and tickets
at the 4 national theatres
(including the Opera):
3 or 5 Goethestrasse –
they do not ask a 20% surcharge as do agencies.

WIEN

0   300 m

U

Roosevelt Platz

Universitätstr.

Rolingasse

Theresien Str.

Maria

Schotten

Wippinger Str. Ring

RING TURM

Franz

Josefs

DONAU

KANAL

Neustorgasse

Heinrichsgasse

Leopoldsgasse

Obere Donaustraße

Hollandstr.

35

Mölker Bastei

DREIMÄDERLHAUS

35

Graben

Tiefer

Salzgries

MARIA AM GESTADE

Morzinpl. Kai

RUPRECHTSKIRCHE

38

Freyung

ALTES RATHAUS

BÖHMISCHE HOFKANZLEI

Judengasse

Maria

NEUES RATHAUS

Rathaus Platz

Dr. Karl Lueger-Ring

PALAIS KINSKY

PALAIS STARHEMBERG

Herren Gasse

13

Am Hof

Judenpl.

UHRENMUSEUM

5

Tuchlauben

Hoher Markt

Rotenturm-

Fleischmarkt

T

L

L

MINORITENKIRCHE

NIEDERÖSTERR. LANDESMUSEUM

Fahnengasse

18

PETERSKIRCHE

6

Wollzeile

22

Schaufler Gasse

Herrengasse

Michaeler-platz

Graben

M

STEPHANSDOM

V

PARLAMENT

Dr. Karl Renner-Ring

VOLKSGARTEN

HOFBURG

INTERNATIONALE KONGRESSHALLE

Heldenplatz

33

MICHAELER KIRCHE

Stallburg Gasse

Spiegelgasse

Stephanspl.

Singer-

straße

MOZART-GEDENKSTÄTTE

DEUTSCHORDENSKIRCHE

NATURHIST. MUSEUM

Burgring

NEUE BURG

M

Josefspl.

AUGUSTINER-KIRCHE

PALAIS LOBKOWITZ

28

DONNERBRUNNEN

KAISERGRUFT

Ballgasse

15

Johannes

FRANZISKANER-KIRCHE

21

Ring

Maria-Theresien-Platz

ALBERTINA

BURGGARTEN

37

2

26

ANNAKIRCHE

15

Park Ring

Messepl.

KUNSTHIST. MUSEUM

Babenberger Str.

30

STAATSOPER

Kärntner Str.

Walfischgasse

Kruger Str.

Schwarzenberg

Schellinggasse

MESSEPALAST

Str.

(Opernpassage)

Mariahilfer

30

Opernring

GEMÄLDEGALERIE DER AKADEMIE DER BILDENDEN KÜNSTE

Kärntner Ring

Schwarzenbergpl.

Lothringer

Schubertring

SCHÖNBRUNN

Getreidemarkt

U

Wienzeile

Wienzeile

30

Karls

Platz

Karlspl.

U

Am Heumarkt

X

Linke

Rechte

Schleifmühl

Gasse

HISTORISCHES MUSEUM

KARLSKIRCHE

Prinz

Straße

RUSS. HELDEN DENKMAL

Margareten

Straße

Gusshaus

Weidner

Wiedner

Hauptstraße

Favoritenstr.

Argentinier

Eugen-Str.

PALAIS SCHWARZENBERG

ÖSTERREICH INFORMATION

Mittelsteigasse

Rienösslgasse

Wiedner

Belvedere

Gasse

Rainergasse

Favoritenstr. straße

Y

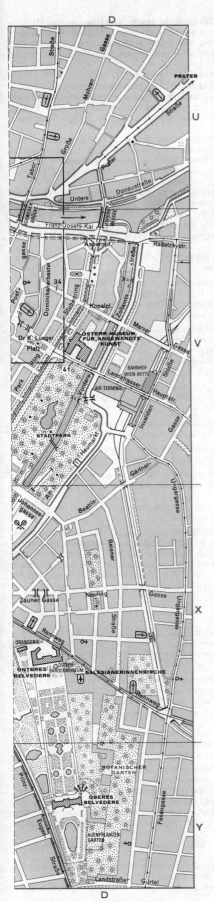

■ ADDITIONAL SIGHTS

Unless otherwise indicated the following sights can be located on the plan pp 164-165.

Historical Museum of the City of Vienna★★ **(Historisches Museum der Stadt Wien) (CX).** – *Open Tuesdays through Fridays 10am to 4pm (7pm Thursdays); 2 to 6pm Saturdays; 9am to 5pm Sundays and holidays.*

Ground Floor. – Maps and a conspectus dealing with the Roman era, as well as pottery, ceramics and bas-reliefs. From Romanesque and Gothic periods: parts of capitals, stained glass windows, frescos, statues, paintings on wood, arms and banners mostly from St Stephen.

First Floor. – Drawings and plans of Vienna. Souvenirs from the siege of 1529 and 1683 (loot taken from the Turks); Vienna until Maria Theresa's death, 1780.

Second Floor. – The Neo-Classical and Biedermeier period are remembered by furniture and by portraits, depicting men of arts and letters (by Waldmüller a portrait of Grillparzer, the poet). The "Vedutenmaler", first half of the 19C (Viennese painters seeking documentary precision), have beautifully depicted their city (*St Stephen* by Rudolf Alt, 1834).

The new phase of urbanism, begun with the opening up of the Ring *(p 152),* is shown (maquette). Paintings by Viennese artists depicting life under Franz-Josef (Makart, Klimt) and Vienna between the two world wars (*Vienna seen from Wilhelminenberg* by Kokoschka, 1931) precede the contemporary works, witnessing Vienna as a cultural centre.

The Opera★ **(Staatsoper) (CV).** – *Guided tours (40 min) in English at 2 and 3pm; 25S; no tours conducted during rehersals; brochure available in English.*

The Opera, inaugurated in 1869 with *Don Juan* by Mozart, was the first public building of the Ring.

Church of St Charles★ **(Karlskirche) (CX).** – Dedicated to St Charles Borromeo, this church was built from 1716 to 1737 to plans by Johann-Bernhard Fischer von Erlach, following a vow by the Emperor Karl VI during the plague of 1713. It is said that it was from the top of the Pincio Hill in Rome *(see Michelin Green Guide to Italy)* that Fischer von Erlach had the inspiration of combining in surprising association Trajan's Column, the Roman portico and the Baroque cupola. Two columns, modelled on Trajan's Column and ornamented with bas-reliefs illustrating the life of St Charles Borromeo, flank a porticoed porch reminiscent of a temple façade. This unit is, in turn, flanked by two squat towers with windows in the lower floors.

The interior has sacrificed decoration to architecture: all attention is drawn to the huge oval **dome**★★, of a remarkable lightness, decorated with frescos by Michael Rottmayr. Huge pilasters divide the walls into panels – symmetry and harmony preside over the interior; the choir, pulpit and portal all interrelate; facing each other are two chapels framed by two smaller ones.

This is a typical Baroque church – with its blend of illusionism, light and colour; where movement is calculated to overwhelm the spectator by a direct emotional appeal.

Gallery of Painting and Fine Arts★ (Gemäldegalerie der Akademie der bildenden Künste) (BX). – *Open 10am to 2pm; Wednesdays 10am to 1pm and 3 to 6pm; Saturdays, Sundays and holidays 9am to 1pm; on Sundays guided tour (1 1/2 hours) in English at 10.30am; closed Mondays; 10S; brochure available in English. Because the gallery has recently been reorganized the works have not been located.*

Throughout the gallery hang Dutch paintings from the 15 to 17C.

The extraordinary **polyptych of the Last Judgement★★** by **Hieronymus Bosch** (1460-1516) is a terrifying work in which monsters are shown with other horrible phenomena symbolizing the sins and suffering of mankind. Note also the *Crowning of the Virgin* by Dieric Bouts (1415-1475).

Among the 15 and 16C Italian School are a *Madonna and Child* from Botticelli's studio and Titian's *Tarquin and Lucretia*.

Lucas Cranach the Elder is represented as much by his early works *(St Francis Receiving the Stigmata)*, as his court paintings *(Holy Family)* and the beautiful enigmatic *Lucretia*, which he painted in 1532. There are also several German primitives such as **Ambroise Holbein**, *The Dormition of the Virgin* and Northern Renaissance art represented by Hans Baldung Grien *(Holy Family)*.

Flemish Baroque is dominated by **Rubens** *(Orithyus Kidnapped by Borée)* – note his 14 oil sketches. Other works of the period are represented by Rubens' assistants Jordaens *(Paul and Barnabus)* and Anthony van Dyck *(Self-Portrait)*. Rembrandt *(Portrait of a Woman)* is always a pleasure to look at. On display are canvases by Pieter de Hooch, a Dutch genre painter and the Italian Mattia Preti; as well as the Dutch masters, Asselijn and Dujardin, who painted Italianate motifs.

The 18C is represented by scenes of Venice by Francisco Guardi (1712-1793) a *Self-Portrait* by Suybleyras and a sketch by Claude Lorrain.

Burggarten (BV). – Formerly the sovereign's private garden, the Burggarten, now public, contains the equestrian statue of the Emperor Franz I, the statue of the Emperor Franz-Josef and the Mozart monument. At the entrance is a statue of Goethe, a giant of world literature who, in his genius, resembled the great Renaissance personalities.

Lobkowitz Palace (CV). – Also known as the Dietrichstein Palace, the palace was built from 1685 to 1687 according to plans by Giovanni Pietro Tencala. Johann-Bernhard Fischer von Erlach added a top floor, ornamented with statues and a main doorway between 1709 and 1711. It was in the Eroica Saal – the Grand Salon – that Beethoven presented the *Eroica Symphony* for the first time in 1804.

Schwarzenberg Palace (CX). – The two great Viennese architects of the Baroque period, Johann-Lukas von Hildebrandt and Johann-Bernhard Fischer von Erlach, collaborated in its building (1697 to 1723). Now arranged, in part, as a hotel.

Church of the Nuns of the Visitation (Salesianerinnenkirche) (DX). – Built from 1717 to 1730 under the direction of Donato Felice Allio, it recalls the Church of St Charles.

Church of St Anne (Annakirche) (CV). – This, the French church of Vienna, achieved its present appearance (marble decoration, stuccos, gold work and paintings) during the first half of the 17C.

Church of the Franciscans (Franziskanerkirche) (CV). – The interior, renovated in the Baroque style during the 18C, contains a fine altarpiece whose central panel, by Wiener Schmidt, represents the Immaculate Conception.

The nearby Franziskanerplatz has a fountain of Moses and is flanked – like the Ballgasse, which opens of the south – by old picturesque houses.

Herrengasse★ (BV). – A pleasant, busy street, linking the Freyung with the Michaelerplatz, the Herrengasse – Lords' Street – still lives in its aristocratic past. It is an important administrative centre with the Landhaus of Lower Austria at No. 13, a palace built in the 16C and reconstructed in the 19C where the Parliament of this Province meets (in the courtyard there is a Renaissance gateway); the Government Palace of Lower Austria (No. 11); the Mollard-Clary Palace (No. 9), which is now the Museum of Lower Austria *(see below)*; the Ministry of the Interior (No. 7); in the former Modena Palace (19C façade).

Donner Fountain★ (Donnerbrunnen) (CV). – The fountain was built by Raphaël Donner from 1737 to 1739.

The central statue, representing Providence, is surrounded by cherubs and fish spurting water. The statues (copies in bronze) round the fountain personify the rivers Traun, Ybbs, Enns and Morava, symbols of the four provinces nearest to the capital. The original statues in lead are at the Barockmuseum *(p 162)*.

Museum of Lower Austria (Niederösterreichisches Landesmuseum) (BV). – *Open 9am to 5pm (noon on Sundays and holidays); closed Mondays, 12 July to 31 August; 10S.*

This is the former Mollard-Clary Palace dating from the end of the 17C. The rooms contain collections dealing with geology, geography, flora and fauna, prehistoric details and modes of life from Vienna and its surrounding area.

The second floor contains religious works of art: sculpted virgins, paintings of Christ's life, an altarpiece from Roggendorf as well as Viennese furniture and costumes.

In the courtyard is a well (1570) decorated with iron work.

Church of St Michael (Michaeler Kirche) (BV). – Dominated in the Michaelerplatz by the concave façade of the Hofburg, this church presents a curious mixture of styles recalling the different times of its construction: the base of the church is Romanesque (nave, transept, right bay of the chancel) the 1792 façade is in the Neo-Classic style, the tower is 1340, the spire is 16C and the apses and side chapels are Gothic. The high altar owes its profuse decoration to the Fall of the Angels – completed in 1781, this was the last religious work of Baroque style effected in Vienna.

In the north arm of the transept rests the Italian Baroque poet, Metastase, the official author of operas during the reign of Maria Theresa.

The Mount of Olives, a magnificent group, carved in stone, dating from the end to the 15C, stands against the outside of the south wall of the church.

Stallburggasse, a street lined with houses of old tiled roofs, offers a picturesque view of St Michael's belfry.

Church of the Minorities (Minoritenkirche) (BV). – This church was begun in the first half of the 14C, but later came under Baroque influence. The chevet is flanked by an octagonal tower and the right side by an elegant ribbed gallery.

The interior is surprising by its almost square design and its three naves of equal height. On the north wall there is a huge mosaic copied from Leonardo da Vinci's *The Last Supper,* and completed on the order of Napoleon I.

Kinsky Palace (BV). – This palace, built between 1713 and 1716 by Johann-Lukas von Hildebrandt for the Marshal, Count Daun, is one of the most remarkable civil architectural buildings of the Baroque period. The façade is richly decorated with armorial bearings, statues, pilasters and sculptured motifs. The doorway and balconies are highly ornate.

Starhemberg Palace (BV). – Now the Ministry of Education and the Arts, this majestic palace dates from the second half of the 17C. It belonged to Count von Starhemberg *(p 147).*

Volksgarten (BV). – This, the oldest public garden in Vienna, was laid out in 1820. Rose gardens, lakes, statues and fine views make it popular; monuments to the poet Grillparzer, and the Empress Elizabeth and the Temple of Theseus are set against floral backgrounds.

Dreimäderlhaus (BUV). – A celebrated house where tradition has it that Schubert courted three young ladies all from the same family.

In the nearby Mölkerbastei, there are remains of Vienna's ancient ramparts, and at No. 8 is the house in which Beethoven stayed in 1804, 1810 and 1812.

Austrian Folklore Museum★★ **(Österreichisches Museum für Volkskunde)** *(Plan p 150* AUV). – *Open 9am to 3pm (noon Saturdays, 1pm Sundays and holidays); closed Mondays; 10S.*

The main floor illustrates traditional Austrian domestic life: beds, buffets, painted chests, sideboards, pottery and ironmongery. Note the amusing porcelain stove in the form of a peasant woman. There is a particularly interesting collection of sleds and toboggans.

The 1st floor exhibits religious and peasant life: masks, headdresses, costumes, musical instruments, cribs (the richest collection in Austria) and votive offerings.

Natural History Museum★ **(Naturhistorisches Museum)** (BV). – *Open 1 May to 31 August 9am to 1pm (4pm Saturdays, Sundays and holidays in summer); closed Tuesdays; 10S; brochure available in English.*

The prehistorical section *(on the mezzanine)* includes, apart from numerous objects from Hallstatt *(p 81),* the celebrated statuette of the so-called Venus of Willendorf, about 25 000 years old. On the 1st floor there are interesting collections of botany and zoology.

Town Hall (Neues Rathaus) (BV). – *Guided tours (45 minutes) 7.30am to 3.30pm Monday through Friday.*

This was completed in 1883 in a Neo-Gothic style. The reception rooms, the council chambers and the huge banqueting hall are visited. Following the German custom, the cellars are now a restaurant and beerhall or *Rathauskeller.*

Church of the Faithful Virgin (Maria Treu or **Piaristenkirche)** *(Plan p 150.* AV). – This church is built in the centre of the Josefstadt quarter. Its beautiful Classical façade faces the Jodok-Fink Platz known more familiarly as the Piaristenplatz. Inside two great round cupolas are decorated with a fresco by Maulpertsch, dating from 1752.

Austrian Museum of Applied Arts★ **(Österreichisches Museum für angewandte Kunst)** (DV). – *Open 10am to 4pm (6pm Thursdays, 1pm Sundays); closed Mondays, Saturdays and holidays; 10S; on Sundays guided tours in English on request (10.30am).*

Exhibited are carpets and tapestries of the 16 to 18C – among which are the *Carpet of the Hunt,* a Persian work of the 16C, and the *Carpet of Mameluk,* an Egyptian work of the same period (room XX) – a collection of Limoges enamels (13 to 16C), jewellery (15 to 19C) and a review of furniture with examples by Riesener and Roentgen with the founding of the Empire or Biedermeier style. Also on display are examples of Europe's leading porcelains and, above all, Old Vienna (1718-1864).

Displays of ceramics, glassware, crystal and a comprehensive collection of "Art nouveau" objects complete this section.

Stadtpark (DV). – This vast and agreeable public garden was opened in 1862 during the planning of the Ring. It contains the famous statue of Johann Strauss.

The Prater★. – *Plan p 151.* This immense green space, which extends between the two arms of the Danube, was once a hunting reserve for the aristocracy. The benevolent Emperor, Josef II, opened the Prater to the public. With its cafés where they could sing and dance, the Prater was extremely popular during the hey-day of the Viennese waltz.

One part of the Prater is devoted to sports and to travelling fairs. The **Giant Wheel** *(20S; children 8S)* or Riesenrad, with a diameter of more than 64 m - 200 ft, dominates the city and the Danube with its familiar silhouette.

Oberlaa Park (Kurpark)★. – *Southeast of the plan p 148.* South of the town the park was arranged for the International Horticulture Exposition of 1974. The tourist will appreciate the calm and serenity offered by the variety of paths lined with beautiful flower beds and fountains. Near the restaurant is a beautiful **view** of the surrounding countryside.

Museum of Modern Art (Museum Moderner Kunst) (BU). – *Open 10am to 6pm; closed Tuesdays; guided tours in English (apply in advance) on Saturdays at 2.30pm and on Sundays at 11am; 10S.*

The museum is located in the former summer palace of the Prince Johann-Adam of Liechtenstein. The palace has kept its disposition and **Baroque decoration,** as can be seen in the state apartment on the 1st floor.

Go directly up to the 2nd floor *(lift)* where the permanent collection of early 20C art is displayed – German Expressionism is well represented. The works of Klimt, Schiele and Kokoschka *(p 162)* are also exhibited.

On the 1st floor the Hahn collection and the Ludwig collection illustrate the major movements of contemporary art and its off-shoots.

Military History Museum (Heeresgeschichtliches Museum) (DY). – *Plan p 151. Open 10am to 4pm; closed Fridays; 10S; brochure available in English.*

Interesting collections show the most glorious phases of the military history of the Habsburg Empire. One section of the museum is devoted to the navy. One room, the Sarajevo Room, recalls the assassination of the Archduke Franz Ferdinand and his wife on 28 June 1914. The bullet scarred car in which the Archduke was riding and his blood-stained uniform are on view.

Birthplace of Schubert (Schubert-Museum) (AT). – *Plan p 150. Open Tuesdays through Friday 10am to 4pm (2 to 6pm Saturdays, 9am to 1pm Sundays and holidays).*

The composer lived here for the first years of his life before moving to No. 3 Säulengasse. A museum is on the 1st floor.

Main Cemetery (Zentralfriedhof). – *Simmeringer Hauptstrasse by ③ of plan p 148.*

Beethoven, Brahms, Gluck, Schubert and Hugo Wolf rest in the "musicians' square" *(Gräbergruppe 32 A)* beside the great masters of the Viennese waltz and operetta: Johann Strauss, father and son, Josef Strauss, Josef Lanner, Karl Millöcker, Franz von Suppé.

St Mark's Cemetery (St. Marxer Friedhof). – *Leberstrasse 6, southeast of plan p 148.*

Buried anonymously in 1791 in a common grave, "the divine Mozart" has but a pathetic and empty tomb topped with a crying cherub.

EXCURSIONS

The Kahlenberg Heights★★ (Höhenstrasse). – *Round tour of 33 km - 21 miles – about 2 hours. Leave Vienna by the Heiligenstädterstrasse (north of the plan p 148), the road for Klosterneuburg, which runs beside the railway.*

By the Klosterneuburg-Kierling station turn left in the Stadtplatz then almost immediately turn left again where the road finally widens; cross the Kierlingbach riverlet and go up towards the abbey.

Leave your car in the Rathausplatz.

Klosterneuburg Abbey (Stift Klosterneuburg). – *Obtain your tickets at the place, near the book shop, from which you reach the Stiftsplatz. Open 9.30 to 11am and 1.30 to 4pm; Sundays and holidays afternoons only; 25S; brochure available in English.*

The apartments contain Empire furniture. The abbey church was renovated in the Baroque period. The former chapter now the Chapel of St Leopold, has an **altarpiece by Nicolas of Verdun★**. This magnificent work has some fifty subjects in champlevé enamel carried out by a goldsmith from Lorraine in 1181. Near the altarpiece is a 12C chandelier from Lombard. The Leopoldstrasse to the south leads to the Weidlingbach Valley, where you cross the Weidlingerstrasse taking in the Höhenstrasse, which is facing you. This winding road rises between villas and then enters the woods, emerging with a **view** of Klosterneuburg Abbey.

Leopoldsberg★★. – This, the most easterly spur of the Wienerwald, overlooks the Danube from 423 m - 1 388 ft. Make for the restaurant terrace in front of the little church (Leopoldskirche), where there is a relief plan of Vienna as it was in 1683, to enjoy a very extended **view★★** over the northern and eastern sections of the city and the plain of Wagram, the Leitha-Gebirge and the Wienerwald hills.

Return to the Höhenstrasse, which you take on your left; then leave your car in the large Kahlenberg car park.

Kahlenberg★. – To the right of the Kahlenberg restaurant (483 m - 1 585 ft), a terrace gives an attractive **view★** over Vienna. The spires of the Cathedral of St Stephen stand out above the city and the Ringturm, which indicates meteorological forecasts by means of luminous signals, can also be seen. In the foreground are the vineyards of Grinzing and the Wienerwald mounds.

Take the Höhenstrasse once again following its wide curves on the heights, then turn to the left on to the Cobenzlgasse to get down to Grinzing.

Grinzing. – This is the best known – *Heurigen* – wine village in the countryside, immediately north of Vienna.

Heiligenstadt. – Admirers of Beethoven will want to go to the central square of this old village (Pfarrplatz) to see at No. 2 the little 17C house (now changed into a *Heurigen*), where the musician lived for some months in 1817.

Leaving the square, at the Probusgasse, you will find the house (No. 6) where the composer wrote his famous letter in 1802 called the *Testament of Heiligenstadt* when in despair over his deafness.

Open 10am to 4pm; Saturdays 2 to 6pm; Sundays and holidays 9am to 1pm; closed Mondays; brochure available in English.

Return to Vienna by the Hohe Warte and the Döblinger Hauptstrasse.

Alternate Route. – *Extra distance 10 km - 6 miles.* After Kahlenberg, tourists who already know Grinzing can continue to follow the Höhenstrasse; about 500 m - 500 yds after leaving the Cobenzlgasse on the left one comes across an interesting **view** of Vienna. Follow the Höhenstrasse as far as the Hauserl am Roan Inn. There is a fine view of Vienna and the Wienerwald from the car park.

Turn round; shortly before the Sieveringer Brücke, turn to the left, and immediately take the Sieveringer Strasse on the right. Return to Vienna by Sievering *(Heurigen).*

The Wienerwald★ (Vienna Woods). – *Round tour of 74 km - 46 miles – about 3 hours – local map p 168.*

Leave Vienna by the Eichenstrasse *(southwest on the plan p 150)*. The road goes through a suburb *(local map p 148)* before reaching the first vine covered slopes of the Vienna Woods.

Perchtoldsdorf, Mödling. – Charming winegrowing villages.

The winding route crosses small rocky and wooded valleys along the banks of the River Mödling and then continues in the woods as far as Heiligenkreuz.

Heiligenkreuz. – *Guided tours (40 minutes) in English 9 to 11am and 1.30 to 5.30pm (4.30pm in winter) Sundays and holidays 11 to 11.30am and 1.30 to 5.30pm (4.30pm in winter); 20S; brochure available in English.* The Abbey of the Holy Cross was founded in the 12C by Leopold Margrave "III the Saint", who installed Cistercian monks here. The arcaded courtyard was rebuilt after the monastery was pillaged by the Turks, but the church has preserved its Romanesque nave and Gothic chancel. The chapter and the cloister with their many small red marble columns form a harmonious architectural picture.

Mayerling. – *Description p 108.*

After Mayerling the road follows the little Valley of St Helen (Helenental) as far as Baden, through rocky, wooded country. The Duke of Reichstadt used to horseback in this little valley.

WIENERWALD

Baden★. – *Description p 51.*

To the north of Baden the road winds between vineyards as far as Gumpoldskirchen.

Gumpoldskirchen. – The vineyards of this village produce the famous Gumpoldskirchner wine, which is much drunk in the *Heurigen.*

Return to Vienna by road No. 17.

EUROPE on a single sheet
Michelin map No. 920
(scale 1/3 000 000)

VILLACH (Carinthia)

Michelin map **426** fold 35 – *Local map p 172* – Pop 52 744 – Alt 501 m - 1 644 ft – 🛈 ☎ 24444.

Villach, gateway to the south, owes its prosperity to the timber industry and international transport.

An overnight stop rather than a holiday centre – with the exception of the radioactive waters of the thermal baths of Warmbad-Villach, Villach nevertheless has a tourist trade owing to its proximity to the Lake of Ossiach and the Villacher Alpe.

Relief Model of Carinthia (Relief von Kärnten). – *In the Schillerpark, Peraustrasse. Open 2 May to 15 October 9am to noon and 2 to 5pm; closed Sundays and holidays; 5S.*

This immense relief model of the province of Carinthia is on a scale of approximately 1/10 000 - 1 in to 275 yds (heights twice enlarged). By studying this the tourist can familiarize himself with the general character of the countryside, often difficult to determine on the spot.

EXCURSION

Road to Villacher Alpe★. – *16 km - 10 miles toll (summer rate) 120S per car.* This modern mountain road is well laid out along the wooded mountainsides and later along the cliff like edge of the Dobratsch; many viewpoints have been constructed overlooking the deep Gail Valley and facing the very jagged crests of the Julian Alps to the south *(make a point of stopping at the car parks numbered 2, 5 and 6).*

When you reach the end of the roadway (alt 1 732 m - 5 682 ft) we suggest that you take the chairlift to the upper platform *(45S Rtn)* and then climb on foot to the top of the **Dobratsch★★** (alt 2 167 m - 7 107 ft). The peak stands alone and provides the famous **panorama★★** of the Karawanken, the Carinthian Lakes, the Julian Alps and the Tauern *(about 2 1/2 hours Rtn from the end of the road, of which 10 minutes are spent in the chairlift and 2 hours walking).*

VOLDERS ★ (Tyrol)

Michelin map **426** fold 31 – 5 km - 3 miles east of Hall in Tirol – *Local map p 90* – Alt 558 m - 1 831 ft

On the green banks of the River Inn, near the motorway, the **Servites' Church** (Servitenkirche) of Volders appears with its red and white decorations as one of the most refreshing examples of Baroque art in the Tyrol.

The edifice, completed in 1654, is built round a central rotunda in a clover shaped plan. The helmet like roofs, intricately interwoven and covering the cupolas, and the bulbed clock tower (1740), whose base is quartered by small towers, characterize the outline of the building of which one can get a full view from the centre of the bridge.

A passage links the church to the monastery, now used as a small seminary for the Servites (a religious order who consecrate themselves in Austria to the parishioners and to the upkeep of pilgrimage sanctuaries).

What one can see of the church interior, beyond the dividing grille, indicates that the builders were able to call on excellent artists to help them: outstanding are the paintings of the cupolas and the picture over the high altar of St Charles Borromeo, patron of the church, attributed to Martin Knoller (1725-1804).

VORAU (Styria)

Michelin map **426** fold 24 – Pop 1 482 – Alt 660 m - 2 165 ft

On a solitary hillock in Joglland the Abbey of Vorau, founded in the 12C, belongs to the monks of St Augustine, who work in several nearby parishes.

The Abbey. – As soon as you enter the main gateway, the monastery buildings spread out before you in remarkable order. The western façade of the church, decorated with fine stuccos and flanked by two towers, is placed between two symmetrical wings.

Monastery Church (Stiftskirche). – This church has suffered from excessive Baroque decorations.

WAIDHOFEN AN DER THAYA (Lower Austria)

Michelin map **426** fold 10 – Pop 5 401 – Alt 510 m - 1 673 ft

Waidhofen is situated on the left bank of the River Thaya in a pleasant countryside.

Parish Church (Pfarrkirche). – The outside gives no hint of the interest of the church's interior decorations, which dates from Baroque times. The vault of the nave is decorated with frescos and surrounded by stuccos whose pastel tones are dominated by gold and violet. The pulpit and the organ tribune are worked with great elegance. To the right of the chancel a 17C chapel contains a Virgin and Child (1440), which is charming, despite the stiffness of the pose.

Town Hall (Rathaus). – This beautiful Renaissance building, situated in the middle of the main square, is crowned with a central bell-turret, and stepped gables at each end of the roof.

WEISSENKIRCHEN (Lower Austria)

Michelin map **426** fold 11 – *Local map p 61* – Pop 1 603 – Alt 206 m - 676 ft

Weissenkirchen in the heart of the Wachau, is noted for its vineyards which climb up the sides of the hills and for the charm of its old houses dominated by a fortified church.

■ **SIGHTS** *time: 1/2 hour*

Leave your car near the church, which is reached by a 16C covered staircase.

Parish Church (Pfarrkirche). – Built in the Gothic style in the 15C, the church was fortified in 1531 to resist the Turkish invasions. A Virgin and Child, opposite the pulpit, is of this period. Go round the church from the left and then pass along the ancient fortifications. From a little terrace covered with vines, there are views of the church's chevet and the Danube Valley.

On your return, take the open air staircase which leads to charming views of the little streets with their overhanging houses. Make for the Wachau Museum.

Wachau Museum (Wachaumuseum). – *Open 1 April to 31 October 10am to 5pm; closed Mondays or Tuesdays when Monday is a holiday; 15S.*

The museum is in the Teisenhofer-Hof, a fortified farm of the 16C, which has a delightful courtyard: arcades support a covered gallery, lined with flowers and sheaves of maize.

WELS (Upper Austria)

Michelin map **426** fold 21 – Pop 51 024 – Alt 317 m - 1 040 ft – 🛈 ☎ 4601

The Innviertel – the northern part of the Danubian Plateau in Austria – is an area rich in agriculture and stock farming, and Wels is therefore an important centre for agricultural markets. Popular fairs are held every year in the town: the largest, an agricultural fair, is held every two years *(first week in September in even years)* as does the *Welster Volksfest,* a popular feast. The old town is situated on the left bank of the River Traun.

■ **SIGHTS** *time: 1 hour*

Leave from the Polheimerstrasse.

Passing beneath the **Ledererturm,** a tower built in 1618, you come to the long **Stadtplatz** with its ornate fountain. Most of the houses on the square have first floors projecting on consoles and are decorated with beautiful wrought iron grilles.

Pass the fountain and leave on your left the **town hall** (Rathaus) with its elegantly carved façade, to follow the picturesque **Minoritengasse,** which goes through the heart of the old town where the houses are supported by arches and vaulted passageways.

The **Kaiserliche Burg,** where the Emperor Maximilian died in 1519 (*p 85*), has been restored and converted into a museum.

Return to the Stadtplatz and continue on to the **parish church** (Stadtpfarrkirche) in whose Gothic style chancel there are 14C stained glass windows behind the high altar.

The Pfarrgasse and Schmidtgasse both lead back to the Stadtplatz. At No. 52 there is an interesting courtyard with two storeys of arcades.

Cross the courtyard of Polheim Château (Schloss Polheim), ornamented with some Renaissance motifs, before returning to your car.

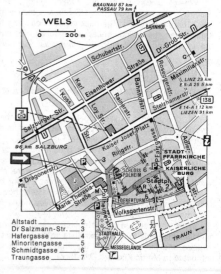

Altstadt	2
Dr Salzmann-Str.	3
Hafergasse	4
Minoritengasse	5
Schmidtgasse	6
Traungasse	7

WIENER NEUSTADT (Lower Austria) _____

Michelin map **426** fold 25 – Pop 35 050 – Alt 265 m - 869 ft

Wiener Neustadt, an important centre for mechanical and textile industries, suffered heavily during the last war owing to its armament factories and military material. Already rebuilt once in the last century after a gigantic fire, the town is richer in historical memories than in monuments. Founded in 1194 by Duke Leopold of Babenberg as a frontier fortress against the Magyars, Wiener Neustadt became the imperial residence from 1440 to 1493 in the reign of Friedrich III. His son, the Emperor Maximilian, was born there in 1459 and his remains rest here, far from the pomp of the magnificent mausoleum at Innsbruck *(p 88)*.

■ **SIGHTS** *time: 1 hour*

Church of St George in the Castle (St. Georgskirche in der Burg). – *To see the court, the "Wappenwand", and the church, apply to the military academy guardroom in the castle (8am to 4pm).*

The church gable, which can be seen from the first court, is covered with 107 carved coats of arms from the House of the Habsburgs – the 15C Wappenwand. These armorial bearings frame the central window of the church and surround the statue of Friedrich III.

The Gothic hall church, built during the reign of Friedrich III and completely restored after the Second World War, lies above the arched entrance. The Virgin on the north side altar and some stained glass fragments (blazons), are the most outstanding remains of the original furnishings. Maximilian lies, anonymously, beneath the high altar.

The New Abbey Church (Neuklosterkirche). – *Ungargasse, near the Hauptplatz.* In this Gothic building whose chancel (first half of the 14C) is higher up than the nave and has Baroque furnishings and decoration. In the apse, behind the high altar, there is the beautiful **tombstone** of the Empress Eleanor of Portugal, the wife of Friedrich III, which was carved by Nikolaus Gerhart of Leyden in 1467.

Join us in our never ending task of keeping up to date.

Send us your comments and suggestions, please.

Michelin Tyre P.L.C.
Tourism Department
81 Fulham Road, LONDON SW3 6RD.

WÖRTHER Lake ★ WÖRTHER SEE (Carinthia) _____

Michelin map **426** folds 35 and 36

Wörther Lake, stretching between Velden and Klagenfurt and over 17 km - 10 miles long, receives little in the way of river floodwaters and is therefore warm – 24-28°C – 75-82°F in summer – a fact which has encouraged the development of resorts such as Velden and Pörtschach *(p 117)*. A screen of low hills sometimes hides the Karawanken, but a short stroll is generally enough to bring again into view to the south the magnificent splendour of this mountain barrier which stretches between Austria, Yugoslavia and Italy.

THE SOUTH BANK OF LAKE WÖRTHER★
From Villach to Klagenfurt – *56 km - 35 miles – about 2 1/2 hours – Local map p 172*

The route proposed, goes through the Drava depression, within sight of the Karawanken (on the way several Bildstock (p 28) can be seen). At Velden do not use the main road going to the resorts of the Austrian Riviera; it continues along the south bank of Wörther Lake (narrow roads). Note the site of the Maria Wörth promontory and the panorama from the Pyramidenkogel.

On leaving Villach *(p 169)* and shortly after crossing the Gail, be certain to turn into the Maria Gail loop road.

Maria Gail. – Inside this little rural pilgrimage church the visitor should look at the **altarpiece★★**, the central panel depicts the Crowning of the Virgin. The work, dating from the beginning of the 16C, only just avoids affectation in its style.

On the north and south walls behind the nave can be seen traces of late Romanesque frescos. There are also good 16C statues of St George and St Florian. While in the church note the inscriptions in the Slovene language, evidence of the existence of a Slav minority in Carinthia.

Farther on towards the east, the road, which continues to rise, affords a wide general view of the Villach basin where the Gail and the Drava converge. Farther on again, beyond a pinewood, there comes into view the beautiful sheet of water that is the Lake of Faak and the decapitated pyramid, the Mittagskogel, standing quite alone (alt 2 143 m - 7 031 ft).

The route next leads down to the bottom of the furrow through which the Drava flows fully, hidden behind a curtain of trees; 500 m - 500 yds before the hamlet of St. Martin *(details on the patron saints p 28)*, a Bildstock, consecrated to this saint, standing at the roadside, depicts in naïve fashion the dividing of the cloak. Beyond the Rosegg Bridge you begin again to get occasional glimpses of the Karawanken.

Velden★★. – Pop 7 458. *Facilities p 42.* The resort of Velden, which lies at the west end of Lake Wörther and possesses a casino, has a long tradition as a halting stage.

The original château which belonged to the Khevenhüller family, was rebuilt in 1891 as an hotel, but the 17C plans were preserved, especially the Baroque fragment formed by the main doorway, surmounted with obelisks and bearing, on the pediment, the family arms *(pp 82 and 113)*.

WÖRTHER LAKE*

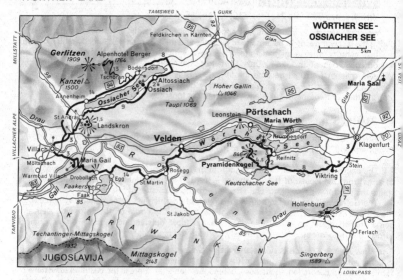

Maria Wörth★. – Pop 1 046. *Facilities p 41.* On their promontory, the belfries of the two pilgrimage sanctuaries of Maria Wörth and the round tower of the charnel-house are placed side by side, within the same surrounding wall.

In the Romanesque choir of the first little sanctuary, known as the "Winterkirche", painted murals of the 11C depict the Apostles. The main church, an amalgamation of different styles, is much decorated inside.

There is a Calvary of the early 16C, a statue of the Virgin above the high altar, and a copy of the Madonna (early 13C), the original being in the Church of St Mary of the People in Rome *(see Michelin Green Guide to Italy).*

Reifnitz. – *Facilities see at Maria Wörth p 41.*

Pyramidenkogel★. – Alt 850 m - 2 789 ft. A good road leads to the summit, which is crowned with a viewing tower – 54 m - 177 ft high *(lift: 20S).* There is a fine **circular view★** over the great central depression of Carinthia, the Karawanken mountain barrier and, far to the west, the jagged Julian Alps (Yugoslavia and Italy). To the northeast lies the Ulrichsberg, looking like a sphinx emerging from the mass of hills. During the Celtic period this was one of the sacred mountains of Carinthia.

In the foreground, you can see the peninsula of Maria Wörth which juts out into the waters of the lake.

Viktring. – *The entrance to the abbey is at the end of the main street of the village which runs north-south.*

Viktring Abbey, founded by the Cistercians in 1142, is laid out round two vast courtyards with superimposed galleries. It was secularized in 1786.

The church, though shortened in 1847, is of exceptional interest for French visitors, since it was closely inspired by the Abbey of Fontenay in Burgundy *(see Michelin Green Guide Bourgogne, in French only)* the model for Cistercian design. Thus one finds at Viktring: the blind nave, with its broken cradle-vaulting extending to the cross of the transept, the arched side aisles in transversal cradles buttressing the main nave and the projecting transept off which open square chapels.

The severity of the reformed Cistercian style was tempered during the 14C when a polygonal chancel replaced the early flat chevet, and above all, between 1380 and 1390 when the high windows lighting the choir received their beautiful stained glass. In the 15C the Chapel of St Bernard was built, with its network vaulting, extending the left arm of the transept.

Hollenburg Castle. – *7 km - 4 miles – from the Stein fork by the Loiblpass Strasse (No. 91). Time: 1/2 hour.* The massive Hollenburg Fortress commands the Valley of the Drava, known in this section as the Rosental.

Turn off the Loiblpass road where it starts to descend in order to bear left into the castle avenue.

Leave the car at the entrance to the fortified covered bridge which leads to the inner court. This is irregular in shape and picturesque with richly carved arcades. Go through a doorway marked "zum Söller" to a small terrace overlooking the Rosental.

Take your car and return onto road No. 91 which brings you from the south to Klagenfurt *(description p 96).*

Michelin map **426** folds 19 and 33 – *Local maps pp 77 and 122* – Pop 7 959 – Alt 757 m - 2 484 ft – ▣ ☎ 2600 – *Facilities pp 42 and 43*

The Zell am See countryside finds its true beauty reflected in the waters of the lake which unites, as in a mirror, the far-off snows of the Tauern heights, the rocks of the Steinernes Meer and the Alpine meadows of the "Grasberge".

The Lake of Zell (Zeller See). – During the glacial period the masses coming from the Tauern heights pushed towards the north, profiting from the weak point offered by the schistose massif opposing them and clearing the way to the Zell corridor and the Plain of Saalfelden. When running water reappeared, blocked by moraine, it could only collect in the present Saalach Valley *(local map p 122)*.

The lake today receives no water from the Saalach or the Salzach. Not fed with glacier water, it warms rapidly in summer to 20°C - 68°F.

EXCURSIONS

Schmittenhöhe★★. – *Alt 1 965 m - 6 447 ft. – 2 km - 1 mile plus about 1 1/2 hours Rtn including 15 min cable-car: summer service every 1/2 hour; 120S Rtn; local map p 77.*

The panorama encompasses the limestone ranges of the Wilder Kaiser, Loferer and Leoganger Steinberge and the glacial beauties of the Tauern heights, the Grossglockner and Grossvenediger.

Kitzsteinhorn★★. – *15 km - 9 miles – plus about 2 1/2 hours Rtn of which 40 min are by cable-car – in summer 8am to 5.20pm; 180S; local map p 77.*
To go to the summit:
– either by cable-car (cable-car transfers at Salzburger Hütte and at Alpincenter Kaprun)
– or by the underground funicular with a change at the Alpincenter Kaprun.

Follow as described below the route along the Kaprun Valley. Leave the car at the lower station of the cable-car and funicular (Gletscherbahn). After transferring to a second cable-car, one arrives at the base of a snow covered ridge (alt 3 029 m - 9 935 ft). Immediately below the actual summit of the Kitzsteinhorn (alt 3 203 m - 10 508 ft) which may only be ascended by mountaineers.

Skiing is practised all year round on the glacial slopes which are well marked and equipped with ski lifts. The Alpincenter Kaprun (alt 2 446 m - 8 023 ft) is the largest skiing area in Austria.

The **panorama**★★, half hidden to the south, extends towards the Grossvenediger, the mountain ranges of the Wetterstein (Zugspitze), the Karwendel and the Kaisergebirge, the Lake of Zell am See and the Saalach gap which appears hemmed in by the Berchtesgaden Alps (Watzmann, Steinernes Meer), and the Dachstein.

For the circular view use the tunnel (300 m - 984 ft) which opens onto a panoramic gallery on the south side of the mountain, in view of the Grossglockner massif.

Valley of the Kaprun★ **(Kaprunertal) and its Dams**★★. – *Local map p 77.* This valley adds to the sparkling glacial summits of the Tauern mountains, the impressive spectacle of dams built up in tiers. These hydro-electric developments, forming the Glockner-Kaprun combine, are among the most outstanding of contemporary Austrian engineering feats.
The complete excursion, using several forms of transport, requires at least 5 hours from Zell am See. It is usually feasible mid-May to mid-October. Rtn excursion fare from Zell am See by the postal car from the Limberg tunnel or Kesselfall Alpenhaus car park (farthest point: bus shuttle service and funicular); 125S in season, 105S out of season.

Leave Zell am See by the Mittersill road; at the entrance to Fürth, bear left.

Kaprun. – Pop 2 604. *Facilities pp 39 and 43.* This township, situated where the valley begins finally to broaden and in view of the Kitzsteinhorn, a snow covered pyramid, owes its recent development to the construction of the hydro-electric undertakings. The Kaprun power station (220 000 kW) lies about 2 km - 1 mile above the town, marking the lower level of the Glockner-Kaprun undertaking. *The machine rooms are open to visitors.*

The road rises in the valley between steep mountainsides; suddenly in front there looms the high wall of the Limberg Dam (Limbergsperre). The Kitzsteinhorn may be ascended from the Gletscherbahn cable-car station *(see above).*

A bus shuttle service connects the Kesselfall Alpenhaus or Limbergstollen car park with the lower station of the Lärchwand funicular.

The upward journey in the funicular provides a view of the valley along which one has just come and Kaprun. From the upper station can be seen the Limberg Dam and, in the background, the Wiesbachhorn, the Bratschenkopf and the Klockerin.

The Limberg Dam (Limbergsperre). – This arched gravity dam rises 120 m - 394 ft above its foundations and is 357 m - 387 yds long at its crest (alt 1 672 m - 5 486 ft). The power station at its foot receives water from the Upper Mooserboden reservoir which it immediately returns behind the dam to the far end of the Wasserfallboden lake reservoir.

This excursion through the valley continues by bus along the Mooserboden road, which includes 1 700 m - about 1 1/2 miles of tunnels, to the Mooser Dam.

On the way one can enjoy, at first from its own level and later from above, the **Wasserfallboden lake reservoir**★ in its isolated setting.

The Dams★**: the Mooser** (Moosersperre) **and the Drossen** (Drossensperre). – Alt 2 036 m - 6 680 ft. Both streams flowing out of the Mooserboden combe have been dammed – one by a gravity dam, the other by an arched type dam, each of which is keyed, as the centre, to the Höhenburg rock.

The **Mooserboden lake reservoir**★★ and the wonderful scenery provided by the icy peaks of the High Tauern are unforgettable.

By following the path along the top of the first dam, you get a surprising **view**★★ of the green waters of the Wasserfallboden Lake below, and in the distance, the walls of the Leoganger Steinberge and the Steinernes Meer.

A gallery over 12 km - 7 miles long, by which the waters from the Pasterze Glacier and the Leiterbach are pumped into the Mooserboden reservoir, is worth seeing. The water is concentrated behind the Margaritze Dam, at the foot of the Grossglockner *(p 78).*

The great Cistercian Abbey of Zwettl stands in a curve of the River Kamp, one of the most romantic river valleys above the Ottenstein Dam.

The Abbey (Stift). – *Open 1 May to 30 September 10 (11am Sundays and holidays) to noon and 2 to 5pm; the rest of the year 10 (Sundays and holidays) to noon 11am and 2 (1pm Sundays and holidays) to 4pm; 20S.*

From the abbey courtyard, which has a fountain at its centre, there is a fine view of the Baroque tower of the monastery church.

To the church built during the 14C in Gothic style, an elegant western façade was added in the 18C. This is decorated with statues and topped by a slender bulbed tower.

The Baroque decoration is continued inside where a profusion of marble and statues harmonize with the architecture of the chancel, framed by fourteen side chapels. The altarpieces are by Martin Altomonte, Paul Troger and Johann Georg Schmidt.

The cloister marks the transition between the Romanesque and Gothic styles. From the monks' ritual washing place, jutting on to a gallery, one appears to be surrounded by small columns and capitals.

INDEX

175

NOTES

(EF 10th)

MANUFACTURE FRANÇAISE DES PNEUMATIQUES MICHELIN
Société en commandite par actions au capital de 1 300 000 000 de F
Place des Carmes-Déchaux - 63 Clermont-Ferrand (France)
R.C.S. Clermont-Fd B 855 200 507
© Michelin et Cie, propriétaires-éditeurs, 1982
Dépôt légal : 8-82 - ISBN 2 06 015 121-X - ISSN : 0293-9436

Printed in France - 7-82-30
Photocomposition : COUPÉ S.A. Sautron
Impression : TARDY QUERCY S.A. - BOURGES Nº 10661